Adventures in japaNese 2

アドベンチャー日本語

Hiromi Peterson & Naomi Hirano-Omizo

4TH EDITION

CHENG & TSUI

Boston

27 26 25 24   8 9 10 11

8th Printing, 2024

Printed in the United States of America

Published by
Cheng & Tsui Co.
25 West Street
Boston, MA 02111-1213 USA
Phone (617) 988-2400 / (800) 554-1963
Fax (617) 426-3669
www.cheng-tsui.com
"Bringing Asia to the World"™

Adventures in Japanese Vol. 2 Textbook, 4th Edition
ISBN: 978-1-62291-066-3

The *Adventures in Japanese* series includes textbooks, workbooks, teacher guides, audio downloads, and a companion website at **cheng-tsui.com/adventuresinjapanese**.

The *Adventures in Japanese* series includes textbooks, workbooks, teacher guides, audio, and a digital edition on Cheng & Tsui FluencyLink™. Visit **cheng-tsui.com** for more information about *Adventures in Japanese* and additional Japanese language resources.

Illustrations
Michael Muronaka, Asuka Hazuki (manga)

Photo Credits
front cover ©SeanPavonePhoto, Fotolia; Level 1 ©iStock.com/tuk69tuk; Radu Razvan/Photos.com; Level 3 ©ULTRA.F Getty Images; xiii ©iStockphoto/Pete Leong; 1, 13, 49, 85, 121, 130, 141, 151(b), 157, 191, 227, 263, 331, 363, 383, 399 ©Datacraft/Imagenavi.com; 24(t) ©Y-Tea Fotolia; 48, 120, 190, 262, 362, 432 ©iStockphoto/hichako; 61 ©iStock.com/gsermek; 69 ©Unlisted Images / Fotosearch.com; 78, 79(b), 156, 178, 374, 387 ©Michele Fujii; 84, 156, 226, 294, 330, 398 ©iStockphoto/-WaD-; 111 ©Unlisted Images / Fotosearch.com; 134(t) ©iStockphoto/suchoa lertadipat; 147 ©Jupiterimages/Getty Images; 167 ©amplion, Fotolia; 180 ©iStock.com/TAGSTOCK1; 241 ©Unlisted Images / Fotosearch.com; 244 ©iStockphoto/ Catherine Yeulet; 247 ©WorkingPENS/Shutterstock.com; 247(l) ©2jenn/Shutterstock.com; 247(r) ©Takayuki/ Shutterstock.com; 253 ©iStock.com/sunstock; 276 ©iStock.com/edge69; 291 ©iStock.com/visualgo; 381(t) ©iStock.com/Nikada; 388 ©iStockphoto/homydesign; 395 ©iStock.com/gangliu10; 413 ©iStock.com/ AlbertSmirnov, ©iStock.com/ARSELA, ©iStock.com/pearleye, ©iStock.com/dendong; 422 ©iStock.com/ AlexeyPushkin, ©iStock.com/Vicgmyr, ©iStock.com/WizData, ©iStock.com/DNY59, ©iStock.com/ Creativestock, ©iStock.com/egal, ©iStock.com/AniaFotKam, ©iStock.com/Lesyy; 429 ©iStock.com/caracterdesign; 489 ©iStock.com/Bercutt

Contents

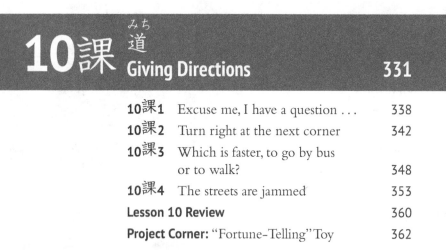

Foreword

As an author of an elementary Japanese textbook for college students, I am keenly aware of the difficulty of writing an elementary textbook. It is time-consuming, energy-consuming and creativity-consuming. Writing an elementary Japanese textbook for high school students must be much harder than writing the counterpart for college students, because it involves a host of age-adequate considerations peculiar to high school students.

Adventures in Japanese has been prepared by highly experienced and knowledgeable high school teachers of Japanese, Hiromi Peterson and Naomi Hirano-Omizo, who know exactly what is teachable/learnable and what is not teachable/learnable for high school students. They know how to sustain students' interest in the Japanese language and its culture by employing so many age-adequate, intriguing activities with a lot of fun illustrations. The grammar explanations and culture notes provide accurate and succinct pieces of information, and each communicative activity is well-designed to assist the students in acquiring actual skills to use grammar and vocabulary in context. In short, *Adventures in Japanese* is an up-to-date high school Japanese textbook conceived and designed in a proficiency-based approach. Among many others, it comes with a teacher's guide which is intended to help a novice high school teacher of Japanese teach Japanese in a pedagogically correct manner from day one.

I am pleased that at long last we have a high school textbook that is both learnable and teachable, and very importantly, enjoyable. I endorse *Adventures in Japanese* wholeheartedly.

Seiichi Makino
Professor Emeritus of Japanese and
Linguistics
Department of East Asian Studies
Princeton University

Welcome to the second volume of *Adventures in Japanese*! We hope you enjoyed your adventure in the first volume of the series. In Volume 1, you learned how to express your basic needs in Japanese through the adventures of Ken and Emi. In Volume 2, dialogues continue to center on Ken, but you will also be introduced to Mari, a student from Japan who shares many cultural insights. Ken and Mari's conversations provide many opportunities to compare Japanese and U.S. customs.

We hope your experience with Volume 2 will be as fulfilling and enjoyable as that with Volume 1. While your studies this year will take you further, our goals remain the same:

1. To create a strong foundation of the Japanese language through the development of the four language skills: speaking, listening, reading, and writing.

2. To strengthen, in particular, your conversational skills.

3. To deepen your understanding of the Japanese people and culture through the study of the language and the many aspects of Japanese culture.

4. To encourage a rediscovery of your own language and culture through the study of Japanese language and culture.

5. To encourage your growth as a culturally sensitive, aware, and responsible world citizen.

These general goals align with the Japanese language national standards and create a foundation upon which to build should you choose to sit for the AP® Japanese Language and Culture exam or other standardized tests. Activities throughout the book will encourage you to make comparisons between your own culture and Japan's, thus strengthening your understanding of both. We have also tried to connect the Japanese language to other disciplines, and you will learn to use Japanese to discuss the weather, geography, mathematics, technology, and more.

Topics
For Volume 2, topics were carefully selected so that you will be able to make maximum use of Japanese after completing the course. Many lessons take you out into the community with Ken and Mari to use Japanese in real-life situations, e.g., at a Japanese restaurant, speaking with Japanese tourists, giving directions, etc. There are also topics drawn from school life, such as sports, illness, and school rules. Many also compare Japanese and U.S. customs around driving, holidays, part-time work, and restaurants. We have also included a traditional Japanese folktale, *The Mouse Wedding,* which illustrates Japanese literary culture and traditional values.

Can-Do Statements
Each lesson starts with a set of Can-Do Statements that state the goals and expectations for the lesson. At the end of each lesson, you will also find a Now I Can... self-assessment checklist to help you determine if you have mastered all of the lesson's goals. Use these to check your own progress.

Review

A list of previously learned vocabulary and grammar will appear at the start of every lesson. These pages also include activities to help you remember and use what you have already learned. In order to be successful with the new lesson, it is important that you review all of these materials first.

Kanji

Volume 1 introduced 60 *kanji*, and Volume 2 introduces 102 additional *kanji*. There are also **Recognition Kanji** that you are only expected to read and know the meanings of, but will not yet need to write. Six characters per lesson are introduced in Lessons 2 and 3, increasing to 10 per lesson in Lesson 4. In addition, many of the other 410 *kanji* used on the AP® Test will appear throughout the lesson dialogues, vocabulary, grammar models, and activities. *Hiragana* readings appear over new *kanji* until the lesson in which they are taught as **Lesson Kanji**.

You will also learn several new readings for previously learned *kanji*, which will appear on the **Lesson Kanji** pages. While *kanji* may first appear complicated, you will soon begin to see patterns emerge in combinations, especially among *on* (Chinese-based) and *kun* (native Japanese-based) readings. On **Lesson Kanji** pages, the *on* readings will be written in *katakana* and the *kun* readings in *hiragana*. Through diligent practice, you will begin to appreciate *kanji* as much as the Japanese do.

Dialogues

A multi-page manga dialogue appears at the beginning of each lesson, modeling the lesson vocabulary and grammar in an authentic Japanese context. The dialogues in the textbook are in formal style, but informal versions are also provided on the companion website at **www.cheng-tsui.com/adventuresinjapanese.** This volume focuses on teaching the formal style of speech, but you may also wish to familiarize yourself with the more natural speaking style of the informal version which is introduced in Lesson 3 and appears in many of the later lessons. You will learn more about informal speech patterns in Volume 3.

Vocabulary and Language in Context

As in Volume 1, the vocabulary has been carefully selected based on frequent and practical use. In Volume 2, new vocabulary is limited to 30-40 words per lesson. Additional vocabulary is provided immediately following lesson vocabulary for those who want to learn even more Japanese.

The Language in Context section uses vocabulary in model sentences based on real-life situations. Use these models to expand and apply your knowledge of the vocabulary in different contexts.

Grammar

The grammatical structures in this volume build on those you learned in Volume 1. We have kept the explanations short so that they are easy for you to understand. You will learn several ways to conjugate verbs in Volume 2. They are organized so that you may smoothly progress from one form to the next. By the end of the volume, you should be able to:

1. Describe an ongoing state or action

2. Grant or ask for permission or prohibit actions

3. State your intentions and your obligations

4. Express your ability to do something and give conditions

5. Compare things and actions

6. Describe the act of giving and receiving favors and gifts

Grammar explanations are all accompanied by model sentences with audio available online to put the grammar in context and exercises to check your ability to use the grammar correctly.

Culture and Language Notes

Understanding culture is essential to learning a language. We have thus included many cultural explanations in the form of Culture Notes. Each of these Culture Notes also contains an activity to help deepen your understanding of Japanese culture through technology, compare it to your own culture, or connect it to another discipline. Lessons in culture can also be drawn from many of the illustrations and photos. In addition, Language Notes will help you understand unique elements of the Japanese language that may be very different from your own language, such as onomatopoeia.

Every other chapter also includes a Japanese Culture Corner which gives you a chance to further compare your culture with Japanese culture. You are encouraged to find answers through various resources, including the Internet, reading materials, or people from Japan!

Project Corners

Japanese culture includes many crafts and games. This text introduces origami, songs, Japanese recipes, games (*hanafuda*), and cultural practices like *rajio taiso*. More Project Corners are available on the companion website at **cheng-tsui.com/adventuresinjapanese**.

Review Questions and Text Chat

After every lesson, there is a list of common questions related to the topics covered. You will ask your partner these questions in Japanese and your partner will answer you without looking at the textbook. You and your partner will take turns asking and responding. You should pay attention to speed, intonation, and pronunciation as these factors matter in communicating successfully and will be assessed by your teacher. You may also practice or check how the questions should be asked using the audio. If you need to review, page numbers are provided to help you find the relevant material pertaining to the question.

There is also an AP®-style Text Chat review activity. You will respond to text messages from Japanese students based on prompts, modeling a real-life exchange about the lesson topics.

It is our hope that upon completing this volume, you will be able to communicate successfully at a basic level, orally and in written form. We also hope that you will learn more about culturally appropriate behavior.

One piece of advice from your teachers:
The key to success in the early years of foreign language study is frequent and regular exposure to the language. Take advantage of class time with your teacher, practice in and outside of class, and keep up with your work. Learn your material well, don't hesitate to try it out, and most of all, enjoy! And, as the Japanese say,

がんばって！

As their sophomore year progresses, Mari helps Ken practice his Japanese, Ken teaches Mari about the U.S., and the two become good friends. Through their conversations and adventures, they learn much about each other's cultures.

KEN Ken Smith is one of the main characters in the *Adventures in Japanese* series. In Volume 2, Ken is a sophomore studying Japanese in a U.S. high school.

Ken is an avid sports fan and athlete. He excels at several sports and also plays the guitar and the piano. Ken is laid-back, but his kind and caring nature is obvious from his interactions with friends and family.

MARI Mari Hayashi is the other main character of Volume 2. She is a 16-year old exchange student from Tokyo, Japan studying at Ken's school and staying with the Green family. She is also a sophomore.

ぼくは　ケンです。

はじめまして。まりです。

Meet the Rest of the Characters

Throughout Volume 2, Ken and Mari will meet several people who help Ken learn Japanese.

EMI
Ken's friend from freshmen year. She moved away, but she and Ken still keep in touch.

IZUMI-SAN
A waitress at a local Japanese restaurant in Ken's hometown.

OGAWA-SAN
A Japanese shopper who comes to the T-shirt store, where Ken works part-time, to buy souvenirs.

INOUE-SAN
A Japanese tourist who stops Ken to ask directions in San Francisco, where Ken is on vacation.

MRS. SMITH
Ken's mother, a 43-year old Japanese woman who has lived in the U.S. for 20 years. She works at the local bookstore.

In *Adventures in Japanese Volume 3*, Ken will experience Japanese culture firsthand as he travels to Tokyo as an exchange student. He hopes you will come along with him!

The following sections outline the ACTFL–World Readiness Standards for Learning Languages (reprinted with permission from *Standards for Foreign Language Learning in the 21st Century*, 2015, by the National Standards in Foreign Language Education Project), and how activities in *Adventures in Japanese Volume 2* align with them. While this is not an exhaustive discussion, it will inform you, the teacher, about how standards may be met in Volume 2. Complete correlations, a full **Scope and Sequence,** as well as supplemental materials including audio and other resources, are available on the companion website at **cheng-tsui.com/adventuresinjapanese**.

I. Communication
Communicate effectively in Japanese in order to function in a variety of situations and for multiple purposes

1.1 Interpersonal Communication. *Learners interact and negotiate meaning in spoken, signed, or written conversations to share information, reactions, feelings, and opinions.* Students practice speaking with one another and the teacher on various topics, often in realistic Communicative Activities which require the exchange of authentic information, such as school rules, restaurant orders, directions, and health. Students are tested using review questions which require proficiency in asking and answering questions on a variety of topics, and engage in simulated written communication through Text Chat activities. Authentic Readings ask students to answer questions that will help them navigate real life situations. Students ask for and give information, state preferences or opinions about food, prices, jobs, sports, family, etc.

1.2 Interpretive Communication. *Learners understand, interpret, and analyze what is heard, read, or viewed on a variety of topics.* At this level, students listen regularly to audio exercises. They listen to and respond to questions from their teacher and classmates on a daily basis. They also gain reading skills through reading authentic materials in each lesson, such as menus, social media posts, recipes, letters, GPS navigation routes, and New Year's wish tablets.

1.3 Presentational Communication. *Learners present information, concepts, and ideas to inform, explain, persuade, and narrate on a variety of topics using appropriate media and adapting to various audiences of listeners, readers, or viewers.* Students may create posters and announcements or present short speeches as part of Culture Note and Authentic Reading activities. Japanese folktales may be presented as part of Lesson 9. Students will also engage in longer presentations using a variety of media in Extend Your Learning activities in Japanese Culture Corners.

II. Cultures
Interact with cultural competence and understanding of Japan

2.1 Relating Cultural Practices to Perspectives. *Learners use Japanese to investigate, explain, and reflect on the relationship between the practices and perspectives of Japanese culture.* Culture Notes cover a variety of topics that demonstrate Japanese patterns of behavior as well as how they are reflected in the language, such as giving gifts, naming conventions, shopping culture, and holiday customs. In addition, students learn many expressions and gestures commonly used by the Japanese, and show how language and non-verbal actions communicate politeness. The Dialogues involve conversations between Japanese and U.S. high school students, explaining differences in their cultural practices.

2.2 Relating Cultural Products to Perspectives. *Learners use Japanese to investigate, explain, and reflect on the relationship between the products and perspectives of Japanese culture.* As students use this volume, they will learn to prepare a Japanese recipe, fold origami, create New Year's cards, read the folktale *Nezumi no Yomeiri*, and play *hanafuda*. Through these activities, students are expected to draw conclusions about the nature of these traditional arts and how they are representative of Japan. Activities in the Culture Notes also encourage a deeper understanding of Japanese cultural products such as food, traditional dress, songs, proverbs, holidays, folktales, and landmarks.

III. Connections
Connect with other disciplines and acquire information and diverse perspectives in order to use the language to function in academic and career-related situations

3.1 Making Connections. *Learners build, reinforce, and expand their knowledge of other disciplines while using Japanese to develop critical thinking and to solve problems creatively.* Japanese Culture Corners at the end of every other lesson encourage students to research topics of Japanese Culture associated with a variety of fields including geography, sociology, and economics. Special "Connect" activities in each lesson also encourage students to use their knowledge of Japanese to answer questions involving other career-based disciplines. In addition, students learn about cooking, music, art (origami), and math (metric system).

3.2 Acquiring Information and Diverse Perspectives. *Learners access and evaluate information and diverse perspectives that are available through Japanese and its culture.* At this level, students will read a folktale in Japanese and several proverbs, gaining insight into how these works reflect aspects of Japanese culture. They are also introduced to honorific forms of speaking *(keigo)* between employees and customers. Authentic Readings in Japanese introduce students to content drawn from real-life. Students are also made aware of many cultural distinctions through the Extend Your Learning corner, for which they must acquire information about a number of diverse topics.

IV. Comparisons
Develop insight into the nature of language and culture
in order to interact with cultural competence

4.1 Language Comparisons. *Learners use Japanese to investigate, explain, and reflect on the nature of language through comparison of the Japanese language and their own.* Language Notes teach students about differences between Japanese and their native language, including words that are difficult to translate such as "to wear," "*yaku*," and "*ao*." Students are also introduced to informal and formal speech styles, as well as verbs of giving and receiving that are used differently with people of different status, illustrating cultural perspectives.

4.2 Cultural Comparisons. *Learners use Japanese to investigate, explain, and reflect on the concept of culture through comparisons of Japanese culture and their own.* Culture Notes and activities also provide information about elements of Japanese culture, such as driving practices, restaurant etiquette, and holidays while encouraging students to compare these with elements from their own culture. Culture Corners at the end of odd-numbered lessons also help students make comparisons.

V. Communities
Communicate and interact with cultural competence in order to participate in multilingual communities at home and around the world

5.1 School and Global Communities. *Learners use Japanese both within and beyond the classroom to interact and collaborate in their community and the globalized world.* Students share their Japanese language skills by sending New Year's greetings to friends and relatives or by making Mother's Day cards in Japanese. They may also perform skits based on the folktale *Nezumi no Yomeiri*. They may share culinary skills and knowledge of Japanese through preparing an *oyakodonburi* recipe. Culture Corners also encourage students to interact with Japanese speakers in their community or online.

5.2 Lifelong Learning. *Learners set goals and reflect on their progress in using Japanese for enjoyment, enrichment, and advancement.* In Volume 2, students engage in many activities that may lead to lifelong enjoyment and enrichment. They include games and crafts such as origami, making Japanese food, and playing *hanafuda*. Lesson topics are drawn from real-life situations outside the classroom, and students learn how to order Japanese food, give directions, and go shopping. Authentic Readings teach students how to interact with Japanese texts they may encounter outside class. Can-Do Statements and self-assessments also encourage students to set goals and reflect on their progress throughout life.

Common Core State Standards

The Reading, Writing, Speaking and Listening, and Language skills acquired and practiced every day in the Japanese language classroom align with the Common Core Anchor Standards for English Language Arts & Literacy in History/Social Studies, Science, and Technical Subjects. Additional activities and questions with the Common Core icon encourage students to read texts closely; to write to explain, to persuade, and to convey experience; and to understand the purpose behind communication. Students will write narratives portraying the meaning of Japanese proverbs, draw comparisons about practices, products, and perspectives in U.S. and Japanese culture, and closely read for details and main ideas.

21st Century Skills

Adventures in Japanese encourages students to develop 21st Century Skills and achieve technology and media literacy through activities and research. These skills are emphasized in activities with the 21st Century Skills icon, and in Extend Your Learning at the end of each Japanese Culture Corner. Students will research Japanese culture online, prepare digital media presentations, and learn to critically view media.

We hope the preceding information has been helpful in providing you, the teacher, with ways in which *Adventures in Japanese Volume 2* meets national language standards. Correlations to each lesson are provided in the Lesson Organizers on the *Teacher's Guide to Go*. Complete Correlations are available online at **cheng-tsui.com/adventuresinjapanese**. The ultimate goal of this text, however, supersedes meeting standards. It is our wish to nurture students who grow to love the language and culture of Japan, integrate them into their lives, and contribute to a more seamless relationship between our nations. We hope that with their appreciation for and understanding of language and culture, they will be better prepared to lead us into a more peaceful and harmonious world.

Acknowledgments

Adventures in Japanese Volume 2 was developed thanks to the efforts and contributions of our friends as well as our colleagues and students at Punahou School and beyond. We express our appreciation to all who contributed in any way, even if we may have failed to mention them below.

First and foremost, we express our sincere thanks to our current and former students who have contributed to the development of the text. They have provided us with a purpose, motivated and taught us, given us ideas and suggestions, and encouraged us in many ways.

We acknowledge Professor Emeritus Seiichi Makino of Princeton University, who has written the foreword, conducted workshops for us, and offered us much support and encouragement throughout the years. We thank Professor Emeritus Masako Himeno of Tokyo University of Foreign Studies for sharing her incredible knowledge of Japanese linguistics and her wisdom, guidance, and support. We are also grateful to our illustrators, former Punahou student Michael Muronaka, and former colleague Emiko Kaylor.

We express our appreciation to Wendi Kamiya for her guidance, and to Kathy Boswell for naming our text. Our warm thanks go to our current and former colleagues at Punahou School, especially Junko Ady, Jan Asato, Hiroko Kazama, Naomi Okada, Alison Onishi, and Aki Teshigahara. We also thank Amanda Nakanishi for coloring our illustrations, and Kyle Sombrero for his technical expertise. We are also grateful to Masako Himeno, Chikako Ikeda, Chitose Nishiyama, Yasuko Suzuki, Miyoko Fujisaki, and Fusako Takishita for their contributions.

We thank Roko Takizawa of the Shobi College of Music for coordinating the audio, and teachers Aruno Tahara, Mahiro Inoue, and their students for their audio contributions. Thank you also to Harry Kubo for his English narration, Akemi Sakamoto, Nobuko Yamamoto, and the students at Yuhigaoka High School.

We are grateful to all those who have contributed to our photo collection, especially Gen and Mutsuko Tsujii. Our thanks also go out to Yoko Tamura, Makiko Hagimoto, Daisuke Ikemizu, Kazuko Muneyoshi, Machiko Ito, Akemi Doi, Mahoko Dai and Akemi Kato, Hisae Hiraki and Masumi Takabayashi, Hiroshima Jogakuin High School, Hiroka Kawasaki, the Okayama Tourism Convention Society, Shitennoji Habikigaoka High School, Yuji Watanabe, Keiko Kameoka, Kenshiro Mori, and Shinji and Kyoko Nakatani.

We express our gratitude to Jill Cheng of Cheng & Tsui Company for her support over many years, as well as her entire staff for their work on this volume. In particular, we recognize editor ShuWen Zhang for her careful and caring work on this volume.

Finally, we express our appreciation to Wes Peterson, whose wisdom, encouragement, and technological expertise will be remembered throughout our "Adventures" journey. We are eternally grateful to our families for their patience, sacrifice, and unwavering support throughout the development of *Adventures in Japanese*.

Hiromi Peterson and Naomi Hirano-Omizo

ふくしゅう
復習
Preliminary Lesson

Can Do!

In this lesson you will review how to:

- say that you want an object or want to do an activity
- combine two sentences into one
- make requests and ask for permission
- write a response to an e-mail or blog post

Online Resources

cheng-tsui.com/
adventuresinjapanese

- Audio
- Vocabulary Lists
- Vocabulary Flashcards
- *Kanji* Flashcards

- Activity Worksheets
- TE Form Review Chart
- Additional Review Dialogue

Kanji
used in this lesson

In this lesson, you will review some key *kanji* from Volume 1.

	Kanji	Meaning	Readings	Examples	
47.	学	study	ガク	だいがく 大学	college
			カッ	しょう がっこう 小 学校	elementary school
48.	校	school	コウ	ちゅう がっこう 中 学校	middle school
41.	年	year	とし	ことし 今年	this year
			ネン	らいねん 来年	next year
37.	先	first, previous	セン	せんせい 先生	teacher
38.	生	be born, person	セイ	せいと 生徒	student
40.	毎	every	マイ	まいにち 毎日	every day
6.	日	sun, day	ニ	にほん 日本	Japan
			ニチ	なんにち 何日	What day of the month?
			ひ	ひ 日づけ	date
			び	にちようび 日曜日	Sunday
			*	ふつか 二日	2nd day of the month
18.	本	origin, book	ホン	ほん 本	book
			ポン	にっぽん 日本	Japan
			もと	やまもと 山本	Yamamoto (surname)

	Kanji	Meaning	Readings	Examples	
60.	語	language	ゴ	に ほん ご 日本語	Japanese language
31.	人	person	ひと	ひと 人	person
			ニン	さん にん 三人	three people
			ジン	に ほん じん 日本人	Japanese (person)
			*	ひと り 一人	one (person)
39.	今	now	いま	いま だ 今田さん	Mr./Mrs. Imada
			コン	こん 今しゅう	this week
			*	きょう 今日	today
43.	大	big	おお(きい)	おお ひと 大きい人	a big person
			ダイ	だい す 大好き	like very much
34.	好	like	す(き)	す 好き	like
27.	来	come	き(ます)	き 来ます	come
26.	行	go	い(く)	い 行きます	go
46.	早	early (time)	はや(い)	はや かわ 早川さん	Mr./Mrs. Hayakawa

Recognition Kanji

こう こう 高校	せい と 生徒	じ 時	じょう ず 上手	へ た 下手
high school	student	o'clock	skillful	unskillful

For a full list of *kanji* from *Adventures in Japanese* 1, go to **cheng-tsui.com/adventuresinjapanese**

*Indicates an irregular reading

Authentic Reading

A new student from Japan is coming to Ken's school. Ken plans to send her an e-mail introducing himself. On a separate sheet of paper, mark the statements below T or F based on his e-mail.

Send

To... mari@yahoo.ne.jp

Cc...

Subject: はじめまして

まりさん、

はじめまして。ぼくは　ケン・スミスです。十五さいで、マッキンリー高校の
一年生です。まりさんは　日本の　どこから　来ましたか。きょ年、
ともだちの　エミさんと　いっしょに　日本語を　べんきょうしました。
今　エミさんは　カナダに　います。ぼくは　日本語が　大好きですが、
とても　むずかしいです。でも、ぼくの　先生は　とても　いいですよ。
今年、もっと　かんじを　ならいたいです。そして、日本語の　じゅぎょうを
たのしみに　して　います。

ケン・スミス

T　F　1. Ken is a high school freshman.

T　F　2. Ken and Emi both studied Japanese last year.

T　F　3. Ken and Emi will be in the same Japanese class this year.

T　F　4. Ken thinks Japanese is difficult so he doesn't like it.

T　F　5. Ken is looking forward to meeting the new student from Japan.

 Write your own e-mail to a new Japanese friend introducing yourself and telling him/her about your Japanese class.

単語 Vocabulary

めいし Nouns

1. 高校一年生〔こうこう いちねんせい〕	first year high school student	6. カナダ	Canada
2. 日本〔にほん〕	Japan	7. 先生〔せんせい〕	teacher
3. きょ年〔きょねん〕	last year	8. 今年〔ことし〕	this year
4. ともだち	friend	9. じゅぎょう	class, instruction
5. 日本語〔にほんご〕	Japanese language	10. はじめて	for the first time

どうし Verbs

11. 来ました [IR くる/きて]	came	13. います [G2 いる/いて]	to exist, to have (animate objects)
12. べんきょうしました [IR べんきょう(を)する]	studied	14. ならいたい [G1 ならう/ならって]	want to learn

ふくし Adverbs

15. とても	very	16. もっと	more

文法 Grammar

From Volume 1, Lesson 6-5

A Adjective Conjugation Review

	い adjectives			な adjectives	
affirmative	大きいです **is big**			しずかです **is quiet**	
negative (is not...)	大きく ないです 大きく ありません			しずかでは ありません しずかじゃ ありません	
additional adjectives	いい	たかい	わかい	好き	きらい*
	小さい	ひくい	きびしい	上手	とくい*
	かわいい	わるい	やさしい	にが手	きれい*
	きたない	ながい	うるさい	下手	じゃま

*Exceptions

B Contrasting Conjunction が

Sentence 1 + が、Sentence 2。   Sentence 1, but Sentence 2.

= Sentence 1。でも、Sentence 2。   Sentence 1. But/However, Sentence 2.

◀))) MODELS

1. ぼくは　日本語が　大好きですが、とても　むずかしいです。
   I love Japanese, but it is very difficult.

2. 私は　サッカー が　好きですが、上手では　ありません。
   I like soccer, but I am not skillful.

READ/WRITE Combine the sentences below using が instead of でも.

1. 先生は　きびしいです。でも、やさしいです。

2. おちゃが　好きです。でも、ミルクが　きらいです。

3. あねは　せがたかいです。でも、あには　せが　ひくいです。

C Verb たい Form

Verb (Stem form) ＋ たい(ん)です。   want to do ～.

たくない(ん)です。   do not want to do ～.

This construction is used most commonly when the subject is first person. It is also used to ask another person of equal or lower status if he/she would like to do something. It is not polite to use this to address people of higher status, especially if you do not know the person well. The particles を or が may follow what is considered the direct object of the sentence. は may also be used if the sentence has a negative ending.

◀))) MODELS

1. 日本へ　行きたいんです。   I want to go to Japan.

2. コーヒーは　のみたく　ないです。   I do not want to drink coffee.

READ/SPEAK Choose the correct form of the verb in the ( ) and the most appropriate particle from the options in the [ ] to best match the information given in English below.

I want to go home early, and I want to see a movie. I don't want to do my homework though.

1. 早く　うち [を　に　は]　（かえります）。

2. えいが [を　へ　は]　（見ます）。

3. でも、しゅくだい [が　へ　は]　（します）。

D Conjoining Sentences with the Verb TE Form *From Vol. 1, Lessons 12-2, 12-4, 12-5*

Sentence 1 [Verb (TE form)], Sentence 2。 Sentence 1 and Sentence 2.

Sentence 1 [I Adjective (-くて)], Sentence 2。 Sentence 1 and Sentence 2.

Sentence 1 [Noun / NA Adjective] ＋で, Sentence 2。 Sentence 1 and Sentence 2.

This construction is used to conjoin two or more sentences into one. The tense of the entire sentence is determined by the tense of the final sentence. と is not used to conjoin sentences.

◀)) MODELS ▶

1. 六時に　おきて、学校へ　行きます。
   I get up at six o'clock and go to school.

2. 日本の　じゅぎょうは　おもしろくて、楽^{たの}しいです。
   Japanese class is interesting and fun.

3. あには　大学生で、今　アメリカに　います。
   My older brother is a college student and is in America now.

4. 母は　テニスが　好きで、父は　ゴルフが　好きです。
   My mother likes tennis and my father likes golf.

READ/SPEAK Change the words in the ( ) to their correct TE forms and connect the two sentences.

1. 学校に　(来ます)。としょかんに　行きました。

2. 私は　高校 (1年生です)。十五さいです。

3. ともだちは　あたまが　(いいです)。スポーツも　上手です。

アクティビティー　Communicative Activities

ペアワーク

A. SPEAK/LISTEN Conjugate the verbs in ( ) and ask a partner if he/she wants to do the following.

Ex. Question:「今年　バスケットが　したいですか。」

　　Answer:「はい、したいです。」or 「いいえ、したくないです。」

しつもん	はい	いいえ
1. 今年　日本へ　(行きます)。		
2. 今年　よく　(べんきょうします)。		
3. 今年　日本語を　よく　(はなします)。		

B. SPEAK/LISTEN/WRITE Ask your partner about what he/she has done today. Ask at least six questions. Write his/her answers in order on a separate sheet of paper.

Ex.　Person A: けさ　何時に　おきましたか。

　　　Person B: ～時に　おきました。

　　　Person A: おきて、(それから)　何を　しましたか。

　　　Person B: おきて、あさごはんを　食べました。

　　　Person A: あさごはんを　食べて、(それから)　何を　しましたか。etc.

C. SPEAK/LISTEN/WRITE Ask your partner the following questions. Your partner should answer in one sentence using the two prompts in the ( ).

しつもん	こたえ
1. うちで　何を　しますか。	(do homework, watch TV)
2. 学校は　どうですか。	(enjoyable, like)
3. ともだちは　どんな　人ですか。	(pretty, smart)

D. SPEAK/LISTEN/WRITE Ask your partner for his/her opinions about the things listed below. Your partner should answer using two descriptive words in one sentence.

Ex. 日本の　車　　　　　　Question: 日本の　車は　どうですか。

　　　　　　　　　　　　　　Answer: 小さくて、ちょっと　たかいです。

1. 日本語の　じゅぎょう　　　　3. カフェテリアの　食べもの
2. あなたの　へや　　　　　　　4. ブログ

E. SPEAK/LISTEN/WRITE Ask your partner the following questions. Your partner should answer each question in one sentence.

何さいですか。何年生ですか。

私は　～さいで、～年生です。

1. 何さいですか。何年生ですか。
2. どんな　ことが　とくいですか。どんな　ことが　にが手ですか。
3. どんな　食べものが　好きですか。どんな　食べものが　きらいですか。

Authentic Reading

Mari wrote the following blog post. Answer the questions below based on her entry.

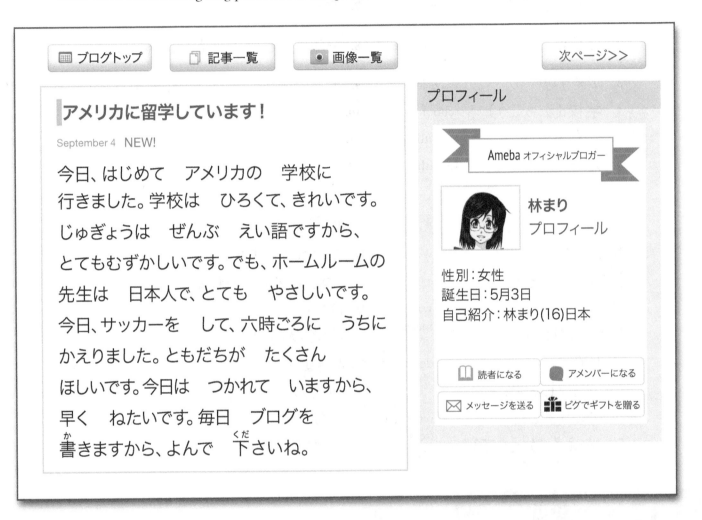

1. What is Mari's impression of her school?

2. Why does Mari think her classes are difficult?

3. What after-school activity does Mari do?

4. What is Mari's wish now?

5. What does Mari ask readers to do for her?

 Write a response to Mari's blog post asking her questions about her family or hobbies and telling her about your own wish. Include the following grammar patterns in your response.

～たい	～て　ください	～から	でも

めいし Nouns

1.	今日〔きょう〕	today	7.	ホームルーム	homeroom
2.	はじめて	for the first time	8.	日本人〔にほんじん〕	Japanese person
3.	アメリカ	America	9.	サッカー	soccer
4.	学校〔がっこう〕	school	10.	うち	(my) house
5.	ぜんぶ	everything	11.	毎日〔まいにち〕	everyday
6.	えい語〔えいご〕	English	12.	ブログ	blog

どうし Verbs

13.	行きました [G1 いく/いきます]	went	17.	つかれています [G2 つかれる/つかれます]	is tired
14.	つくりたいです [G2 つくります/つくって]	want to make	18.	ねたい [G2 ねる/ねます]	want to sleep
15.	して [IR する/します]	do	19.	かきます [G1 かく/かきます]	write
16.	かえりました [G1 かえる/かえって]	returned (to a place)	20.	よんで ください [G1 よむ/よみます]	Please read.

文法 Grammar

From Volume 1, Lesson 9-4

A Verb ほしい "To Want" Something

Something ＋ が ＋ ほしいです。   **want (something)**

Something ＋ は ＋ ほしくないです。   **do not want (something)**

The particle が follows the noun one wants. は may be used in negative sentences. It is impolite to use this construction in a question when addressing people of higher status.

 MODELS

1. 友達が たくさん ほしいです。   I want a lot of friends.

2. あかい ぼうしは ほしくないです。   I do not want a red hat.

READ/WRITE Choose the correct particle from the options in the ( ). Then, write the correct form of ほしいです in the [ ] based on the information given in English sentences below.

I don't want food now. I want water. And later I want soup.

今、食べもの (は　が)　[　]。お水 (を　が)　[　]。そして、あとで
スープ (を　が)　[　]。

B Causation Sentence Connector から

From Volume 1, Lesson 9-3

Sentence 1 (Reason) ＋から、　**Sentence 2 (Result)** 。

= Sentence 1 (Reason), so Sentence 2 (Result).

The conjunction から follows a reason or cause. The reason must appear first in this sentence structure, but the second sentence may be omitted if it is understood. When the first portion (reason) of the sentence ends with an い Adjective, the です before から is often omitted. If a noun or な Adjective precedes です in the first portion, です must not be dropped.

◀)) MODELS

1. 今日は　つかれて　いますから、早く　ねたいです。
   I am tired today, so I want to go to bed early.

2. 日本語は　おもしろいから、好きです。
   Japanese is interesting, so I like it.

3. しけんは　明日ですから、今ばん　べんきょうします。
   I have an exam tomorrow, so I'll study tonight.

READ/WRITE Rewrite the sentences below on a separate sheet of paper. Drop です when necessary.

1. ともだちは　日本人 (です) から、日本語を　話します。

2. テストが　むずかしかった (です) から、かなしいです。

3. 日本の　食べものが　好き (です) から、日本に　行きたいです。

From Volume 1, Lesson 11-2

C Making Requests with the Verb TE Form

Verb (TE form) ＋ ください。　　　　　**Please do ～.**

This construction is used to politely request a favor.

◀)) MODELS

1. ちょっと　まって　ください。　　　Please wait a minute.

2. ここに　来て　ください。　　　　Please come here.

D TE Form Verbs in Permission Questions and Responses

Verb (TE form) + も　いいです(か)。　　　　　**You may; May I ～?**

This construction is used to ask for or grant permission. This construction, when used in a statement form, is not generally used directly to give permission to people of higher status.

((•)) MODELS

1. トイレに　行っても　いいですか。　　May I go to the bathroom?

2. お水を　のんでも　いいですよ。　　You may drink water.

READ/SPEAK Change the verbs in the ( ) to the correct form and choose the correct ending in the [ ] based on context to complete the dialogues below.

1. 「この　ドアを　(あけます) [も　いいですか / ください]。」

　　「はい、(はいります) [も　いいですか / ください]。」

2. 「おんがくを　(ききます) [も　いいですか / ください]。」

　　「すみません、もう　一ど　(言います) [も　いいですか / ください]。」

アクティビティー　Communicative Activities

ペアワーク

A. SPEAK/LISTEN/ WRITE You and your partner are going shopping. Ask him/her what items he/she wants or doesn't want at the stores you are visiting and why. He/she should respond with at least two reasons. Write down his/her responses on a separate sheet of paper.

Ex.　Question:　日本語の　本が　ほしいですか。

　　　Answer:　はい。かんじが　よく　分からなくて、もっと　べんきょう
　　　　　　　　したいですから。

1. シャツ
2. スマートフォン
3. テレビゲーム
4. ざっし

クラスワーク

B. READ/SPEAK/LISTEN Play Simon Says with your class. You may use these example commands.

たって　ください。　　　　　～を　かして　ください。

すわって　ください。　　　　～へ　行って　ください。

～を　あけて　ください。　　～を　見せて　ください。

～を　しめて　ください。　　～を　見て　ください。

じこしょうかい
Self-Introduction

✓ Can Do!
In this lesson you will learn to

- identify the main islands and cities of Japan
- say where you live, where you were born, and where your family members are employed
- describe the locations of people and objects
- share your own hobbies, likes, dislikes, strengths, and weaknesses and those of others using action verbs

Online Resources

cheng-tsui.com/
adventuresinjapanese

- Audio
- Vocabulary Lists
- Vocabulary and *Kanji* Flashcards
- Study Guides
- Activity Worksheets

Let's Review

In this lesson you will learn how to introduce yourself in Japanese. Review these words, phrases, and grammatical structures you already learned to help you talk about yourself.

めいし Nouns

1. 十六さい	16 years old		11. 今	now	
2. 高校一年生	high school sophomore		12. 大学四年生	college senior	
3. スポーツ	sports		13. 毎日	every day	
4. やきゅう	baseball		14. 本や	bookstore	
5. とうきょう	Tokyo		15. うち	home	
6. かぞく	family		16. 車	car	
7. 父	(own) father		17. へや	room	
8. 母	(own) mother		18. ベッド	bed	
9. デパート	department store		19. つくえ	desk	
10. あね	(own) older sister		20. ねこ	cat	

どうし Verbs

21. はなして [G1 はなします]	to talk; to speak
22. あって [G1 あります]	to exist, to have (for inanimate objects)
23. いて [G2 います]	to exist, to have (for animate objects)
24. ねて [G2 ねます]	to sleep

-い けいようし -I Adjectives

25. ひろい	spacious	26. きたない	dirty, messy

-な けいようし -NA Adjectives

27. 好き	like	29. きれい	pretty, clean
28. 大好き	like very much, love	30. きらい	dislike

ふくし -Adverbs				
31. もう ＋ Aff.	already	**33.** いつも	always
32. まだ ＋ Neg.	not yet	**34.** すこし	a little

Expressions

35. どうぞ　よろしく　おねがいします。	Glad to meet you. [lit., Please take good care of me.]

ぶんぽう Grammar

36. Noun / NA-Adjective で、～。　　　　　～ and ～.

しゅみは　スポーツで、やきゅうが　好きです。

My hobby is sports and I like baseball.

37. Verb (TE form)、～。　　　　　～ and ～.

こうえんに　プールが　あって、毎日　およいで　います。

There is a pool at the park and I swim (there) every day.

38. I-Adjective (TE form -くて)、～。　　　～ and ～.

うちは　ひろくて、きれいです。　　The house is spacious and pretty.

WRITE/SPEAK/LISTEN Practice introducing yourself in Japanese! Write about yourself using the prompts below and give your self-introduction speech to your class.

1. Introduce yourself with your name, age, and grade in one sentence. Use the correct expressions.

2. Say where (city) your home is and where your school is.

3. Describe your room, mentioning its size (large, small, spacious, etc.) and whether you like it or not.

4. Tell what your hobby is and what you like to do.

5. End your speech with the appropriate Japanese expression.

まりさん、マッキンリー高校へ　ようこそ。

Welcome to McKinley High, Mari!

自己紹介します。
私は　林 まりです。
十六歳で、
高校一年生です。

趣味は　スポーツで、
特に　野球が
好きです。

東京で　生まれました。
家族は　東京に
住んで　います。

父は
銀行に　勤めて　いて、
母は　デパートで
働いて　います。

姉は　もう
結婚して　いて、
赤ちゃんが　います。

赤ちゃんは
まだ　一歳です。
姉は　今　仕事を
して　いません。

兄は　大学四年生で、りょうに　住んで　います。

毎日　本屋で　アルバイトを　して　います。

皆さんは　グリーンさんを　知って　いますか。
私は　今　グリーンさんの　家に　ホームステイを　して　います。
グリーンさんに　ついて　少し　話します。

家は　とても　広くて、きれいです。
家族は　車を　二台　持って　います。

部屋の 中に
きれいな ベッドや
机が あります。

白い 猫が 一匹 いて、
いつも ドアの 所に
寝て います。

家の 前に
公園が あります。

そして、
公園に プールが あって、
私は 毎日 プールで
泳いで います。
私は 泳ぐことが 大好きです。

どうぞ よろしく
お願いします。

会話 かいわ Dialogue

🔊 **READ/LISTEN** Where does Mari live now?

まりさんは　今　どこに　住んで　います か。

私は　グリーンさんの　家に　住んで　います。

文型 ぶんけい Sentence Patterns

READ Find one of these sentence patterns in the dialogue.

1. Action Verb (TE Form) ＋ います　　　　　is doing ~ [continuation of an action]
2. Stative Verb (TE Form) ＋ います　　　　　[state]

単語 たんご Vocabulary

1. 電話番号 でんわばんごう

telephone number

2. 住所 じゅうしょ

address
アドレス refers to e-mail addresses.

3. (Place で) 生まれました う
[G2 うまれる／うまれて]

was born (in ～)

4. (Place に) 住んで
います
<ruby>住<rt>す</rt></ruby>

[G1 すむ／
すみます]

live (in), reside (in)

すみます means "will live,"
"will reside" (future only).

5. (Place に) 勤めて
います
<ruby>勤<rt>つと</rt></ruby>

[G2 つとめる／
つとめます]

is employed (at 〜)

6. (Place で) 働いて
います
<ruby>働<rt>はたら</rt></ruby>

[G1 はたらく／
はたらきます]

is working (at 〜)

7. (Place で) （アル）バイト(を)
して います

[IR (アル)バイト(を)する／します]

is working part-time [for students]

8. (Person と) 結婚 (を)
して います
<ruby>結婚<rt>けっこん</rt></ruby>

[IR けっこん(を)する／します]

is married (to 〜)

9. 持って います
<ruby>持<rt>も</rt></ruby>

[G1 もつ／もちます]

have, possess, hold, carry

When a possesser is animate and the possessed is inanimate, もっています is may be used instead of あります.

10. 知って います／ 知りません
<ruby>知<rt>し</rt></ruby> <ruby>知<rt>し</rt></ruby>

[G1 しる／しりません]

know　　do not know

しります means "to get to know" and しっています "know."
"Do not know" is しりません. しっていません is never used.

11. 習^{なら}って　います
[G1 ならう／ならいます]

is learning

12. ホームステイを　します
[G1 する／して]

will do a homestay

追加単語^{ついかたんご} Additional Vocabulary

1. べっきょして　います   is separated
2. りこんして　います   is divorced
3. どくしんです   is single

読^よみましょう　Language in Context

◀))) READ/LISTEN/SPEAK Read these sentences in Japanese. Tell a classmate whether you work part-time and who in your family has a smartphone.

よしくんは　ファストフードで
アルバイトを　して　います。

川本先生は　スマートフォンを
持^もって　います。

文法 Grammar

A Expressing Occurring and Continuing Actions or States with TE Form

Verb TE form ＋います。

The Verb -て います form combines the TE form of verbs and います, which may conjugate in any way. TE forms of あります and います are not used as - て forms. The interpretation of this construction varies depending on the verb that appears in the TE form.

The verbs appearing in this pattern may mean:

1. An action is / is not / was / was not occurring, or continuing.

のんで います	is drinking
のんで いません	is not drinking
のんで いました	was drinking
のんで いませんでした	was not drinking

2. As a result of an action, a state exists. Often verbs that do not express continuity cannot take on this meaning.

すみます	will live	すんで います	live/reside, is living/residing
けっこんします	will marry	けっこんして います	is married
もちます	will carry	もって います	have, possess, is carrying
つとめます	will be employed	つとめて います	is employed
しにます	will die	しんで います	is dead
しります	will get to know	しって います*	know*

*The negative of しって います is not しって いません, but しりません.

◀)) MODELS ▷

1. 「今　何を　して　いますか。」　　　　"What are you doing now?"
   「お昼ご飯を　食べて　います。」　　　"I am eating lunch."
2. 姉は　結婚して　います。　　　　　　My older sister is married.
3. 今　お金を　持って　いません。　　　I do not have any money now.
4. 「この　人を　知って　いますか。」　"Do you know this person?"
   「いいえ、知りません。」　　　　　　　"No, I do not know him/her."

READ/SPEAK Choose the correct word in the ( ) based on the information given in English:
My older sister is working at a coffee shop now. She lives in our house with us now. She is not married. She does not know my friend.

1. あねは　今　きっさてんで　(はたらきます / はたらいて　います)。

2. あねは　今　私たちと　うちに　(すみます / すんで　います)。

3. あねは　今　(けっこんしません / けっこんして　いません)。

4. あねは　私の　ともだちを　(しりません / しって　いません)。

B "Already" Adverb もう & "Not Yet" Adverb まだ

◀))) MODELS

♻

1. 「もう　お昼ご飯を　食べましたか。」   "Have you already eaten lunch?"

  「いいえ、まだです。」   "No, not yet."   **or**

  「いいえ、まだ　食べて　いません。」   "No, I have not eaten yet."

2. 「この　漢字を　もう　習いましたか。」 "Have you already learned this *kanji*?"

  「いいえ、まだ　習って　いません。」   "No, I have not learned it yet."

READ/SPEAK Choose the correct word in the ( ) to complete the dialogue.

先生：おひるごはんを　(もう / まだ)　食べましたか。

まり：はい、(もう / まだ)　食べました。

ケン：いいえ、(もう / まだ)　(食べません / 食べて　いません / 食べませんでした)。

文化ノート　Culture Notes

田中速雄

A. Japanese Names

In Japan, first names are chosen based on auspicious meanings or positive associations. Traditionally, birth order, connection to meaning of the family name, number of strokes in the *kanji* characters, or the season of birth is considered. Middle names are not given. Currently, some common Japanese first names for boys are Hiroto, Ren, and Takuya. Common girls' names are Hina, Momoko, and Yuka. Recently, names that resemble Western names in sound and appearance have also become popular and are generally written in *katakana*.

Last names are used far more frequently than first names in Japan, which are generally only used between close friends or with younger family members. Some common Japanese surnames are Tanaka, Nakamura, and Yamada.

B. Regions of Japan

Japan is a volcanic archipelago formed by four main islands and hundreds of smaller ones. Its latitudes span the distance from Maine to Florida.

Lavender Farm, Furano, Hokkaido

ほっかいどう
北海道

Enjoy a variety of seasonal outdoor sports and learn more about the history of Japan's first inhabitants in Hokkaido. This northernmost island is home to volcanoes, hot springs, and flat open spaces rarely seen in other parts of Japan. Many descendants of the original inhabitants of Japan, the Ainu, call this island their home. The winters are cold with lots of snow, and summers often cool and dry, relatively unaffected by つゆ, the rainy season. Sapporo is the island's largest city.

ほんしゅう
本州

Explore the center of modern Japanese culture in Honshu. Shop, eat, and experience the variety of Japan's largest island. Honshu is home to the major urban centers of Tokyo, Yokohama, Osaka, and Nagoya and historic cities such as Kyoto, Nara, and Hiroshima. It is the seventh-largest and second most-densely populated island in the world, with a climate that is mostly temperate, though it varies greatly across the island. Due to the island's large size and population, it is further divided into five regions (from Northeast to Southwest): Tohoku, Kanto, Chubu, Kansai (sometimes called Kinki), and Chugoku.

Imperial Palace area, Chiyoda, Tokyo

しこく
四国

Experience the beauty of nature on a walking tour of Japan's sacred temples and shrines in Shikoku. Shikoku takes its name from its four prefectures (*shi* [four], *koku* [countries]), and is the smallest and least populated of Japan's main islands. It is less urban than the rest of Japan, and is popular for its untouched natural beauty. The climate is subtropical, but mountains divide the island into north and south, with the sparsely populated south receiving significantly more rainfall during つゆ. Its largest city is Matsuyama.

Motoyama, Reihoku, Kochi

きゅうしゅう
九州

If you're interested in visiting a traditional Japanese inn or taking a dip in a natural hot spring, consider visiting Kyushu. The southernmost of the four main islands, Kyushu, is the home of many volcanoes and famous hot springs. According to Japanese mythology, it is the origin of Japan's Imperial Family. Like Shikoku, its climate is largely subtropical, but the rainy season affects the whole island.

Volcano, Sakurajima, Kagoshima

おきなわ
沖縄

Chatan Sunset Beach,
Mihama, Okinawa

Check out Okinawa if you like the beach and want to experience a culture distinct from the rest of Japan. South of the four main islands lie the Ryukyu Islands, including Okinawa, the largest of these islands. Okinawa has warm winters and hot, humid summers. Its culture has elements distinct from the rest of Japan, and after WWII it was occupied by the U.S. until being returned to Japan in 1972. Okinawa's capital is Naha.

 Be a travel agent! Research a city in Japan and create a travel brochure to attract tourism. Be sure to include information such as geographical features, climate, activities, and landmarks.

アクティビティー　Communicative Activities

ペアワーク

A. SPEAK/LISTEN/WRITE Interview your partner and take notes on a separate sheet of paper.

しつもん	こたえ
1. どこで　うまれましたか。	
2. 今　どこに　すんで　いますか。	
3. お父さんは　どこに　つとめて　いますか。	
4. 今　アルバイトを　して　いますか。	
5. どこで　はたらいて　いますか。	
6. 今　百ドルを　もって　いますか。	
7. かんじを　ならって　いますか。	
8. かんじを　百　しって　いますか。	
9. おねえさんは　けっこんして　いますか。	
10. 〜さんを　しって　いますか。	

ペアゲーム

B. SPEAK/LISTEN/WRITE On this and the next page, there are two identical pictures with names missing on each. Look at one picture as your partner looks at the other and ask each other what each person whose name appears in your picture is doing. Record your answers on a separate sheet of paper.

Ex. Person A: ～さんは　今　何を　して　いますか。

Person B:　　～さんは　Verb-て　います。

1. ゆきお　　3. 一ろう　　5. 大すけ　　7. けんじ　　9. としかず
2. しんー　　4. あきら　　6. まこと　　8. けんた

バイクに　のります [G1] to ride a motor bike, うんてん(を)　します to drive [IR]

Ex. Person A: ～さんは　今　何を　して　いますか。

Person B:　　　～さんは　Verb-て　います。

   1. えみ　　　**3.** さち子　　**5.** みち子　　**7.** ゆか

   2. あい　　　**4.** まゆみ　　**6.** なおみ　　**8.** ゆう子

バイクに　のります [G1] to ride a motor bike, うんてん(を)　します to drive [IR]

会話 Dialogue

🔊))) **READ/LISTEN** What are Mari and Ken looking for?

猫は　どこに
いますか。

机の　下に
います。

文型 Sentence Patterns

READ Find these sentence patterns in the dialogue.

1. Topic は　　　　　Something の Position に　　います／あります。
2. Something の　　　Position に　Subject が　　います／あります。

単語 Vocabulary

1. 上
うえ

on, above, on top of

2. 下
した

under, below

3. 中
なか

inside

4. 外
そと

outside

5. 前 <ruby>前<rt>まえ</rt></ruby>

in front of

6. 後ろ <ruby>後<rt>うし</rt></ruby>ろ

back, behind

7. 右 <ruby>右<rt>みぎ</rt></ruby>

right side

8. 左 <ruby>左<rt>ひだり</rt></ruby>

left side

9. そば

by, nearby

10. 間 <ruby>間<rt>あいだ</rt></ruby>

between

11. となり

next (to)
(two similar animate or inanimate objects)

12. 近く <ruby>近<rt>ちか</rt></ruby>く

vicinity, nearby

13. 遠く <ruby>遠<rt>とお</rt></ruby>く

far away

14. 所 <ruby>所<rt>ところ</rt></ruby>

place
ドアの ところに います。

追加単語 <ruby>追加単語<rt>ついかたんご</rt></ruby> Additional Vocabulary

1. 横 <ruby>横<rt>よこ</rt></ruby>　　side

2. 向こう <ruby>向<rt>む</rt></ruby>こう　　beyond

3. 手前 <ruby>手前<rt>てまえ</rt></ruby>　　this side

4. 真ん中 <ruby>真<rt>ま</rt></ruby>ん<ruby>中<rt>なか</rt></ruby>　　middle

5. 近所 <ruby>近所<rt>きんじょ</rt></ruby>　　neighborhood

6. 庭 <ruby>庭<rt>にわ</rt></ruby>　　garden

🔊 **READ/LISTEN/SPEAK** Read these sentences in Japanese. Say who you are sitting by in your Japanese class. Say what is by the door.

お母さんは　かれんさんと　ふみや
さんの　あいだに　たって　います。

ごみばこは　ドアの
ところに　あります。

ぶんぽう
文法　Grammar

A Location Markers + Position Verbs　います/ あります

Topic は	Location		に	います。[for animate objects]
	Noun の	Position		
		うえ above したした below なか inside そと outside まえ front うしろ back みぎ right ひだり left そば nearby となり next あいだ between		あります。[for inanimate objects]

| Location | | に | Subject が | います。[for animate objects] |
| Noun の | Position | | | あります。[for inanimate objects] |

This new construction is an expansion of the N1 は　Place に　あります/います and Place に　Noun が　あります/います patterns. In the first grammatical structure, the emphasis is on where the topic is located. In the second, the emphasis is on what/who exists.

MODELS

1. 家の　外に　木が　たくさん　あります。
   There are many trees outside (my) home.

2. 私の　後ろに　ジョン君が　います。
   John is behind me.

3. 家は　本屋と　パン屋の　間に　あります。
   My house is between the bookstore and the bakery.

READ/SPEAK Choose the correct word in the ( ) to complete the sentences.

1. ケン：ねこ(は / が)　どこに　いますか。

   まり：あそこに　ねこ(は / が)　いますよ。

2. ケン：母(は / が)　車(の / に)　外(に / で)(います / あります)が、
   　　　宿題(は / が)　車(に / の)　中(に / で)(います / あります)。

B Place Words ——————————————

Location　　に　　　　　　　います。　　[for animate objects]
Noun　　　の　ところに　あります。　　[for inanimate objects]

When indicating the existence of an object at a certain location, the place word に + existence verb is used. When indicating the existence of an object at a location which is not a place, e.g., a person or thing, ところ is attached to create a "place word" as the location of existence.

MODELS

1. 犬が　ドアの　ところに　います。
   The dog is where the door is.

2. 宿題は　先生の　ところに　あります。
   The homework is at the teacher's (place).

3. 一時に　あの　木の　ところで　待って　いますよ。
   At 1 o'clock, I will be waiting where the tree is (by the tree).

READ/SPEAK Choose the correct particle in the ( ) to complete the dialogue.

まり：ごみばこ(は / が)　どこ(に / で)　ありますか。
ケン：ドア(の / に)　ところ(に / で)　ありますよ。

文化ノート　Culture Notes

ぶん か

A. Japanese Proverb 「石の　上にも　三年」

いし うえ さんねん

いし means "a stone." This proverb means that even a stone becomes warm after sitting on it for three years. It is a proverb used to express that perseverance overcomes all things.

B. Inside the Japanese Home

Especially in large cities, many Japanese people live in apartments or condominiums. Most modern Japanese homes are now designed in a more Western-style while retaining some elements of the traditional Japanese home.

For example, each house or apartment usually has at least one Japanese-style room with straw mat flooring (たたみ), floor cushions (ざぶとん), and a knee-high table. Larger houses may also include other traditional features. Families may receive guests, or gather in this room to watch television or eat if there is no separate formal dining space. Most homes do not have dedicated home offices, and personal laptops are often kept in a bedroom on a small desk.

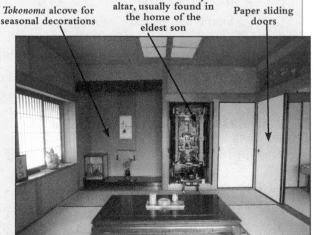

Tokonoma alcove for seasonal decorations

A Buddhist family altar, usually found in the home of the eldest son

Paper sliding doors

Tatami mats and *zabuton*

A traditional-style room in a Japanese house

 Check the Internet for photos of the interior, exterior, and landscaping of several Japanese homes. Find a photograph or make a model and label the various objects commonly found in a Japanese home. Write a short description in Japanese using location words to indicate where each object is.

アクティビティー　Communicative Activities

ペアワーク

A. SPEAK/LISTEN/WRITE Choose picture A or B on the next page and ask your partner where the missing items listed under the heading "Find" are. Draw in the items according to the locations your partner gives you on a separate sheet of paper and compare. Take turns. Are the drawings accurate?

Ex. 「〜は　どこに　あります／いますか。」

Picture A

Find:

ごみばこ
ごきぶり
バット
男の子
犬
25セント
本

Picture B

Find:

ギター
ねこ
ボール
木
ぼうし
女の子
一ドル

B. SPEAK/LISTEN Ask what each person/animal is doing now and where it is being done.

Ex. 「〜は　今　どこで　何を　して　いますか。」

ジョン	
ローラ	
ケン	
犬	
ねこ	

1課3
<small>か</small>

The baby is still one

会話 Dialogue
<small>かいわ</small>

🔊 **READ/LISTEN** How old is the baby?

> 赤ちゃんは
> いくつですか。

> まだ
> 一歳です。

文型 Sentence Patterns
<small>ぶんけい</small>

READ Find one of these sentence patterns in the dialogue.

1. Verb Dictionary Form 　まだ＋ Affirmative predicate。 　　still
　　　　　　　　　　　　　　　もう＋ Negative predicate。 　　(not) any more

♻ **2.** Verb Dictionary Form 　まだ＋ Negative predicate。 　　(not) yet
　　　　　　　　　　　　　　　もう＋ Affirmative predicate。 　　already

単語 Vocabulary
<small>たんご</small>

<small>いえ</small>
1. 家

house

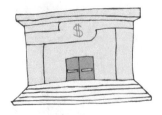

<small>ぎんこう</small>
2. 銀行

bank

<small>こうえん</small>
3. 公園

park

4. 寮
（りょう）

dormitory

5. 赤ちゃん
（あか）

baby

6. 〜ちゃん

Used instead of 〜さん when addressing or referring to young/ small/cute animals or children.

7. まだ＋ Aff.

still

8. もう＋ Neg.

(not) any more

9. (topic)に　ついて

about (a topic)

10. しょうかい(を)　します
[IR する／して]

to introduce

11. じこしょうかい(を)　します
[IR する／して]

to do a self-introduction

追加単語 Additional Vocabulary
（ついかたんご）

1.	アパート	apartment	**4.**	郵便局（ゆうびんきょく）	post office
2.	マンション	condominium	**5.**	映画館（えいがかん）	movie theater
3.	ホテル	hotel	**6.**	ガソリンスタンド	gas station

🔊 **READ/LISTEN/SPEAK** Read these sentences in Japanese. Say what grade you are in and whether you are still a middle school student or already a high school student.

みかさんは　もう
小学生では　ありません。

まいさんは　まだ
小学生です。

<ruby>文法<rt>ぶんぽう</rt></ruby> Grammar

A Adverbs まだ and もう

まだ＋ Affirmative predicate。	still
もう＋ Negative predicate。	(not) any more
もう＋ Affirmative predicate。	already
まだ＋ Negative predicate。	(not) yet

♻ 🔊 MODELS ▷

1. 「お<ruby>兄<rt>にい</rt></ruby>さんは　まだ　サンフランシスコに　<ruby>住<rt>す</rt></ruby>んで　いますか。」
   "Is your older brother still living in San Francisco?"

   「いいえ、<ruby>兄<rt>あに</rt></ruby>は　もう　サンフランシスコに　<ruby>住<rt>す</rt></ruby>んで　いません。」
   "No, my older brother is not living in San Francisco any more."

2. 「もう　<ruby>宿題<rt>しゅくだい</rt></ruby>を　しましたか。」
   "Have you done your homework already?"

   「いいえ、まだ　して　いません。」
   "No, I have not done it yet."

READ/SPEAK Choose the correct word in the ( ) to complete the sentences.

1. まり：(もう / まだ)　本を　ぜんぶ　よみましたか。

　　ケン：いいえ、(もう / まだ)　ぜんぶ　よんで　いません。

2. まり：(もう / まだ)　本を　よんで　いますか。

　　ケン：いいえ、(もう / まだ)　ぜんぶ　よみましたよ。

B Verb Dictionary Form

The verb dictionary form is the form you would use to look up a verb in a dictionary. It is also used in many grammatical structures. It is the plain, non-past affirmative verb form.

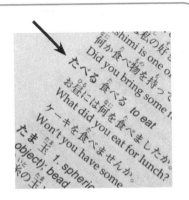

Group 1 Verbs

Group 1 verbs are identified by the verb stem, which is the portion of the verb that remains after dropping -ます. If there are two or more *hiragana* characters remaining in the verb stem after dropping ます and the final sound of the verb stem is an *-i* ending sound, the verb can usually be categorized as Group 1. To obtain the dictionary form, change the *-i* ending verb stem to its corresponding *-u* sound.

MODELS

[-i ます]	MASU form	Meaning	Dictionary form
[み]	のみます	to drink	のむ
	よみます	to read	よむ
	やすみます	to rest, be absent	やすむ
[に]	しにます	to die	しぬ
[び]	あそびます	to play	あそぶ
[い]	あいます	to meet	あう
[ち]	かちます	to win	かつ
[り]	分かります	to understand	分かる
	しります	to get to know	しる
	あります	to be (inanimate)	ある
[き]	ききます	to listen, hear	きく
	行きます	to go	行く
	あるきます	to walk	あるく
[ぎ]	およぎます	to swim	およぐ
[し]	はなします	to talk, speak	はなす

Group 2 Verbs

Group 2 verbs can be identified by a verb stem (verb without ます) ending in an "–*e* sounding" *hiragana,* or a stem with only one *hiragana.* There are some exceptions that must be learned as special verbs. Group 2 dictionary forms are created by replacing -ます with る.

	MASU form	Meaning	Dictionary form
[-*e* ます]	見えます	can be seen	見える
	きこえます	can be heard	きこえる
	食べます	to eat	食べる
[One hiragana]	見ます	to see, watch	見る
	います	to be (animate)	いる
	ねます	to sleep	ねる
[Special verbs]	おきます	to get up	おきる

Group 3 Irregular Verbs

Only きます, します and a noun ＋します verbs belong to this group. Memorize the individual dictionary forms as they do not follow any rules.

MASU form	Meaning	Dictionary form
来(き)ます	to come	来(く)る
します	to do	する
べんきょう(を)します	to study	べんきょう(を)する

READ/WRITE Write the verbs in their dictionary forms in *hiragana* on a separate sheet of paper.

1. 見ます   3. します   5. ねます

2. のみます   4. およぎます   6. 来ます

文化(ぶんか)ノート Culture Notes

A. Age

Traditionally, Japanese babies were considered to be a year old at birth. Japanese people also traditionally believed that everyone aged a year at New Year's. Today, however, this system is rarely used, unless counting ages for special celebrations.

B. Chinese Zodiac

A Japanese person can determine someone's age by asking what Chinese zodiac animal's year they were born in. There are twelve animals in the Chinese zodiac which create a repeating cycle. See a list of the zodiac animals and associated birth years at **cheng-tsui.com/adventuresinjapanese**.

C. Traditional Birthday Celebrations:

For young adults in Japan, the twentieth birthday signifies a "coming of age." On the second Monday of January, 成人の日 (せいじんのひ) is celebrated to recognize all those who have turned twenty during the last year. Young women wear bright, festive kimono and young men wear Western suits or traditional *hakama* kimono to congratulatory ceremonies held at local government offices. Afterwards, they have parties or go out with friends or family to celebrate.

やくどし marks another significant birthday for the Japanese. It is celebrated when a man turns 41, as according to the traditional way of counting age, this is when he turns 42. The 42nd year of life is believed to be dangerous, because read in Japanese, 42 is しに, a form of the verb しにます, which means "to die." In order to chase away the possibility of death at this age, the Japanese celebrate with friends and family. Other ages that are considered dangerous for males are 25 and 61. For women, ages that are considered challenging years are 19, 33, and 37.

 Interview a person in your community from another country. Ask them what birthdays are significant in their culture and how they are celebrated. Then, plan a birthday party for someone in your family or a friend with a cultural twist borrowed from another culture. Draw a picture or find photos online of what the celebration may look like.

アクティビティー Communicative Activities

ペアワーク

A. SPEAK/LISTEN Choose one of the following sets of questions and ask your partner the questions in the left-hand column in Japanese. He/she should answer in Japanese according to the information given in the right-hand column. Switch roles for the second set of questions and answers.

しつもん	こたえ
Who?	My older brother.
Name?	His name is Mike.
Age?	He is already 20 years old.
Which college?	He goes to college in California.
Does he live in a dormitory?	He still lives in a dormitory.
Does he have a car?	He does not have a car.
Does he want to buy a car?	He wants to buy a car.
Is he working part-time?	He is working part-time at a bookstore.

しつもん	こたえ
Who?	My older sister.
Name?	Her name is Lisa.
Age?	She is 25 years old.
Married?	She is already married.
Baby?	She already has a baby.
Age of baby?	Her baby is still one.
Where does she live?	She lives by a park.
Job?	She is not working now.

ペアゲーム

B. READ/WRITE Recreate the gameboards below on a separate sheet of paper. Play Tic-Tac-Toe with your partner by changing the -*masu* form of the verbs in the grid to the dictionary form. For more game boards, go to **cheng-tsui.com/adventuresinjapanese**.

a.

のみます	しにます	見ます
おきます (to get up)	ねます	かちます
休みます	はなします	かきます

b.

います	来ます (to come)	かえります
あいます	よみます	食べます
行きます	分かります	します

Authentic Reading

C. READ/WRITE Read this pen-pal e-mail from Hana Tagawa, a Japanese high school student, and answer the following questions in Japanese on a separate sheet of paper.

UNDERSTAND

1. Is Hana's room spacious?

2. Where is Hana's desk?

3. What instrument does Hana have in her room?

4. What animal sits near Hana all the time?

APPLY

5. If Hana offered to host you at her home, would you accept? Why?

WORKBOOK   page 5

2:30 PM

Inbox (7)

田川ハナ

私の　へや

私の　へやに　ついて　しょうかいしましょう。私の　へやは　せまいですが、きれいですよ。

まどは　大きくて、まどの　そばに　つくえが　あります。まどからとおくに　山が　見えます。つくえの　ひだりに　ギターがあります。犬が　いつも　私のそばにすわって　います。私はこの　へやが　大好きです。

会話 <small>かいわ</small> Dialogue

🔊 **READ/LISTEN** What does Mari like to do?

まりさんは　何を　するのが
好きですか。

私は　泳 <small>およ</small> ぐことが　特 <small>とく</small> に　好きです。

文型 <small>ぶんけい</small> Sentence Patterns

READ Find one of these sentence patterns in the dialogue.

1. Verb Dictionary Form ＋の／こと　が　好きです。   I like to do ~.
2. Verb Dictionary Form ＋の／こと　は　楽 <small>たの</small> しいです。   It is fun to do ~.

単語 <small>たんご</small> Vocabulary

1. 特 <small>とく</small> に

especially

2. 両親 <small>りょうしん</small> ／御両親 <small>ごりょうしん</small>

(one's own)
parents

(someone else's)
parents

3. 正 <small>ただ</small> しい

[い Adjective]

is correct

4. ちがいます
[G1 ちがう]

is wrong, to differ

5. 質問
[Noun]

question

しつもんを　します
[IR する]

to ask a question

6. 答え
[Noun]

answer

こたえます
[G2 こたえる]

to answer

追加単語 Additional Vocabulary

1. そふ　　　　(one's own) grandfather

2. そぼ　　　　(one's own) grandmother

3. あね　　　　(one's own) older sister

4. あに　　　　(one's own) older brother

読みましょう　Language in Context

🔊 **READ/LISTEN/SPEAK** Read these sentences in Japanese. Ask what your partner enjoys doing.

日本語を　話すのは
楽しいです。

ゴルフを　することが　とくに
好きです。

文法 Grammar

ぶんぽう

A Verb Nominalizer の／こと

Verb Dictionary form ＋ の／こと　が　好きです。

Verb Dictionary form ＋ の／こと　は　楽しいです。

たの

This construction is used to describe or comment upon some action or state. The action or state being described is used in its verb dictionary form, followed by の or こと, which nominalizes the verb form. の or こと are nouns which literally mean "(the) act (of)." Generally, using こと is more formal than using の. こと is often used in writing while の is used more often in speaking. In sentences that end with a verb, choose こと, not の before です。Example: しゅみは　本を　よむこと (not の)　です。

◀)) MODELS

うた　うた
1. 母は　歌を　歌うのが　好きです。
   My mother likes to sing.

べんきょう　たの
2. 日本語を　勉強するのは　楽しいです。
   Studying Japanese is fun.

よ　きら
3. 私は　本を　読むのが　嫌いです。
   I dislike reading books.

あさ　たいへん
4. 朝　七時に　学校へ　来ることは　大変です。
   It is difficult to come to school at 7:00.

か
5. 日本語を　書くことは　むずかしいです。
   Writing Japanese is difficult.

6. しゅみは　アニメを　見ることです。
   My hobby is watching anime.

READ/SPEAK Given the context, change the verb in the ( ) to the correct form.

はな
1. 日本語を　(話します)ことが　好きです。

2. (食べます)ことが　大好きです。

たの
3. ダンスを　(します)ことは　楽しいです。

4. しゅみは　(およぎます)ことです。

きら
5. 早く　(おきます)ことが　嫌いです。

ぶん か

A. Swimming

Swimming is a popular pastime in Japan, an island country striped with rivers. Swimming in Japan has its origins as a martial art; samurai were trained to swim silently underwater while carrying weapons. Today it is also a required part of physical education classes, and most Japanese elementary schools have their own pool.

There are both public and private pools in Japan, and they are especially popular among young families during the hot summer. Rules for pool usage vary from pool to pool, but commonly include the following:

1. Wear a swim cap

2. No shoes in the locker room

3. Cover all tattoos

4. Remove all make-up

5. No food or drinks

 Is swimming a required part of physical education at your school? Write a short paragraph explaining why you think Japan's swimming requirements are or are not appropriate for your school.

B. Japanese Proverb 「となりの　花は　赤い」
はな　　あか

となり means "next door" or "neighbor." This proverb means that the neighbor's flowers are red. Its equivalent in English is "The grass is greener on the other side of the fence." This proverb suggests that once you own something (even if it previously looked attractive), it loses its appeal and other things that you do not possess become more attractive.

アクティビティー　Communicative Activities

ペアワーク

A. SPEAK/LISTEN/WRITE Ask your partner if he/she thinks the activities below are fun or uninteresting. On a separate sheet of paper, track his/her answers using a chart like the one below.

Ex. 歌を　歌います

「歌を　歌うの(or こと)は　楽しいですか。つまらないですか。」

しつもん	たのしい	つまらない
1. ダンスを　します		
2. 日本語を　ならいます		
3. ともだちと　はなします		
4. 本を　よみます		
5. えいがを　見ます		
6. はしります		
7. およぎます		
8. かんじを　かきます		
9. 学校に　来ます		
10. 何を　することが　特に　楽しい／つまらないですか。」		

B. SPEAK/LISTEN/WRITE Interview your partner about activities his/her family member likes and dislikes. Write his/her answers on a separate sheet of paper in a chart like the one below.

Ex. 「お父さんは　何を　するの(or こと)が　好きですか。」

人	好きな　こと	きらいな　こと
お父さん		
お母さん		
Your choice		

WORKBOOK page 7

Review Questions

Ask your partner these questions in Japanese. Your partner should answer in Japanese. Check your answers using the audio.

About you   Review pages 22–23, 30–31, 36–38, 43

1. Where were you born?

2. Where are you living now?

3. Is your mother employed at a school?

4. Is your father working at a bank?

5. Are you working at a part-time job?

6. Please introduce yourself.

7. Do you want to live in a college dormitory?

8. Are you still an eighth grader (middle school second grader)?

9. What kind of person do you want to marry?

10. Have you already eaten lunch?

11. What do you like to do?

Location: (Use location and position words.)   Review pages 36–38

12. Where is your house?

13. What is near the door?

14. Where is the teacher now?

15. Is there a park near your house?

16. Where is Hokkaido? Do you know?

17. Where is Okinawa? Do you know?

Opinions   Review pages 36–38, 43

18. Please tell (speak to) me about Tokyo. Where is it?

19. Please tell (speak to) me about your school. (Give two descriptions in one sentence.)

20. Is coming to school fun?

Text Chat

You will participate in a simulated exchange of text-chat messages. You should respond as fully and as appropriately as possible. You will have a conversation with Mayu Tanaka, a Japanese high school student, for the first time.

9月 5日 7:46 PM

はじめまして。田中 まゆです。
15歳で、高校一年生 です。
どうぞ よろしく。

Introduce yourself.

9月 5日 7:51 PM

私の しゅみは、カラオケですが、
何を することが 好きですか。

Respond and give details.

9月 5日 7:56 PM

どこに すんで いますか。そして、
どんな ところですか。

Respond and use two descriptive words.

Can Do!
Now I can . . .

- ☐ identify the main islands and cities of Japan
- ☐ name my place of residence, where I was born, and talk about where my family members are employed.
- ☐ describe the locations of various people and objects
- ☐ share what some of my and my family's and friends' hobbies, likes, dislikes, strengths and weaknesses are by using action verbs

Cities in Japan

RESEARCH Use books, the Internet, or interview a Japanese member of your community to answer the following questions.

Determine

1. What is the old name for Tokyo?

2. What is the second largest city in Japan?

3. Which ancient capital is famous for its shrines, temples (including one gilded with 24-karat gold), and geisha district?

4. What city hosted the 1998 Winter Olympics?

5. Which city in Japan hosts a famous snow and ice festival?

Compare

6. Does your hometown or state have a sister-city in Japan? What is it? Do they share any similarities (climate, population, traditional crafts)?

7. What is the distance from Wakkanai to Okinotorishima? What is the distance between the northernmost and the southernmost city of your own country?

Apply

8. Japan is home to many internationally recognized historical sites and landmarks, such as the Shiretoko Peninsula, Mt. Fuji, the Hiroshima Peace Memorial, and Itsukushima Shrine. Why do you think the preservation of such landmarks is important? What are some historic landmarks in your own country?

Extend Your Learning
VISUAL AND TECHNOLOGY LITERACY

Which city in Japan would you most like to visit? Why? Take photos or screenshots of the Japanese city from the Internet and make a short presentation to your class. Be sure to include the city's location, climate, population, traditional arts and festivals, and any other important information.

学校の きそく
School Rules

✓ **Can Do!**
In this lesson you will learn to:

- describe how you and others are dressed
- grant and ask for permission
- tell others what they may or may not do
- state reasons for going somewhere
- answer negative yes/no questions

Online Resources

cheng-tsui.com/
adventuresinjapanese

- Audio
- Vocabulary Lists
- Vocabulary and *Kanji* Flashcards
- Study Guides
- Activity Worksheets

In this lesson you will learn how to talk about school rules, explain your reason for doing something, and describe your school's dress code. Review these words, phrases, and grammatical structures you already learned to help you talk about your school life.

めいし Nouns

1. 学校	school		8. 本	book	
2. 男	male		9. 何	what?	
3. 小さいの	small one		10. 中	inside	
4. アメリカ	America		11. 一時	one o'clock	
5. としょかん	library		12. ところ	place	
6. どこ	where?		13. お昼ご飯（おひるごはん）	lunch	
7. たてもの	building		14. くつ	shoes	

どうし Verbs

15. 行きたいんです [G1 いく／いきます／いって]	want to go
16. 〜が　いります [G1 いる／いって]	need 〜
17. はなして [G1 はなす／はなします]	to talk, to speak
18. 食べ [G1 たべる／たべます／たべて]	to eat [stem form]
19. 行きましょう [G1 いく／いきます／いって]	let's go

-い けいようし -I Adjectives

20. いい	good, okay		22. 白い	white
21. みじかい	short [for length]		23. きびしい	strict

ふくし -Adverbs

24. とても	very

Others

25. でも	However		26. それから	And then, In addition

Expressions	
27. あ、はい、はい。	Oh, yes, yes.
28. どうも　ありがとう。	Thank you very much.
29. あ、いいですね。	Oh, that sounds good.
30. じゃ、またね。	Well, see you again.

ぶんぽう　Grammar	
31. Sentence 1＋が、Sentence 2。	Sentence 1, but Sentence 2.
32. Sentence 1＋から、Sentence 2。	Sentence 1, <u>so</u> Sentence 2.
33. Verb (Stem form)＋たい(ん)です。	I want to do 〜 .
	[ん is inserted when one explains to the listener what one wants to do.]

A. SPEAK/LISTEN Tell your partner the following things in Japanese.

1. Give a reason why you like your school.

2. Compare two of your classes using が.

3. State what you want to do tonight.

B. READ/WRITE Complete the sentences below according to the English prompts by filling in the appropriate word in the ( ). Write your answers on a separate sheet of paper.

1. 日本語は　むずかしいです(　　)、おもしろいです。
The Japanese language is difficult, but it is interesting.

2. 天気(てんき)が　いい(　　)、外(そと)で　お昼(ひる)ご飯(はん)を　食べましょう。
The weather is good, so let's eat lunch outside.

3. 今　食べ(　　)んです。
I want to eat now.

4. 一時に　食べに　行(　　)。
Let's go eat at one o'clock.

In this lesson, you will learn some *kanji* related to positions, age, and the first person, as well as review some key *kanji* from Volume 1.

	Kanji	Meaning	Readings	Examples	
61.	私	I	わたし	わたし 私	I (polite)
			わたくし	わたくし 私	I (formal)
62.	才	- years old	サイ	ごさい 五才	5 years old
63.	上	top	うえ	やま うえ 山の上	top of mountain
			ジョウ	じょうず 上手	skillful
64.	下	under	した	め した 目の下	under the eye
			くだ(さい)	み 見て く だ 下さい	Please look.
			カ	ち か てつ 地下鉄	subway
				へた 下手	unskillful
65.	右	right	みぎ	みぎ て 右手	right hand
66.	左	left	ひだり	ひだり て 左手	left hand

Review Kanji					
23.	父 father	ちち	父	one's own father	
		とう	お父さん	someone else's father	
24.	母 mother	はは	母	one's own mother	
		かあ	お母さん	someone else's mother	
44.	小 small	ちい(さい)	小さい人	a small person	
		ショウ	小学生	elementary school student	
45.	中 inside, middle	なか	車の中	inside the car	
		チュウ	中学生	middle school student	

New Reading					
27.	来 to come	くる	来る	come	
		こ(ない)	来ない	do not come	
38.	生 be born	う(まれる)	生まれました	was born	

Recognition Kanji

歳 - years old [formal]

WORKBOOK page 171

きそくが たくさん あります

There are many rules

会話 Dialogue
^{かいわ}

🔊 **READ/LISTEN** What color are Ken's pants? What else is he wearing?

ケンさんは　白い　シャツを
着て、青い　ズボンを
はいて　います。そして、黒と
赤の　ぼうしを　かぶって
います。

文型 Sentence Patterns
^{ぶんけい}

READ Find one of these sentence patterns in the dialogue.

1. "wear"	シャツを	着て　います	is wearing a shirt
2.	くつを	はいて　います	is wearing shoes
3.	イヤリングを	して　います	is wearing earrings
4.	ぼうしを	かぶって　います	is wearing a hat
5.	めがねを	かけて　います	is wearing glasses

単語 Vocabulary
^{たんご}

1. 着て　います
[G2 きる／きます]

is wearing [above the waist or on the entire body]

2. はいて　います
[G1 はく／はきます]

is wearing [below the waist]

3. して　います
[IR する／します]

is wearing [accessories]

4. かぶって　います

[G1 かぶる／かぶります]

is wearing [on, or draped over the head]

5. かけて　います

[G2 かける／かけます]

is wearing [glasses]

6. ふく 服

clothing

7. Ｔ(ティー)シャツ

T-shirt

8. ズボン

pants

9. ショートパンツ
or ショーツ

shorts

10. セーター

sweater

11. ワンピース

dress

12. スカート

skirt

13. せいふく

uniform

14. くつ下 or
ソックス

socks

15. ゆびわ

ring

16. めがね

eyeglasses

17. サングラス

sunglasses

18. ネックレス

necklace

19. イヤリング

earrings

20. ピアス

pierced
(earrings)

追加単語　Additional Vocabulary

つい か たん ご

1.	水着 ぎ	bathing suit	7. ジャケット	jacket
2.	アクセサリー	accessories; jewelry	8. せびろ or スーツ	suit
3.	ブレスレット	bracelet	9. こん色 いろ	navy blue [a common color for Japanese uniforms]
4.	ユニフォーム	sports uniform	10. ぬぐ [G1 ぬぎます]	to take off [articles used with verbs きる, はく, かぶる]
5.	ストッキング	stockings	11. はめる [G2 はめます]	to insert; fit on to (something) [i.e., rings and gloves]
6.	サンダル	sandals	12. とる [G1 とります]	to take off [articles used with verbs する, かける, はめる]

読みましょう　Language in Context

よ

🔊 **READ/LISTEN/SPEAK** Read these sentences in Japanese. Describe at least three things you are wearing today, including the colors of the items.

あそかちゃんは　ぼうしを
かぶって　います。

山田さんは　青い　シャツを
あお
着て、ベージュの　スカートと
き
くつを　はいて　います。

文法 Grammar

A Verbs of Wearing

The Japanese verb "to wear" varies according to where or how an object is worn on the body.

For example, 着ます is used to describe things worn above the waist or on the entire body.

はきます	will wear (below the waist)
します	will wear (accessories)
かぶります	will wear (on or draped over the head)
かけます	will wear (glasses)

With verbs of wearing, the MASU form is an imperfect tense, which means that an action will take place in the future. -ています is used to describe one's present state or a habitual state, or that the action of wearing is occurring at the present moment.

着ます	will wear	着て います	is wearing or wears
着ません	will not wear	着て いません	is not wearing or does not wear

MODELS

1. 父は 青い シャツを 着て います。
   My father is wearing a blue shirt.

2. あの 生徒は 黒い ズボンを はいて います。
   That student is wearing black pants.

3. 姉は 白い ネックレスを して います。
   My older sister is wearing a white necklace.

4. 弟は いつも ぼうしを かぶって います。
   My younger brother always wears a hat.

5. 母は めがねを かけて います。
   My mother is wearing glasses.

READ/WRITE In each ( ), choose the correct verb from the choices given in the box below. You may use the same verb twice. Write your answers on a separate sheet of paper.

着て はいて して かぶって かけて

まりさんは 今 白い シャツを （1）、青い スカートを （2）、

黒い くつを （3） います。そして、ぼうしは （4） いませんが、

ネックレスを （5） います。めがねは （6） いません。

B Review of Colors

All color words in Japanese can be expressed as nouns. When noun forms of color words are used, the color word is followed by の before the word it modifies. Some color words also have い adjective forms, which do not take の.

Ex. a white shirt　白い　シャツ　or　白の　シャツ

NOTE: When talking about something that is "black and white," white is always listed first in Japanese, unlike in English.

(Ex. a black and white shirt　白と　黒の　シャツ)

い Adjectives		Nouns			
白い	white	白	white	みどり	green
黒い	black	黒	black	むらさき	purple
赤い	red	赤	red	ピンク	pink
青い	blue	青	blue	グレイ	gray
黄色い	yellow	黄色	yellow	金色	gold
茶色い	brown	茶色	brown	銀色	silver

READ/WRITE Read the English description below. Write the correct color words in the (　) to match the description on a separate sheet of paper.

Ken is wearing a blue and white shirt, and green pants. His shoes are red. He is wearing a pink cap and a gold pierced earring.

ケンさんは　（ 1 ）と　（ 2 ）の　シャツを
着て、(3)の　パンツを　はいて　います。
くつは　（ 4 ）です。そして、(5) の　ぼうしを
かぶって　いて、(6)の　ピアスを　して
います。

A. Uniforms

Uniforms were introduced to Japanese schools with the influence of Western culture in the Meiji Period (1868–1912). Today uniforms are worn at most junior high and high schools. While traditional uniforms resembled military-style uniforms, they have evolved with the changing fashion of the times. Nowadays uniforms typically consist of a blazer, shirt, and skirt or trousers.

Students typically wear both summer (なつふく) and winter uniforms (ふゆふく). Some schools also have あいふく, uniforms which are worn during times of transition between the cold winters and hot summers of Japan. Japanese students often wear uniforms even during non-school hours and are easily identifiable by school according to the uniforms they wear.

Uniforms are not limited to students, but are also commonly worn by health care professionals and law enforcement officers. There are many other types of occupations which also require uniforms. Some examples are: department store employees, taxi drivers, and sales clerks.

 Create a Venn diagram of occupations in your country and Japan where uniforms are required. What is the purpose of wearing uniforms at work? What conclusion can you draw about the practice of wearing uniforms in Japan? Write a brief paragraph to accompany your Venn diagram.

B. Cosplay

Cosplay (コスプレ) originated in Japan, home of "*kawaii*" pop culture. The word cosplay comes from the combination of the English words "costume" and "play." Some young adults dress up as video game or anime characters or don gothic or frilly fashions. As the popularity of cosplay grows in Japan, more and more businesses cater to cosplay customers. Costumes, supplies, and wigs can also be purchased online, some for under $100, while custom-made costumes may cost several thousand dollars.

Popular gathering places for cosplay in Tokyo are Akihabara, the "electronic and pop culture town" of Japan, and Harajuku, long known as a fashionable but quirky hang-out site for young people. Young Japanese who love to engage in cosplay enjoy the escape to a world of fantasy. At places such as Akihabara, they are able to connect to others who share their interest in Japanese pop culture.

 Should you engage in cosplay, how would you choose to dress and why? Research examples of cosplay in Japan online, then design your own costume. Draw yourself in your costume, or if you already own one, take a photo and share it with your class.

ペアワーク

A. SPEAK/LISTEN Ask your partner if any of your classmates are wearing the following. He/she should respond based on fact.

Ex. 白い　Tシャツ

質問：だれが　白い　Tシャツを
　　　着て　いますか。

答え：～さんが　白い　Tシャツを
　　　着て　いますよ。

　or　～さんです。

　or　だれも　着て　いません。　No one is wearing (it).

1. 白い　Tシャツ	8. ピアス
2. ぼうし	9. せいふく
3. めがね	10. ワンピース
4. とけい	11. ショートパンツ
5. 黒い　くつ	12. 赤い　セーター
6. 白い　ソックス	13. スカート
7. サングラス	14. 青い　ズボン

クラスワーク

B. WRITE/LISTEN Write your name and describe what you are wearing today from head to toe in one sentence, using color descriptions for each item on a separate piece of paper. Your teacher will collect the self-descriptions from each student and read them at random. Try to guess who is being described and record your answers.

Ex. 白い　シャツを　着て、青い　ズボンを　はいて、赤と　白の

　　ぼうしを　かぶって　います。

WORKBOOK page 15

2課2
May we wear hats in the classroom?

会話 Dialogue

🔊 READ/LISTEN Are students allowed to wear hats in the classroom?

> きょうしつ
> 教室で
> ぼうしを　かぶっても
> いいんですか。

> いいえ、
> かぶっては
> いけません。

文型 Sentence Patterns

READ Find one of these sentence patterns in the dialogue.

1. Verb (TE Form)	＋も　いいです。	Permission: may, allowed to
2. い Adjective (TE Form －くて) ＋も	かまいません。	(I/We) don't mind if...
3. な Adjective	＋で ＋は　いけません。	Prohibition: may not, should not, is not allowed
4. Noun	＋で ＋は　だめです。	It is no good if...

単語 Vocabulary

きそく
1. 規則

rule, regulation

じゆう
2. 自由
[な Adj.]

free, liberal

3. いけません

won't do, must not do

4. かまいません

(I) do not mind if ...

5. ガムを　かみます
[G1 かむ／かんで]

to chew gum

6. ごみを　すてます
[G2 すてる／すてて]

to litter, to throw away trash

7. <ruby>運転<rt>うんてん</rt></ruby>(を)　します
[IR する／して]

to drive

車を　うんてんします to drive a car

8. Personに　<ruby>会<rt>あ</rt></ruby>います
[G1 あう ／ あって]

to meet someone

9. Personに　<ruby>聞<rt>き</rt></ruby>きます
[G1 きく ／ きいて]

to ask someone

10. ぜったい(に)

absolutely

<ruby>追加単語<rt>ついかたんご</rt></ruby> Additional Vocabulary

1. まんが　　　　　　　comics

2. けしょうを　します　to wear makeup

3. マニキュアを　します　to polish one's nails

4. たばこを　すいます　　to smoke

<ruby>読<rt>よ</rt></ruby>みましょう　Language in Context

🔊 **READ/LISTEN/SPEAK** Read these sentences in Japanese. Say two things you are allowed to do in your English or Social Studies class. Then say two things you are NOT allowed to do.

ここで　たばこを
すっては　いけません。

このスリッパを
はいても　いいですか。

A Granting Permission with Descriptions ─────

Verb TE form	＋も　いいです／かまいません。
い Adjective (-くて)	＋も　いいです／かまいません。
な Adjective / Noun ＋ で	＋も　いいです／かまいません。

This sentence construction allows the speaker to ask for, or grant permission to do something. The question form is usually used to receive permission from people of higher status, but not for granting them permission. The verb -て form is followed by the particle も and いいです (translated as "all right if," or "may") or かまいません (translated as "don't mind if").

◄)) MODELS

1. 「この　学校では　ショートパンツを　はいても　いいですか。」
   "May I wear shorts at this school?"

   「はい、かまいません。」
   "Yes, I don't mind."

2. プレゼントは　高くても　かまいませんか。
   Do (you) mind if the present is expensive?

3. パーティーは　一時でも　いいです。
   It is ok if the party is at 1 o'clock.

READ/SPEAK Change the word in the ( ) to its correct TE form. Then choose the correct particle.

1. 「すみません、質問を　(聞きます)[も／は]　かまいませんか。」

2. 「パーティーの　音楽は　(うるさいです)[も／は]　いいですか。」

3. 「パーティーは　(日曜日です)[も／は]　いいですか。」

B Expressing Prohibition with だめです／いけません ─────

Verb TE form	＋は　だめです／いけません。
い Adjective (-くて)	＋は　だめです／いけません。
な Adjective / Noun ＋ で	＋は　だめです／いけません。

This sentence construction expresses prohibition and is used by people of higher status to people of lower status. The verb -て form is followed by the particle は, then いけません (translated as "must not"), or だめです (translated as "It is not good if..."). だめです is most often spoken in informal situations, while いけません expresses very strong prohibition.

1. 図書館で 話しては だめです。　　You must not talk in the library.

2. スカートは 短くては いけません。　　Skirts should not be (too) short.

3. この 本では だめです。　　This book will not do.

READ/SPEAK Change the word in the ( ) to its correct TE form. Then choose the correct particle.

1. 教室で ガムを (かみます)[も / は] いけません。

2. ショートパンツを (はきます)[も / は] いけません。

3. パーティーが (一時です)[も / は] だめです。

文化ノート　Culture Notes

Japanese School Handbooks

School handbooks, called 生徒手帳, are issued to junior high and high school students. They are often small pocket-sized handbooks that vary widely in content and appearance, depending on the school.

Some schools issue new 生徒手帳 every year while others issue one for the entire duration of the students' attendance at the school.

Some common features of the 生徒手帳, are an ID, the school song, school motto, and a message from administrators. They may also include detailed school rules regarding dress codes, absences, part-time work, establishments that are off limits, a calendar, and a memo section.

Write an e-mail to a Japanese student, explaining the type of ID you use and how you use it. Is it a school ID or a driver's license? Do you have a school-issued calendar organizer and set of rules?

アクティビティー　Communicative Activities

ペアワーク

A. SPEAK/LISTEN You are planning to have a party at your partner's house. Ask your partner whether the following things are allowed. Your partner will respond based on fact.

Ex. 質問： パーティーは 十二時でも いいですか。

　　答え： はい、十二時でも いいですよ／かまいませんよ。

　　or　いいえ、十二時では だめですよ／いけませんよ。

1. パーティーは　日曜日でも　いいですか。

2. パーティーは　おそくても　いいですか。

3. パーティーで　ソーダを　飲んでも　いいですか。

4. パーティーで　カラオケを　しても　いいですか。

5. パーティーで　うるさくても　いいですか。

B. SPEAK/LISTEN Ask your partner about your school rules. Conjugate the words in the ( ) and use the appropriate grammar patterns based on the example below.

Ex. 質問：　この　学校で　スカートを　はいても　いいですか。

答え：　はい、はいても　いいです。でも、短くては　いけません。

　　　or　いいえ、はいては　いけませんよ。

1. ガムを　（かみます）

2. ぼうしを　（かぶります）

3. Tシャツを　（着ます）

4. サングラスを　（かけます）

5. かみのけは　（長い）

6. ピアスを　（します）

7. ケータイを　（使います to use）

8. コンピュータゲームを　（します）

9. ソーダを　（飲みます）

10. ごみを　（すてます）

Authentic Reading

C. READ/WRITE Read the blog post on the next page about school rules by Momoko Tanaka, a Japanese high school student, and answer the questions below.

UNDERSTAND

1. Does this blog writer like Japanese school dress codes?

2. Are students allowed to wear colored shoes or socks to school?

IDENTIFY

3. In what month do students at this school have to change to winter uniforms?

4. What kind of buttons must the students wear on their uniforms?

APPLY

5. What is your opinion about the school rules? Which rule do you think is the most strict?

WORKBOOK page 17

次ページ>>

プロフィール

Ameba オフィシャルブロガー

田中ももこ
プロフィール

性別：女性
誕生日：1月12日
自己紹介：田中ももこ (17) 日本

📖 読者になる　　💬 アメンバーになる

✉ メッセージを送る　　🎁 ピグでギフトを贈る

「学校のきそく」 ブログ

December 4　NEW!

今年から　私は　あたらしい　高校に
行っていますが、きそくが　とても
きびしいんですよ。ふゆの　せいふくは
10月から　5月までで、なつの
せいふくは　6月から　9月までです。

1. 学校では　せいふくだけ　きます。
2. せいふくの　ボタンは　学校の
   ボタンだけです。
3. ブラウスは　白だけ　いいです。
4. スカートは　ひざまでで、
   みじかくては　だめです。
5. くつは　白の　スニーカーだけ
   いいです。
6. くつ下は　白だけ　いいです。
7. セーターと　ベストは、くろか
   こんか　白か　グレーだけいいです。

日本の　学校は　大変で〜す！

最新の記事

秋のファッション

友達と買い物！

好きな料理

テスト

日本、ライブします

最近の事

新しい学校

家族の写真

始めまして〜

一覧を見る

2課3

I'll go borrow a book

会話 Dialogue
かいわ

🔊 READ/LISTEN   Where is Mari going? What will she go there to do?

本を　借りに
行きます。

としょかん
図書館へ　何を
しに　行きますか。

文型 Sentence Patterns
ぶんけい

READ Find this sentence pattern in the dialogue.

Placeへ	Verb (Stem Form)に	Direction Verb。
うみ 海へ	およ 泳ぎ　　に	行きます。

I will go to the beach to swim.

単語 Vocabulary
たんご

か
1. 借ります

[G2 かりる／かりて]

to borrow, rent (from)

き
2. 気を　つけて

[G2 きを　つける／
きを　つけます]

to be careful

えいがかん
3. 映画館

movie theater

4. 証明書
<ruby>証明書<rt>しょうめいしょ</rt></ruby>
I.D.

5. 運転免許
うんてんめんきょ
driver's license

6. パスポート
passport

7. ところで
by the way

ついかたんご
追加単語 Additional Vocabulary

1. お金を　引き出します
ひ　だ
to withdraw money (e.g., from a bank)

2. ゆうびんきょく
post office

3. ゆうびんを　出します
だ
to mail

4. 切手
きって
postage stamp

5. 動物
どうぶつ
animal

6. 動物園
どうぶつえん
zoo

読みましょう　Language in Context
よ

🔊 **READ/LISTEN/SPEAK** Read these sentences in Japanese. Where will you go this weekend? Tell a classmate why you will go there in one sentence.

これを　食べに
行きましょう。

プールへ　およぎに
行きました。

文法　Grammar

A Coming and Going Verbs 行きます / 来ます / かえります

Verb (STEM Form)＋に　　**Direction verb。**

行きます

来ます

かえ
帰ります

This pattern expresses going, coming, or returning somewhere for the purpose of doing something. The place of destination is followed by に or へ, followed by the purpose (a verb stem form, or a noun). The purpose is followed by the purpose particle に, which is then followed by any of the three directional verbs.

MODELS

1. 友達の　うちへ　勉強しに　行きます。

   I will go to my friend's house to study.

2. ここに　本を　借りに　来ました。

   I came here to borrow a book.

3. 父は　お昼ご飯を　食べに　うちに　帰りました。

   My father returned home to eat lunch.

When a verb is of the noun ＋を　します type, the noun may replace the verb stem as the purpose. There is no change in meaning. See examples below.

1. 水泳を　しに　行きます。　　　　I will go to swim.

   or 水泳に　行きます。　　　　　I will go swimming.

2. 食事を　しに　行きます。　　　　I will go to eat.

   or 食事に　行きます。　　　　　I will go eat.

READ/SPEAK Change the verbs in the ( ) to their correct stem forms.

1. 学校へ　(勉強します)に　来ます。

2. 四時に　モールへ　友達に　(会います)に　行きます。

3. きのう　友達は　お金を　(借ります)に　うちに　来ました。

文化ノート　Culture Notes

Going to the Movies in Japan

Going to the movies in Japan is an experience that may be quite different from what you may be used to. Ticket prices are high, but are generally cheaper later in the evening compared to afternoon matinees. Discounts are available for students, senior citizens, and the disabled, and on certain days, women can also receive a ladies' discount. When purchasing a ticket you will be shown a theater seating chart and can select your seat. Many theaters also offer tickets and seat reservations online.

Foreign movies may be shown in the original language, or they may be dubbed or have subtitles. Japanese movie audiences are also quiet, and do not laugh loudly, or comment during the movie. At the end of the movie, most Japanese movie-goers will stay until all of the credits are finished before quietly filing out of the theater.

Check the Internet for a movie theater in Japan, pick a movie that is playing, then check the show times, ticket prices, and concessions sold there. Write a short blog entry comparing the theater to one in your area. Be sure to include the information from your research and pictures if you choose.

アクティビティー　Communicative Activities

ペアワーク

A. SPEAK/LISTEN Ask your partner if he/she goes to the following places. If so, ask your partner the purpose for which he/she goes there.

Ex. 図書館

　　Aさん: ところで、 ～さんは　図書館へ　行きますか。

　　Bさん: はい、行きますよ。

　　Aさん: 何を　しに　行きますか。

　　Bさん: 宿題を　しに　行きますよ。

図書館	銀行	本屋	映画館	スーパー
公園	スタジアム	デパート	大学	友達のうち

Authentic Reading

B. READ/WRITE Look at the movie theater sign board above and answer the following questions.

UNDERSTAND

1. Are the ticket prices for college students and high school students the same?

2. What is the difference in price to see 2-D movies and 3-D movies?

IDENTIFY

3. What do you think プレミアシート means?

APPLY

4. How much would your ticket cost if you wanted to see a 3-D movie?

5. About how much would it cost in dollars? Look up the current exchange rate.

WORKBOOK page 19

会話^{かいわ} Dialogue

🔊 READ/LISTEN When and where will Mari and Ken meet?

一時に　門^{もん}の
ところで
会いましょう。

あ、はい。でも、
一時半^{はん}でも
かまいませんか。

はい、一時半^{はん}でも
かまいませんよ。

文型^{ぶんけい} Sentence Patterns

READ Find one of these sentence patterns in the dialogue.

1. 聞^きこえませんか。　　　　　Can't you hear? [Negative question]

　　はい、聞^きこえません。　　　Yes (= I agree with your statement), I cannot hear.

　　いいえ、聞^きこえます。　　　No (= I disagree with your statement), I can hear.

2. いいんですか。　　　　　　　Is it really all right?

3. 〜だけ　　　　　　　　　　　only 〜

1. 〜が 見えます

〜 can be seen, visible

2. 〜が 聞こえます

〜 can be heard, audible

3. 門

gate

4. 本当〔ほんとう〕に

really, truly [Adverb]

5. 本当ですか。

Is it true/real?

ほんとう is a noun and means truth.

6. 〜だけ

only 〜

だけ replaces を, が, は and is used with へ, に, で, etc.

読みましょう Language in Context

🔊 **READ/LISTEN/SPEAK** Read these sentences in Japanese. Say what the only language(s) you speak at home are.

「分かりませんか。」
「はい、分かりません。」

女の 生徒だけ います。

A Answering Negative Questions

「食べませんでしたか。」「はい、食べませんでした。」

The Japanese answer affirmatively or negatively to the stated form of the verb rather than to the action implied. For example, when responding to the question 「きのう　うみへ　行きませんでしたか。」, the response would be, 「はい、行きませんでした。」 "Yes, I agree with your assumption that I didn't go to the beach." Or, 「いいえ、行きました。」 "No, I disagree with your assumption that I didn't go to the beach, I went." Do not confuse this form with the negative invitation form. When responding to an invitation, one should answer as one would in English.

MODELS

ごく　　はな
1.「中国語を　話しませんか。」　　　"Don't you speak Chinese?"

はな
「いいえ、話します。」　　　"No, I do speak (it)."

えい　　はな
2.「英語で　話しては　いけませんか。」　　　"Must I not speak in English?"

「はい、だめです。」　　　"Yes, it is not allowed."

READ/SPEAK Choose the correct verb form in response to the negative questions.

しゅくだい
1. 先生：宿題を　しませんでしたか。

ケン：はい、（しました / しませんでした）。

かんじ　し
2. 先生：この　漢字を　知りませんか。

し　　　　し　　　　　　し
ケン：いいえ、（知ります / 知っています / 知りません）。

B Particle Replacer 〜だけ

〜だけ　　**only** 〜

だけ replaces を, が, は and is used with other particles such as へ, で, に, から.

MODELS

1. まりさんだけ　スカートを　はいて　いました。
Only Mari was wearing a skirt.

2. ピアスを　一つだけ　しても　いいです。
You may wear only one pierced earring.

3. 小さいのだけ　しても　いいです。
You may wear only a small one.

べんきょう
4. ケンさんは　学校でだけ　勉強します。
Ken studies only at school.

READ/WRITE Rewrite the each of the following sentences on a separate sheet of paper. Use だけ in the correct locations to match the information given below. Replace or retain particles as needed.

In my family, only my mother speaks Japanese well. My father speaks only a little Japanese and speaks only at home.

1. 母は　日本語を　よく　話_{はな}します。

1. 母は　日本語を　よく　話します。
2. 父は　日本語を　少_{すこ}し　話_{はな}します。
3. 父は　うちで　日本語を　話_{はな}します。

C Inviting Explanation with 〜んです

「いいんですか。」

The んです ending is frequently used in speaking. When it appears in a question form, it serves the purpose of inviting an explanation from the listener. When used in a statement form, it suggests that the speaker feels obligated to explain himself.

🔊 MODELS

1. 今晩_{ばん}　映画_{えいが}に　行きたいんです。　　I really want to go to a movie.
2. この　車を　運転_{うんてん}しても　いいんですか。　May I really drive this car?

READ/SPEAK Choose the correct word for each given situation from the options in the ( ).

1. A Japanese student said that Japanese school rules are strict.

日本の　学校の　きそくは　(きびしい / きびしいん)です。

2. A Japanese student is surprised that U.S. students can wear earrings at school, and asks about it.

アメリカの　学校で　ピアスを　しても　(いい / いいん)ですか。

文化_{ぶんか}ノート　Culture Notes

Japanese Neighborhoods

Japan is a mountainous country and most of its land is unsuitable for building. The general population tends to be concentrated in urban centers, such as Tokyo, Yokohama, Nagoya, Osaka, and Kyoto, with houses sitting close together and in some cases even touching! An assortment of housing styles can be found both in the city and countryside, ranging from single-family homes (both traditional

and modern in style) and small town-house type apartments to condominium complexes tens of stories high.

A young girl greets her neighbors.

Neighborhood blocks are ordered and named, but the majority of neighborhood streets are unnamed. This system can be difficult to navigate for those who do not have a good sense of the area. Streets may also be quite narrow, allowing only enough room for one car or only a bicycle or pedestrian to pass through.

In the past, many of these neighborhoods formed tight-knit communities. Today, people in Japan move far more frequently, and as a result this sense of community has diminished. Still, many neighborhoods in both rural and urban regions form communities around Shinto shrines, business organizations, or neighborhood associations. These communities [usually] have police boxes or こうばん, where two or three police officers are assigned to cover the neighborhood throughout the day and night. Usually quite approachable, they assist others with finding their way around the neighborhoods, as many of the homes are not numbered in order and finding the addresses requires the resources of the knowledgeable police officer at the こうばん.

A こうばん in Shiga Prefecture

 Research a little more about police officers in Japan and in your community. Write a job description for a Japanese police officer assigned to a neighborhood こうばん and one for a police officer assigned to the area in which you live. How are they similar and different? Write a brief summary of your findings.

アクティビティー Communicative Activities

ペアワーク

A. SPEAK/LISTEN On a separate sheet of paper, sketch of a view of the outdoors from one of the windows of your home. Take turns describing the view to your partner, who will draw a picture based on your description. Compare sketches to see whether you communicated successfully.

Ex. A: まどから　何が　見えますか。

B: まどから　〜が　見えます。

B. SPEAK/LISTEN Ask your partner the following negative questions. He/she should answer based on the facts.

Ex. 質問：昨日　おすしを　食べませんでしたか。

　　答え：はい、食べませんでした。or いいえ、食べましたよ。

1. きのう　おすしを　食べませんでしたか。	2. きのう　日本語の　しゅくだいを　しませんでしたか。	3. きのう　テレビを　見ませんでしたか。
4. けさ　あさごはんを　食べませんでしたか。	5. テキストを　かりて　もかまいませんか。	6. 今　食べても　かまいませんか。
7. 十ドル　かしませんでしたか。	8. 中学一年生では　ありませんか。	9. 今日は　金曜日では　ありませんか。

C. SPEAK/LISTEN/WRITE Ask your partner the following questions. He/she should answer based on the facts using だけ appropriately in his/her responses.

Ex. 質問：今　何人の　人が　スカートを　はいて　いますか。

　　答え：三人だけ　です。

1. 今　何人が　スカートを　はいて　いますか。	
2. うちに　車が　何台　ありますか。	
3. 今　お金を　いくら　持って　いますか。	

4. 今　えんぴつを　何本　持って　いますか。	
5. 教室に　何人が　めがねを　かけて　いますか。	
6. 今　教室に　先生が　何人　いますか。	

D. READ/SPEAK/LISTEN/WRITE Suggest doing the following activities with your partner. Decide on a mutually agreeable time and place to meet and write your plans on a separate sheet of paper.

Ex. お昼ご飯が (or を)　食べたいです。

Aさん：お昼ご飯を　食べに　行きましょう。

Bさん：はい、行きましょう。

Aさん：何時に　会いましょうか。

Bさん：十二時半に　会いましょう。

Aさん：どこで　会いましょうか。

Bさん：門の　ところで　会いましょう。

1. えいがが(or を)　見たい です。

2. フットボールの　しあいが(or を)　見たいです。

3. バスケットボールが(or を)　したいです。

4. およぎたいです。

5. たんじょう日の　プレゼントを(or が)　かいたいです。

Lesson 2
Review

Review Questions

🔊 Ask your partner these questions in Japanese. Your partner should answer in Japanese. Check your answers using the audio.

Clothing and Uniforms Review pages 60–61

1. Do you like to wear uniforms?

2. Do you always wear a ring?

3. Are you wearing white socks today?

4. Don't you sometimes wear glasses?

5. Is it all right to wear shoes inside your home?

School Rules Review pages 66–67, 77

6. Are your school rules strict? Are they liberal?

7. Is eating allowed in the school library?

8. Is it ok to wear sunglasses in school?

9. Are you not allowed to wear shorts in school?

10. Are you allowed to chew gum in class?

11. Do you speak only in Japanese in (your) Japanese classroom?

Your Plans Review pages 72, 77

12. I want to go to the library to borrow books. What do I need?

13. Are you going to meet your teacher today?

14. Are you going to the movie theater to see a movie this weekend?

15. Are you going to study only Japanese tonight?

About You Review pages 77–78

16. Don't you have your driver's license?

17. Can you hear a phone (ringing)?

Text Chat

You will participate in a simulated exchange of text-chat messages. You should respond as fully and as appropriately as possible. You will have a conversation with Kana Murata, a Japanese high school student, about school rules.

9月　20日　10:27 AM

私は　学校に　せいふくを　きて　行きますが。何を　きて　行きますか。

Describe two items you are wearing now, including their colors.

9月　20日　10:32 AM

としょかんに　何を　しに　行きますか。

Respond by giving two examples.

9月　20日　10:36 AM

学校の　きそくは　きびしいですか。

Give your opinion and the one rule you dislike the most.

Can Do!

Now I can . . .

- ☐ describe how I and others are dressed
- ☐ grant and ask for permission
- ☐ tell others what they may or may not do
- ☐ state my reasons for going somewhere
- ☐ answer negative yes/no questions

花札 Cards
<small>は な ふ だ</small>

Background

Hanafuda are traditional Japanese playing cards popular among all ages and used to play several different games. Unlike *go, shogi,* and *mah-jong,* which originated in China, *hanafuda* is a uniquely Japanese creation that evolved from *kai-awase* (matching pictures on shells game) and playing cards introduced by the Portuguese in the late 1500s. Quintessentially Japanese in its stylized depiction of the seasons, the colorful cards bear pictures of Japanese flora, fauna, *tanzaku* (strips of paper for writing poems), and Japanese symbols of good luck. In addition to the traditional decks, there are now many themed decks and online versions available.

Cards

A *hanafuda* deck consists of 48 cards. There are 12 different suits, four cards in each. Each suit bears a seasonal flower or plant representing one of the 12 months of the year. Each card has a face value that falls into one of four different categories: Light beams-20 points, animals-10 points, *tanzaku* or *tan* (red or blue strips of paper)-5 points, and *kasu* (junk)-1 point. There is one red and black colored junk card of the *yanagi* or *ame* suit sometimes called the *gaji*. The *gaji* acts like a joker and can take any card of any suit. Also included with each deck is a blank card that can be used to replace a lost or bent card.

A うぐいす (nightingale) card from the うめ (plum) deck representing February

A たんざく card from the ふじ (wisteria) deck representing April

A がじ (joker) card from the やなぎ or あめ deck representing November

The Game

There are numerous ways of playing and scoring *hanafuda*, and they vary among regions. Therefore, it is best to establish the rules before playing. The five most common ways of playing are: *Bakappana* (Matching Flowers or Fool Flowers), *Hachi-hachi* (Eighty-eight), *Koi-koi* (Come on), *Kabu* (Nine), and *Mushi* (Honeymoon *Hanafuda*). *Hachi-hachi* is the most popular version, but it is also the most complicated. *Bakappana* is the simplest version, and therefore favored by beginners who wish to familiarize themselves with the cards and rules.

For a complete set of printable *hanafuda* cards and directions on how to play *Bakappana*, visit the companion website at
cheng-tsui.com/adventuresinjapanese

うんてん
運転
Driving

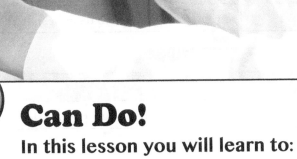

Can Do!
In this lesson you will learn to:

- recognize some informal speech styles
- politely tell others to not do a certain action
- communicate how an action is done
- talk about driving and commuting

Online Resources

cheng-tsui.com/
adventuresinjapanese

- Audio
- Vocabulary Lists
- Vocabulary and *Kanji* Flashcards
- Study Guides
- Activity Worksheets

In this lesson you will learn how to discuss commuting and transportation. Review these words, phrases, and grammatical structures you already learned to help you talk about driving with your friends.

めいし Nouns

1. もん	gate	5. お昼ご飯	lunch	
2. 先月	last month	6. あれ	that one over there	
3. うんてんめんきょ	driver's license	7. あそこ	over there	
4. 自動車	car	8. ところ	place	

どうし Verbs

9. うんてんして [IR うんてんする／うんてんします]	drive
10. とりました [G1 とる／とって]	took
11. 食べに [G2 たべる／たべます／たべて]	to eat [purpose]
12. 行きましょう [G1 いく／いきます／いって]	let's go
13. 行って [G1 いく／いきます]	go
14. います [G2 いる／いて]	be, exist (animate)

-い けいようし I Adjectives

15. すごい	terrific, terrible [Used to describe extremes.]

ふくし Adverbs

16. ちょっと	a little	17. あまり＋Neg.	(not) very

じょし Particles

18. Aや　B	A and B and alike	19. も	also

Expressions	
20. わあ	Wow!
21. さあ	Well . . .
22. 大じょうぶですか。	Is it okay?/ Are you okay?
23. 大じょうぶですよ。	It's okay.
24. あっ	Oh!
25. ごめんなさい。	I'm sorry.
26. そうです。	That's right.

ぶんぽう Grammar	
27. Verb TE form＋も　いい(ん)ですか。	Is it alright if ～?
としょかんで　食べても　いいんですか。	Is it alright if I eat in the library?
28. Verb TE form＋下さい。	Please do ～.
食べて　下さい。	Please eat it.
29. Verb TE form＋は　いけません。	You must not ～.
としょかんで　食べては　いけません。	You must not eat in the library.

WRITE Write out what Ken and Mari are saying in each scene using the words, phrases, and grammatical structures you reviewed above.

1.

2.

3.

Kanji
used in this lesson

In this lesson, you will learn some basic *kanji* for common nouns and verbs and review key *kanji* from Volume 1.

	Kanji	Meaning	Readings		Examples	
67.	名	name	な	名前 (なまえ)	name	
			メイ	有名 (ゆうめい)	famous	
68.	外	outside	そと	車の外 (くるま そと)	outside of the car	
			ガイ	外国語 (がいこくご)	foreign language	
69.	前	front	まえ	名前 (なまえ)	name	
				木の前 (き まえ)	in front of the tree	
			ゼン	午前 (ごぜん)	a.m.	
70.	話	to speak	はな(す)	話す (はな)	speak	
			ワ	電話 (でんわ)	telephone	
71.	書	to write	か(く)	書く (か)	write	
			ショ	教科書 (きょうかしょ)	textbook	

	Kanji	Meaning	Readings	Examples	

72. 何　what　　なに　　何人 (なにじん)　what nationality?

　→　何

　　　　　　　　なん　　何月 (なんがつ)　what month?

Review Kanji

54. 見　look, see　み(る)　見ます (み)　look

58. 食　to eat　た(べる)　食べましょう。(た)　Let's eat.
　　　　　　　ショク　食事を します (しょくじ)　To have a meal

59. 言　to say　い(う)　もう一ど言って 下さい。(い)(くだ)　Please say it again.

New Reading

22. 手　person　シュ　運転手 (うんてんしゅ)　driver

Recognition Kanji

夕方 (ゆうがた)　early evening

漢字 (かん)(じ)　Chinese character

WORKBOOK　page 175

運転するのは下手です ...

You're not a good driver ...

ケンさんは
もう　運転しても
いいんですか。

はい、

ぼくは　先月
運転免許を
取りました。

見せて　下さい。

わあ、
すごいですねえ。

私は　今から
食堂へ　行きます。
ケンさんは？

ぼくは　今から　外へ
食べに　行きます。

いっしょに
行きませんか。
自動車に　乗って
下さい。

大丈夫ですか。
ちょっと
こわいですねえ。

心配しないで
下さい。

シートベルトを
して 下さい。さあ、
出かけましょう。

危ない!

信号は 黄色でしたよ。
行っては いけませんよ。

大丈夫ですよ。

あっ、ケンさん、
角を 速く まがらないで
下さいよ。

ごめんなさい。

あれは
救急車<ruby>救急<rt>きゅうきゅう</rt></ruby>車ですか。

そうです。あそこに
パトカーも　警官<ruby>警官<rt>けいかん</rt></ruby>も　いますね。
事故<ruby>事故<rt>じこ</rt></ruby>ですよ。

<ruby>気<rt>き</rt></ruby>を　つけて　下さいね。
あまり　スピードを
<ruby>出<rt>だ</rt></ruby>さないで　下さい。

はい、レストランに
<ruby>着<rt>つ</rt></ruby>きましたよ。

ケンさん、
<ruby>急<rt>きゅう</rt></ruby>に　<ruby>止<rt>と</rt></ruby>まらないで
下さいよ。

ごめんなさい。

さあ、
<ruby>早<rt>はや</rt></ruby>く　<ruby>降<rt>お</rt></ruby>りて　下さい。

To read an informal version of the conversation,
go to cheng-tsui.com/adventuresinjapanese

会話 Dialogue
かいわ

🔊 **READ/LISTEN** Where is Mari going? Will Ken go with her?

私は　今から　食堂へ　行く。ケンは？
どう

ぼくは　今から　行かないよ。

文型 Sentence Patterns
ぶんけい

READ Find this sentence pattern in the dialogue.

Verb NAI Form: Informal negative nonpast form

Group 1 Verb	飲みません	→飲まない
Group 2 Verb	食べません	→食べない
Group 3 Verb	来ません	→来ない
	しません	→しない

単語 Vocabulary
たんご

1. こうつうじこ

traffic accident

2. しんごう

traffic lights

3. 赤, 黄色, 青
あか　きいろ　あお

red, yellow, green

あお is used to describe green traffic lights.

4. パトカー

police car

5. 救急車
<ruby>きゅうきゅうしゃ</ruby>

ambulance

6. 道
<ruby>みち</ruby>

street, road

います is used instead of あります to describe an occupied moving vehicle.

7. 角
<ruby>かど</ruby>

corner

8. 運転手 or ドライバー
<ruby>うんてん</ruby>

driver

9. かぎ

key

追加単語 Additional Vocabulary
<ruby>ついかたんご</ruby>

1.	おまわりさん	police officer	**3.** サイレン	siren (sound)
2.	こうばん	police box	**4.** オートバイ	motor bike

読みましょう Language in Context
<ruby>よ</ruby>

🔊 **READ/LISTEN/SPEAK** Read these sentences in Japanese. Say which side of the car drivers in your country sit on while driving.

道に　パトカーが
<ruby>みち</ruby>
二台　いますよ。
<ruby>だい</ruby>

運転手は　車の
<ruby>うんてん</ruby>
右に　います。

A Verb NAI form : Informal Negative Non-past form

do not do ～, will not do ～, is not going to do ～

The formal negative nonpast form is -ません. Its informal equivalent is the NAI form. The NAI form is used in informal situations, such as when one talks with family or close friends. The meaning of a sentence remains the same whether one uses formal or informal endings. The NAI form is also used before extenders in certain sentence patterns, as in the - ない + でください negative request pattern, "Please do not do (such and such)."

1. Group 1 Verbs

To obtain the NAI form, change the *-i* ending sound of the stem to the corresponding *-a* ending sound and add -ない. Verbs that have stems ending in い change to -わない.

 MODELS

[-i ます]

	MASU form -i	Meaning	Dictionary form -u	NAI form -a
[み]	のみます	to drink	のむ	のまない
	よみます	to read	よむ	よまない
	やすみます	to rest, be absent	やすむ	やすまない
[に]	しにます	to die	しぬ	しなない
[び]	あそびます	to play	あそぶ	あそばない
[い]	あいます	to meet	あう	あわない
[ち]	かちます	to win	かつ	かたない
[り]	わかります	to understand	わかる	わからない
	しります	to get to know	しる	しらない
	かえります	to return (place)	かえる	かえらない
[り]	あります	to be (inanimate)*	ある	ない*
	がんばります	to do one's best	がんばる	がんばらない
	はしります	to run	はしる	はしらない
[き]	ききます	to listen, hear	きく	きかない
	かきます	to write	かく	かかない
	いきます	to go	いく	いかない
	あるきます	to walk	あるく	あるかない
[ぎ]	およぎます	to swim	およぐ	およがない
[し]	はなします	to talk	はなす	はなさない

* ない is the NAI form of あります. It is an exception.

2. Group 2 Verbs

Group 2 verbs can be identified by a verb stem (verb without ます) that ends in an "-e sounding" *hiragana* or a verb stem that contains only one *hiragana*, with some exceptions. Group 2 verb's NAI forms are created simply by adding ない after removing the -ます.

	MASU form	Meaning	Dictionary form	NAI form
[-e ます]	みえます	can be seen	みえる	みえない
	まけます	to lose	まける	まけない
[One *hiragana*]	みます	to see, watch	みる	みない
	います	to be (animate)	いる	いない
	ねます	to sleep	ねる	ねない
[Special verbs]	おきます	to get up	おきる	おきない
	かります	to borrow	かりる	かりない
	おります	to get off, to get out	おりる	おりない

3. Group 3 Irregular Verbs

Only 来ます, します and noun +します verbs belong to this group. You must memorize the NAI form individually, as they do not follow rules.

	MASU form	Dictionary form	NAI form
to come	きます	くる	こない
to do	します	する	しない
to type	タイプ(を)します	タイプ(を)する	タイプ(を)しない

READ/SPEAK Change the following verbs to the negative NAI form.

1. 話しません   3. 言いません   5. ありません

2. 見ません   4. 来ません   6. しません

Language Note

A. あお

Do you remember that the color あお can mean both blue and green? Traditionally, it referred to a blue-green color, but is often translated as "blue" in English. For example, "go" traffic lights, the ocean, and sprouting leaves are all considered あお in Japanese.

B. Onomatopoetic Street Sounds

Some examples of Japanese onomatopoetia for street sounds are the sound of a screeching car, キキーッ, an emergency vehicle's siren, ピーポーピーポー, and a honking car, プップー.

アクティビティー Communicative Activities

ペアワーク

A. READ/SPEAK/LISTEN You are taking driving lessons from a driving instructor (your partner). Tell the instructor that you see/hear the things below. The instructor gives you directions on what to do.

Ex.　　You:　　　しんごうが　あおです。

　　Instructor:　　行って　下さい。

　　　　You:　　　はい、行きます。

Words you may use: ゆっくり slowly, きを　つけて be careful, とまって to stop

1. 車の　かぎが　ありません。
2. 道^{みち}に　パトカーが　三台^{だい}　います。
3. きゅうきゅう車の　サイレンが　聞^きこえます。
4. しんごうが　赤^{あか}/ 黄色^{きいろ}/ 青^{あお}です。
5. こうつうじこです。

ゲーム Tic-Tac-Toe

B. READ/WRITE Play Tic-Tac-Toe with a 3x3 chart. Take squares by changing the -ます form of each verb to its -ない form. Find more words and answers at **cheng-tsui.com/adventuresinjapanese**.

のみます	しにます	見ます
おきます	ねます	あそびます
休みます	話します	はきます

WORKBOOK page 29

3課2
Don't worry

会話 Dialogue
<small>かい わ</small>

🔊 **READ/LISTEN** What does Mari think about Ken's driving?

文型 Sentence Patterns
<small>ぶんけい</small>

READ Find one of these sentence patterns in the dialogue.

1. Verb (NAI Form) ＋ で 下さい。　　Please do not do ~.

2. Formal Speech Style　　　　　　　　Informal Speech Style

Verbs:		
行きます。	→ 行く。	will go / be going
行きません。	→ 行かない。	will not go / is not going
行きますか。	→ 行く？↗	Will you go? / Are you going?
行って 下さい。	→ 行って。	Please go.

単語 Vocabulary
<small>たん ご</small>

1. うん

Yes. (Informal)

2. ううん

No. (Informal)

3. けっして ＋ Neg.

never

4. 心配(を) する
しんぱい

[IR しんぱい(を) します/して]

to worry

5. けんか(を) する

[IR けんか(を) します/して]

to have a fight

6. Place に 入る
はい

[G1 はいります/はいって]

to enter (a place)

7. Place を 出る
で

[G2 でます/でて]

to exit, get out of (a place)

8. 使う
つか

[G1 つかいます/つかって]

to use

読みましょう Language in Context
よ

🔊 **READ/LISTEN/SPEAK** Read these sentences in Japanese. Ask a teacher and a friend not to enter a room in Japanese. How would you address each person?

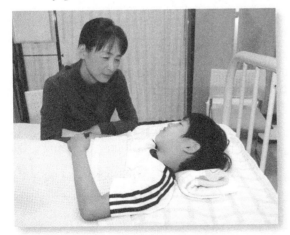

心配しないで 下さい。
しんぱい

先生は 部屋に 入って います。
へや　　はい

A Making Negative Requests with NAI form

Verb NAI form ＋で 下さい。 **Please do not do ~. [Negative request]**

The polite negative imperative pattern is used when one politely asks the listener not to do something. It is translated as "please don't do . . ." The extender で 下さい is attached to the verb –NAI form.

◀)) MODELS

1. 宿題を 忘れないで 下さい。
   しゅくだい わす
   Please don't forget (your) homework.

2. 教室で ぼうしを かぶらないで 下さい。
   きょうしつ
   Please don't wear (your) hat in the classroom.

3. 英語で 話さないで 下さい。
   えい
   Please don't speak in English.

READ/SPEAK Change the verb in the ( ) to its correct NAI form to mean, "Please do not ~."

1. 後ろの ドアから (入る)で 下さい。
   うし はい

2. 前の ドアから (出る)で 下さい。
   で

3. 友達と (けんかを する)で 下さい。
   ともだち

4. レストランで ケータイを (使う)で 下さい。
   つか

B Informal Conversation

When Japanese people speak with family and friends, they use the informal speech style. Use of the informal style indicates a close relationship between the speaker and listener. The dictionary form is the informal style of –ます. The NAI form is the informal style of –ません. A question may be formed in informal speech by ending the informal sentence with a rising intonation. This form is used by males or females. Verb and い Adjective forms are introduced here for recognition purposes only. な Adjective and Noun forms will be introduced later.

	Formal Speech Style	→	Informal Speech Style	
Verbs:	行きます。	→	行く。	will go / be going
	行きません。	→	行かない。	will not go / is not going
	行きますか。	→	行く?↗	Will you go? / Are you going?
	行って 下さい。	→	行って。	Please go.
	行かないで 下さい。	→	行かないで。	Please do not go.

い Adjectives:　あついです。　　　→　あつい。　　　It is hot.

　　　　　　　　あつくないです。　　→　あつくない。　It is not hot.

　　　　　　　　あついですか。　　　→　あつい？↗　　Is it hot?

MODELS

1. 「行く？↗」　　　　　　　　　　　"Are you going?"

「うん、行く。」　　　　　　　　　"Yes, I will go."

2. 「今　お昼ご飯　食べる？↗」　　"Are you going to eat lunch now?"

「ううん、今は　食べない。」　　"No, I won't eat now."

3. 「その　コーヒー　熱い？↗」　　"Is that coffee hot?"

「ううん、熱くないよ。」　　　　"No, it is not hot."

READ/WRITE/SPEAK Ken is talking to a Japanese visitor, Mr. Tanaka. Change the following informal conversation style to a formal style and write it on a separate sheet of paper.

田中：うんてんめんきょを　持って　いる？

ケン：うん、持って　いる。

田中：うんてんは　むずかしい？

ケン：ううん、むずかしくない。心配しないで。

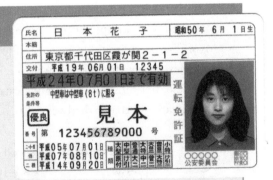

A Japanese driver's license for family-sized cars.

文化ノート　Culture Notes

A. Driver's Licenses

In the major cities of Japan, public transportation is so reliable and efficient that many people do not own cars or have driver's licenses.

Different types of operational licenses are available for family-sized cars, heavy trucks, and motorcycles. Sixteen-year-olds may apply for motorcycle licenses, a standard driver's license can be obtained at 18 years or older, and drivers of heavy trucks must be 20 years old or older.

Courses at driving schools are rigorous and costly. However, most Japanese people enroll in private driver's education. Drivers do not have to take a road test if they receive certification from an accredited driving school that ensures that the driver has ample experience on the road.

B. Driver's Marks

New drivers in Japan must attach a yellow and green arrow-shaped sticker on the front and back of their car to indicate that they are still inexperienced. The new driver's mark must remain on the car for at least one year after receiving a license. This sticker is called the 初心者(しょしんしゃ)マーク, the "new, first-time driver's mark" or the 若葉(わかば)マーク, the "young leaf mark." A four-leaf, green, yellow, and orange mark may be affixed to cars driven by senior citizens.

しょしんしゃ
初心者マーク

New, first-time driver's mark

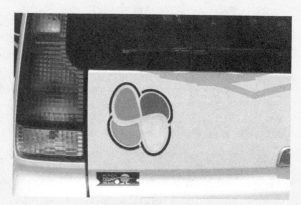

こうれいしゃ
高齢者マーク

Senior citizen driver's mark

C. Speed Regulations

Since Japan uses the metric system, all speed limits are posted in kilometers. Typical speed limits are 80–100 km per hour on expressways, 40 km in city limits, and 30 km on smaller, narrower roads. In other areas, posted limits may be 50–60 km per hour. The Japanese are known to often drive slightly over the speed limit. However, traffic cameras set up to catch speeding vehicles, especially on bigger thoroughfares, are common. All signs are in Japanese, but most follow international markings and also include English, particularly on major roadways.

 Convert the following speed limits to miles. 1 kilometer = .6214 miles

Expressways: 80–100 km/hour = _____ miles per hour

City limits: 40 km/hour = _____ miles per hour

Smaller roads: 30 km/hour = _____ miles per hour

Other streets: 50–60 km/hour = _____ miles per hour

Now record the speed limits in your area and convert them to kilometers.

アクティビティー　Communicative Activities

ペアワーク

A. READ/SPEAK/LISTEN Role play with a partner. You are breaking the rules. Your partner is a supervisor who will politely warn you to stop. Apologize and promise never to do it again. Find more situations on the companion website at **cheng-tsui.com/adventuresinjapanese**.

Ex. You are eating.　「ここで　食べないで　下さい。」
　　　　　　　　　　「すみません。　けっして　ここで　食べません。」

図書館（としょかん）で：A student and a librarian

1. コーラを　飲（の）まないで　下さい。	2. うるさく　しないで　下さい。	3. ごみを　すてないで　下さい。
4. ガムを　かまないで　下さい。	5. 走（はし）らないで　下さい。	6. ぼうしを　かぶらないで　下さい。
7. 食べないで　下さい。	8. 寝（ね）ないで　下さい。	9. 話さないで　下さい。

B. READ/SPEAK/LISTEN Ms. Kawamoto and Ken do not know each other well. Change the following conversation between them to the formal speech style by changing the parts in red.

ケンさん、今　お昼ご飯を　食べる？

ううん、まだ　食べない。図書館へ　行く。

図書館で　何を　する？

WI-Fiを　使いに　行く。

いつ　食べる？

一時ごろに　食べる。

じゃ、この　おむすびを　食べて。

どうも。

Authentic Reading

C. READ/SPEAK Study the Japanese sign and answer the following questions.

UNDERSTAND

1. Can you enter this area? Why or why not?

2. What do you think is occurring in the area of this sign?

IDENTIFY

3. What do you think 立入禁止 means?

APPLY

4. When you see this sign, what are you expected to do?

WORKBOOK　page 31

会話 Dialogue

🔊 **READ/LISTEN** What is Mari asking Ken to do or not to do?

文型 Sentence Patterns

READ Find one of these sentence patterns in the dialogue.

1. 早く 寝ました。   I went to bed early.

    急に 止まりました。   I stopped suddenly.

2. この 道を 行きます。   I will go along this road.

単語 Vocabulary

1. あぶない

[い Adj.]

dangerous

2. 安全

[な Adj.]

safe

3. こわい

[い Adj.]

scary

4. 早く / 速く
<ruby>早<rt>はや</rt></ruby>

early/quickly

5. 急に
<ruby>急<rt>きゅう</rt></ruby>

suddenly

きゅう is a な adjective
meaning "urgent" or "sudden."

6. を

through, along

7. Place に / で 止まる
<ruby>止<rt>と</rt></ruby>
[G1 とまります / とまって]

to stop

8. Place で / を まがる
[G1 まがります / まがって]

to turn at/along (a place)

9. スピードを 出す
<ruby>出<rt>だ</rt></ruby>
[G1 だします / だして]

to speed

<ruby>追加単語<rt>ついかたんご</rt></ruby> Additional Vocabulary

1. <ruby>交差点<rt>こうさてん</rt></ruby>　　　　intersection

2. <ruby>横断歩道<rt>おうだんほどう</rt></ruby>　　　pedestrian crossing

読_よみましょう Language in Context

🔊 **READ/LISTEN/SPEAK** Read these sentences in Japanese. Answer the question on the left, then say one more thing about this scene in the photo on the right that is different from your country.

山本さんは　安全_{あんぜん}に
運転_{うんてん}して　いますか。

道_{みち}の　左を　運転_{うんてん}します。

文法_{ぶんぽう}　Grammar

A Adverbial Usage of Adjectives ────────

Some adverbs are derived from い adjectives and な adjectives. When い adjectives become adverbs, the final い is dropped and replaced by く. When な adjectives become adverbs, に is added to the adjective. - く and に are never used together. Observe how each type is formed below. Note that いい (good) becomes よく (well, often) when used as an adverb.

a. い Adjective (- い)　→　い Adjective (- く) [Adverb]

		→		
はやい	is early	→	はやく	early
おそい	is slow, is late	→	おそく	slowly, late
いい	is good	→	よく	well
うるさい	is noisy	→	うるさく	noisily

b. な Adjective　→　な Adjective ＋ に [Adverb]

		→		
しずか	is quiet	→	しずかに	quietly
じゆう	is free, is liberal	→	じゆうに	freely
きれい	is pretty, is clean	→	きれいに	neatly
きゅう	is urgent, is sudden	→	きゅうに	suddenly

Remember! Adverbs describe verbs, adjectives, and other adverbs. Adjectives describe nouns.

1. 早く 起きて 下さい。   Please wake up early.

2. ゆうべ おそく 寝ました。   I went to bed late last night.

3. 図書館では 静かに 勉強して 下さい。   Please study quietly in the library.

4. ここでは 自由に 話しても いいです。   You may talk freely here.

5. よく 出来ました。   You did well. [lit., It is well done.]

READ/SPEAK Change the word in the ( ) to the correct adverbial form.

1. 姉は 毎日 (いい) 勉強を します。

2. 母は 絵を (きれい) かきます。

3. 父は 車を (安全) 運転します。

4. ぼくは けっして (早い) 起きません。

B Moving "Through" Places ───────────────

Place + を + direction/ movement verb "along, through"

The particle を marks the direct object in a sentence. In Japanese を may be used with verbs of direction, or words that suggest movement from one place to another. Such cases in Japanese are translated into English as "through" or "along." This usage suggests that the movement is occurring along or through the location preceded by を.

Compare:

1. 公園を 走ります。   I run through the park.

2. 公園に/へ 走ります。   I run to the park.

3. 公園で 走ります。   I run at/in the park.

4. 毎日 公園を 走ります。   I run through the park every day.

5. この 道を 歩きましょう。   Let's walk along this road.

6. この 角を 左に まがって 下さい。   Please turn left along this corner.

READ/SPEAK Insert the correct particle in the ( ). (/) indicates two possible answers.

1. 私は　毎日　この　道(　)　歩いて、学校に　行きます。

2. 私は　友だちを　道(　)　二十分　待って　いました。

3. 「すみません、運転手さん、ここ(　)　待って　いて　下さい。」

4. 「すみません、角(　/　)　右に　まがって　下さい。」

文化ノート　Culture Notes

Police in Japan

Police officers in Japan generally are well respected by the community. In addition to tending to crime, another major responsibility of Japanese police is to assist the public with directions, as some streets and buildings in Japan are not named, or do not have posted signs. Many police are stationed at こうばん near train stations, and often assist those who are lost.

パトカー Police car

Police uniforms in Japan do not vary widely across the country. Most are dressed in dark navy or gray uniforms with button-down blue or white shirts, trousers, a protective vest, and a duty belt. Male and female officers wear similar uniforms, with the exception of headgear. Male officers usually wear caps while female officers wear derby shaped hats.

Marked police cars are black and white. Most are medium or larger sized Japanese-made cars.

Search the Internet for pictures of police uniforms and cars in your country. Write a cultural note comparing your country's police officers to Japanese police officers. Consider their uniforms, community presence, and the way they are regarded.

Language Note

"Police"

There are many words in Japanese used to refer to "police"(警官 and 警察) or "police officers" (警察官 and お巡りさん). The first few terms all include the same *kanji*, 警 (けい), which means to "admonish," "warn," or "prohibit." The second two terms, suggest "circulating" or "going around." Traditionally, police officers patrolled around the neighborhood on foot or by bike; this is to some extent the case today as well. お巡りさん is often used to refer to police who are posted at こうばん. What are some terms for police officers in your own country?

ペアワーク

A. READ/SPEAK/LISTEN You are driving and your driving instructor is worried about your driving. Your instructor warns you about your driving. You apologize and promise never to do it again.

Ex. Instructor: ここで　食べないで。

You: すみません。けっして　ここで　食べません。

1. きゅうに　とまらないで。

2. かどを　きゅうに　まがらないで。

3. うるさい　おんがくを　きかないで。

4. きいろの　しんごうで　とまって。

5. スピードを　ださないで。

6. 前を　よく　見て。

7. 大きい　こえで　うたわないで。

8. あんぜんに　うんてんして。

B. SPEAK/LISTEN/WRITE You are driving with a friend and run into traffic. Explain what you see from your window and create a short conversation appropriate to the situation. Choose one to present to your class!

Choices: 交通事故, パレード, 映画のロケ (movie location), 火事 (fire)

Ex.

Aさん: 人が たくさん いますね。 何ですか。
Bさん: 工事 (construction)ですね。
Aさん: 何を 作って いますか。
Bさん: 何でしょうか。 大きい 建物ですね。
Aさん: 気を つけて 下さいね。
Bさん: はい、ゆっくり 運転します。

1.

2.

3.

4.

Authentic Reading

C. READ/WRITE/SPEAK Read the social media posts by Tadashi Oda, a Japanese high school student, and answer the following questions on a separate sheet of paper. Discuss your answers with your class.

UNDERSTAND

1. What did Tadashi see today?

2. Explain how it happened.

3. What was the condition of the drivers involved?

IDENTIFY

4. Who came to the scene to assist?

APPLY

5. How would you comment on Tadashi's social media post?

WORKBOOK page 33

小田正 · 2h
今日 私は こうつうじこを 見ました。

小田正 · 2h
うしろの 車が スピードを 出して いて、前の 車が きゅうに 止まりました。前の 車の うんてん手は 大じょうぶ でしたが、うしろの 車の

小田正 · 2h
うんてん手は みちに いました。 すぐ パトカーが 三台 来て、 きゅうきゅう車も 来ました。 とても こわかったです。

What time do you leave home?

会話 Dialogue

🔊 READ/LISTEN What time does Ken leave for school in the morning? How does he get there?

文型 Sentence Patterns

READ Find one of these sentence patterns in the dialogue.

1. Place ＋ を 出ます。   I will leave (a place).
2. Vehicle ＋ から/を おります。 I will get out of (a vehicle).
3. Place ＋ へも 行きます。   I will go to (a place), too.

単語 Vocabulary

1. vehicle に 乗る
[G1 のります/のって]
to ride (vehicle)

2. vehicle を/から おりる
[G2 おります/おりて]
to get off, to get out (vehicle)

3. シートベルトを する
[IR します/して]
to wear a seat belt

4. 出^でかける
[G2 でかけます/でかけて]

to go out

Used only to describe persons who are leaving.

5. Place を/から 出^でる
[G2 でます/でて]

to leave (a place)

6. Place に 着^つく
[G1 つきます/ついて]

to arrive (at a place)

7. 教^{おし}える
[G2 おしえます／おしえて]

to teach

読^よみましょう Language in Context

🔊 **READ/LISTEN/SPEAK** Read these sentences in Japanese. Look at the photo at the left. What do you notice about disembarking from a bus in Japan? Is it different from your own country?

バスを おりて います。

学校に 着^つきました。

A　Use of に and を/から

Use に after place words with the verbs 乗ります, 入ります and 着きます. This may be equated to using に after place words (destinations) with the directional verbs 行きます, 来ます and かえります. Do not use the particle へ with 乗ります, 入ります or 着きます.

🔊 MODELS ▷

1. はやく　車に　乗って　下さい。 　　　Please get in the car quickly.

2. 部屋に　入って　下さい。 　　　　　　Please enter the room.

3. 八時に　学校に　着きました。 　　　　I arrived to school at 8:00.

With the verbs おります and 出ます, を, or から, are used after the place of departure. When から is used, there is an emphasis on departing from the place/vehicle with a definite destination. When を is used, the statement simply describes leaving or disembarking.

Compare: 　A.　1. Vehicle ＋ を ＋ おります 　　　to get out of (a vehicle)

　　　　　　　　2. Vehicle ＋ から ＋ おります 　　to get out from (a vehicle)

　　　　　　B.　1. Place ＋ を ＋ 出ます 　　　　　to leave (a place)

　　　　　　　　2. Place ＋ から ＋ 出ます 　　　to leave from (a place)

4. 学校の　前で　バスを　おりました。
I got off the bus in front of the school.

5. バスから　おりて、図書館へ　行きました。
I got off from the bus and went to the library.

6. 七時に　うちを　出ました。
I left (my) home at 7:00.

7. 日曜日に　うちから　出ませんでした。
I did not leave from (my) home on Sunday.

READ/SPEAK Choose the correct particle for the (　). (　/　) indicates two possible answers.

1. 毎日　七時に　うち(　/　)　出て、八時ごろに　学校(　)　着きます。

2. うちの　前で　バス(　)　のって、学校の　前で　バス(　)　おります。

3. バスは　たいてい　道(　)　ゆっくり　うんてんします。

B Double Particles

Particles such as も (also) and だけ (only) belong to a special category of particles that either replace or attach to other particles. These particles replace the particles を, が or は, but are attached to other particles such as に, へ, で, から, まで, etc.

◀))) MODELS

1. 土曜日に　映画に　行きました。日曜日にも　映画に　行きました。
   I went to a movie on Saturday. I went to a movie on Sunday, too.

2. 学校で　宿題を　しました。うちでも　しました。
   I did my homework at school. I did it at home, also.

3. 東京へも　京都へも　行きたいです。
   I want to go to both Tokyo and Kyoto.

4. 日本語の　クラスでだけ　日本語を　話します。
   I speak Japanese only in Japanese class.

Usage of も

In general, when the particle も appears after a noun (or a noun and a particle) in a sentence, it follows a related sentence or pre-supposed sentence in which a similar noun has been named. See the example below. It is important that も follows the correct noun, or noun + existing particle

1. A. 父は　日本へ　行きました。　　　My dad went to Japan.

   B. 母も　日本へ　行きました。　　　My mom also went to Japan.

2. A. 父は　先月　京都へ　行きました。　Last month, my dad went to Kyoto.

   B. 父は　大阪へも　行きました。　　My dad went to Osaka, too.

READ/WRITE/SPEAK Write the correct particle in the (　). One particle per parenthesis. Each sentence means "both ~ and ~."

1. 私は　今日　お金(　)　かぎ(　)　わすれました。

2. 父は　先月　日本(／)(　)　中国(／)(　)　行きました。

3. 母は　うち(　)(　)　外(　)(　)　日本語を　話します。

4. 車の　シートの　上(　)(　)　下(　)(　)　ごみが　あります。

5. アメリカに　ヨーロッパ(　)(　)　アフリカ(　)(　)　アジア(　)(　)
   たくさんの　人が　来ました。

文化ノート　Culture Notes

Transportation to School

Students in Japan commute to school by many different modes of transportation depending on where they live. In cities and suburban areas, elementary school students who go to public schools often gather together to walk to school, since schools are located in their neighborhoods.

Middle school and high school students may also walk to their schools, ride bicycles, or catch public transportation. Students who attend far-away private schools usually commute by train, subway, or public buses.

Although some private kindergarten or pre-schools may own buses designed in the shape of cute, colorful characters or animals, students do not generally commute by school bus.

 Be a sociologist! Take a survey among at least 20 of your classmates and friends detailing the ways they commute to school. Create a graph or a pie chart from the data and compare it to what you know about how Japanese students commute. Why do you think there are differences? Write a brief summary of your findings.

アクティビティー　Communicative Activities

ペアワーク

A. READ/SPEAK/LISTEN/WRITE Take turns asking and answering the following questions with your partner. Record his/her answers on a separate sheet of paper.

1. 朝　何時ごろに　うちを　出ますか。
2. 学校に　何時ごろ　着きますか。
3. 学校へ　何に　乗って　来ますか。
4. どこで　車/バスから　おりますか。

B. READ/SPEAK/LISTEN Take turns asking and answering the following questions with your partner. Use ～も～も to indicate two possible correct answers in one sentence.

1. 週末　どこへ　行きましたか。
2. 映画館は　どこに　ありますか。
3. どこで　コンピューターを　使いますか。
4. この　学校の　生徒は　毎日　どこから　来て　いますか。

C. READ/LISTEN/SPEAK You are going to a party and you take your friend with you. You drive to your friend's house to pick him/her up. Answer your friend's questions below appropriately in Japanese.

1. 本とうに　うんてんめんきょを　もって　いますか。
2. うんてんめんきょを　見せて　下さい。
3. うんてんめんきょを　いつ　とりましたか。
4. だれが　うんてんを　おしえましたか。
5. うんてんの　しけんは　むずかしかったですか。
6. うんてんは　安全ですか。
7. じゃ、出かけましょうか。
8. シートベルトを　して　いますか。

D. READ/LISTEN/SPEAK You are a driver's education teacher. Give your student (partner) instructions. Your student repeats what he/she is supposed to do or responds appropriately.

Ex. 先生：さあ、車に　乗って　下さい。

　　　生徒：はい、車に　乗ります。

先生	生徒
1. かりめん(permit)を　見せて　下さい。	
2. 車に　乗って　下さい。	
3. シートベルトを　して　下さい。	
4. 学校を　出て　下さい。	
5. 黄色の　しんごうで　止まって　下さい。	
6. 次の　かどで　左に　まがって　下さい。	
7. スピードを　出さないで　下さい。	
8. 前を　よく　見て　下さい。	
9. よく　出来ました。　学校に　着きましたね。	
10. 車を　おりて　下さい。	

Lesson 3
Review

Review Questions

🔊 Ask your partner these questions in Japanese. Your partner should answer in Japanese. Check your answers using the audio.

Driving Safely   Review pages 95–96, 100–101, 107–108

1. Do you always wear a seatbelt? Please don't forget! (formal)

2. Do you always wear a seatbelt? Please don't forget! (informal)

3. Do your parents drive fast?

4. Do your parents drive safely?

5. Does your mother/father always stop at a yellow light?

Your Commute   Review pages 100–101, 114

6. Do you come to school by (riding the) bus?

7. What time do you leave home every morning?

8. What time do you arrive at school every day?

9. Where do you get off the bus/out of the car (at school) every day?

10. Are you returning home early today?

11. Can you hear an ambulance? There's probably an accident.

12. Traffic accidents are scary, aren't they? Please be careful.

About You   Review pages 100, 108, 114–115

13. Do you want (your) license?

14. Do you drive a car?

15. Do you walk along the streets nearby? Please don't walk in dangerous places.

16. Is the outside of your school safe? Let's be careful!

Text Chat

You will participate in a simulated exchange of text-chat messages. You should respond as fully and as appropriately as possible. You will have a conversation with Kaito Mori, a Japanese high school student, about driving.

10月07日　12:01 PM

毎あさ　何時ごろに　うちを
でて、　何時ごろに　学校に
つきますか。

Answer the question and give your opinion.

10月07日　12:09 PM

私は　うんてんしませんが、アメリカ
では　何歳から　うんてんしても
いいんですか。

Answer the question and give your situation.

10月07日　12:14 PM

日本は　こうつうじこが　おおいです
が、そちらは　どうですか。

Answer and give two reasons.

Can Do!
Now I can . . .

- ❑ recognize some informal speech styles
- ❑ politely tell others to not do a certain action
- ❑ communicate how an action is done
- ❑ talk about driving and commuting

Driving and Transportation in Japan

RESEARCH Use books, the Internet, or interview a Japanese member of your community to answer the following.

Determine

1. Why do the Japanese drive on the left side of the street?

2. List five models of Japanese cars you can find in your country (e.g., Honda Accord). What are these models called in Japanese?

Compare

3. What types of mass transportation are available in your area? How much do they cost? Are they reliable?

4. What types of mass transportation are available in Japan? How much do they cost? Are they reliable?

5. What percentage of Japanese people own a car? What percentage of people in your country (in your city and overall)?

6. What percentage of Japanese people use mass transportation? What percentage of people in your country (in your city and overall)?

7. How much does a gallon of gasoline cost in your area? How much does a gallon of gasoline cost in Japan? (Remember, Japan uses liters, so make sure you convert to the correct units.)

Infer

8. Based on the information above, give some possible reasons why the percentage of people who drive in Japan versus in your own country is different or similar.

Extend Your Learning

CREATIVE THINKING AND PROBLEM SOLVING

In a small group, brainstorm a list of common problems connected with driving and transportation in your region. Based on your research and the Culture Notes in this lesson, propose at least three solutions for any of these problems based on practices in Japan. For each solution, create a list of pros and cons for adopting it in your region.

レストランで
At a Restaurant

✓ Can Do!
In this lesson you will learn to:

- order food at a Japanese restaurant
- describe how things appear to you
- say what you have to do or do not have to do
- express your desire to try and do something
- use chopsticks properly

Online Resources

cheng-tsui.com/
adventuresinjapanese

- Audio
- Vocabulary Lists
- Vocabulary and *Kanji* Flashcards
- Study Guides
- Activity Worksheets

In this lesson you will learn how to order and pay for food in a Japanese restaurant. Review these words, phrases, and grammatical structures you already learned to help you talk about dining out in a restaurant.

めいし Nouns				
1. レストラン	restaurant		5. (お)はし	chopsticks
2. 何人さま (なんにん)	how many (people)?		6. さかな	fish
3. 二人 (ふたり)	two (people)		7. いくらぐらい	about how much?
4. おなか	stomach		8. お金	money

どうし Verbs	
9. 行きましょう [G1 行く／行って]	let's go
10. いけません	won't do
11. わすれました [G2 わすれる／わすれて]	forgot
12. かして　下さい [G1 かす／かします]	please lend

-い けいようし -i Adjectives	
13. おいしい	delicious, tasty
14. おいしかった	was delicious, was tasty

-な けいようし -na Adjectives	
15. 好きじゃないんです	do not like

Expressions	
16. ちょっと、ちょっと	Just a minute, just a minute.
17. おなかが　すきました。	I am hungry.
18. いただきます。	[Expression used before a meal.]
19. いいえ、けっこうです。	No, thank you.
20. ごちそうさま。	[Expression used after a meal.]
21. おねがいします。	Please do it.
22. ありがとう　ございました。	Thank you very much. [for something done in the past.]
23. すみませんが . . .	Excuse me, but . . .

ぶんぽう　Grammar

24.　Sentence 1 + から、Sentence 2。　Sentence 1, so Sentence 2.

おなかが　すきましたから、早く　食べたいです。

I am hungry, so I want to eat early.

A. WRITE Write out what Ken and Mari are saying in each scene using the words and phrases you reviewed above.

1.

2.

3.

B. WRITE/SPEAK/LISTEN Using the review vocabulary and grammar, write a short conversation between two characters from your favorite television show going out to dinner. Act out the script in class or create a video and share it with the class.

Kanji
used in this lesson

In this lesson, you will learn the *kanji* for size and different levels of school.

	Kanji	Meaning	Readings	Examples		
73.	門	gate	モン	もん 門	gate	門 → 門 → 門
74.	聞	to listen, hear	き(く) ブン	き 聞く しんぶん 新聞	listen newspaper	門 → 門 + → ＝聞
75.	雨	rain	あめ	あめ 雨	rain	→ 雨 → 雨
76.	電	electricity	デン	でんしゃ 電車	train	→ 雨 + 雨 → → 甩 ＝電
77.	魚	fish	さかな	さかな 魚	fish	→ → 魚
78.	肉	meat	にく	にく 肉	meat	→ → → 肉

	Kanji	Meaning	Readings	Examples	
79.	安	cheap	やす(い)	やす 安い　cheap	
80.	高	tall expensive	たか(い) コウ	たか　ひと 高い人　tall person たか　ほん 高い本　expensive 　　　　book こうこう 高校　high school	
81.	帰	to go back	かえ(る)	かえ 帰る　return	 road　hand on broom ＝帰
82.	買	to buy	か(う)	か　もの 買い物　shopping	 net shell　＝買

New Reading				
56.	牛	cow	うし ギュウ	うし 牛　cow ぎゅう　にく 牛肉　beef

WORKBOOK page 179

お昼を食べに行きましょうか。 **Let's go out to lunch!**

ごちそうさま。
おいしかったですね。

おなかが
いっぱいです。

今日は　ぼくが
ごちそう　しますよ。

ありがとう。

じゃ、私が
チップを　払（はら）いましょう。

いくらぐらい
置（お）かなければ
なりませんか。

だいたい
十五パーセント
ぐらいです。

すみません、
お勘定（かんじょう）を
お願（ねが）いします。

ありがとう
ございました。

あちらの　レジで
お願（ねが）いします。

あっ、まりさん

さいふを　忘（わす）れました。

すみませんが、
お金を　貸（か）して　下さい。

明日　返（かえ）しますから。

はいはい。

To read an informal version
of the conversation,
go to cheng-tsui.com/
adventuresinjapanese

かいわ

会話 Dialogue

🔊 **READ/LISTEN** What food is Mari going to order? What is Ken going to order?

う〜ん ... おいしそうですねえ。

何に　しますか。

私は　にぎりずしに　します。

ぼくは　親子どんぶりに

肉うどんを　食べます。

ぶんけい
文型 Sentence Patterns

READ Find one of these sentence patterns in the dialogue.

1. おいし＋そうです。　　　　　looks delicious

2. something に します。　　will have something. / decide on something.

3. something に something　　~ and ~ [A particle to combine two or more nouns.]

1. う〜ん	2. （おいし）そうです	3. 〜にします	4. 〜に〜	5. メニュー
Yummm . . .	looks (delicious)	decide on ~	~ and ~ (as a set)	menu

6. うどん

thick white noodles in broth

7. 肉うどん (にく)

うどん topped with beef

8. ざるそば

buckwheat noodles

Served cold.

9. ラーメン

Chinese noodle soup

Also called ちゅうかそば.

10. 親子どんぶり (おや)

chicken and egg over a bowl of steamed rice.

おや means "parent" and 子 means "child."

11. とんかつ

pork cutlet

12. カレーライス or ライスカレー or カレー

curry rice

13. （お）みそしる

soup flavored with *miso* (soybean paste).

や　にく
14. 焼き肉

や　とり
15. 焼き鳥

16. にぎりずし

meat grilled over a fire

やきます means to cook or to grill.

grilled skewered chicken

bite-sized rectangles of rice topped
with fish, vegetables, or egg

にぎります means "to grasp."

ついかたんご
追加単語　Additional Vocabulary

1. ぎょうざ

や
2. 焼きそば

3. そうめん

Japanese pot stickers

fried noodles

thin white noodles served cold

よ
読みましょう　Language in Context

🔊 **READ/LISTEN/SPEAK** Read these sentences in Japanese. Tell your partner what food you would
order from the vocabulary list above.

これに　します。

おいしそうです。

文法 Grammar

A Making Selections

Noun ＋に します

This construction is used when the subject chooses an item, or decides on a certain item. This is often used in restaurants or other situations that require selecting one thing over others.

MODELS

1. ぼくは ピザと コーラに します。
   I will have pizza and a coke.

2. 私は おすしに しましょう。
   (I guess) I'll have sushi.

3. 「何に しますか。」 「そうですねえ... 肉うどんに します。」
   "What will you have?" "Let me see . . . I'll have beef *udon*."

READ/SPEAK Choose the correct particle from among は, に, と.

1. 何( ) しますか。

2. 私( ) おすし( ) します。

3. ぼく( ) おすし( ) ラーメン( ) します。

B Describing Appearance

い Adjective [Stem Form]/な Adjective/Verb [Stem Form] ＋そうです

This construction is used to describe the appearance of the subject under discussion. It suggests that the statement is not a fact, but an opinion based on the speaker's observations.

Some adjectives take irregular forms in this construction. いいです becomes よさそうです which means "looks good" and ないです becomes なさそうです which means "looks like there is not/does not exist." In addition, only certain verbs can be used with そうです. Nouns are not used with そうです.

MODELS

1. 今日は あつそうですね。
   It looks hot today, doesn't it?

2. あの 学生は 頭が よさそうですね。
   That student over there looks smart, doesn't he?

3. この レストランは 静かそうですねえ。
   This restaurant looks quiet, doesn't it!

4. あの　人は　テニスが　上手そうですねえ。
   That person looks skillful at tennis!

5. あの　人は　お金が　なさそうです。
   That person looks like he doesn't have any money.

6. 今日は　雨が　ふりそうですねえ。
   It looks like it will rain today!

7. あかちゃんが　なきそうです。
   The baby looks like she will cry.

READ/SPEAK Complete each sentence using the form of the word in the ( ) which means "looks like."

1. おすしは　(おいしい)です。

2. この　レストランの　シェフは　(上手)ですね。

3. ケンさんは　おすしを　ぜんぶ　(食べます)ですよ。

4. ケンさんは　お金が　(ない)ですよ。

C Set Connector Particle に

Noun に Noun　　　　"~ and ~"

The particle に may be used to combine two or more nouns that are usually considered part of a set. に implies that one or more than one object has been added to the first object.

((•)) MODELS

1. 朝ご飯は　毎日　パンに　コーヒーです。
   Every day, my breakfast is bread and coffee.

2. 「何を　買いましたか。」「シャツに　ズボンを　買いました。」
   "What did you buy?"　　　　"I bought a shirt and pants."

スィーツ

READ/SPEAK Emi describes her daily breakfast in two different ways.
Choose the correct particles in the ( ) to complete each sentence.

1. 私(は / の)　朝ご飯(は / に)　たいてい
   パン(と / に)　ミルク(X / に)です。

2. 私(は / の)　朝ご飯(は / に)　たいてい
   パン(を / に)　食べて、ミルク(X / を)　飲みます。

A. ざるそば

Zarusoba is a popular noodle dish in Japan, especially during the summer when it can be found at almost any Japanese restaurant. The noodles are made from a combination of buckwheat and wheat flour, and have a grayish brown color. They are served cold on a bamboo mat in a square or round lacquered box. Thin strips of *nori* (dried seaweed) are sprinkled over the noodles. A soy-based dipping sauce accompanies the noodles in a small dish, along with condiments such as minced *negi* (green onions) and *wasabi* (Japanese horseradish).

To eat the noodles, add your desired condiments to the dipping sauce, then dip a few noodles at a time into the broth with your chopsticks. As you eat, make a slurping sound to show that you're enjoying the noodles. At certain restaurants, the broth in which the *soba* was boiled is provided in a small, often square, teapot-shaped container. It may be added to the dipping sauce, then drunk as a broth after the meal.

B. Varieties of Sushi

Sushi traditionally comes in a variety of forms, and as its popularity abroad has increased, many new, creative variations have become available in Japan and throughout the world. However, the common ingredient in all sushi is rice. Traditionally, the rice is flavored with vinegar and other condiments to add flavor and preserve the food.

にぎりずし **Hand-molded sushi**
Nigirimasu means "to grasp" or "to mold". Perhaps the most iconic form of sushi, *nigirizushi* commonly comes in two forms. The first is made of a rectangular bed of hand-molded rice covered with a piece of seafood, egg, or vegetables. The second type is known as *gunkan*, meaning "warship", as it resembles the shape of a battleship. It uses the same bed of hand-molded rice, surrounded by *nori* (seaweed) and filled with a topping such as fish roe. In America, this sushi often contains other ingredients mixed with mayonnaise.

ちらしずし **Scattered sushi**
Chirashimasu means to "scatter." With this kind of sushi, slices of raw fish, shrimp, sliced egg, seaweed, and vegetables are "scattered" on top of rice. The ingredients and style may vary in different regions of Japan. Pictured is an example typically found around Tokyo. In southern Japan, the ingredients may be mixed in with the rice. This is sometimes called *mazegohan* (mixed rice) or *gomokuzushi* (5 ingredient sushi).

まきずし Rolled sushi

Makimasu means "to roll." One of the most popular varieties of sushi outside of Japan, this type is made by rolling the ingredients in rice and an outer covering. Most *makizushi* is rolled in *nori*, though layers of rice, egg, fish roe, or sesame seeds may also be an outer layer. This style is called *uramaki* (inside-out roll).

いなりずし Pouch sushi

This is sushi stuffed with flavored rice in deep fried tofu (or sometimes egg) pockets. It is called "*inari*" after a Shinto god who was believed to enjoy fried tofu.

手まきずし Hand-rolled sushi

Temaki sushi is a type of *makizushi* rolled in cones of *nori* and rice with fresh ingredients such as raw fish and vegetables. Easy to make, creative versions of this sushi have recently appeared in many sushi bars at home and abroad.

C. Westernized Sushi

As in all cases where food from one culture is introduced to another area of the world, creative modifications of the original dish occur. Sushi is no different. Across North America, many local ingredients and tastes have been incorporated into traditional Japanese recipes. In Hawaii, where a community of Japanese immigrants has long been established, sushi rice is often sweeter, and recipes include local ingredients such as tuna flakes, fish cakes, dried gourd, and spam. One notable specialty is the Hawaiian version of *inarizushi*, often called "cone sushi," which may include green beans and carrots with the rice inside the fried tofu shell.

However, the most popular form of Westernized sushi is probably the California roll, named after the state where it was created and made with crab and avocado. The California roll is often served *uramaki* style (inside-out roll), as the rice is not encased in *nori*. In addition, there are Philadelphia (Philly) rolls (salmon, cream cheese, and cucumber), Seattle rolls (salmon, avocado, and cucumber), spider rolls (fried soft-shell crab, cucumber, avocado), and many more regional creations.

 Online, find a menu for a sushi restaurant in your area. Identify at least one kind of "traditional" sushi and one kind of local or non-traditional sushi not described above. Write a short paragraph describing the ingredients of each and how they reflect local tastes and cultures. Include photographs.

トンカツ定食

天ぷら定食

ハンバーグ定食

ステーキ定食

焼き鳥定食

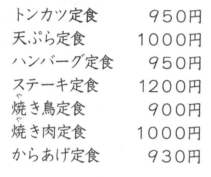

メニュー

定食

ごはん、みそしる、つけものつき

トンカツ定食	950円
天ぷら定食	1000円
ハンバーグ定食	950円
ステーキ定食	1200円
焼き鳥定食	900円
焼き肉定食	1000円
からあげ定食	930円

丼

カツどん	700円
親子どんぶり	600円
天どん	700円
牛どん	700円

うどん、そば

中華そば*	350円
焼きそば	400円
ざるそば	350円
天ぷらそば	450円
月見うどん	400円
肉うどん	450円

お飲み物

コーラ	280円	ジュース	280円

焼き肉定食

からあげ定食

親子どんぶり

中華そば

天ぷらそば

*The term 中華そば is used at restaurants that do not specialize in ramen (Chinese-style noodles), such as this one, and only offer one style of ramen. The term ラーメン is used at ラーメンや, where a variety of ramen noodles are served.

136

アクティビティー Communicative Activities

Authentic Reading

A. READ/SPEAK Read the menu on the previous page and answer the following questions.

UNDERSTAND

1. What kinds of food does this restaurant serve?

2. How many kinds of *soba* are served at this restaurant?

IDENTIFY

3. What is the most expensive dish? What is the least expensive?

4. How much does *oyakodonburi* cost?

5. What does 定食 mean?

APPLY

6. Which dish would you like to order?

ペアワーク

B. SPEAK/LISTEN/WRITE Ask your partner what he/she will have today from the menu on the previous page. Write down your partner's response on a separate sheet of paper.

Ex.
しつもん
質問：どれが　おいしそうですか。
こた
答え：～が　おいしそうです。
しつもん
質問：何に　しますか。
こた
答え：そうですねえ...　　私は　～に　します。

クラスワーク - うた

C. LISTEN/SPEAK Listen to this Japanese song about Japanese food and sing along with your class.

WORKBOOK page 43

おやこどんぶり

津川 圭一 作詩
作曲者 不詳

4課2
You don't have to eat with chopsticks

会話 (かいわ) Dialogue

🔊 **READ/LISTEN** Does Mari tell Ken he has to eat his noodles with chopsticks?

うどんは
はしで
食べなければ
なりませんか。

いいえ、
おはしで
食べなくても
いいんですよ。

文型 (ぶんけい) Sentence Patterns

READ Find one of these sentence patterns in the dialogue.

1. Verb [NAI form] (-な)ければ　　　なりません　　　have to do ~
　　　　　　　　　　　　　　　　いけません

2. Verb [NAI form] (-な)くても　　　いいです　　　it's ok not to ~
　　　　　　　　　　　　　　　　かまいません

単語 Vocabulary

1. チップ

tip

2. テーブル

table

3. (お)かんじょう

a check; bill

4. レジ

cash register

5. だいたい

generally,
approximately
[Adv.]

6. なりません

(it) won't do

7.	%
1	いっパーセント
2	にパーセント
3	さんパーセント
4	よんパーセント
5	ごパーセント
6	ろくパーセント
7	ななパーセント
8	はっパーセント
9	きゅうパーセント
10	じ(ゅ)っパーセント
?	なんパーセント

8. 食べなければ
なりません

[G2 食べる]

have to/ should eat

Lit. If (you) do not eat, it
won't do.

9. 食べなくても
いいです

[G2 食べる]

do not have to/
no need to eat it

Even if (you) do not eat, it
is okay.

10. 予約(を)
します
<ruby>予約<rt>よやく</rt></ruby>

[IR よやく(を) する]

to make a reservation

11. 注文(を)　します
<ruby>注文<rt>ちゅうもん</rt></ruby>

[IR ちゅうもん (を)　する]

to order

12. 置きます
<ruby>置<rt>お</rt></ruby>

[G1 おく]

to put, leave

13. 払います
<ruby>払<rt>はら</rt></ruby>

[G1 はらう]

to pay

追加単語 Additional Vocabulary
ついかたんご

1. とりけします [G1 とりけす]　　　　to cancel

読みましょう　Language in Context
よ

 READ/LISTEN/WRITE Read these sentences in Japanese. Say what you think the man in the picture on the right asked to get the response in the caption.

おべんとうは　おはしで
食べなければ　なりません。

チップを　おかなくても
いいです。

文法　Grammar
ぶんぽう

A　Must/Have to: Using the Verb Nai Form

Verb NAI form (-な) ければ　なりません / いけません

This construction is used when you want to express that you "have to (do)" or "must (do)" something. It is constructed by dropping the final -い of the verb *nai* form and adding the extender -*kereba narimasen* or -*kereba ikemasen*.

◀ MODELS

1. 今　授業に　行かなければ　なりません。
じゅぎょう
I have to go to class now.

2. 明日までに　この　本を　読まなければ　なりません。
よ
I have to read this book by tomorrow.

3. 早く　帰_{かえ}らなければ　いけませんよ。

   I have to return home early, you know.

4. 明日　試験_{しけん}が　ありますから、勉強_{べんきょう}しなければ　なりません。

   Since I have an exam tomorrow, I have to study.

READ/WRITE Change the verb in the ( ) to create a sentence which means "have to do ~." Write the answers on a separate sheet of paper.

1. お水は　毎日　(飲_のみます)　なりません。

2. 毎日　(食べます)　いけません。

3. 日本語を　(べんきょうします)　なりません。

B Do Not Have to: Using the Verb Nai Form in Negative Sentences

Verb NAI form (-な)くても　いいです / かまいません

This is the negative equivalent of the previously introduced permission pattern. It is formed by taking the verb nai form, dropping the final -い、 and adding -くても　いいです／ -くても　かまいません。 Literally, it translates to "It is all right even if (you) don't," but is often used in situations where English speakers would say "(You) don't have to."

This pattern is an appropriate negative reply to a question asked in the なければ なりませんか pattern.

Ex. 「明日　行かなければ　なりませんか。」 "Do I have to go tomorrow?"

「いいえ、行かなくても　いいですよ。」 "No, you don't have to go."

1. お昼ご飯_{ひる　はん}を　食べなくても　いいです。

   I don't have to eat lunch.

2. 明日　学校へ　来なくても　いいです。

   You don't have to come to school tomorrow.

3. 「今日　出_ださなければ　なりませんか。」

   "Do (we) have to turn (it) in today?"

「いいえ、今日　出_ださなくても　かまいません。」

   "No, I don't mind if you don't turn it in today."

4. 漢字で　書かなくても　いいです。

   It is all right even if you don't write in *kanji*.

READ/SPEAK Choose the correct sentence ending to complete each sentence based on fact.

1. そばは　はしで　(食べなければ　なりません / 食べなくても
   いいです)。

2. 日本で　チップを　(おかなければ　なりません / おかなくても
   いいです)。

3. レストランで　お金を　(はらわなければ　なりません / はらわなくても
   いいです)。

文化ノート　Culture Notes
<ruby>文化<rt>ぶんか</rt></ruby>

A. Chopstick Etiquette

Chopsticks are versatile eating utensils. As you master their use, you must be careful to observe chopstick etiquette. Observe the do's and don'ts below. Note that there are basically three types of chopsticks in Japan: those used at casual restaurants or included with *bento* (disposable wooden chopsticks), those used at more formal restaurants or at home (often lacquered, plastic, or polished wood), and those used for cooking (longer in length, often wooden). Regardless of the formality of the meal or the chopsticks you use, the rules below should always be followed.

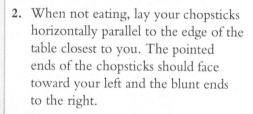

Do	Do NOT
1. Pick up your food without stabbing it.	1. Vertically rub the chopsticks together in your open palms.
2. When not eating, lay your chopsticks horizontally parallel to the edge of the table closest to you. The pointed ends of the chopsticks should face toward your left and the blunt ends to the right.	2. Scrape chopsticks against each other.
	3. Stick chopsticks vertically into a bowl of rice, as it is reminiscent of practices associated with death in Japan.
	4. Pass food to or from another person from chopstick to chopstick. This too, is associated with traditional funeral practices.
3. Place the pointed ends of the chopsticks on a はしおき or chopstick rest. Using a はしおき keeps the tips of your chopsticks sanitary as they do not make contact with the table.	5. Suck the tips of the chopsticks.
	6. Use chopsticks to slide dishes across the table.

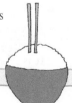

B. 天ぷら

The popular Japanese food known as *tempura* is said to have originated with the Portuguese missionaries who arrived in Japan during the latter part of the 16th century. It is made by frying fish, shrimp, squid, or vegetables (e.g., eggplant, green peppers, sweet potatoes, pumpkin, green beans, mushrooms, lotus root, carrots, etc.) in a light batter. When eaten, *tempura* is dipped in a soy-sauce-based broth. Grated *daikon* radish and ginger may be added to the dipping sauce for greater flavor. The word *tempura* is written in Japanese as 天ぷら, but it is not related to "heaven" in any way, though you may think it is heavenly to eat!

 Create a list of do's and don'ts about using Western utensils for Japanese students, then create a Venn diagram comparing chopsticks and Western utensils, including characteristics, usage, and rules of etiquette.

アクティビティー Communicative Activities

ペアワーク

A. SPEAK/LISTEN/WRITE On a separate sheet of paper, complete the schedule of events by writing down what time you had to or will have to perform the following actions. Then ask a partner about his/her schedule for today and write down the times they tell you. When finished, compare what you and your partner wrote down to check your answers.

My schedule for today:
私は 今日 _____に 起きなければ なりませんでした。
私は 今日 _____に うちを 出なければ なりませんでした。
私は 今日 _____に 学校へ 来なければ なりませんでした。
私は 今日 _____に 家へ 帰らなければ なりません。
私は 今日 _____に 寝なければ なりません。

B. SPEAK/LISTEN Ask your partner these questions. Your partner gives complete answers based on fact. Mark whether he/she answers affirmatively or negatively on a separate sheet of paper.

Ex. 質問：今日　日本語の　宿題を　しなければ　なりませんか。

答え：はい、しなければ　なりません。

or いいえ、しなくても　いいです。

しつもん	はい	いいえ
1. 今日　日本語の　しゅくだいを　しなければ　なりませんか。		
2. 今日　ばんごはんを　うちで　食べなければ　なりませんか。		
3. 日曜日に　学校へ　行かなければ　なりませんか。		
4. 今日　早く　うちへ　帰らなければ　なりませんか。		

C. SPEAK/LISTEN With a partner, role play the following. You are in Japan and a Japanese friend wants to take you to a Japanese restaurant. Ask your partner the following questions about what you should do there. He or she will respond affirmatively or negatively.

Ex.

「くつ下を　はかなければ　なりませんか。」

「はい、はかなければ　なりません。
or 「いいえ、はかなくても　いいです。」

1. レストランの　予約を
　　しなければ　なりませんか。
2. たたみに　すわらなければ
　　なりませんか。
3. おはしで　食べなければ
　　なりませんか。
4. チップを　おかなければ
　　なりませんか。
5. おかんじょうは　はらわなければ
　　なりませんか。

WORKBOOK　page 45

会話 <small>かいわ</small> Dialogue

🔊 **READ/LISTEN** What does Mari ask Ken to try? Why does Ken decline?

ケンさん、
にぎりずしを 一つ
食べて みませんか。

いいえ、
けっこうです。
ぼくは 魚<small>さかな</small>が 好き
じゃないんですよ。

文型 <small>ぶんけい</small> Sentence Patterns

READ Find one of these sentence patterns in the dialogue.

1. Verb (TE Form) + みます。   will try doing ~
2. Verb (TE Form) + みましょう。   Let's try doing ~
3. Verb (TE Form) + みませんか。   Would you like to try doing ~? [Invitation]
4. Verb (TE Form) + みて 下さい。   Please try doing ~. [Request]
5. Verb (TE Form) + みたいです。   I want to try doing ~.

単語 Vocabulary

1. さいふ

wallet

2. (食べて) みます

<small>Do not use kanji 見ます here.</small>

will try (eating)

3. ごちそう(を) します

[IR ごちそう(を) する]

to treat (someone) to a meal

<table>
<tr><td colspan="2">5.</td><td>General counter</td></tr>
</table>

5.	General counter	
	Used for small objects that take the ひとつ, ふたつ series, but used more conversationally	
1		いっこ
2		にこ
3		さんこ
4		よんこ
5		ごこ
6		ろっこ
7		ななこ
8		はっこ
9		きゅうこ
10		じ(ゅ)っこ
?		なんこ？

4. 返します
[G1 かえす]

to return (something)

追加単語　Additional Vocabulary

1. わりかんに　しましょう。　　Let's split the cost.

2. えんりょしないで　下さい。　Please make yourself at home. Please do not hesitate.

読みましょう　Language in Context

🔊 **READ/LISTEN/SPEAK**　Read these sentences in Japanese. Make a suggestion to a partner that he/she try something new.

この　お店に　入って
みましょう。

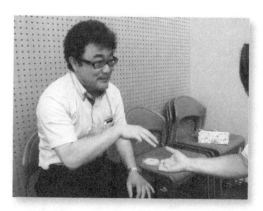

これを　食べて　みませんか。

文法 Grammar
ぶんぽう

A To Try Doing: Verb-て＋みます

Verb (TE Form) + みます

This pattern is constructed by taking the verb in its TE form and attaching みます or other conjugated forms of みます. It means "try to do (something)" It is generally used in a context where the subject will "do something and find out (something about it)." The kanji 見 is not used for this みます because this みます means "to try," not to see with one's eyes.

食べて　みます。	I'll try eating.
食べて　みましょう。	Let's try eating. / Let me try eating.
食べて　みませんか。	Would you like to try eating (it)? [Invitation]
食べて　みて　下さい。	Please try eating. [Request]
食べて　みたいです。	I want to try eating.

 MODELS

1. おすしを　食べて　みましょう。
   Let's try eating sushi.

2. この　ドレスを　着て　みます。
   き
   I will try wearing this dress.

3. この　くつを　はいて　みて　下さい。
   Please try wearing these shoes.

4. 私は　来年　日本へ　行って　みたいです。
   I want to try going to Japan next year.

READ/SPEAK Complete each sentence using the form of the verb in the ( ) which means "want to try to do ~."

1. 日本へ　（行きます）　みたいです。

2. 日本で　おすしを　（食べます）　みたいです。

3. 日本人と　日本語で　（話します）　みたいです。

4. 日本語で　（よやくを　する）　みたいです。

Tipping in Japan

In most restaurants in Japan, tipping is not required or expected. However, some restaurants and other service-oriented businesses may automatically include a service charge indicated on the receipt. In international tourist situations, tipping a tour guide or driver is acceptable. If tips are offered, they should always be placed in envelopes, as it is considered crude to hand cash to others for services.

 Many Japanese people are uncertain about how to tip when they travel. Write a short article that could be used in the restaurant section of a guidebook for your city instructing Japanese tourists about when to tip, how much to tip, and how to go about leaving a tip. Is it necessary to tip at all food establishments? How much is recommended? Does the amount of tip left vary by situation? Who tips? When is the tip left? How?

Language Note

やき

Many people from outside Japan are familiar with the word *"teriyaki."* The word *"yaki"* comes from the verb *"yakimasu"* or *"yaku,"* which means "to burn, bake, roast, toast, broil, grill, char, or fry." Any food prepared in these ways often includes the word *"yaki,"* e.g., *yakisoba, misoyaki, yakiniku, shioyaki, sukiyaki, yakitori,* etc. Can you think of any others? The left radical of the kanji for *yaki* (焼), which is the fire radical, also clearly indicates the meaning of this character.

焼
fire radical

アクティビティー　Communicative Activities

ペアワーク

A. SPEAK/LISTEN Tell a partner your impression of the following things based on the cues given. Your partner will suggest that you try it.

Ex. This cake looks delicious.

　　Aさん: この　ケーキは　おいしそうですねえ。

　　Bさん: そうですねえ。じゃ、食べて　みましょう。

1.
looks delicious
おいし(い)

2.
looks interesting
おもしろ(い)

3.
looks cheap
安(い)

4.
looks good
いい or よ(い)

5.
looks fun
たのし(い)

6.
looks delicious
おいし(い)

7.
looks cold
つめた(い)

8.
looks expensive
高(い)

B. SPEAK/LISTEN You are working at a store and want to sell the items below to a customer. You recommend that the customer try them. The customer (your partner) decides to try them and comments on them. Switch roles.

Ex. Tシャツ

この　Tシャツは　とても　いいですよ。きて　みませんか。

じゃ、ちょっと　きて　みましょう。
あ、ちょっと　小さいですね。

1. チョコレート
2. ジュース
3. ペン
4. サングラス
5. コンピューター
6. 車
7. ぼうし

WORKBOOK　page 47

会話 かいわ Dialogue

🔊 **READ/LISTEN** How does the server greet Ken? Is it different from how a friend would greet him?

ウェイトレス： いらっしゃいませ。
何人様 さま ですか。

ケン： 二人です。

ウェイトレス： どうぞ　こちらへ。
メニューを　どうぞ。

単語 Vocabulary

1. ウェイター
waiter

2. ウェイトレス
waitress

3. こちら, そちら, あちら, どちら?
here, there, over there, where?
Polite equivalent of ここ, そこ, あそこ, どこ.

4. いらっしゃいませ。
Welcome.

5. どうぞ　こちらへ。
This way, please.

6. ごちゅうもんは?
May I take your order?
Lit. What is your order?

7. ほかに　何か？

Anything else?

8. それだけです。

That's all.

Lit. It is only that.

9. すみません。

Excuse me.

[to get someone's attention]

<ruby>読<rt>よ</rt></ruby>みましょう　Language in Context

🔊 **READ/LISTEN/SPEAK** Read these sentences in Japanese. With a partner, practice greeting customers at a restaurant as a server.

いらっしゃいませ。　　　　　　どうぞ、こちらへ。

<ruby>文化<rt>ぶんか</rt></ruby>ノート　Culture Notes

A. Teens and Restaurant Culture in Japan

Japanese teens enjoy gathering at inexpensive restaurants that serve Western foods, such as hamburgers, fried chicken, pastas, and pizzas, or shops that serve sweets, such as cakes, doughnuts, and ice cream. Also popular with younger adults are *yakiniku* (Korean-style grilled beef) restaurants.

Families enjoy going out for meals at *famiresu,* or family restaurants mainly located in suburban areas. Here children and their families find a variety of food choices to suit the tastes of all generations at a reasonable cost.

B. Western Food in Japan

The Japanese love to explore foods from other cultures, and just as Japanese food has been "westernized," so too have many foreign foods been "Japanized" using local ingredients and cooking styles. Portions are also often smaller in Japan, and good presentation is stressed. Chinese and Korean foods like ramen have long been part of the Japanese diet, and more recently many American and Italian dishes have been adapted by the Japanese.

Nattoo (fermented soy beans) sauce over spaghetti

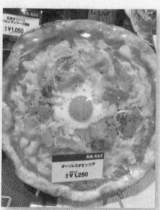

Raw egg pizza

Sandwiches filled with sweetened red bean paste and whipped cream

C. Service in Japanese Restaurants

When customers enter a restaurant in Japan, they should expect a quick, loud welcome of *"irasshaimase."* Unlike most Western restaurants, one waiter/waitress is not assigned to a table, so any waiter or waitress may help you. Customers must call out for the waitress when they need help. When food arrives at the table, the waiter/waitress may not be the same one that took your order, so they will ask who ordered each dish. Tips are not expected. As you exit, you will receive a hearty thank you for your patronage.

 Online, find a menu for a local restaurant specializing in some kind of ethnic food (i.e., Chinese, Japanese, Mexican, French, Thai, Indian, etc.), then research common Americanized foods in that cuisine. Note differences between the "authentic" food and the food served at this restaurant. Why would this food be popular in America? Imagine you are a chef at this restaurant and create a dish that might appeal to local American tastes. Write a simple recipe to share with your classmates. If you wish, actually prepare it and bring it to school to share with your class!

アクティビティー Communicative Activities

ペアワーク

Role play with your partner. (ウェイ represents the waiter/waitress and きゃく is the customer.)

1. ウェイ：いらっしゃいませ。何人様ですか。

   きゃく：一人です。

   ウェイ：どうぞ　こちらへ。メニューを　どうぞ。

   After a while.

   ウェイ：御注文は？

   きゃく：ラーメンと　ギョウザに　します。

   ウェイ：ほかに　何か？

   きゃく：それだけです。

2. きゃく：すみません。お勘定を　お願いします。

   ウェイ：ありがとう　ございました。あちらの　レジで
   　　　　お願いします。

3. ケン／まり：　いただきます。

   Ken eats Chinese noodles and Mari eats sushi.

   　　まり：　おすし、一つ　どうぞ。

   　　ケン：　ありがとう。でも、
   　　　　　けっこう。
   　　　　　ぼく、おなかが
   　　　　　いっぱい。

   ケン／まり：　ごちそうさま。

Review Questions

🔊 Ask your partner these questions in Japanese. Your partner answers in Japanese. Check your answers using the audio.

Eating out   Review pages 132, 133, 140, 141, 147

1. What do you generally order at a Japanese restaurant?

2. Do I have to make reservations at an expensive restaurant?

3. How much (what percentage) tip do you have to leave at an American restaurant?

4. Do I have to leave a tip in Japan?

5. Japanese foods are delicious looking, aren't they?

6. Is it all right if I don't eat with chopsticks at a Japanese restaurant?

7. What kind of sushi would you like to try and eat?

8. Have you tried to order sushi at a restaurant?

9. Do you want to try going to a Japanese restaurant?

At School   Review pages 128, 133, 141

10. I forgot my money. Please lend me $10.00. I will return it tomorrow.

11. At the school cafeteria, do you have to pay at the register?

12. How many hamburgers did you eat for lunch?

Weather   Review pages 132, 133

13. Does the weather look like it will be good tonight?

14. Does it look like it will rain tomorrow?

Text Chat

You will participate in a simulated exchange of text-chat messages. You should respond as fully and as appropriately as possible. You will have a conversation with Mariko Yamamoto, a Japanese high school student, about a meal.

11月 20日　09:47 PM

日本で　どんな　ものを
食べて　みたいですか。

Give at least two examples.

11月 20日　09:53 PM

日本で　チップを　おかなくても
いいです。アメリカは？

Respond and give details.

11月 20日　09:59 PM

アメリカで　高校生は　レストランで
はたらいても　いいですか。

Respond.

Can Do!
Now I can . . .

❏ order food at a Japanese restaurant

❏ describe how things appear to me

❏ say what I have to do or do not have to do

❏ express my desire to try and do something

❏ use chopsticks properly

Cooking 親子どんぶり
<ruby>おや</ruby><ruby>こ</ruby>

Oyakodonburi is a simple but favorite dish of the Japanese. *Oyako* means "parent and child," which refers to the fact that this dish contains both chicken (parent) and egg (child). *Donburi* is the word for the kind of bowl that holds this dish. Other favorite *donburi* dishes include *tanindonburi* (beef and egg) and *katsudon* (pork cutlet). *Donburi* dishes, or *donburimono*, are generally served with soup and pickled vegetables.

Let's try and make some delicious *oyakodonburi!*

Ingredients (Serves 4)
4 servings of cooked short-grain rice separated
    into 4 bowls
¾ pound of chicken thighs cut into bite-sized pieces
½ cup onions, thinly sliced
4 eggs, well beaten
thinly sliced *nori* seaweed for garnish (optional)

Broth
¼ cup soy sauce
¼ cup *mirin**
1 ¾ cups water
2 teaspoons *katsuo dashi* powder

*mirin – a sweet and sour condiment made of corn syrup, water, rice wine, and vinegar. May substitute 3 tablespoons of rice wine with 1 tablespoon of sugar.

Preparing the broth
1. Boil water for the broth in a saucepan.
2. When water comes to a boil add the *katsuo dashi* and *mirin*.
3. Reduce heat and carefully add soy sauce to taste.
4. Set the broth aside for later.

Preparing the dish
1. Add a small amount of oil to the frying pan and heat the pan.
2. Add the onions to the frying pan and cook on low heat until soft.
3. When the onions soften, add the chicken and cook on medium heat for 2-3 minutes.
4. Add the broth to the chicken and onions and boil for 2-3 minutes.
5. Immediately lower the heat and skim off any foam and fat that may have risen to the top of the broth.
6. Separate the chicken and onions into 4 portions.
7. Add one portion of chicken and onions to a new frying pan and heat for 1 minute.
8. Pour 1 beaten egg over the chicken and onions and put a lid on the frying pan. Cook on low heat for 20-30 seconds.
9. Repeat steps #7 and 8 for the remaining 3 portions.
10. Gently pour the mixture over rice and garnish with *nori* (optional).
11. Cover the bowls with lids (if you have them) and serve hot!

いただきましょう!!!

げんき
元気
Wellness

5課

 **Can Do!**

In this lesson you will learn to:

- talk about illnesses you may have experienced
- discuss what you are or are not able to do
- communicate your intentions and plans
- talk about what you and others are expected to do

Online Resources

cheng-tsui.com/
adventuresinjapanese

- Audio
- Vocabulary Lists
- Vocabulary and *Kanji* Flashcards
- Study Guides
- Activity Worksheets

In this lesson you will learn how to express what you are and are not able to do. Review these words, phrases, and grammatical structures you already learned to help you talk about your health.

めいし Nouns				
1. 先週 しゅう	last week	5. おなか	stomach
2. ねつ	fever	6. くすり	medicine
3. よる	night	7. びょうき	illness
4. こと	thing [intangible]	8. あたま	head

どうし Verbs	
9. 休んで います [G1 やすむ／やすみます／やすまない]	is absent
10. あって [G1 ある／あります／ない]	have, there is
11. ねる [G2 ねます／ねて／ねない]	to sleep
12. 飲まなければ なりませんでした [G1 のむ／のみます／のんで]	had to drink, take (medicine)
13. 行かない [G1 行く／行きます／行って]	do not go
14. しんぱいしなくても いいです [IR しんぱいする／します／して]	no need to worry

-い けいようし -I Adjectives	
15. いたくて（いたい）	painful, sore

-な けいようし -NA Adjectives			
16. 大丈夫 じょうぶ	all right	17. 大変 たいへん	hard, difficult

ふくし -Adverbs	
18. もう ＋ Affirmative	already
19. あまり ＋ Negative	(not) very
20. ちょっと	a little
21. よく	well

Expressions	
22. どう　しましたか。	What happened?
23. お大事に。	Please take care.

A. WRITE Write out what Ken and Mari are saying in each scene using the words, phrases, and grammatical structures you reviewed above.

1.

2.

3.

B. WRITE Imagine that you have the flu. Write an e-mail to your Japanese teacher naming two of your symptoms and telling him/her you will be absent from school. Ask your teacher what kind of homework you will have to do while you are absent.

In this lesson, you will learn the *kanji* for health and intervals of time.

	Kanji	Meaning	Readings	Examples		
83.	元	origin	ゲン	げんき 元気	healthy	二 + 〰 → 儿 = 元
84.	気	spirit	キ	びょうき 病気	illness	〰 → 〰 +
				てんき 天気	weather	〰 → 米 = 気
85.	週	week	シュウ	いっしゅうかん 一 週 間	one week	用 + 口 +
				こんしゅう 今 週	this week	
				らいしゅう 来 週	next week	〰 → 〰 = 週
				せんしゅう 先 週	last week	
				まいしゅう 毎 週	every week	
				しゅうまつ 週 末	weekend	
86.	間	between	あいだ	ひと くるま あいだ 人 と 車 の 間	between (a) person and (a) car	門 → 門 +
		interval	カン	いちじかん 一時間	one hour	〰 → 日 = 間
87.	出	to go out	で (る)	で うちを出る	leave home	〰 → 出 → 出
				でき 出来ません	can't do	
				でぐち 出口	exit	
		to turn in	だ (す)	だ 出して くだ 下さい	Please turn (something) in.	

	Kanji	Meaning	Readings	Examples	
88.	午	noon	ゴ	<ruby>午前一時<rt>ごぜんいちじ</rt></ruby>	1:00 a.m. ▽ + 二 + 十 = 午
89.	後	behind	うし(ろ)	<ruby>車<rt>くるま</rt></ruby> の <ruby>後<rt>うし</rt></ruby>ろ	behind the car
		later	あと(で)	<ruby>後<rt>あと</rt></ruby>で	later
		after	ゴ	<ruby>午後一時<rt>ご ご いちじ</rt></ruby>	1:00 p.m.
90.	飲	to drink	の(む)	<ruby>水<rt>みず</rt></ruby>を<ruby>飲<rt>の</rt></ruby>む	drink water 食 + 𝕽 → 㐬 = 飲
91.	事	thing (intangible)	こと ごと ジ	どんな<ruby>事<rt>こと</rt></ruby>？	What kind of things? 一 + 口 +
				<ruby>仕事<rt>し ごと</rt></ruby>	job
				<ruby>食事<rt>しょく じ</rt></ruby>	meal
				<ruby>大事<rt>だい じ</rt></ruby>	important
				<ruby>事務所<rt>じ む しょ</rt></ruby>	office
92.	回	- time(s)	カイ	<ruby>一日<rt>いちにち</rt></ruby>に <ruby>三回<rt>さん かい</rt></ruby>	three times a day (👄 → 口)×2= 回

Recognition Kanji

<ruby>病気<rt>びょう き</rt></ruby>　illness

<ruby>度<rt>ど</rt></ruby>　- time(s) - degree(s)

WORKBOOK page 183

学校を　休んで　いますね

You haven't been at school

もう　一週間も
学校を　休んで
いますね。

もしもし、
ケンさん、
どう　しましたか。

ああ、まりさん
ですか。

風邪を　ひきました。
具合が　悪いんです。

大丈夫ですか。

先週は　熱が
三十九度も　あって、夜
寝る　ことが
出来ませんでした。
お腹も　痛くて、
何も　食べる　ことが
出来ませんでした。

そうですか。
薬を　飲んで　いますか。

毎日　三度も
薬(くすり)を　飲まなければ
なりませんでした。

大変(へん)でしたねえ。

明日　日本語の
試験(しけん)が　ある　はずですが、
学校へは　行かない　つもりです。
頭(あたま)が　痛(いた)くて　漢字も　単(たん)語も
覚(おぼ)える　ことが　出来ません。

そうですか。
あまり　心配(しんぱい)しないで
下さいね。

仕方(しかた)が　ないですよ。
よく　休んで　下さい。
じゃ、お大事に。

To read an informal version of the conversation,
go to cheng-tsui.com/adventuresinjapanese

5課1
I can't go to school

会話 Dialogue
<small>かいわ</small>

🔊 **READ/LISTEN** Why was Ken absent? How does he feel?

今日　学校を　休んで　いましたね。どう　しましたか。

お腹が　痛くて、何も　食べる　ことが　出来ませんでした。
<small>なか　いた</small>

大丈夫ですか。
<small>じょうぶ</small>

文型 Sentence Patterns
<small>ぶんけい</small>

READ Find one of these sentence patterns in the dialogue.

1. Noun ＋が　出来ます。   be able to do (an activity)
2. Verb (Dictionary Form) ＋こと＋が　出来ます。   be able to do (an action)

単語 Vocabulary

1. 具合が　悪いです
<small>ぐ あい</small>
<small>わる</small>

condition is bad, feel sick

2. 風邪を　ひきました
<small>か ぜ</small>
[G1 かぜをひく]

caught a cold

3. ストレスが　いっぱいです

is very stressed
ストレスが　ありません。 have no stress

4. 問題
<ruby>問題<rt>もんだい</rt></ruby>

problem

5. 変
<ruby>変<rt>へん</rt></ruby>

[な Adjective]

strange, weird, unusual

6. ひきます

[G1 ひく]

to play (a string instrument)

7. 〜が 出来ます

[G2 できる]

be able to do 〜

<ruby>追加単語<rt>ついかたんご</rt></ruby> Additional Vocabulary

1. インフルエンザ　flu

2. せきが 出る　to cough

3. ねんざ(を) しました。　(I) sprained (something).

4. ほねを おりました。　(I) fractured a bone.

5. ふきます　to play (a wind instrument)

6. たたきます　to play (a percussion instrument)

<ruby>読<rt>よ</rt></ruby>みましょう　Language in Context

🔊 READ/LISTEN/SPEAK Read these sentences in Japanese. Say three things you are not able to do when you are sick.

ピアノを <ruby>少<rt>すこ</rt></ruby>し
ひくことが 出来ます。

<ruby>具合<rt>ぐあい</rt></ruby>が <ruby>悪<rt>わる</rt></ruby>いです。

A Expressing Ability 出来ます (Informal)

Noun ＋が　出来ます。　　　**can do, be able to do (something)**

)) MODELS ▷

1. 母は　少し　日本語が　出来ます。
   My mom can speak a little Japanese.

2. 父は　全然　料理が　出来ません。
   My father cannot cook at all.

READ/SPEAK Fill in the ( ) with the appropriate word based on what you are able to do.

1. (　)が　まあまあ　出来ます。

2. (　)が　あまり　出来ません。

3. (　)が　全然　出来ません。

B Expressing Ability ことが　出来ます (Formal)

Verb (dictionary form)＋ことが　出来ます。

This form is used to express one's ability to do something. It is used more frequently in writing than in speaking. It is also used in more formal speech.

)) MODELS ▷

1. 手が　痛くて、書くことが　出来ません。
   My hands hurt, and I am not able to write.

2. 「ピアノを　ひくことが　出来ますか。」
   "Are you able to play the piano?"

   「少し　出来ますが、まだ　下手です。」
   "I can play a little, but I'm still unskillful at it."

READ/SPEAK Answer the questions below based on fact.

1. フランス語を　話すことが　出来ますか。

2. 漢字を　いくつ　読むことが　出来ますか。

文化ノート Culture Notes

Centigrade and Fahrenheit

The Japanese follow the metric system. In measuring temperature, therefore, the Centigrade (せっし), rather than Fahrenheit (かし) scale, is used. Normal body temperature, which is 98.6 degrees in Fahrenheit, is 37 degrees in Centigrade.

Conversion Formula: Centigrade $°C = (Fahrenheit °F - 32) \times 5 / 9$

 Online, look up the current temperatures of eight major cities on at least four different continents. Create a table that shows the names of the cities in Japanese and English with temperatures in both Centigrade and Fahrenheit. Then choose one city and plan a trip. Answer the following questions in Japanese: Where do you want to go and why? What will you pack and why? Describe each item of clothing in detail.

Centigrade °C	Fahrenheit °F
20	68.0
25	77.0
28	82.4
30	86.0
32	89.6
33	91.4
34	93.2
35	95.0
36	96.8
37	98.6

アクティビティー Communicative Activities

クラスワーク

A. SPEAK/LISTEN/WRITE Ask your classmates the questions below until you find a person who can answer affirmatively. Record his/her name on a separate sheet of paper.

質問：泳ぐことが　出来ますか。

答え：はい、出来ます。 or いいえ、出来ません。

質問	名前
1. 左手で　書くことが　出来ますか。	
2. ギターを　ひくことが　出来ますか。	
3. 日本の　歌を　歌うことが　出来ますか。	
4. 車を　運転することが　出来ますか。	
5. スペイン語を　話すことが　出来ますか。	

ペアワーク

B. SPEAK/LISTEN Your partner does not look well. Ask him/her what is the matter and express sympathy according to his/her answers. Take turns.

Ex. headache   Aさん: どう　しましたか。

            Bさん: 頭（あたま）が　痛（いた）いんです。

            Aさん: 大丈夫（だいじょうぶ）ですか。

            Bさん: ええ、大丈夫（だいじょうぶ）です。

1. stomachache   **2.** sore throat   **3.** high fever   **4.** caught a cold

5. toothache   **6.** voice is funny   **7.** left foot is sore   **8.** headache

C. SPEAK/LISTEN Tell your partner about a problem. Your partner should tell you what he/she thinks and respond accordingly. Take turns.

     Aさん: 病気で　学校へ　行くことが　出来ません。

     Bさん: 仕方（しかた）が　ありませんね。心配（しんぱい）しなくても　いいですよ。

1. 今日は　お金を　忘（わす）れて、ランチを　買うことが　出来ません。

2. 具合（ぐあい）が　悪（わる）くて、私は　食べることが　出来ません。

3. 私は　漢字を　おぼえることが　出来ません。

4. 明日　試験（しけん）が　ありますが、ねつが　あって、勉強（べんきょう）することが　出来ません。

5. 夏休（なつ）みに　日本へ　行くつもりですが、まだ　日本語が　下手です。

6. 風邪（かぜ）で　ゆうべは　全然（ぜんぜん）　寝（ね）ることが　出来ませんでした。

WORKBOOK page 57

会話 Dialogue
かい わ

🔊 **READ/LISTEN** What did Mari send to Ken? Did he see it yet?

もしもし、ケンさん?メールを
おくりましたが、見ましたか。

すみません。具合が 悪いから、
ぐあい　　わる
まだ 見て いません。

おもしろい 動画を 見ましたから、
どうが
リンクを おくりました。

じゃ、 後で 見て みますね。

文型 Sentence Patterns
ぶんけい

READ Find one of these sentence patterns in the dialogue.

1. Sentence + が ...   [Softens the statement.]

2. Reason [Noun] + で   because of ~

単語 Vocabulary

1. もしもし

Hello.
Used in telephone conversations.

2. 電話を かけます
[G2 でんわを かける]

to make a phone call

3. 間違えました
ちが
[G2 まちがえる]

made a mistake

4. ～を 送<ruby>おく</ruby>る

[G2 おくります]

to send e-mail

5. (person) から ～を もらう

[G1 もらいます]

to receive e-mail (from someone)

6. 充 電<ruby>じゅう</ruby>する

[IR じゅうでんします]

to charge (battery)

7. 動画<ruby>どうが</ruby>

online video

8. (reason) で

because of (reason)

9. 残念<ruby>ざんねん</ruby>ですが . . .

It is regrettable, but . . .

Used to decline invitations.
Literally, It's disappointing, but . . .

10. Sentence +

が . . .

[Softens the
statement.]

追加単語<ruby>ついかたんご</ruby> Additional Vocabulary

1.	メールアドレス	e-mail address	**4.**	ファイル	file
2.	ブログ	blog	**5.**	いんさつする	to print
3.	アプリ	app	**6.**	コピーする	to copy

読<ruby>よ</ruby>みましょう Language in Context

🔊 **READ/LISTEN/SPEAK** Read these sentences in Japanese. Say one thing that might be a good reason for not being able to turn in your homework.

もしもし、風邪<ruby>かぜ</ruby>で 学校へ
行くことが 出来ません。

ゆうべ 充 電<ruby>じゅう</ruby>しましたが...

A Softening Sentences with が

Sentence + が ...

Japanese people tend to avoid directness in their speech. They often end sentences with が and leave the sentences incomplete. The listener compensates by empathizing with the speaker and mentally completes the sentence in his/her own mind. Often the unmentioned portion of the sentence suggests a request or something the speaker does not want to express directly. The listener must respond accordingly. が does not literally mean "but" in this case, but merely softens the directness of the sentence.

◀))) MODELS

1. 「もしもし、山本ですが . . .」
   "Hello, this is Yamamoto. [Expecting words from the listener.]"

2. 「先生、宿題が よく 分からないんですが . . .」
   "Teacher, I don't understand the homework. (Can you help me?)"

READ/SPEAK Complete the Japanese sentence to match the English.

1. 「もしもし、(　　　　　)ですが . . .」
   "Hello, this is [own name]."

2. 「先生、この 漢字を まだ (　　　　　)が . . .」
   "Teacher, we have not learned this *kanji* yet. [Can you teach it to us?]"

B Reason Particle で

(Reason [Noun]) で   because of (reason)

When the reason can be expressed in a single noun, it may appear in this sentence construction, with the noun (reason) followed by the particle で, which is then followed by a sentence that expresses the consequence.

◀))) MODELS

1. 山本さんは 病気で 三日 学校を 休んで います。
   Yamamoto has been absent from school for three days because of illness.

2. 父は 仕事で 東京へ 行きました。
   My father went to Tokyo for work.

READ/SPEAK Give an appropriate reason in the ( ) for each sentence.

1. 今日 (　)で のどが 痛いです。

2. 今朝 (　)で 学校に 遅く 着きました。

3. 今週は たくさんの 試験や (　)で 忙しかったです。

文化ノート　Culture Notes

（ぶんか）

> よろしく
> おねがいします。

A. Phone Conversations

Having a phone conversation in any foreign language can be challenging, as you cannot see the speakers' facial expressions, gestures, or environmental context to help with communication. In Japanese, phone conversations tend to be more polite and formal than face-to-face conversations. Japanese people will also bow or use other body language, as if speaking to the other person face-to-face.

On the phone, the listener will respond often with あいづち, such as 「はい」,「そう?」,「ええっ」,「ほんとうですか」, or 「そうですか」to indicate that they are listening. If you do not use these often enough, your phone partner may ask you (politely) if you are following the conversation. Japanese people rarely end phone conversations with 「さようなら。」. Rather, they will end with expressions such as 「では、また。」, 「それでは、来週。」,「しつれいしました。」, or 「よろしく　おねがいします。」.

 Practice one of the phone dialogues in the textbook in Japanese. What body language would you use? Try to add あいづち and body language as you speak. Record a video of the performance and share it with your class.

B. Cell Phone Etiquette in Japan

Cell phones are highly popular in Japan. Smartphones (スマートフォン) in particular are popular for their increasingly extensive functions, such as the ability to watch television programs, listen to music, or write blog posts.

When in public, Japanese people are expected to turn their cell phones to silent mode, or マナーモード (manner mode). The expression "manner mode" shows a respect for others, as any activity on the phone that produces noise that may annoy others is considered to be rude. Texting, browsing the Internet, reading or writing e-mails, or playing games without sound however, are acceptable.

On trains, subways, and buses in Japan, passengers are frequently reminded through announcements and signs that their phones should be turned to "manner mode." Cell phone usage is particularly discouraged near priority seats in trains, as those seats may be occupied by passengers who may have pacemakers or other medical devices that are affected by the electromagnetic energy released by cell phones. For the same reason, cell phones must be turned off completely at hospitals.

C. Japanese Emoticons

Japanese emoticons are called 絵文字 (picture writing) or 顔文字 (face writing). The original Japanese emoticons used in e-mails are composed of punctuation marks, numbers, and alphabets that are put together to form facial expressions. They are used to express the writer's emotions or mood. Some examples are: (^_^) or (˄▽˄). Japanese mobile phone providers also offer many emoticons and graphics on their electronic devices, much like those found on smartphones in the U.S. and other countries.

 Write a short e-mail to a classmate in Japanese about a topic of your choosing and create an *emoji* that fits your message. Cc your teacher!

Language Note

Moshi moshi もしもし

The term もしもし is used most often in answering phones, as "Hello!" would be in English. It is also sometimes used as a way to confirm whether or not another person is listening to the speaker. The expression is said to be derived from the verb "もうします," a humble form of the word "to speak." At many businesses, phone calls are answered with はい instead of もしもし. Would you answer your private phone differently than at your place of work?

アクティビティー　Communicative Activities

ペアワーク

A. SPEAK/LISTEN You call your friend and invite him/her to an event. Carry on a telephone conversation. Your friend may either accept or decline your invitation. Switch roles.

Ex. There is a basketball game on Saturday starting at 6 p.m.

You: もしもし、(First name)さんですか。

Friend: はい、そうです。

You: バスケットボールの　試合が　ありますが、いっしょに行きませんか。

Friend: いつですか。

You: 土曜日の　午後六時です。

Friend: 残念ですが...

School dance Friday, 8:00 p.m.	Concert Saturday, 7:30 p.m.	Movie 8:20 p.m.	Play (げき) 6:30 p.m.

B. SPEAK/LISTEN Carry on a telephone conversation in the following situations. Use your own names.

1. You try to call けんじ, but by mistake you call someone else. The person who answers the phone tells you that you have the wrong number. You admit you made a mistake and apologize.

2. You call your friend. Your friend complains and asks why you did not call last night. You explain that you called many times, but he or she didn't answer.

3. Your friend was absent from school today. You call him or her and ask why he or she was absent. Your friend gives you a reason.

C. SPEAK/LISTEN/WRITE Take turns with your partner asking and answering the following questions about technology. Record his/her answers on a separate sheet of paper.

しつもん 質問	こた 答え
1. 先生に メールを 時々 送りますか。	
2. だれから メールを よく もらいますか。	
3. メールに すぐ 答えますか。	
4. どんな アプリを いつも 使いますか。	
5. 動画を 毎日 見ますか。	
6. ブログを して いますか。	
7. たいてい どこで パソコンを 充電しますか。	

WORKBOOK page 59

<ruby>会話<rt>かいわ</rt></ruby> Dialogue

🔊 READ/LISTEN   Why doesn't Ken plan to go to school tomorrow? What will he miss?

<ruby>風邪<rt>かぜ</rt></ruby>で まだ <ruby>熱<rt>ねつ</rt></ruby>が
高いから、
学校へは 行かない
つもりです。

明日 <ruby>試験<rt>しけん</rt></ruby>が
あるはずですね。
学校へ 行きますか。

<ruby>文型<rt>ぶんけい</rt></ruby> Sentence Patterns

READ Find one of these sentence patterns in the dialogue.

1. Verb (Dictionary form) ＋つもりです。   I plan/intend to do ~.
2. Verb (NAI form) ＋つもりです。   I do not plan/intend to ~.
3. Verb (Dictionary form) ＋はずです。   is expected to do ~, I expect ~
4. Verb (NAI form) ＋はずです。   is not expected to do ~, I do not expect ~

<ruby>単語<rt>たんご</rt></ruby> Vocabulary

1. (行く／行かない) つもりです

plan to go, do not plan to go

Not used to ask about the intentions or plans of a person
of higher status.

2. (行く／行かない) はずです

I expect that he/she will/will not go.
He/she is expected to/not to go.

3. (クラスを) <ruby>取<rt>と</rt></ruby>る

[G1 とります]

to take (a class)

4. (<ruby>運転<rt>うんてん</rt></ruby>めんきょを) <ruby>取<rt>と</rt></ruby>る

to get (a driver's license)

5. おぼえる

[G2 おぼえます]

to memorize

おぼえています

remember

6. <ruby>仕方<rt>しかた</rt></ruby>が ないです/ありません。

It cannot be helped.

7. もちろん

of course

<ruby>読<rt>よ</rt></ruby>みましょう Language in Context

🔊 **READ/LISTEN/SPEAK** Read these sentences in Japanese. Tell a classmate what classes you plan to take next school year.

<ruby>漢字<rt></rt></ruby>を <ruby>全部<rt>ぜんぶ</rt></ruby>
おぼえるはずです。

もうすぐ <ruby>運転<rt>うんてん</rt></ruby>めんきょを
<ruby>取<rt>と</rt></ruby>るつもりです。

文法 Grammar

A Intention Extender -つもりです

Verb Dictionary Form +つもりです。   plan to do ~, intend to do ~

Verb NAI Form +つもりです。   do not plan to ~, do not intend to ~

This construction is used to express an intent, or a plan to perform some action in the future. The subject of a つもり sentence is generally first person. The second and the third person are used only in questions. The dictionary form precedes the extender つもりです. Negation occurs before the extender つもり, not after. i. e., 食べないつもりです. The past tense is formed after つもり, i.e., 食べるつもりでした. It is not polite to use 〜つもりですか when asking a superior ask about his/her intentions or plans.

◀)) MODELS

1. 今日　三時ごろ　帰るつもりです。
   Today, I plan to return home at about 3 o'clock.

2. 今晩　十二時まで　寝ないつもりです。
   Tonight, I don't plan to go to bed until 12 o'clock.

3. 昨日　買い物に　行くつもりでしたが、行きませんでした。
   I was planning to go shopping yesterday, but I didn't go.

4. ケーキを　食べないつもりでしたが、昨日 パーティーで　食べました。
   I was not planning to eat cake, but I ate some at the party yesterday.

READ/SPEAK Choose the correct response to match the English sentences.

1. 今年　日本へ　(行く / 行かない) つもり(です / でした)が、
   行くことが　出来ませんでした。

   I planned to go to Japan this year, but I couldn't go.

2. 来年　日本へ　(行く / 行かない) つもり(です / でした)。

   I don't plan to go to Japan next year.

3. 今年　インドへ　(行く / 行かない) つもり(です / でした)が、
   行かなければ　なりませんでした。

   I didn't plan to go to India this year, but I had to go.

4. 来年　イタリアへ　(行く / 行かない) つもり(です / でした)。

   I plan to go to Italy next year.

B Supposition Extender はずです

Verb Dictionary form/NAI form +はずです。　　**to expect, is/is not expected to do**

The supposition pattern is used when the speaker expects that a certain action or event will occur. Negation occurs with the verb (NAI form), not at the end of the extender. The subject of a はず sentence is generally a third person. If the subject is the first person, then the sentence implies that someone else has an expectation that the speaker will do something.

◀)) MODELS ▷

1. 明日　試験が　あるはずです。
   Tomorrow, there is supposed to be an exam.

2. 明日　試験は　ないはずです。
   Tomorrow, there is not supposed to be an exam.

3. 東京には　午後一時ごろに　着くはずでした。
   It was expected to arrive in Tokyo at about 1 p.m.

4. 友子さんは　土曜日の　パーティーには　来ないはずでしたよ。
   Tomoko was not expected to come to Saturday's party.

READ/SPEAK Choose the correct responses from the options in the ( ) based on the English cues.

1. 今朝　薬を　(飲む / 飲まない)はず(です / でした)が、忘れました。
   I was supposed to take (my) medication this morning, but I forgot.

2. 今晩　薬を　(飲む / 飲まない)はず(です / でした)が、飲みます。
   Tonight, I was not supposed to take medicine, but I will take it.

3. 新しい　薬は　(安い / 安くない)はず(です / でした)。
   The new medicine is supposed to be cheap.

文化ノート　Culture Notes

School Absenteeism 登校拒否

Japan's schools deal with a relatively high percentage of school absences. Recent statistical reports show that 2.7% of junior high school students are absent for more than a month at a time. Although reasons for high absenteeism are not clear, some point to the emphasis on academic performance in a highly exam-centered curriculum, which creates anxiety, frustration, and boredom for students. Another reason often cited is bullying.

Be a reporter! Ask a school administrator for the percentage of absenteeism at your school. What do you think is the main cause of absenteeism in your school? Is there a difference from Japan? Why? Write a short news report about absenteeism in your country's high schools.

Language Note

仕方がない
(しかた)

The expression 仕方がない, which literally means "there is nothing that can be
(しかた)
done about it," is a reflection of the Japanese social culture. A less formal version
of this expression is しょうがない. Since the Japanese feel that much of what
they encounter in life is out of their control, they are often recognized as people
who exhibit qualities of exceptional endurance, perseverance, acceptance, and
passiveness. Are there similar expressions in English?

アクティビティー　Communicative Activities

ペアワーク

A. SPEAK/LISTEN Ask your partner if he/she plans to do the following things in the future.

Ex. 来年　日本語を　取りますか。
　　　　　　　　　と
しつもん
質問：来年　日本語を　取るつもりですか。
　　　　　　　　　　と
こた
答え：はい、もちろん　取るつもりです。
　　　　　　　　　と

1. 休みに　日本へ　行きますか。	
2. 休みに　アルバイトを　しますか。	
3. 休みに　日本語を　勉強しますか。 (べんきょう)	
4. 大学へ　行きますか。	

B. SPEAK/LISTEN/WRITE Ask what your partner plans to do at the following times. Your partner
should answer using つもりです. Write his/her answers on a separate sheet of paper

Ex. この　クラスの　後で
しつもん
質問：この　クラスの　後で　何を　するつもりですか。
こた
答え：この　クラスの　後で　お昼ご飯を　食べるつもりです。
　　　　　　　　　　　　　　ひる　はん

質問 (しつもん)	質問 (しつもん)
1. 学校の　後で	3. この　週末 (まつ)
2. 今晩　うちで (ばん)	4. 冬休みに (ふゆ)

C. READ/SPEAK/LISTEN You have a schedule like the one below. Your friend asks you when each event is. You are not quite sure, but you answer based on the information you have.

Ex. math exam

質問：数学の　試験は　いつですか。

答え：明後日　あるはずです。

スケジュール

Baseball game – tomorrow
Math exam – the day after tomorrow
Keiko's birthday party – this weekend
Social studies paper – next week
Concert – 15th of next month

Authentic Reading

D. READ/SPEAK Read the social media post by Ryosuke Sugawara, a Japanese high school student, and answer the following questions.

UNDERSTAND

1. What happened to Ryosuke last night?

2. What kind of symptoms did he have this morning?

3. Who took Ryosuke to the hospital?

4. How many times per day does he have to take medication?

IDENTIFY

5. How many degrees is 39°C in Fahrenheit?

APPLY

6. Do you think it's a good idea for Ryosuke to go back to school tomorrow?

WORKBOOK　page 61

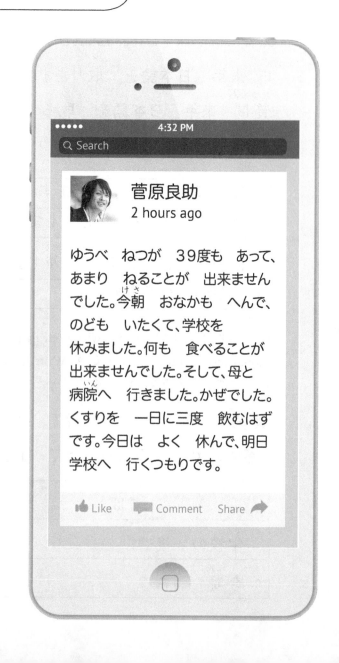

4:32 PM

Search

菅原良助

2 hours ago

ゆうべ　ねつが　３９度も　あって、あまり　ねることが　出来ませんでした。今朝　おなかも　へんで、のども　いたくて、学校を　休みました。何も　食べることが　出来ませんでした。そして、母と　病院へ　行きました。かぜでした。くすりを　一日に三度　飲むはずです。今日は　よく　休んで、明日　学校へ　行くつもりです。

👍 Like　　💬 Comment　　Share ➤

会話 (かいわ) Dialogue

 READ/LISTEN Where did Ken go yesterday? What did he get there?

具合(ぐあい)は　まだ　悪(わる)いんですか。

はい、昨日(きのう)病院(びょういん)へ　行って、薬(くすり)を　もらいましたよ。一日に　三度も　飲まなければ　いけません。

そうですか。お大事に。

文型 (ぶんけい) Sentence Patterns

READ Find one of these sentence patterns in the dialogue.

1. Counter　も   as many/long/high as 〜

2. 一日に　三度/三回   three times per day

♻ **Past tense review:**

い Adjectives あつかったです。   was hot

                 あつくなかったです。or　あつくありませんでした。   was not hot

な Adjectives しずかでした。   was quiet

                 しずかではありませんでした。   was not quiet

1. 一日に 三度/三回	2. counter も	3. 何度も/何回も 〔なんども/ なんかいも〕	4. どのぐらい
three times per day	as many/long as 〜	many times	about how long/ far/often?

度 is more formal and used in writing.

回 is used more for speaking

	5. degree(s), time(s) 〜度〔ど〕	6. time(s) 〜回〔かい〕	7. minute(s) 〜分	8. hour(s) 〜時間
一	いちど	いっかい	いっぷん(かん)	いちじかん
二	にど	にかい	にふん(かん)	にじかん
三	さんど	さんかい	さんぷん(かん)	さんじかん
四	よんど	よんかい	よんぷん(かん)	よじかん
五	ごど	ごかい	ごふん(かん)	ごじかん
六	ろくど	ろっかい	ろっぷん(かん)	ろくじかん
七	ななど	ななかい	ななふん(かん)	ななじかん
八	はちど	はっかい	はっぷん(かん)	はちじかん
九	きゅうど	きゅうかい	きゅうふん(かん)	くじかん
十	じゅうど	じゅっかい	じゅっぷん(かん)	じゅうじかん
？	なんど	なんかい	なんぷん(かん)	なんじかん

	9.	10.	11.	12.
	day(s) 〜日(間)	week(s) 〜週間	month(s) 〜か月	year(s) 〜年(間)
一	いちにち	いっしゅうかん	いっかげつ	いちねん(かん)
二	ふつか(かん)	にしゅうかん	にかげつ	にねん(かん)
三	みっか(かん)	さんしゅうかん	さんかげつ	さんねん(かん)
四	よっか(かん)	よんしゅうかん	よんかげつ	よねん(かん)
五	いつか(かん)	ごしゅうかん	ごかげつ	ごねん(かん)
六	むいか(かん)	ろくしゅうかん	ろっかげつ	ろくねん(かん)
七	なのか(かん)	ななしゅうかん	ななかげつ	ななねん(かん)
八	ようか(かん)	はっしゅうかん	はっかげつ	はちねん(かん)
九	ここのか(かん)	きゅうしゅうかん	きゅうかげつ	きゅうねん(かん)
十	とおか(かん)	じゅっしゅうかん	じゅっかげつ	じゅうねん(かん)
？	なんにち(かん)	なんしゅうかん	なんかげつ	なんねん(かん)

追加単語 Additional Vocabulary
(ついかたんご)

1. 〜びょう　　　　　　　　〜 second(s)

読みましょう　Language in Context
(よ)

🔊 **READ/LISTEN/WRITE** Read these sentences in Japanese. Write a sentence saying how many times you have been sick this year.

一日に　三回　薬を
飲まなければ　なりません。
(くすり)

熱が　三十九度も　あります。
(ねつ)

A　Emphatic Particle も ───────────────

Counter も　　　　　**as many/long/high as ～**

When も follows a number and counter, it places an emphasis on the amount being mentioned. The suggestion is that the amount given is more than expected.

🔊 MODELS

1. 学校を　三日も　休みました。
   I was absent from school for as many as three days.

2. 熱が　三十九度も　ありました。
   ねつ
   I had a fever as high as 39 degrees.

READ/SPEAK Say the words in the (　) in Japanese.

1. (　3 weeks　)も　風邪を　ひいて　いました。 2. (　5 days　)も　病気で
   かぜ
   学校へ　行くことが　出来ませんでした。3. (　14 hours　)も　寝ました。
   ね

B　Open-ended Counter も ───────────────

Question Counter も　　　　　**many ～**

When a question word counter, such as 何度, 何回, 何人, etc. is followed by も, it suggests that there are many of the items being named. The counter must be appropriate for the item.

🔊 MODELS

1. メールを　何回も　見ます。
   I look at the mail many times.

2. 姉は　何か月も　日本を　旅行して　います。
   あね　　　　　　　　　　　りょ
   My older sister has been traveling in Japan for many months.

READ/SPEAK Say the words in the (　) in Japanese.

1. (　many years　)も　日本語を　勉強して　いますが、まだ　下手です。
   べんきょう

2. (　many people　)も　私の　ブログを　見て　います。

3. (　many weeks　)も　病気でした。

C Expressing Duration of Time

Duration of Time に ＋ **Number of Times.**

When expressing that some action is done a certain amount of times within a period of time, this sentence pattern is used. Duration of time words, such as 一年, 三か月, 四時間 are followed by the particle に, then by a number of times or a unit smaller than the original durational word. The counter for number of times is 度〔ど〕 (more formal) or 回〔かい〕. Examples are 二度, 三度, or 一回, 四回.

◄)) MODELS

1. 一日に　四回も　薬<ruby>を<rt>くすり</rt></ruby>　飲まなければ　なりませんでした。

   I had to take medicine as often as four times per day.

2. 日本語の　クラスは　一週間に　何日　ありますか。

   How many days per week do you have your Japanese class?

3. 一日に　どのぐらい　<ruby>勉強<rt>べんきょう</rt></ruby>しますか。

   About how long do you study in a day?

READ/SPEAK Say the words in the ( ) in Japanese.

1. 日本語の　クラスは　(　five days a week　)　あります。

2. 毎日　(　one hour　)　ぐらい　メールを　して　います。

3. (　Once a month　)　ぐらい　おばあさんと　おじいさんに　<ruby>会<rt>あ</rt></ruby>います。

<ruby>文化<rt>ぶんか</rt></ruby>ノート　Culture Notes

Home Cold Remedies in Japan

Each culture has its own folk remedies. There are many folk remedies in Japan passed down from one generation to the next. Among these are specially brewed teas with うめぼし (dried pickled plum), or しょうが (ginger) and seared ねぎ (green onions). The addition of honey to teas is also said to be beneficial. Special soups such as みそしる with だいこん (white Japanese radish) or rice gruel and egg are also commonly served to those who are ill.

 What home remedies have been passed down to you from your family? Give specific ingredients and instructions on how they are prepared and consumed. If you don't have any home remedies in your family, check online or interview a member of your community. Share the home remedy with your classmates.

Language Note

薬 <ruby>くすり</ruby>を飲 <ruby>の</ruby>む。 Taking medication

In Japanese, the expression to "take medication" is くすりをのむ, literally, "to drink" medicine. Why is this? Traditionally, Japanese indeed "drank" their medication, as most medications were herbs taken in liquid or a powdered form which had to be swallowed with liquid. This expression is only used for medication that is taken orally.

アクティビティー Communicative Activities

ペアワーク

A. SPEAK/LISTEN Interview your partner using the following questions.

質問<ruby>しつもん</ruby>： 一日に　どのぐらい　うちで　勉強<ruby>べんきょう</ruby>しますか。

答<ruby>こた</ruby>え： (だいたい)　一日に　二時間ぐらい　うちで　勉強<ruby>べんきょう</ruby>します。

1. 一日に　どのぐらい　テレビを　見ますか。
2. 一日に　どのぐらい　うちで　勉強<ruby>べんきょう</ruby>しますか。
3. 一日に　どのぐらい　メールしますか。
4. 一日に　何時間ぐらい　寝<ruby>ね</ruby>ますか。
5. 一週間に　何回ぐらい　ハンバーガーを　食べますか。
6. 一週間に　何回ぐらい　運動<ruby>うんどう</ruby>(exercise)を　しますか。
7. 一か月に　何回ぐらい　映画<ruby>えいが</ruby>を　見ますか。

B. SPEAK/LISTEN Ask your partner about the Japanese school schedule. Your partner should answer the questions based on the information he/she knows.

質問<ruby>しつもん</ruby>：日本の　学校は　何月に　始<ruby>はじ</ruby>まりますか。

答<ruby>こた</ruby>え：日本の　学校は　一四月に　始<ruby>はじ</ruby>まる はずです。

1. 日本の　学校は　何月に　終<ruby>お</ruby>わりますか。
2. 日本の　学校の　夏休<ruby>なつ</ruby>みは　何か月ぐらいですか。
3. 日本の　学校の　冬休<ruby>ふゆ</ruby>みは　どのぐらいですか。

C. SPEAK/LISTEN Your friend has been absent from school. Call him/her and ask the reason for his/her absence. Your friend should give a reason by conjoining the sentences below.

Ex. 風邪を　ひきました。熱が　高いです。

You: もしもし、(own name) ですが . . .

Friend: ああ、(friend's name) ですか。

You: 二日も　学校を　休んでいますが、どう　しましたか。

Friend: かぜを　ひいて、熱が　高いんです。

You: お大事に。

1. おなかが　痛いんです。食べることが　出来ません。
2. のどが　痛いんです。話すことが　出来ません。
3. 熱が　高いんです。寝ることが　出来ません。

Authentic Reading

D. READ/WRITE Read this prescription envelope and answer the following questions in Japanese on a separate sheet of paper.

UNDERSTAND

1. How many times a day should this person take this medication?

2. How soon after each meal should this medication be taken?

3. Should this person take this medication before sleeping?

IDENTIFY

4. Who is this prescription for?

5. Where did this person receive this prescription?

APPLY

6. What would you do if you were still not well after three days of taking this medication?

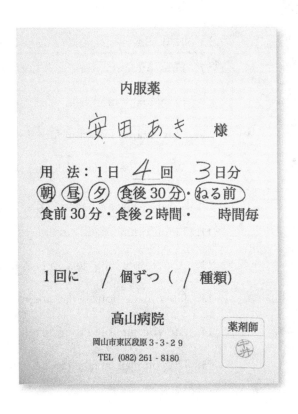

WORKBOOK page 63

Lesson 5
Review

Review Questions

🔊 Ask your partner these questions or say these statements in Japanese. Your partner should answer in Japanese. Check your answers using the audio.

Illnesses   Review pages 164, 171, 178, 184–185

1. Did you catch a cold?

2. I don't feel well now because of a fever.

3. Are you supposed to take medication every day?

Ability   Review page 166

4. Can you play the piano?

5. What kind of sports can you play?

6. Can your mother/father understand Japanese?

Leisure   Review pages 177, 184–185

7. How often do you check (look at) your e-mail in a day?

8. How many months is your summer vacation?

9. How many times a month do you go to watch a movie?

10. What do you plan to do this weekend?

Daily Life   Review pages 171, 177-178, 184–185

11. I didn't understand yesterday's Japanese homework. (Can you help me?)

12. About how long do you plan to study tonight?

13. How many hours a day are you supposed to charge your cell phone/smartphone?

14. Are you supposed to have a Japanese exam tomorrow?

15. Do you plan to take Japanese next year?

Text Chat

You will participate in a simulated exchange of text-chat messages. You should respond as fully and as appropriately as possible. You will have a conversation with Asuka Ueda, a Japanese high school student, about illness.

11月 28日　08:16 AM

お元気ですか。私は　今週
三日も　学校を　休みました。

Ask the reason and ask how she is.

11月 28日　08:28 AM

薬を　一日に　四回も　飲まなければ
なりませんでした。

Show your sympathy and ask what kind of symptoms she had.

11月 28日　08:33 AM

この　週末 忙しいですか。

Tell what exam you are supposed to have next week and tell what you plan to to do this weekend.

Can Do!
Now I can ...

☐ talk about illnesses I may have experienced

☐ discuss what I am or am not able to do

☐ communicate my intentions and plans

☐ talk about what I am and others are expected to do

Health Care in Japan

RESEARCH Use books, the Internet, or interview a Japanese member of your community to answer the following.

Determine

1. Japan has the longest life expectancy in the world. What is the average life expectancy? Is it different for men and women?

2. What percentage of the population in Japan is more than 65 years old?

3. What is the average fertility rate in Japan?

4. Among the countries of the world, how does Japan's health rank? Near the top, or near the bottom?

5. Alternative medicine is common in Japan. Name at least two kinds of alternative medicine practiced in Japan.

6. What country can most of Japan's alternative medical practices and medicines be traced to?

Compare

7. When you are sick, do you go to the doctor for medicine or the local pharmacy? Are there any over-the-counter medications available in your country that cannot be purchased or brought to Japan?

8. How often do you visit your doctor? Do Japanese people visit doctors, clinics, and hospitals more than people in your country?

Apply

9. If you were to live in Japan as an exchange student for a year, would you need medical coverage? How do you think seeing a doctor in Japan would be different than at home? Would you prefer to see a doctor in your own home country or in Japan? Why?

Extend Your Learning
COLLABORATION AND PROBLEM SOLVING
In a small group, research issues that increase the cost of health care in your country, and solutions for these issues adopted in Japan and other countries. Choose at least 3 issues and propose solutions for them. Create a presentation explaining the problems and arguing for your solutions. Begin and end your presentation in Japanese.

お正月
New Year's

✔ Can Do!

In this lesson you will learn to:

- discuss year-end festivities
- share experiences that you or others have had in the past
- communicate taking and bringing things or people to certain destinations
- talk about the giving and receiving of gifts

Online Resources

cheng-tsui.com/
adventuresinjapanese

- Audio
- Vocabulary Lists
- Vocabulary and *Kanji* Flashcards
- Study Guides
- Activity Worksheets

In this lesson you will learn how to talk about holiday celebrations. Review these words, phrases, and grammatical structures you already learned to help you.

めいし Nouns			
1. 外	outside	4. 今年 ^{ことし}	this year
2. 本当の ^{とう}	the real one	5. 歌 ^{うた}	song
3. 買い物 ^{もの}	shopping	6. ギター	guitar

どうし Verbs	
7. 見た [G2 見る／見ます／見ない]	saw
8. ありません [G1 ある／あって／ない]	there is not
9. して　います [IR する／します／して／しない]	is doing
10. 出来ません [G2 出来る／出来て／出来ない]	cannot do
11. 行った [G1 行く／行きます／行って／行かない]	went
12. 行って　みたい [G1 行く／行きます／行かない]	want to try to go
13. 歌った [G1 うたう／うたいます／うたって／うたわない] ^{うた}	sang
14. ない [G1 ある／あります／あって]	there is not
15. 教えて　下さい [G2 おしえる／おしえます／おしえない] ^{おし}	Please teach.
16. ひきます [G1 ひく／ひいて／ひかない]	I will play [musical instrument].

-い けいようし I Adjectives			
17. さむそう[さむい]	looks cold	18. いそがしい	busy

-な けいようし NA Adjectives			
19. きれい	pretty	20. 大好き	like very much

ふくし Adverbs			
21. 本当に (とう)	really, truly	22. いつも	always

Others			
23. でも、	However,	24. ～だけ	only

ぶんぽう Grammar	
25. ～の　前に	before ～
26. どんな　事	what kind of things?
27. Dictionary form ＋ことが　出来ません。	cannot do ～

A. WRITE Write out what Ken and Mari are saying in each scene using the words, phrases, and grammatical structures you reviewed above.

B. WRITE/SPEAK Write a text conversation you may have with a real or imaginary friend who lives in a place where winter weather conditions are different from where you live. For example, if you live in Wisconsin, text a friend in Hawaii. Ask what he/she can and cannot do where he/she lives during the winter.

In this lesson, you will learn the *kanji* related to holiday celebrations.

	Kanji	Meaning	Readings	Examples		
93.	正	correct	ただ（しい） ショウ	ただ 正しい しょうがつ お正月	is correct the New Year	一 → 丁 → 下 → 正 → 正
94.	寺	temple	てら でら ジ	てら お寺 やまでら 山寺 ほんがんじ 本願寺	temple mountain temple *Honganji* Temple	→ 土 + → 寸 = 寺
95.	時	time ~ o'clock	とき ジ	ときどき 時々 よじ 四時	sometimes four o'clock	→ 日 十 寺 = 時
96.	待	to wait	ま（つ）	ま 待って くだ 下さい。	Please wait.	→ 十 寺 = 待
97.	持	to hold	も（つ）	も 持って い 行く	take something	→ 十 寺 = 持
98.	教	to teach	おし（える） キョウ	おし 教えて くだ 下さい。 きょうしつ 教室 きょうかしょ 教科書	Please teach (me). classroom textbook	+ → = 教

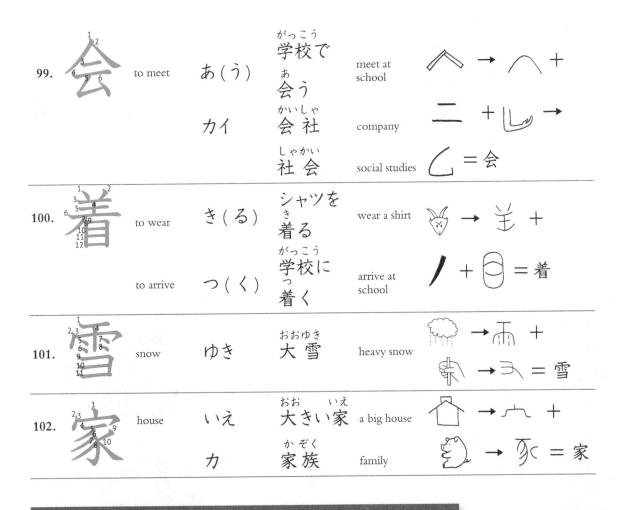

99. 会	to meet	あ(う)	がっこうで 学校で ぁ 会う	meet at school	
		カイ	かいしゃ 会社	company	
			しゃかい 社会	social studies	
100. 着	to wear	き(る)	シャツを き 着る	wear a shirt	
	to arrive	つ(く)	がっこうに 学校に っ 着く	arrive at school	
101. 雪	snow	ゆき	おおゆき 大雪	heavy snow	
102. 家	house	いえ	おお いえ 大きい家	a big house	
		カ	かぞく 家族	family	

New Reading

13. 火 fire び はなび
花火 firework

Recognition Kanji

あ
明けましておめでとうございます。　Happy New Year!

たまだ
玉田さん　Mr./Mrs. Tamada

としだま
お年玉　New Year's monetary gift

ときどき
時々　sometimes

メリークリスマス。
明けましておめでとうございます。

Merry Christmas! Happy New Year!

外は
寒（さむ）そうですねえ。

明日は　たぶん
雪が　ふるでしょう。

まりさんは
雪を　見たことが
ありますか。

はい、ありますよ。
東京（とうきょう）では
よく　降（ふ）りますよ。

そうですか。
もうすぐ
クリスマスですねえ。

日本人は
クリスマスに　プレゼントを
あげますか。

はい、あげます。
そして、お正月に
子どもに　お年玉を
あげますよ。

いいですねえ。
お正月の　前に　日本人は
いつも　どんな　事を
して　いますか。

To read an informal version of the conversation,
go to cheng-tsui.com/adventuresinjapanese

196

そうじや 買い物や
料理を しますから、本当に
忙しいんです。私は いつも
母を 手伝いますが、
今年は 出来ません。

クリスマスの 前に
アメリカ人は いつも
どんな 事を
して いますか。

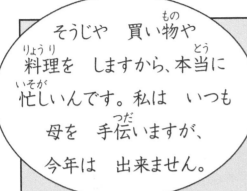

私の 家族は クッキーを
作って、クリスマスツリーを
買って、おばあさんの 家に
プレゼントを 持って
行きます。

クリスマスツリーは
きれいですねえ!
ケンさんは
クリスマスの 歌を
日本語で 歌った こと
が ありますか。

いいえ、ありません。
教えて 下さいよ。ぼくが
ギターを 弾きますから。
ギターを 持って
来ますね。

♪♪♪ ジングルベル ジングルベル 鈴が なる、
そりは すすむよ、はやての ように、
ジングルベル ジングルベル そりは ゆく、
雪けり すすむ その 楽しさよ ♪♪♪

会話 (かいわ) Dialogue

🔊 **READ/LISTEN** What is Mari asking Ken about? What do you think he will do next?

> ケンさんは
> クリスマスの 歌(うた)を
> 日本語で 歌(うた)った
> ことが ありますか。

> いいえ、まだ
> ないんです。

文型 (ぶんけい) Sentence Patterns

READ Find one of these sentence patterns in the dialogue.

1. Verb (TA Form) ＋ことが あります　　have done ～ [Experience]
2. Verb (TA Form) ＋ことが ありません　　have never done ～ [Experience]
   or ことが ない〈ん〉です

単語 Vocabulary

1. (お)正月(しょうがつ)

New Year

Lit., the proper month.

2. (お)餅(もち)

pounded rice cakes

3. 神社(じんじゃ)

shrine (Shinto)

4. (お)寺(てら)

temple (Buddhist)

5. 教会
<ruby>教会<rt>きょうかい</rt></ruby>

church (Christian)

6. クリスマスツリー

Christmas tree

7. <ruby>写真<rt>しゃしん</rt></ruby>を　とります
[G1 とる/とって]

to take a photo

8. <ruby>作<rt>つく</rt></ruby>ります
[G1 つくる／つくって]

to make

9. もうすぐ

very soon

10. <ruby>初<rt>はじ</rt></ruby>めて
〔はじめて〕

(for the) first time

<ruby>追加単語<rt>ついかたんご</rt></ruby>　Additional Vocabulary

1. モスク
mosque

2. シナゴーグ
synagogue

3. <ruby>大晦日<rt>おおみそか</rt></ruby>
New Year's Eve (December 31st)

4. クリスマスイブ
Christmas Eve

5. <ruby>年賀状<rt>がじょう</rt></ruby>〔ねんがじょう〕
New Year's card

6. <ruby>着物<rt>もの</rt></ruby>〔きもの〕
kimono [Japanese traditional wear]

7. かざります[G1 かざる]
to decorate

8. つつみます [G1 つつむ]
to wrap

9. クリスマスプレゼント
Christmas present

10. サンタクロース
Santa Claus

🔊 **READ/LISTEN/SPEAK** Read these sentences in Japanese. Then tell your partner one place you have been and one place you have never been to before.

着物を　着たことが
あります。

日本に　行ったことが
ないんです。

文法 Grammar

Ⓐ Verb TA Form

The verb TA form has two main functions. It may be used to express a plain perfect verb form (past tense, plain equivalent of –ました), or it may be used preceding an extender as a past form.

1. Group 1 verbs

To obtain the TA form, change the TE or DE sound of the verb TE form to TA or DA.

 MODELS

[-i ます]

	MASU form -i	Meaning	TE form	TA form
[み]	のみます	to drink	のんで	のんだ
[に]	しにます	to die	しんで	しんだ
[び]	あそびます	to play	あそんで	あそんだ
[い]	あいます	to meet	あって	あった
[ち]	かちます	to win	かって	かった

[り]	はしります	to run	はしって	はしった
[き]	かきます	to write	かいて	かいた
	いきます	to go	いって *	いった *
[ぎ]	およぎます	to swim	およいで	およいだ
[し]	はなします	to talk	はなして	はなした

* Irregular TE and TA forms

Do you remember the TE form song? Find it on **cheng-tsui.com/adventuresinjapanese**.

2. Group 2 verbs

Group 2 verb's TA forms are created simply by adding た after removing the –ます.

	MASU form	**Meaning**	**TE form**	**TA form**
[-e ます]	たべます	to eat	たべて	たべた
[One *hiragana*]	みます	to see, watch	みて	みた
[Special verbs]	おきます	to get up	おきて	おきた
	かります	to borrow	かりて	かりた

3. Group 3 Irregular verbs

Only 来ます, します and noun +します verbs belong to this group. To obtain the TA form, change the TE sound of the verb TE form to the TA sound.

MASU form	**Meaning**	**TE form**	**TA form**
きます	to come	きて	きた
します	to do	して	した
りょこう(を)します	to travel	りょこう(を)して	りょこう(を)した

READ/WRITE Change the verbs to their correct TA forms using *hiragana* on a separate sheet of paper.

1. 話します   3. 行きます   5. 買います   7. 旅行^{りょ}します
2. 読^よみます   4. 着ます   6. 来ます   8. 泳^{およ}ぎます

B Experiential ことが あります

Verb TA Form ＋　ことが　あります。　　　　　have done ～ [Experience]

あります／ない(ん)です。　have never done ～

The verb TA ことが あります pattern is often called the "experiential pattern." Literally, it means "to have done the act of . . ." It is usually expressed in English as "ever done (something)" or "never done (something)." Negation occurs at the end of the extender. The extender never appears in the perfect (past) form, since it is already preceded by the past verb form of TA. In this usage, the time expressed cannot be too close to the present. Example: 「きのう　おすしを　食べたことが　あります。」 "I have eaten sushi yesterday." is unacceptable, as in English.

◀))) MODELS

1. 私は　まだ　日本へ　行ったことが　ありません。
   I have not gone to Japan yet.

2. 「にぎりずしを　食べたことが　ありますか。」
   "Have you ever eaten *nigirizushi*?"

   「いいえ、　まだ　ないんです。」
   "No, not yet."

READ/SPEAK/WRITE Change the verb in the (　) to its correct TA form and choose the correct sentence ending in the [ ] based on fact. Rewrite the sentences on a separate sheet of paper.

1. おもちを　(食べます)ことが　[あります／ないんです]。

2. クリスマスカードを　(送おります)ことが　[あります／ありません]。

3. 日本から　年賀状がじょうを　(もらいます)ことが　[あります／ないです]。

文化ぶんかノート　Culture Notes

A. Nengajoo 年賀状がじょう

Traditional New Year cards are greetings sent on postcards called ねんがじょう. Although New Year's greetings may now be sent electronically, many Japanese people still prefer to exchange commercially printed or handmade cards, which can be purchased at stationery stores or post offices. Many ねんがじょう feature the New Year's zodiac animal or other auspicious symbols, such as pine trees or bamboo. ねんがじょう are exchanged not only between family, friends, and colleagues, but also companies and business associates.

おせちりょうり

B. New Year's in Japan (お正月)

New Year's (お正月) is the most celebrated holiday in Japan. Many businesses close for several days while families and friends gather to celebrate the arrival of the New Year.

Preparation for New Year's however, begins weeks before. End-of-year parties, housecleaning, writing New Year's cards, preparing special foods (おせちりょうり), decorating business entryways with かどまつ (a pine and bamboo standing decoration) and homes with しめかざり (rice straw rope with white strips of sacred paper) and かがみもち (two-layered decorated もち) all add to the festive spirit of the season.

On New Year's Eve, it is customary to listen to the bells (じょやのかね) rung at midnight at Buddhist temples. According to Buddhist belief, the bells are rung 108 times to purify the 108 sins of man. At home, many people eat としこしそば to celebrate crossing over to the next year with long life. Families also enjoy watching the こうはくうたがっせん (Red and White Song Contest) on television.

On New Year's morning and on following days, many people go to nearby shrines and temples to pray for a good year. Some dress in beautiful kimono for this occasion.

かどまつ

Research more details about お正月. Choose one aspect of Japanese New Year's that is of interest to you, such as one of the foods, activities, or decorations. Create a short slide show and share it with your class.

アクティビティー Communicative Activities

クラスワーク

A. READ/WRITE On a separate sheet of paper, number 1–30. Use *hiragana* to write the correct TA forms of the following verbs as quickly as you can in 2 minutes.

1. 飲みます	11. つとめます	21. おぼえます
2. 聞きます	12. 出かけます	22. はきます
3. 話します	13. 書きます	23. まがります
4. 運転します (うんてん)	14. 読みます	24. よやくします
5. 帰ります	15. 言います	25. 会います
6. 見ます	16. たちます	26. あります
7. 買います	17. すわります	27. かちます
8. かります	18. おきます (get up)	28. まけます
9. 来ます	19. おきます (put)	29. はたらきます
10. 休みます	20. 出します	30. およぎます

ペアワーク

B. SPEAK/LISTEN Ask a partner if he/she has ever done the following using ～たことが あります.

Ex. 日本へ　行きましたか。

しつもん
質問：日本へ　行ったことが　ありますか。

こた
答え：はい、あります。 or いいえ、ありません／ないです。

き　　　き 1. 着物を　着ましたか。	なら 5. ピアノを　習いましたか。
あそ 2. 日本の　ゲームを　遊びましたか。	じんじゃ 6. 神社へ　行きましたか。
うんてん 3. 車を　運転しましたか。	7. おもちを　食べましたか。
うた 4. カラオケを　歌いましたか。	がじょう 8. 年賀状を　もらいましたか。

Authentic Reading

がじょう
C. READ/SPEAK Read the 年賀状 (New Year's card) and answer the questions below.

UNDERSTAND

1. What is the meaning of the message written on the front of the card?

IDENTIFY

2. Who is the sender?

3. Who is the recipient?

4. How much did the postage cost?

APPLY

5. If you were to send a New Year's card to a Japanese person next year, what animal design would you use in your drawing?

WORKBOOK　page 71

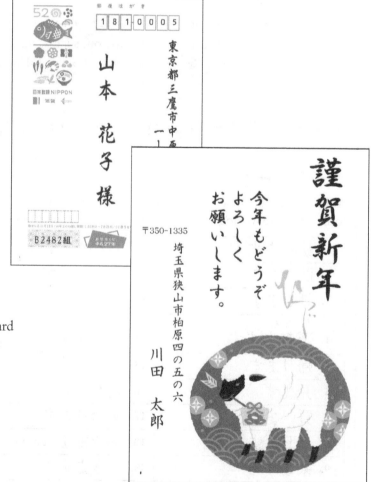

会話　Dialogue
_{かいわ}

🔊 **READ/LISTEN** In the dialogue, what is the weather like today? What will it be like tomorrow?

明日の　天気は
どうでしょうか。

寒いでしょうね。
_{さむ}

たぶん　雪でしょう。

文型　Sentence Patterns
_{ぶんけい}

READ Find at least one of these sentence patterns in the dialogue.

明日	＋でしょう。↘ It is probably tomorrow.	＋でしょう。↗ It is tomorrow, isn't it?
明日じゃない or 明日ではない	＋でしょう。↘ It is probably not tomorrow.	＋でしょう。↗ It is not tomorrow, is it?
さむい	＋でしょう。↘ It is/will probably be cold.	＋でしょう。↗ It is cold, isn't it?
さむくなかった	＋でしょう。↘ It was probably not cold.	＋でしょう。↗ It was not cold, was it?
雨が　降る _ふ	＋でしょう。↘ It will probably rain.	＋でしょう。↗ It will rain, won't it?
雨が　降らなかった _ふ	＋でしょう。↘ It probably did not rain.	＋でしょう。↗ It did not rain, did it?

Pay close attention to the directional arrows indicating intonation. The intonation of a sentence can change the meaning: ↘ dropping intonation　↗ rising intonation.

1. (お)天気

weather

2. あめ
雨

rain

3. ゆき
雪

snow

4. ふ
降る

[G2 ふります/ふって]

(rain, snow) to fall

5. くも
曇り

[noun]

cloudy (weather)

くも
曇る [G1 くもります]

to become cloudy

6. は
晴れ

[noun]

clear (weather)

は
晴れる

[G2 はれます]

to clear up

7. かぜ
風

[noun]

wind

8. おんど
温度

temperature (general)

〜ど counter for degree(s)

9. 〜でしょう ↘

probably 〜

10. 〜でしょう ↗

Isn't it 〜?

An invitation for the listener to
agree with the speaker.

11. たぶん [adverb]

probably

ついか たんご
追加単語　Additional Vocabulary

1. くも
雲

cloud [noun]

2. 台風 [たいふう]

typhoon

3. つなみ
津波

tsunami

4. ハリケーン

hurricane

5. よほう
天気予報

weather forecast

6. 地震 [じしん]

earthquake

READ/LISTEN/SPEAK Read these sentences in Japanese. Say what the weather will probably be like tomorrow.

 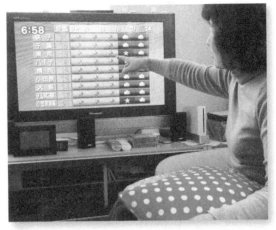

今日　雨が　降^ふるでしょう。↗　　明日　東京^{とうきょう}は^は　晴れでしょう。↘

文法^{ぶんぽう} Grammar

A Verb NAKATTA Form

The verb *nakatta* form is the plain negative past form equivalent of the polite ませんでした form. It may be used at the end of informal sentences or precede extenders. For all verbs, drop the final ない of the −ない form, then replace with −なかった.

 MODELS

Group 1 verbs

[−i ます]

	MASU form	Meaning	DIC. form nonpast	NAI form neg. nonpast	TA form past	NAKATTA form neg. past
	-i		-u	-a	(TE form)	-a
[み]	のみます	to drink	のむ	のまない	のんだ	のまなかった
[に]	しにます	to die	しぬ	しなない	しんだ	しななかった
[び]	あそびます	to play	あそぶ	あそばない	あそんだ	あそばなかった
[い]	あいます	to meet	あう	あわない	あった	あわなかった
[ち]	かちます	to win	かつ	かたない	かった	かたなかった

			DIC.	NAI	TA	NAKATTA
[り]	かえります	to return (place)	かえる	かえらない	かえった	かえらなかった
	あります	to exist (inanimate)	ある	*ない	あった	*なかった
[き]	かきます	to write	かく	かかない	かいた	かかなかった
	いきます	to go	いく	いかない	*いった	いかなかった
[ぎ]	およぎます	to swim	およぐ	およがない	およいだ	およがなかった
[し]	はなします	to talk	はなす	はなさない	はなした	はなさなかった

* Special forms

Group 2 verbs

	MASU form	Meaning	DIC. form nonpast	NAI form neg. nonpast	TA form past	NAKATTA form neg. past
[-e ます]	たべます	to eat	たべる	たべない	たべた	たべなかった
[One *hiragana*]	みます	to see, watch	みる	みない	みた	みなかった
[Special verbs]	おきます	to get up	おきる	おきない	おきた	おきなかった
	かります	to borrow	かりる	かりない	かりた	かりなかった
	おります	to get off	おりる	おりない	おりた	おりなかった
	できます	to be able to	できる	できない	できた	できなかった

Group 3 Irregular verbs

MASU form	Meaning	DIC. form nonpast	NAI form neg. nonpast	TA form past	NAKATTA form neg. past
きます	to come	くる	こない	きた	こなかった
します	to do	する	しない	した	しなかった

READ/WRITE Change the verbs to their correct NAKATTA forms on a separate sheet of paper.

1. 降ります

2. 飲みます

3. 会います

4. 来ます

5. 歩きます

6. 見ます

7. 勉強を します

8. 話します

Verb Dict. form /NAI form /TA form /NAKATTA form

I Adjective (-い) / (-くない) / (-かった) / (-くなかった)　　+でしょう。↘　**probably~**

NA Adjective / Noun じゃない **or** ではない　　　　　　　でしょう?↗　**Isn't it~ ?**

When でしょう appears at the end of a sentence with a falling intonation, the sentence takes on the meaning of "probably." If でしょう is said with a rising intonation, however, it is an invitation for the listener to agree with the speaker, much like ね at the end of a sentence.

◁)) MODELS

1. 明日は　たぶん　くもりでしょう。↘　　　It will probably be cloudy tomorrow.

2. 明日は　雨が　降らないでしょう。↘　　　It will probably not rain tomorrow.

3. 風は　強くなかったでしょう。↘　　　The wind was probably not strong.

4. 雪の　京都は　きれいでしょう。↗　Snow-covered Kyoto is pretty, isn't it?

5. おさしみは　食べないでしょう?↗　　You don't eat raw fish, do you?

6. もう　この　本は　読んだでしょう?↗You've already read this book, haven't you?

READ/SPEAK Change the words in the ( ) to their correct plain forms. Then choose the correct sentence-ending intonation from the choices in the [ ] based on the English cues in < >.

1. さっぽろは　明日　雪が　(降ります)でしょう [↗　↘]。<probably>

2. 名古屋は　昨日　雨が(降りませんでした)でしょう [↗　↘]。<probably>

3. おきなわは　昨日　雨が　(降りました)でしょう [↗　↘]。<Didn't it ~ ?>

4. 東京は　今　(寒くありません)でしょう [↗　↘]。<Didn't it ~ ?>

文化ノート　Culture Notes

A. (O)mochi　(お)もち

On New Year's morning, many families enjoy bowls of steaming おぞうに for breakfast. The featured ingredient of おぞうに is もち, a type of glutinous rice cake. The word もち is part of the verb もちます, meaning "to have" or "possess." Combined with its sticky consistency, which symbolizes family unity, and its round shape, suggesting fulfillment and continuity, もち is considered good luck to have at the New Year.

A bowl of おぞうに made with もち

Traditionally, families gathered to watch もちつき (もち pounding). At this event, special glutinous rice (もちごめ) is steamed and emptied into mortars (うす) and huge wooden mallets (きね) are used to soften and pound the rice, which is then shaped into little balls or cut into small pieces. Some families now make もち with a *mochi*-making machine, or purchase it from confectionaries or other stores.

B. Otoshidama　お年玉

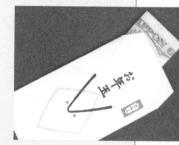

Otoshidama (お年玉) is a monetary gift that adults often give to children at the New Year. Just as Western children look forward to receiving Christmas gifts, Japanese children enjoy receiving their little packets of money on New Year's. As children get older, the amount of money they receive increases. Little children may receive the equivalent of a few dollars in each packet, while teens may receive much more, depending on the generosity of the givers. Some working adults may even give お年玉 to elderly relatives who no longer have incomes. All お年玉 are presented in attractive little envelopes.

Envelope containing お年玉

What kinds of gifts do you like to receive on special holidays? What kinds of gifts do you like to give? Do you like the Japanese practice of お年玉? Write a short persuasive paragraph explaining which custom you prefer and why.

アクティビティー　Communicative Activities

ペアワーク

A. READ/SPEAK/LISTEN/WRITE Ask your partner if his/her family plans to do the following things for the holidays. Record his/her answers on a separate sheet of paper in a chart like the one below.

質問：(family member) は　パーティーに　行くつもりですか。

答え：ええ、たぶん　行くでしょう。↘

　　or　いいえ、たぶん　行かないでしょう。↘

質問	はい	いいえ
1. お正月に　神社に　行くつもりですか。		
2. 年賀状を　日本の　ともだちに　送るつもりですか。		
3. クリスマスに　クッキーを　作るつもりですか。		
4. 大みそか (New Year's Eve) に　花火を　見るつもり ですか。		
5. お正月に　おもちを　食べるつもりですか。		

B. READ/SPEAK/LISTEN/WRITE Your partner has the following map with weather information on it. Ask him/her for the information and record it in a chart like the one below.

Ex. Tokyo

しつもん
質問1:「明日の　東京の
　　　　　お天気は　どうですか。」

こた
答え1:「東京は　雨でしょう。↘」

しつもん
質問2:「明日の　東京の　温度は
　　　　　どのぐらいですか。」

こた
答え2:「五度ぐらいでしょう。↘」

しつもん
質問3:「明日　東京は　寒いでしょうか。」

こた
答え3:「ええ、寒いでしょう。↘」

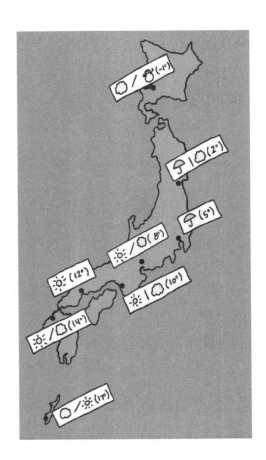

Place	Weather	Temperature	Cold or not
Ex. 東京	雨	5℃	さむい
1. 沖縄			
2. 北海道			
3. 広島			
4. 福岡			
5. 大阪			
6. 名古屋			
7. 仙台			

WORKBOOK　page 73

<ruby>会話<rt>かいわ</rt></ruby> Dialogue

🔊 **READ/LISTEN** What does Ken plan to do today?

今日　何を　しますか。

おばあさんに　プレゼントを
持って行く　つもりです。

<ruby>文型<rt>ぶんけい</rt></ruby> Sentence Patterns

READ Find one of these sentence patterns in the dialogue.

	to take	to bring	to take/bring home
1. Thing を	持って 行きます	持って 来ます	持って 帰ります
2. Person/Animal を	連れて 行きます	連れて 来ます	連れて 帰ります

<ruby>単語<rt>たんご</rt></ruby> Vocabulary

1. そうじ(を)　する

[IR] to clean up

2. <ruby>洗濯<rt>せんたく</rt></ruby>(を)　する

[IR] to do laundry

3. <ruby>料理<rt>りょうり</rt></ruby>(を)　する

[IR] to cook

4. (さらを) 洗う
[G1 あらいます]
to wash (dishes)

5. 手伝う
[G1 てつだいます]
to help

6. 持って 行きます
[G1 もって 行く]
to take (things)

7. 持って 来ます
[IR もって 来る]
to bring (things)

8. 持って 帰ります
[G1 もって 帰る]
to take/bring (things) back home

9. 連れて 行きます
[G1 つれて 行く]
to take (animate)

10. 連れて 来ます
[IR つれて 来る]
to bring (animate)

11. 連れて 帰ります
[G1 つれて 帰る]
to take/bring (animate) back home

追加単語 Additional Vocabulary

1. ごみを 出す [G1 だします]
to take out the garbage

2. 家事
housework, chores

3. 庭仕事
yard work

4. ごちそう
a big meal, feast

READ/LISTEN/SPEAK Read these sentences in Japanese. Say what you do to help out at home.

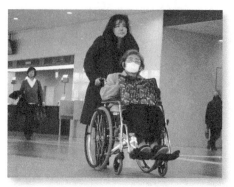

もうすぐ　部屋を
そうじする　つもりです。

お母さんは　おばあさんを
病 院に 連れて 行きました。

文法　Grammar

A Expressing Taking / Bringing / Returning Something

Inanimate object を	持って	行きます。	to take something (elsewhere)
Inanimate object を	持って	来ます。	to bring something (toward the speaker)
Inanimate object を	持って	帰ります。	to return (home) with something
Animate object を	つれて	行きます。	to take someone* (somewhere)
Animate object を	つれて	来ます。	to bring someone* (toward the speaker)
Animate object を	つれて	帰ります。	to return (home) with someone*

*Or something animate (animals, etc.)

To express that someone (subject) will bring, take, or return somewhere with an inanimate or animate object, use the structure above. If the place is included, it is followed by に or へ. Use 行きます, 来ます, or 帰ります based on the relative location of the speaker at the time.

🔊 MODELS

1. パーティーに　おすしを　持って行きました。

I took sushi to the party.

2. パーティーに　友達を　連れて来ても　いいですか。

May I bring my friend to the party?

READ/SPEAK You are talking about yesterday's party with your friend in class. Complete the following sentences by choosing the correct responses.

1. 昨日<ruby>の</ruby>　パーティーに　おすしを　(持って / つれて)(行きました /
来ました / 帰りました)。
<small>きのう</small>

2. 昨日<ruby>の</ruby>　パーティーに　友達<small>ともだち</small>を　(持って / つれて)(行って / 来て /
帰って)も　よかったです。
<small>きのう</small>

3. パーティーの　食べ物<small>もの</small>が　たくさん　ありましたから、次<small>つぎ</small>の　クラスに
(持って / つれて)(行きました / 来ました / 帰りました)。

4. パーティーの　食べ物<small>もの</small>が　たくさん　ありましたから、うちにも
(持って / つれて)(行きました / 来ました / 帰りました)。

Torii gates at Fushimi Inari Shrine in Kyoto

文化ノート　Culture Notes
<small>ぶんか</small>

Religions in Japan

Japan's two major religions are Shinto and Buddhism. Both religions co-exist and many Japanese people engage in the rituals and follow the teachings of both religions. For example, a businessman may have a Buddhist altar at his home at which he, his mother, or wife pray daily and offer incense and food to their ancestors. At his company office, a small Shinto shrine that enshrines a deity to protect the company's business may be displayed.

Shinto is the native Japanese religion. Those who practice Shinto worship many gods, many of whom represent facets or objects of nature. Shinto shrines range from large and elaborate to small and simple, and can be found readily throughout Japan. Events relating to milestones in life, such as the birth of children, weddings, and special birthdays, are usually celebrated at Shinto shrines.

Buddhism, which has its roots in India, arrived in Japan during the sixth century via China and Korea. Buddhism focuses on the influence of a person's current life on life after death. Thus, funerals and services marking funeral anniversaries are held at temples (お寺). Many sects of Buddhism exist in Japan.

Many other newer religions based on Buddhism, Shintoism, Western religions, and folk superstition, or combinations of them, have also sprung up in recent years. Very small groups of followers of Christianity, Islam, Hinduism, and Judaism also exist in Japan.

 Be a sociologist! Research the percentages of followers of the various religions of Japan. Then research the percentages of followers of various religions in your country. Make observations based on your data and write a brief report.

アクティビティー　Communicative Activities

ペアワーク

A. SPEAK/LISTEN/WRITE Ask your partner who does the following things at his/her home and how many times a week. Write his/her answers in a chart like the one below on a separate sheet of paper.

Ex. 家を　そうじします。

質問1:だれが　家を　そうじしますか。

答え1:(たいてい)　母が　します。

質問2:一週間に　何回ぐらい　家を　そうじするんですか。

答え2:一週間に　一回ぐらい　家を　そうじします。

うちの　仕事	だれ?	一週間に　何回?
1. 家を　そうじします。		
2. あなたの　部屋を　そうじします。		
3. スーパーで　買い物を　します。		
4. 洗濯を　します。		
5. おさらを　洗います。		

B. SPEAK/LISTEN You partner is planning a class party. Ask if you can bring the following things. Your partner should answer and give a reason.

「〜を　持って／連れて　来ても　いいですか。」

Yes Answer:「はい、(ぜひ)　持って／連れて　来て　下さい。」

No Answer:「いいえ、(ぜったい)　持って／連れて　来ないで　下さい。」

1. おすし	5. 飲み物
2. 紙の　おさら, コップ, おはし, ナプキン	6. 兄弟
3. 友達	7. デザート
4. ピザ	8. (映画の　名前)

Authentic Reading

C. READ/WRITE Read the wish tablet (絵馬) and answer the following questions in Japanese.

UNDERSTAND

1. What does the writer wish for?

2. When does the writer want this wish to come true?

IDENTIFY

3. When was the wish written?

4. Do you think the writer of this wish tablet is male or female?

APPLY

5. If you were to write a wish tablet, what would you wish for?

WORKBOOK page 75

6課4
What kind of presents do you give your friends?

会話 Dialogue
かいわ

🔊 **READ/LISTEN** What holiday is Mari asking about? What will Ken give to his friends?

> クリスマスに　友達に
> ともだち
> どんな　プレゼントを
> あげますか。

> そうですねえ。
> ぼうしや　ギフトカードなど
> あげます。

文型 Sentence Patterns
ぶんけい

READ Find one of these sentence patterns in the dialogue.

1. Giver は Receiver (equal) に Something を あげます。 give (equal)
2. Giver は Receiver (lower status) に Something を やります。 give (lower status)
3. Giver は Receiver (me) に Something を くれます。 give (me)

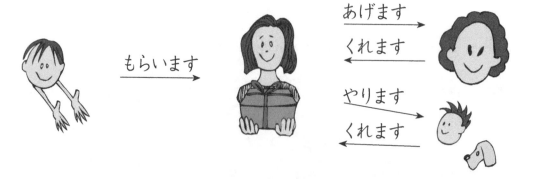

もらいます　　あげます　　くれます　　やります　　くれます

1. おじさん

uncle,
middle-aged man

2. おばさん

aunt,
middle-aged woman

3. いとこ

cousin

4. しんせき

relatives

5.

Bound Objects

1	いっさつ
2	にさつ
3	さんさつ
4	よんさつ
5	ごさつ
6	ろくさつ
7	ななさつ
8	はっさつ
9	きゅうさつ
10	じゅっさつ
?	なんさつ

6. あげます

[G2 あげる/あげて]

to give (to an equal)

7. やります

[G1 やる/やって]

to give (to a person of
lower status)

8. くれます

[G2 くれる/くれて]

give (to me or to my family)

9. もらいます

[G1 もらう/もらって]

receive, get from

🔊)) **READ/LISTEN/SPEAK** Read these sentences in Japanese. Tell a partner about a gift you received.

おばさんが　本を一さつ　　ぼくは　^{ともだち}友達に　Tシャツを
くれました。　　　　　　もらいました。

^{ぶんぽう}
文法　Grammar

A Giving Words あげます and やります ——————

Giver は　　**Receiver** (equal) に　　**Something** を　　あげます。

Giver は　　**Receiver** (lower status) に　　**Something** を　　やります。

Both あげます and やります mean "give." あげます is used when a giver gives to an equal and やります is used in limited situations when the receiver is a person of a lower status (i.e., a parent to his/her own child). やります may also be used when the receiver is an animal and is almost always used when the receiver is inanimate, as in giving water to a plant.

🔊)) MODELS ▷

1. クリスマスプレゼントを　だれに　あげますか。
   Who do you give Christmas presents to?

2. 母は　毎日　犬に　食べ^{もの}物を　やります。
   My mother gives food to the dog every day.

READ/SPEAK Choose the correct words in the ( ) to complete the sentences.

1. ^{ともだち}友達(に / を)　プレゼント(に / を)　(あげました / やりました)。

2. 水(に / を)　ねこ (に / を)　(あげました / やりました)。

3. ^{おとうと}弟 (に / を)　ゲーム(に / を)　(あげました / やりました)。

B Giving / Receiving Word くれます

Giver は **Receiver (me)** に **Something** を くれます。

Giver (outsider) は **Receiver (my family member)** は **Something** を くれます。

The Japanese system of verbs of giving and receiving is a reflection of a society which functions on horizontal and vertical relationships. The verb you select is dependent on the relative status of the giver and receiver, or whether the giver is an outsider or member of one's own in-group.

くれます means "to give" and is used when someone gives something to the speaker or when an outsider gives something to the speaker's family or a member of his/her in-group.

◀)) MODELS

1. 友達が 私に プレゼントを くれました。
   My friend gave me a present.

2. 田中さんは 妹 に 本を 一冊 くれました。
   Mr. Tanaka gave my younger sister concert tickets.

READ/WRITE Choose the correct verb in the ( ) to complete the sentences and write them on a separate sheet of paper.

1. 友達は ぼくに プレゼントを (あげました / やりました / くれました)。

2. ぼくは 友達に プレゼントを (あげました / やりました / くれました)。

3. ぼくは 犬に 水を (あげました / やりました / くれました)。

C Receiving Word もらいます

Receiver は **Giver** に／から **Something** を もらいます。

もらいます means "receive, get." Note that くれます expresses an action of someone *giving* to the speaker or an outsider *giving* to the speaker's family member whereas もらいます means that someone has *received* something from someone else. The particle に or から may follow the giver when the verb is もらいます.

◀)) MODELS

1. 私は おばあさんに お金を もらいました。
   I received some money from my grandmother.

2. ジョンさんは 友達から おむすびを 一つ もらいました。
   John received one rice ball from his friend.

3. 先生に 宿題を いつも たくさん もらいます。
   I always receive lots of homework from the teacher.

READ/SPEAK Choose the correct verbs based on the information given in English below.

I gave chocolates to my friend and my friend gave me a gift card.
I even gave a cap to my dog!

あげました　　やりました　　くれました　　もらいました

1. 私は　友達(ともだち)に　チョコレートを　（　　　）。

2. 友達(ともだち)は　私に　ギフトカードを　（　　　）。

3. 私は　友達(ともだち)から　ギフトカードを　（　　　）。

4. 私は　犬にも　ぼうしを　（　　　）。

文化(ぶんか)ノート　Culture Notes

Christmas in Japan

Because Christianity is not widely practiced in Japan, Christmas is not a national holiday. However, Japan has adopted some aspects of a secularized Christmas. Businesses, taking the opportunity to increase sales, display winter scenes of decorated trees, teddy bears, and Santa Claus.

Colorful light displays, known as "illumination" イルミネーション, in the urban areas of Japan add to the festive mood of the winter holidays. Young couples enjoy Christmas as it is considered a romantic time of the year and some families decorate small trees at home.

The Japanese enjoy fried chicken as their Christmas meal, and most families purchase beautifully decorated Christmas cakes for dessert. Gifts may be exchanged among close friends and family members, especially children. As in other countries, many Japanese children wait for the arrival of Santa Claus.

Christmas also coincides with another traditional gift giving season in Japan called おせいぼ, a time when adults purchase gifts for business associates, clients, others such as parents, doctors, or landlords. おせいぼ serves as an expression of gratitude for those who have shown kindness toward the giver. This practice however, is not as common among the younger generation.

 How do you celebrate winter holidays at your home? Take a photo of your celebration (or draw one) and write a caption for your photo. Describe when, where, and with whom it was taken, and provide information about the event.

アクティビティー Communicative Activities

ペアワーク

A. SPEAK/LISTEN/WRITE Ask what Christmas presents or birthday presents your partner received from the following people. Write down your partner's responses on a separate sheet of paper.

Ex. 「お父さんから　何の　プレゼントを　もらいましたか。」

「私は　父から　〜を　もらいました。」

1. Grandfather/Grandmother	4. Sibling
2. Aunt/Uncle	5. Cousin
3. Father/Mother	6. Other

* 何も　もらいませんでした。　I did not receive anything.

Now, ask your partner what Christmas or birthday presents he/she gave to the following people.

Ex. 「お父さんに　何を　あげましたか。」

「私は　父に　〜を　あげました。」

1. Grandfather/Grandmother	4. Sibling
2. Aunt/Uncle	5. Cousin
3. Father/Mother	6. Other

* 何も　あげませんでした。　I did not give anything.

クラスワーク

＿＿＿＿さんへ、

B. SPEAK/LISTEN The teacher will give everyone a sheet of paper like the one on the left. Write your name in the blank. The teacher will collect the papers and re-distribute them. You should receive a sheet of paper with a classmate's name on it. Draw a sketch of a present you think he/she would like. The teacher will then collect the "presents" and deliver them. After you receive your "present," try to find the person who gave it to you. Ask your classmates:

「〜さんは　私に　このプレゼントを　くれましたか。」

Later, each student will tell the whole class what he/she received:

「私は　〜さんに／から　〜を　もらいました。」

Make a comment about the gift.

Lesson 6
Review

Review Questions

🔊 Ask your partner these questions in Japanese. Your partner should answer in Japanese. Check your answers using the audio.

Your Experiences   Review pages 200–202

1. Have you ever been to a shrine or temple?

2. Have you ever watched fireworks at your home on New Year's?

3. Have you ever made *mochi*?

Weather   Review pages 206–209

4. About how many degrees is the temperature now?

5. How will the weather be tomorrow?

6. Is it raining (or snowing) now?

Around the Home   Review pages 212–213

7. Do you wash dishes every night at home?

8. How many times a month do you clean your room?

9. Can you cook?

10. Who does the laundry at home?

Holidays   Review pages 200–202, 220–221

11. Have you ever received a New Year's card from Japan?

12. What do you plan to give to your friends for Christmas/another holiday?

13. What did your father/mother give you for Christmas/another holiday last year?

14. Who usually gives your pet （ペット）food?

Things You Do   Review pages 212–214

15. Do you always take food to friends' parties?

16. Have you ever brought a dog/cat home?

17. Do you bring your Japanese textbook to school every day?

Text Chat

You will participate in a simulated exchange of text-chat messages. You should respond as fully and appropriately as possible. You will have a conversation with Mika Kanda, a Japanese high school student, about a holiday party.

12月 14日　10:04 PM

クリスマスイブに　何を
しますか。

List two activities.

12月 14日　10:09 PM

クリスマスに　プレゼントを
あげますか。もらいますか。

Respond and name one item for each question and describe them.

12月 14日　10:15 PM

うちで　クリスマスパーティーを
しますか。

Respond and describe.

Can Do!
Now I can . . .

- ☐ discuss year-end festivities
- ☐ share experiences that I or others have had in the past
- ☐ communicate taking and bringing things or people to certain destinations
- ☐ talk about the giving and receiving of gifts

Project
Corner

年賀状(がじょう)〔ねんがじょう〕
New Year's Card

Let's make a *Nengajoo*!

Things you need: 4×6 white unlined index card, black pen, colored pens or pencils.

Neatly write a New Year's message, the appropriate New Year's date, and your name with a black pen as shown below. Draw a design for the New Year in the blank space. Note the locations of the wording on the card.

賀正
二〇二〇年一月一日
なまえ

明けましておめでとう
二〇二〇年元旦
なまえ

賀正(がしょう), 謹賀新年(きんがしんねん)
Happy New Year, 2020年

元旦(がんたん) First day of the year, 一月一日(いちがつついたち) January 1

謹賀新年
二〇二〇年元旦
なまえ

明けましておめでとう
2020年1月1日
な ま え

アルバイト
Part-time Job

7課

✓ Can Do!

In this lesson you will learn to:

- shop for clothing
- ask and respond to questions about what you prefer
- compare two or more items

Online Resources

cheng-tsui.com/
adventuresinjapanese

- Audio
- Vocabulary Lists
- Vocabulary and *Kanji* Flashcards
- Study Guides
- Activity Worksheets

Let's
Review

In this lesson you will learn how to choose and purchase clothing. Review these words, phrases, and grammatical structures you already learned to help you talk about shopping.

めいし Nouns

1. Tシャツ屋（や）	T-shirt store		7. 青（あお）	blue	
2. アルバイト	part-time job		8. Mサイズ	medium size	
3. ねずみ	mouse		9. Sサイズ	small size	
4. どれ?	which one?		10. これ	this	
5. 色（いろ）	color		11. ドル	dollars	
6. みどり	green		12. セント	cents	

どうし Verbs

13. 見せて　下さい [G2見せる／見せます]	please show me
14. あります [G1ある]	there is
15. はらっても　いいですか [G1はらう]	May I pay? Is it all right if I pay?

-い けいようし I Adjectives

16. かわいい	cute	18. 安い	cheap	
17. 大きい	big	19. 高い	expensive	

Others

20. どんな	what kind of?	22. じゃ、	Then,	
21. 犬の	dog's	23. でも、	However, But	

Expressions	
24. いらっしゃいませ。	Welcome.
25. そうですねえ . . .	Let me see . . . [let me think about this a little]
26. すみません。	Sorry, Excuse me.
27. かまいません	does not matter; don't mind (if)

ぶんぽう Grammar	
28. 〜は　いかがですか。	How about 〜? [Polite]
29. 〜を　下さい。	Please give me 〜.
30. Verb TE form　みて　下さい。	Please try doing 〜.
31. Sentence 1　＋から、Sentence 2	S1, so S2.

A. WRITE Write out what Ken and the customer are saying in each sentence using the words, phrases, and grammatical structures you reviewed above.

1. 　2. 　3.

B. READ/WRITE Your Japanese friend is shopping for souvenirs at an amusement park and wants to buy you a T-shirt. She texts you with some questions. Write a short message in Japanese based on the information given in English below.

Ask her if there are any mouse design T-shirts. Tell her you would like a red shirt, but do not mind a white one. Ask her to please buy you a small size. You also want her to buy a shirt for your friend's birthday. Tell her to try and buy a green one and ask if you may pay her later.

In this lesson, you will learn the *kanji* for travel and shopping.

	Kanji	Meaning	Readings	Examples	
103.	英	British	エイ	えいご 英語	English language
104.	国	country	くに	ちいさいくに 小さい国	a small country
			ぐに	やまぐに 山国	mountainous country
			コク	がいこく 外国	foreign country
			ゴク	ちゅうごく 中国	China
105.	犬	dog	いぬ	いぬ 犬	a dog
			ケン	あきたけん 秋田犬	an Akita dog
106.	青	blue	あお	あおうみ 青い海	a blue ocean
107.	番	number	バン	いちばん 一番	No. 1

	Kanji	Meaning	Readings	Examples		
108.	方	person (polite)	かた	あの方 かた	that person over there	
			がた	夕方 ゆうがた	early evening	
		alternative	ホウ	犬の方が 好きです。 いぬ ほう す	I prefer dogs.	
109.	色	color	いろ	何色 なにいろ	What color?	
110.	屋	store	や	本屋 ほんや	book store	
111.	売	to sell	う(る)	売って いる う	is selling	
112.	読	to read	よ(む)	本を読む ほん よ	read a book	
			ドク	読書 どくしょ	reading	

$0 \rightarrow \mathord{\backslash} +$

$卍 \rightarrow \times = 方$

$\mathord{/} + 囗 +$

$\mathord{\mathrm{c}} = 色$

$\Gamma \rightarrow \mathord{\mathsf{P}} + 一 +$

$\mathsf{L} + 土 = 屋$

$\rightarrow 士 +$

$\rightarrow \mathord{\mathsf{儿}} = 売$

$言 + 売 = 読$

Recognition Kanji

同じ おな   same

一生懸命 がんばります
いっしょうけんめい

I will work very hard

いらっしゃいませ。
何を さしあげましょうか。

Tシャツを
見せて 下さい。

どんな デザインが
いいですか。この
猫や 犬の デザインは
いかがですか。
ねこ

猫の
ねこ
デザインの 方が 犬のより
かわいいですねえ。

ねずみのは
いかがですか。

猫と 犬と
ねこ
ねずみの デザインの
中では どれが 一番
お好きですか。

そうですねえ...
この 中では
ねずみのが 一番
いいですね。

ねずみの　デザインのは
白と　青だけです。
白と　青とでは　どちらが
お好きですか。

白は　青ほど
好きでは　ありません。
青の　Mサイズを　下さい。
アメリカの　Mサイズは
日本の　Mサイズと
同じですか。

そうですねえ...
くらべて　みて
下さい。

違(ちが)いますね。
アメリカの　サイズの　方が
もっと　大きいですね。
じゃ、Sサイズを　下さい。

お土産(みやげ)ですから、
箱(はこ)に　入れて
下さい。

すみません。
ふくろだけですが...

でも、これは
セールですから、
おねだんは
お安いですよ。

会話 かいわ Dialogue

🔊 READ/LISTEN   Which animal design does the customer like more?

猫（ねこ）の　デザインと
犬の　デザインとでは
どちらが　お好きですか。

犬の　デザインの　方が
猫（ねこ）の　デザインより　好きです。

文型 ぶんけい Sentence Patterns

READ Find one of these sentence patterns in the dialogue.

1. Noun 1 と　N2 と

   Noun 1 と　N2 (と)で　　　　　} どちら(orどっち)の方が　　〜predicate ＋ か。

   Noun 1 と　N2 (と)では　　　　　　　Which is more 〜, Noun 1 or Noun 2?

2. Noun 1 の方が　N2 より　(もっと)　〜predicate。Noun 1 is more 〜 than Noun 2.

3. Noun 2 より　N1 の方が　(もっと)　〜negative predicate。

単語 Vocabulary

1. AとBで

between
A and B

2. どっち

which (one of two)?
[Informal]

3. どちら

which (one of two)?

Polite form of どっち.

4. こちら, そちら, あちら

this one, that one,
that one over there

Polite equiv. of これ, それ, あれ.

5. (〜の)方〔ほう〕

alternative

〜のほうが　好きです。

(I) prefer 〜.

6. 〜より

more than 〜

Bは　Aより　高いです。

B is more expensive than A.

7. もっと

more

もっと　高いです。

(It) is more expensive.

8. ずっと

by far

ずっと　高いです。

(It) is far more expensive.

9. りょう
両 方〔りょうほう〕

both

りょう方　好きです。

(I) like both.

10. どちら(orどっち)も＋
Neg.

neither, not either 〜

どちら(orどっち)も　好きではありません。

(I) do not like either.

11. お好きですか。

Do you like it?

Polite form of 好きですか。

12. Superiorに　さしあげます

[G2 さしあげる]

to give (to a superior)

Humble form of あげます

13. 何を　さしあげましょうか。

May I help you?

Lit., What shall I give you?

ついかたんご
追加単語　Additional Vocabulary

1. てんいん　　　　　　　　store clerk

2. (お)きゃく(さま)　　　customer, guest [お and さま added for politeness.]

))) **READ/LISTEN/SPEAK** Read these sentences in Japanese. Then answer the question on the right comparing the prices of the vegetables.

<ruby>赤<rt>あか</rt></ruby>い　車の　方が　青い
車より　もっと　大きいです。

だいこんと　ピーマンと
どちらの　方が　高いですか。

<ruby>文法<rt>ぶんほう</rt></ruby>　Grammar

A Interrogative Question Word どちら / どっち

Noun 1 と　**Noun 2** と

Noun 1 と　**Noun 2** (と)で　　どちら (or どっち) の方が　～predicate＋か。

Noun 1 と　**Noun 2** (と)では　**Which is more ～, Noun 1 or Noun 2?**

When asking a question that solicits a comparison between two nouns, this pattern is used. Both alternatives (nouns) are listed before the question is asked. The interrogative (question word) used in comparing two nouns is どちら or どっち. どちら is slightly more formal than どっち. Note that some portions of this pattern are optional. The particle が follows the interrogative word.

))) MODELS

1. こちらと　そちらと　どちらの　方が　お好きですか。
   Which do you like better, this or that?

2. Lサイズと　Mサイズとで　どっちの　方が　いいですか。
   Which is better, the large size or the medium size?

3. 青い　シャツと　<ruby>赤<rt>あか</rt></ruby>い　シャツとでは　どちらの　方が　高いですか。
   Which is more expensive, the blue shirt or the red shirt?

READ/SPEAK Fill in the ( ) with the correct particle. Choose the correct word in the [ ].

1. 友達：犬の　シャツ（　）　ねこの　シャツ（　）　［どっち　どちら］の
   　　　方が　［好き　お好き］ですか。

2. 店員：犬の　シャツ（　）　ねこの　シャツ（　）　［どっち　どちら］の
   　　　方が　［好き　お好き］ですか。

B Comparing Nouns with ～方が ～より ───

> **Noun 1 の　方が (or は)　Noun 2 より　（もっと）　～predicate。or**
>
> **Noun 2 より　Noun 1 の　方が　（もっと）　～～predicate。**
>
> **Noun 1 is more ～ than Noun 2.**
>
> This construction is used when comparing two nouns. The noun followed by は or の方が is the subject, and the noun that is comparatively less (い adjective/な adjective) than the subject is followed by より. The use of もっと is optional.
>
> 🔊 MODELS
>
> 1. 「犬と　猫と　どちらの　方が　好きですか。」
>   "Which do you like better, dogs or cats?"
>
>   「犬の　方が　好きです。」
>   "I like dogs better."
>
> 2. 私は　犬の　方が　猫より　好きです。
>   I like dogs more than cats.
>
> 3. 赤い　シャツより　青い　シャツの　方が　いいです。
>   The blue shirt is better than the red shirt.
>
> 4. 日本語の　方が　ずっと　むずかしいです。
>   Japanese is far more difficult.

READ/WRITE/SPEAK This person prefers dogs to cats. Fill in the ( ) with the word 犬 or ねこ in Japanese. Rewrite the sentences on a separate sheet of paper.

1.（　）の　方が　もっと　好きです。

2.（　）の　方が　（　）より　もっと　好きです。

3.（　）より　（　）の　方が　もっと　好きです。

文化ノート　Culture Notes

A. Omiyage (お土産)

Gift-giving is an important ritual in Japan, and one of the many ways Japanese people maintain social relationships. The giving of おみやげ (souvenir gifts) is a good example of this system.

When travel was less common, friends, family, and colleagues would sometimes give a traveler money as a departing gift. In return, the traveler would bring back a small gift unique to the place that was visited. Though おせんべつ (departing monetary gift) is not always given these days, Japanese travelers still maintain the custom of bringing back gifts for family, friends, and co-workers.

Popular おみやげ include foods (often sweets such as cookies, crackers, or red-bean buns) special to the region that are individually wrapped and carefully packaged. These are sold in gift shops, train stations, and airports throughout popular tourist areas. おみやげ may also include small trinkets or T-shirts. Those who want to spend more buy designer items such as wallets and purses when abroad.

B. Part-time Jobs (アルバイト)

The number of students and housewives who work part-time in Japan has increased significantly in recent years. Some high school students now work part-time after school, on weekends, or during short spring, summer, and winter breaks. However, some schools still prohibit students from working part-time as this trend has affected participation in after-school and weekend club activities.

Common jobs for young adults are working at fast-food restaurants, convenience stores, and supermarkets. Students who work part-time are said to have an アルバイト or バイト. These terms come from the German word *arbeit*, which means "work." Wages earned by students are usually used as spending money for themselves.

In Japan, it is still common for married women to stay at home to care for the family. In recent years, some housewives are taking on part-time jobs in addition to caring for the needs of the family. Such part-time jobs are referred to as パート. These women may work at supermarkets, fast food restaurants, convenience stores, small shops, factories, or in home care.

 Write an article about part-time work in your country. Where do most teenagers you know work? Are there differences and similarities between part-timers in Japan and America? Write a blog post about your findings in Japanese and share it with your class.

Language Note

Japanese Proverb [花<ruby>はな</ruby>より団子<ruby>だんご</ruby>]

The proverb はなより　だんご literally means "Dango (sweet rice ball dumplings) rather than flowers." In other words, people must put their practical needs (such as food) before aesthetics.

Recently, 花より男子 (Boys Over Flowers), which is read as はなよりだんご, has become a popular television series based on an equally popular *manga*. Although 男子 is correctly read だんし、the だんご reading can be derived from the combination of 男 and 子. The pun on the word だんご ("dumpling" and "boys") has helped make the proverb famous.

アクティビティー　Communicative Activities

ペアワーク

A. SPEAK/LISTEN Using the cues below, ask your partner comparative questions. Take turns asking and answering questions.

Ex. 日本, アメリカ　(広<ruby>ひろ</ruby>い)

質問<ruby>しつもん</ruby>：日本と　アメリカとでは　どちら(or どっち)の　方が　広<ruby>ひろ</ruby>いですか。

答え<ruby>こた</ruby>：アメリカの　方が　日本より　もっと　広<ruby>ひろ</ruby>いです。

1. (かみが　長<ruby>なが</ruby>い)	2. (頭<ruby>あたま</ruby>が　いい)	3. (高い)
ひな　　えり		¥8000　¥3000
4. (年を　取<ruby>と</ruby>って　います)	5. (太って　います)	6. (おもしろい)
65　70		00

B. SPEAK/LISTEN/WRITE Interview each other using the cues below. Answer based on facts.
Write your partner's response on a separate sheet of paper.

Ex. 犬, 猫 (好き)

質問：犬と　猫とで　どちら(or どっち) の　方が　好きですか。

答え：犬の　方が　猫より　もっと　好きです。or

　　　両方　好きです。or どちら(or どっち)も　好きではありません。

1. チョコレートアイスクリーム, バニラアイスクリーム (好き)	4. 数学, 英語 (むずかしい)
2. コーラ, ソーダ (好き)	5. バイオリン, ギター (やさしい)
3. 魚, 牛肉 (好き)	6. お父さん, お母さん (きびしい)

C. READ/SPEAK/LISTEN Role play the following conversation between a store clerk and a customer.
You may replace the words in the ( ) with other words.

店員：いらっしゃいませ。何を　さしあげましょうか。

客：(くつ)を　見せて下さい。

店員：どんな　(くつ)が　お好きですか。

客：白い　(くつ)が　ほしいんですが . . .

店員：この　(くつ)は　いかがですか。

客：ちょっと　(大きい)ですね。ほかのを
　　　見せて　下さい。

店員：では、こちらは　いかがでしょうか。

客：ああ、いいですね。じゃ、これを
　　　下さい。おいくらですか。

店員：セール中ですから、おねだんは
　　　お安いですよ。(50)ドルです。

<ruby>会話<rt>かいわ</rt></ruby> Dialogue

🔊 **READ/LISTEN** What colors does the shirt come in? Which one does the customer like the least?

白の　シャツと　青の　シャツと　どちらの　方が　お好きですか。

白の　シャツは　青の　シャツほど　好きではありません。

<ruby>文型<rt>ぶんけい</rt></ruby> Sentence Patterns

READ Find this sentence pattern in the dialogue.

Noun 1 は　Noun 2 ほど　Negative predicate.　　　Noun 1 is not as 〜 as Noun 2.

<ruby>単語<rt>たんご</rt></ruby> Vocabulary

1. 〜ほど＋ Neg.

(not) as 〜 as

ねこは　犬ほど　良くないです。

Cats are not as good as dogs.

2. (お)ねだん

price

[お for politeness]

3. デザイン

design

4. セール(<ruby>中<rt>ちゅう</rt></ruby>)

on sale

(at a markdown)

5. いろいろ

various [な Adj.]

いろいろな　いろ various colors
　いろいろ　あります。
　There is a variety.

6. ほか

other

ほかの　いろ other colors
ほかに　何か? Anything else?

7. ありがとうございました。

Thank you very much.

[Used after one has received something,
or after a deed has been done.]

8. くらべる

[G2 くらべます／くらべて]

to compare

N1と　N2を　くらべます。
(I) compare N1 and N2.

N1を　N2と　くらべます。
(I) compare N1 to N2.

9. 同じ

〔おなじ〕

same

N1と　N2は　同じです。
N1 and N2 are the same.

N1は　N2と　同じです。
N1 is the same as N2
同じ　色 same color

10. ちがう

[G1 ちがいます]

is different, is wrong

N1と　N2は　ちがいます。
N1 and N2 are different.

N1は　N2と　ちがいます。
N1 is different from N2.
ちがう　色 different/wrong color

読みましょう　Language in Context

READ/LISTEN/SPEAK Read these sentences in Japanese. Restate the sentence on the right using the
~方が　~より structure.

高林さんの　シャツと
平木さんの　シャツは　同じです。

右の　ゆかたは　左の　ゆかた
ほど　好きではありません。

A Comparing Nouns in Negative Sentences

Noun 1 は　Noun 2 ほど　Negative Predicate。

This construction is used to compare two nouns in a negative-ending sentence, similar to the English structure "not as . . . as . . ." The noun followed by は is the one that is comparatively less (い adjective / な adjective). ほど follows the noun that is comparatively more (い adjective / な adjective). The predicate must <u>always</u> appear in the negative form.

◀))) MODELS ▶

1. アメリカは　カナダほど　広くありません。
　　ひろ
   America is not as spacious as Canada.

2. 私は　兄や　姉ほど　頭が　良くないです。
   　　 あに 　あね 　　あたま
   I am not as smart as my older brother and older sister.

3. 白いのは　黒いのほど　好きではありません。
   　　　 くろ
   I don't like the white one as much as the black one.

4. 日本の　サイズは　アメリカの　サイズほど　大きくありません。
   Japan's sizes are not as big as America's sizes.

READ/SPEAK Choose the correct word in the ( ) to create a factual statement.

1. アメリカは　ロシア（より / ほど）
　 （ひろい / ひろくない）です。

2. おじいさんは　子ども（より / ほど）
　 年を　取って（います / いません）。
   　と

3. 犬は　牛（より / ほど）
　 （大きい / 大きくない）です。

4. 日本語の　先生は　私
　 （より / ほど）日本語が
　 上手（です / では
　 ありません）

文化ノート Culture Notes

(ぶんか)

A. Clothing Sizes

Clothing sizes in Japan and the U.S. differ slightly. For T-shirts, American sizes are generally one size larger than Japanese sizes. In most cases the sizing does not run from XS through XL, but from SS, S, M, L to LL though some brands do follow the XS, XL marking. In Japan, shoes are sized by metric measurement. While in Japan, it is best to try on clothing for fit.

T-Shirt Sizes:

Japan	SS	S	M	L	LL	
U. S.		XS	S	M	L	XL

*Shoe Sizes:

Japan (cm)	22	22.5	23	23.5	24	24.5	25	25.5	26	26.5	27	27.5
U.S. Women's	5.5	6	6.5	7	7.5	8	8.5	9	9.5	10	10.5	11

Japan (cm)	25	25.5	26	26.5	27	27.5	28	28.5	29	29.5	30	31	32
U.S. Men's	7	7.5	8	8.5	9	9.5	10	10.5	11	11.5	12	13	14

*Note: It is very difficult to find larger shoe sizes in Japan.

Expand the conversion charts above to include clothing sizes in other countries by searching the Internet. Record all the information in a new chart. Then research average sizes for men and women in each category. Are the average sizes comparable? Share your findings with your class.

B. Trying on Clothes in Japan

While shopping for clothing in Japan, approach a clerk when you are ready to try on some clothes. The clerk will lead you to a dressing room. The floor of the dressing room is generally slightly elevated and carpeted; almost all dressing rooms require you to remove your shoes before entering. Some shops also may provide you with a face covering to protect the clothing from makeup stains.

Language Note

A. ありがとうございます

Note that in Japanese, the word "thank you" has a present and past tense form. It is important to know that when a gift was given or a favor was done in the past, the past tense form ありがとうございました is used.

B. Prefix お

When お precedes words in Japanese, it adds a level of politeness shown to the listener. Do not use お unless you have seen or heard it being used with a word. How is politeness shown when speaking to customers in your own country?

アクティビティー Communicative Activities

ペアワーク

A. READ/SPEAK/LISTEN Using the cues below, take turns asking your partner questions. He/she should answer your questions using ほど.

Ex. 日本, アメリカ (広い)

質問：日本と　アメリカとで　どちら(or どっち)の　方が　広いですか。

答え：日本は　アメリカほど　広くないです。

1. 日本語, スペイン語 (むずかしい)

おはよう。　Buenos días.

4. ひこうき, 自動車 (あぶない)

2. 秋, 冬 (寒い)

5. すもうとり, あなた (大きい)

YOU

3. あなたの字, 先生の字 (きれい)

YOU

6. ごきぶり, ねずみ (多い)

B. SPEAK/LISTEN/WRITE Find out things you do and don't have in common with your partner while carrying on a conversation in Japanese. Record the answers on a separate sheet of paper.

「〜さんと　私は　どこが　同じでしょうか。」

「〜さんと　私は　どこが　ちがうでしょうか。」

C. SPEAK/LISTEN Take turns interviewing your partner using the cues below. He/she should answer using の　方が and より.

Ex: Two school subjects　（好き）

質問：日本語と　数学とで　どちら(or どっち)の　方が　好きですか。

答え1：(日本語)の　方が　(数学)より　好きです。

答え2：(数学)は　(日本語)ほど　好きではありません。

1. Two sports（上手）

2. Two school subjects（成績が　いい）

3. お父さん, お母さん（きびしい）

4. Two movies（好き）

5. Two singers（好き）

6. Two TV programs（おもしろい）

7. Two friends（せが　高い）

8. 土曜日, 日曜日（忙しい）

Authentic Reading

D. READ/WRITE Read the セールのちらし (sales ad) at right and answer the questions below.

UNDERSTAND

1. What type of ad is this?

IDENTIFY

2. In what sizes are the shirts available?

3. How much does each shirt normally cost?

4. What is the sale price of one shirt?

APPLY

5. What would be the total cost if you were to buy a shirt in every color, size, and type available?

WORKBOOK　page 87

7課3
I like the mouse design best

<ruby>会話<rt>かいわ</rt></ruby> Dialogue

🔊 **READ/LISTEN** What three choices of design are there? Which one will the customer choose?

猫<rt>ねこ</rt>と　犬と　鼠<rt>ねずみ</rt>の デザインの　中では どれが　一番 お好きですか。

そうですねえ... この　中では　鼠<rt>ねずみ</rt>のが 一番　好きですね。

<ruby>文型<rt>ぶんけい</rt></ruby> Sentence Patterns

READ Find one of these sentence patterns in the dialogue.

1. N1と N2と N3(と)で　どれ/何/どこ/だれ/いつ etc. が　一番　～ですか。
2. ～ (の中)で　～が　一番　～predicate。

単語　Vocabulary

1. どれ

which one
(of three or more)?

どれが　好きですか。

Which one do you like?

2. (～の中)で

among ~

この　シャツの　中で

Among these shirts,

3. この中で

among these

4. 一番〔いちばん〕

the most

～が　一番　好きです。

I like ～ the most.

5. 世界（せかい）
world

6. 国（くに）
country, nation

7. 州（しゅう）
state

8. 市（し）
city

9. 島（しま）
island

10. さあ
Well . . .
[Used when one does not know or is unsure of the answer.]

追加単語（ついかたんご） Additional Vocabulary

1. もっとも   the most

2. 町〔まち〕   town

3. 村〔むら〕   village

読みましょう Language in Context

READ/LISTEN/SPEAK Read these sentences in Japanese and answer the questions.

赤（あか）い　はしと　黒（くろ）い　はしと
みどりの　はしで　どれが　一番
好きですか。

この中で　何が　一番
ほしいですか。

A Comparing Three or More Objects

Noun 1と Noun 2と Noun 3(で/の中)	どれ 何	
Category (の中)	だれ	が 一番 〜ですか。
Place (の中)	で どこ	
この中／その中／あの中	いつ etc.	

When comparing three or more objects, the objects are listed before the question. Other than listing the individual choices, a category (color, food, subject, etc.) may be named, from which a choice would have to be named in the answer. The question word is most often どれ, but may also be なに, だれ, どこ, etc., depending on the question. The particle following the interrogative (question) word is が. 一番 must precede the い adjective or な adjective.

◀)) MODELS

1. 赤と 白と 黒では どの 色が 一番 好きですか。
   あか   くろ
   Which color do you like best, red, white, or black?

2. 「魚と 豚肉と チキンでは どれが 一番 いいですか。」
        ぶた
   "Which is best, fish, pork, or chicken?"

   「私は 魚に します。」
   "I will have fish."

3. 「日本語と 中国語と ドイツ語では どれが 一番 難しいですか。」
                                              むずか
   "Which is most difficult, Japanese, Chinese, or German?"

   「さあ... 日本語でしょう。」
   "Hmm . . . probably Japanese."

4. 「この クラスで だれが 一番 背が 高いですか。」
                              せ
   "In this class, who is the tallest?"

   「マイクさんです。」
   "Mike is."

READ/LISTEN/SPEAK/WRITE Rewrite and complete the following sentences with the correct particle in the ( ) and the correct question word in the [ ] on a separate sheet of paper.

1. 牛 ( ) 犬 ( ) ねずみ ( )、[　　　] が 一番 小さいですか。

2. 家族 ( )、[　　　] が 一番 年を 取っていますか。

3. アメリカの しゅう ( )、[　　　] が 一番 広いですか。

4. 一週間 ( )、[　　　] が 一番 忙しいですか。

B Superlative 一番 ─────────────────

～(の 中)で ～が 一番 (い **adjective** / な **adjective** / **Verb**)。

This construction is used when three or more nouns are being compared. It singles out one noun as the one that is most (い adjective / な adjective / Verb) among at least three items. The particle で follows a category or group of items from which one is being singled out as the superlative. 一番〔いちばん〕 is the required superlative that precedes the い adjective, な adjective or verb.

🔊 MODELS

1. この 中で これが 一番 好きです。
   Among these, I like this best.

2. 「先生の 中で だれが 一番 きびしいですか。」
   "Among the teachers, who is the strictest?"
   「体育の 先生です。」
   "My P.E. teacher is."

3. 「アメリカの 大学で どこが 一番 いいですか。」
   "Among American colleges, what is the best?"
   「さあ...よく 知りません。」
   "Well . . . I don't know"

READ/SPEAK Complete the sentences with the correct particle in the ( ).

1. 白 ( ) 青 ( ) 赤 ( )、白 ( ) 一番 好きです。

2. 動物 ( ) 中 ( )、犬 ( ) 一番 好きです。

3. この 中 ( )、みどり ( ) シャツ ( ) 一番 好きです。

4. この シャツの 中 ( )、どれ ( ) 一番 好きですか。

文化ノート　Culture Notes

Shopping Districts in Japan

Tokyo is a metropolis composed of many diverse districts. Certain areas of Tokyo are known for their collections of specialized shops. Perhaps the best known is Akihabara, which boasts dozens of shops featuring electronics. Recently, however, Akihabara has become better known as the center of the anime/manga world. Dozens of cosplay shops, maid cafes, and video game-related businesses occupy the crowded streets. Other specialty districts in Tokyo include

Shoppers walking around Akihabara.

Kanda (for books), Tsukiji (for fish and seafood), and Okachimachi and Ueno (for wholesale food markets). Kappabashi is known for its many shops that sell restaurant supplies, such as pots, pans, dishes, cooking utensils, and the plastic food samples found in restaurant display windows throughout Japan.

Osaka's Nipponbashi, also known as Denden Town, is touted as Osaka's answer to Akihabara. Traditionally, it was known as the area for shoppers to buy furniture and tools.

Kyoto features many shops stocked with traditional Japanese arts and crafts. The Higashi-yama district is noted for its steep, narrow, pebble-paved lanes that lead to the famous Kiyomizudera temple grounds. Many traditional crafts, pottery and specialty foods and restaurants can be found there.

 Online, look for photos of the shopping districts mentioned above and the products sold there. Then write a short composition about what you would buy if you were to visit one of these shopping districts on a trip in the future.

アクティビティー　Communicative Activities

ペアワーク

A. READ/SPEAK/LISTEN Take turns asking your partner the following questions.

1. 一番　好きな　色は　何色ですか。
2. 牛肉と　ぶた肉と　魚で　どれが　一番　好きですか。
3. 家族の　中で　一番　背が　高い　人は　だれですか。
4. 一番　旅行したい　国は　どこですか。
5. 英語と　数学と　外国語で　どの　科目が　一番　むずかしいですか。

ペアゲーム

B. READ/WRITE/SPEAK/LISTEN Recreate the game boards below on a separate sheet of paper and play Tic-Tac-Toe with a partner. Follow the directions preceding each game.

ゲーム1: What is the antonym (opposite)?

1. 暑^{あつ}い	4. 早い	7. 黒^{くろ}い
2. 大きい	5. 長^{なが}い	8. うるさい
3. やさしい	6. 近^{ちか}い	9. 新^{あたら}しい

ゲーム2: Give the correct answer in a complete sentence.

1. 世界^{せかい}で どの海^{うみ}が 一番 大きい?	4. 世界^{せかい}で どの国が 一番 大きい?	7. 世界^{せかい}で どの山が 一番 高い?
2. 日本と 中国と アメリカとで どこが 一番 小さい?	5. イタリアと インドと ロシアで どこが 一番 広^{ひろ}い?	8. 春^{はる}と 夏^{なつ}と 冬^{ふゆ}とで いつが 一番 暑^{あつ}い?
3. 自転車^{じてん}と 車と 飛行機^{ひこうき}とで 何が 一番 はやい?	6. 北海道^{ほっかいどう}と 沖縄^{おきなわ}と 京都^{きょうと}とで どこが 一番 寒^{さむ}い?	9. 日本と 中国と かん国とで どの 国が アメリカに 一番 近^{ちか}い?

ゲーム3: Answer in a complete sentence using はい or いいえ.

1. ひこうきの方が車より はやいですか。	4. あきは ふゆほど さむくないですか。	7. 学校は 家より せまいですか。
2. スペイン語は日本語 ほどむずかしくない ですか。	5. 犬は ぶたほど あたまが 良くないですか。	8. だいたい 子どもより おばあさんの 方が しずかですか。
3. レストランの 方が カフェテリアより 安いですか。	6. はる休みは ふゆ休みより みじかいですか。	9. アラスカは ハワイより あついですか。

会話 Dialogue

🔊 READ/LISTEN What was the total cost of the customer's purchase? How will he pay?

おいくらですか。

税金が
かかりますから、
全部で
三十ドル五十セント
です。

クレジットカードで
払っても
いいですか。

はい、どうぞ。

単語 Vocabulary

1. (お)みやげ

2. はこ

3. (container)に 入れる
[G2 いれます]

4. ふくろ

souvenir gift

box

to put in 〜

(paper) bag

5. 税金〔ぜいきん〕

tax

6. おつり

change (from a larger unit of money)

7. クレジットカード

credit card

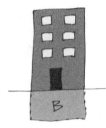

8. 地下

basement

9. かかる

[G1 かかります]

to require (tax), to take (time)

12.

Floor	
?F	なんがい?
10F	じゅっかい
9F	きゅうかい
8F	はっかい
7F	ななかい
6F	ろっかい
5F	ごかい
4F	よんかい
3F	さんがい
2F	にかい
1F	いっかい
B1F	ちかいっかい

10. 売って　います

[G1 うる／うります]

is selling

11. また　どうぞ。

Please come again.

追加単語　Additional Vocabulary

1. レシート　　　receipt

2. しょうひぜい　sales tax

3. 現金 or キャッシュ　　　cash

4. 小切手　　　　　a check

🔊 **READ/LISTEN/SPEAK** Read these sentences in Japanese. Say in Japanese how much change is being returned in U.S. dollars and/or cents in the photo on the right.

地下一階で　食べ物を
売って　います。

30円の　おつりです。

文化ノート　Culture Notes

A. Japanese Department Stores

Most of the early Japanese department stores (デパート) grew out of businesses that originally sold kimono. To this day, department stores feature quality kimono and traditional accessories. Other department stores were established as the railway systems in major cities expanded. Department stores owned by private railway companies were built alongside terminal stations, creating convenient shopping stops for commuters. Although department stores now face competition from expanding supermarkets, convenience stores, and other businesses, the Japanese still patronize department stores when they shop for gifts.

Department stores, particularly in major urban cities, are several stories high. The basement floors feature groceries, ready–made foods, sweets, and *omiyage*–type delicacies. The ground floor usually features cosmetics and fashion wear. Men's, women's, and children's fashions, house wares, gift items, folk crafts, and stationery items, and kimono wear occupy most of the floors. The upper floors may also house toys, sportswear, garden, pet, and aquatic supplies. A variety of restaurants usually occupy the top floor. Rooftop floors may feature gardens and open air space for customers to enjoy. Services such as foreign exchange, travel reservations, and event ticket sales are also offered at major department stores.

B. Kimono 着物

The word "kimono" literally means "thing to wear" (きるもの). There are many varieties of kimono and the type of kimono that a person wears depends on the occasion or purpose, and the age and gender of the person wearing it. Before the arrival of Western clothes, Japanese men and women wore kimono on a daily basis. Now, they are worn by the Japanese only on special occasions, such as New Year's Day, *Shichi-Go-San* (a winter celebration for children who are 3, 5, and 7 years old), Coming of Age Day, college graduations, weddings, and funerals.

People who engage in traditional Japanese art forms, such as martial arts, tea ceremony, dramatic arts, or flower arranging, also wear kimono while practicing their art. During the summer, Japanese men, women, and children also enjoy wearing *yukata* (a light cotton kimono) to festivals.

A man and woman in wedding kimono

Kimono on display at a department store.

C. Credit Cards in Japan

Japan is mostly a cash-based society although credit and debit cards are more widely used now than in the past. Credit cards issued outside of Japan are less readily accepted than those issued in Japan. However, larger businesses, restaurants, and hotels do accept international credit cards. Smaller businesses may still prefer cash transactions, so it is wise to always carry cash when traveling in Japan. ATMs located in post offices and most convenience stores accept international credit cards but will likely charge a service fee.

 You are planning to take a trip to Japan and need to alert your credit card company that you will be traveling abroad. Choose a credit card company and use the Internet or visit your local bank to find out how you can use your credit card overseas. Write a brief summary of your findings and preparations.

アクティビティー　Communicative Activities

ペアワーク

A. READ/SPEAK/LISTEN/WRITE Ask your partner where in the Japanese department store each item on your shopping list is sold. Write the answers on a separate sheet of paper.

Ex. T-shirt

客 すみません。Tシャツは

　　何階で　売っていますか。

店員：Tシャツですか。Tシャツは

　　～かい✓/がいで売っています。

Aさんの　お買い物	何階
1. おべんとう	
2. バッグ	
3. シャツ	
4. 男の人の　ズボン	
5. ペン	
6. ネックレス	
7. かさ	
8. ゆびわ	
9. アイスクリーム	

Bさんの　お買い物	何階
1. 女の人の　ズボン	
2. 魚	
3. くつ	
4. おはし	
5. けしゴム	
6. とけい	
7. 男の人のジャケット	
8. やさい	
9. ぼうし	

階	商品
8F	
7F	
6F	
5F	
4F	
3F	
2F	
1F	
B1F	
B2F	

クラスワーク

B. SPEAK/LISTEN/WRITE Find a classmate who fits one of the following descriptions. Record his/her name on a separate sheet of paper. See if you can find someone for each description.

<ruby>質問<rt>しつもん</rt></ruby>：コーラより　お水の　方が　好きですか。

1. お水の　方が　コーラより　好きです。
2. チーズバーガーより　てりやきバーガーの　方が　好きです。
3. 犬の　方が　ねこより　好きです。
4. 中国<ruby>料理<rt>りょうり</rt></ruby>は　日本<ruby>料理<rt>りょうり</rt></ruby>ほど　好きではありません。
5. 食べ<ruby>物<rt>もの</rt></ruby>の　中で　ピザが　一番　好きです。
6. パスポートを　持って　います。
7. レモネードを　<ruby>売<rt>う</rt></ruby>ったことが　あります。
8. レストランで　アルバイトを　して　います。
9. 日本の　Sサイズの　シャツを　着ることが　出来ます。
10. Tシャツの　<ruby>店<rt>みせ</rt></ruby>で　<ruby>働<rt>はたら</rt></ruby>いたことが　あります。

Authentic Reading

C. READ/WRITE Study the receipt and answer the questions below in Japanese on a separate sheet of paper.

UNDERSTAND

1. What type of store is this receipt for?

IDENTIFY

2. When did the buyer go shopping?

3. Name two items that the buyer purchased.

4. What was the total cost of the purchase?

APPLY

5. Did the buyer pay with cash or credit card?

毎度ありがとうございます

 DAIMARU

大丸梅田店(06)6343-1237

領収書

5月18日16時43分＊通番: 1002-5027+
423-6015-250　服用品

シャツ	1300	1	1300
靴下	500	2	1000
セーター	2000	1	2000
お買上高　4			4300

合計	4300
お預り金	5000
お釣銭	700
（うち消費税等	XX)
売場名：プライド	11000

販売員：田中

00　現金　　売上
会員募集中・お買い物にうれしい

新しいカード　DAIMARU CARD
（大丸カード）誕生。詳しくは
１０階クレジットサービスセンターまで

Review Questions

Ask your partner these questions in Japanese. Your partner should answer in Japanese. Check your answers using the audio.

About you   Review pages 238, 250–251

1. Are you taller than I am?

2. Among your family, who is the most skillful at sports?

Comparing countries and languages
Review pages 237–238, 243–244, 250–251

3. Which is more difficult, Chinese (language) or Japanese (language)?

4. Among foreign languages, which is the easiest?

5. To which country in the world do you most want to travel?

6. Please compare your country and Japan.

Shopping   Review pages 229, 236–237, 245

7. What T-shirt size do you wear?

8. What do you prefer, a white shirt or a blue shirt?

9. (Take the role of a sales clerk.) Welcome! May I help you?

Foods   Review pages 238, 250–251

10. Do you like tea more than cola?

11. Among beef, pork, chicken, and fish, which do you like best?

12. Among Japanese foods, what do you like best?

Text Chat

You will participate in a simulated exchange of text-chat messages. You should respond as fully and as appropriately as possible. You will have a conversation with Kai Mitsuwa, a Japanese high school student, about part-time jobs.

01月 07日 11:41 AM

私は 今 コンビニで
アルバイトを して います。

Respond and ask why.

01月 07日 11:48 AM

アルバイトを した ことが
ありますか。

Respond and explain.

01月 07日 11:53 AM

レストランの アルバイトと
ファストフードの アルバイトと
どちらの 方が 好きですか。

Respond and give two reasons.

 Can Do!
Now I can . . .

- ☐ shop for clothing
- ☐ ask and respond to questions about what I prefer
- ☐ compare two or more items

Shopping in Japan

RESEARCH Use books, the Internet, or interview a Japanese member of your community to answer the following.

Determine

1. Name four major department stores in Japan.

2. Choose one of the Japanese department stores from above. How many floors does it have? How many floors are dedicated to women's clothing? How many to men's clothing? How many to food? How many to toys and games? How many to home goods?

3. Find a department store with a restaurant floor. What type of food do they offer? Is it all Japanese food? If not, what other types of food can you eat there?

4. Where could you likely purchase a kimono in Japan?

5. Where would you go to purchase manga in Japan? Where would you go to purchase used manga? Name at least one store for each.

Compare

6. 100円 shops are quite popular in Japan. What kinds of items can you purchase at a Japanese 100円 shop? Is there an equivalent shop in your own country? Are the same items sold in 100円 shops as the equivalent store in your own country?

7. When shopping for clothes in Japan, what must you do when you want to try them on? What is the general practice in your own country? Are there any differences or similarities?

8. What is the percentage of Japanese people who have credit cards? What percentage of people in your country?

Infer

9. Online shopping has become quite popular in the U.S. in recent years while many Japanese people do not shop online at all. Why do you think a Japanese person would go to a department store instead of shopping online?

Extend Your Learning
COLLABORATION AND INNOVATION

In a group, create a plan to open a Japanese-style department store in your area. Choose a name and location, then create a directory of the store showing what will be sold in English and Japanese. Make a presentation explaining the store's features and what demands it could satisfy in your community.

スポーツの試合
しあい
Going to a Game

8課

Can Do!
In this lesson you will learn to:

- discuss sporting events
- explain that you will pick up someone or something at a certain location
- relate what you can or cannot do
- express what you would like someone else to do

Online Resources

cheng-tsui.com/
adventuresinjapanese

- Audio
- Vocabulary Lists
- Vocabulary and *Kanji* Flashcards
- Study Guides
- Activity Worksheets

In this lesson you will learn how to invite a friend to a sporting event. Review these words, phrases, and grammatical structures you already learned to help you talk about sports.

めいし Nouns					
1. バスケットボール	basketball		9. 外	outside	
2. しあい	sports game		10. よる	night	
3. (お)みせ	store		11. 十一時	11 o'clock	
4. 二階	second floor		12. どっち	which (one of two)?	
5. 今晩	tonight		13. ぼく達	we [used by males]	
6. 午後七時	7 p.m.		14. チーム	team	
7. 六時半ごろ	about 6:30		15. 足	foot, leg	
8. 家	house		16. 三分	three minutes	

どうし Verbs	
17. 来ました [IR くる]	came
18. あります [G1 ある]	there is
19. 見に [G2 みる]	to see [Purpose]
20. 行きませんか [G1 いく]	won't you go? [Invitation]
21 行きましょう [G1 いく]	let's go
22. 待って　います [G1 まつ]	is waiting
23. 帰らなければ　なりません [G1 かえる]	have to return
24. まけて　います [G2 まける]	is losing
25. かちます [G1 かつ]	win

-い けいようし I Adjectives				
26. つよい	strong		28. すごい	terrific
27. せが　高い	tall			

-な けいようし NA Adjectives				
29. 足が 速そう	looks fast		30. 大事	important

ふくし Adverbs	
31. もちろん	of course
32. ぜったい	absolutely

Expressions	
33. じゃ、	Then, [Informal]
34. 良かったですねえ。	How nice! [Past event]

ぶんぽう Grammar	
35. Verb TE form ＋ みました。	tried doing ～
36. Sentence 1 [Noun] ＋ で、Sentence 2。	S1 and S2.
37. ～だけ	only ～

A. WRITE Write out what Ken and Mari are saying in each scene using the words, phrases, and grammatical structures you reviewed above.

1.

2.

B. READ/WRITE Think back to a time when you did not know how to play a sport, but tried it anyway. Write a short blog post about the experience in four sentences. Tell how old you were and what grade you were in (in one sentence), and whether you were skilled at it or not.

Kanji
used in this lesson

In this lesson, you will learn the *kanji* for sports and hobbies.

	Kanji	Meaning	Readings	Examples	
113.	友	friend	とも	ともだち 友達 — friends	
114.	足	foot, leg	あし	みぎあし 右足 — right foot/leg	
115.	点	point(s)	テン	はってん 八点 — 8 points	
116.	半	half	ハン	はんぶん 半分 — a half くじはん 九時半 — 9:30 はんにち 半日 — half day はんとし 半年 — half year	
117.	所	place	ところ ショ	ところ しずかな所 — a quiet place じゅうしょ 住所 — address じむしょ 事務所 — office	
118.	映	projection	エイ	えいが 映画 — movie	日＋口＋ 人＝映

Kanji	Meaning	Readings	Examples	
119. 画 _{1 4} ₃ _{2 6} _{7 5 8}	picture	ガ	えいが 映画	movie
			まんが 漫画	manga
120. 取	to take (something)	と(る)	にほんご 日本語を と 取っている	is taking Japanese 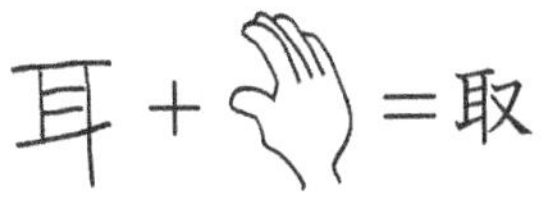
			くるま と 車 を取りに い 行く	to go get the car
121. 入	to enter	はい(る)	はい 入って くだ 下さい。	Please enter. 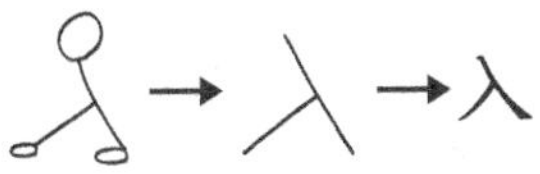
	to put in	い(れる)	い 入れて くだ 下さい。	Please put in.
		いり	いりぐち 入口	entrance
122. 走	to run	はし(る)	はし 走った。	(I) ran. 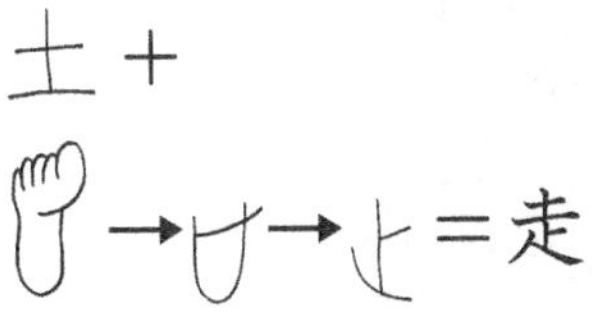

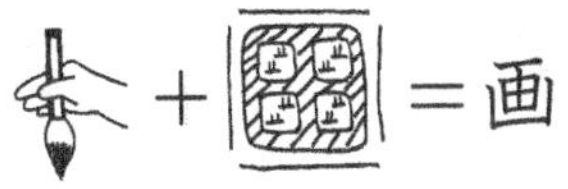

画筆 + 図 = 画

耳 + 手 = 取

人 → 入 → 入

土 +
足 → 止 → 止 = 走

Recognition Kanji			
と 戸	door	きど 木戸さん	Mr./Mrs. Kido
ひとたち 人達	people	ともだち 友達	friend

WORKBOOK page 195

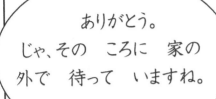

ありがとう。
じゃ、その ころに 家の
外で 待って いますね。

夜は 十一時までに
帰らなければ
いけません。

いいですよ。

どっちの チームの
方が 強いですか。

もちろん ぼく達の
チームですよ。

あの 五番の
ユニフォームの 選手は
ぼくの 友達ですよ。

あの 背が 高い
選手ですか。
足が 速そうですね。
試合は かてますか。

さあ...
分かりません。

To read an informal version of the conversation, go to cheng-tsui.com/adventuresinjapanese

会話 〔かいわ〕 Dialogue

🔊 **READ/LISTEN** What is Ken inviting Mari to do?

> 今晩〔ばん〕 バスケットボールの
> 試合〔しあい〕に 行きませんか。

> 試合〔しあい〕は 何時に
> 始〔はじ〕まりますか。

> 六時半です。

文型 〔ぶんけい〕 Sentence Patterns

READ Find one of these sentence patterns in the dialogue.

1. 試合〔しあい〕が 始〔はじ〕まります。　　　　The game will start. [Intransitive Verb]

2. 試合〔しあい〕を 始〔はじ〕めます。　　　　(Someone) will start the game. [Transitive Verb]

単語 Vocabulary

1. 時間〔じかん〕

time

2. 場所〔ばしょ〕

location, place

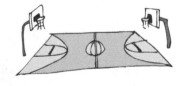

3. 体育館〔たいいくかん〕

gym

たいいく P.E.

4. 運動場
<ruby>運動場<rt>うんどうじょう</rt></ruby>

athletic field

うんどう sports
うんどうぐつ sports shoes
うんどう(を)する to exercise

No.1	いちばん	No.6	ろくばん
No.2	にばん	No.7	ななばん
No.3	さんばん	No.8	はちばん
No.4	よんばん	No.9	きゅうばん
No.5	ごばん	No.10	じゅうばん

5. No. ～

6. ユニフォーム

(sports) uniform

7. 選手
<ruby>選<rt>せん</rt></ruby>手
〔せんしゅ〕

(sports) player

8. 試合に 出る
<ruby>試合<rt>しあい</rt></ruby>に 出る
[G2 でます]

to participate in a (sports) game
しあいを する to have a game

9. おうえん(を) する
[IR おうえん(を) します]

to cheer

10. ～が 始まる
～が <ruby>始<rt>はじ</rt></ruby>まる
[G1 はじまります]

(something) begins, starts

(something)を はじめる
(someone) will start, begin
(something)

11. ～が 終わる
～が <ruby>終<rt>お</rt></ruby>わる
[G1 おわります]

(something) finishes, ends

(something)を おわる
(someone) will finish (something)

追加単語 Additional Vocabulary
ついかたんご

1. 陸上 (りくじょう)　　track
2. チアリーダー　　cheerleader
3. プロ　　professional
4. アマ(チュア)　　amateur
5. スタジアム　　stadium
6. ドーム　　dorm
7. きょうぎじょう　　field
8. トーナメント　　tournament

読みましょう　Language in Context

 READ/LISTEN/SPEAK Read these sentences in Japanese. Say what time a sporting event at your school starts and what time it ends.

プロサッカーの　試合が (しあい)
今　始まりました。(はじ)

高校野球の　試合は (やきゅう) (しあい)
今　終わりました。(お)

文法　Grammar
ぶんぽう

A Intransitive and Transitive Verbs

In Japanese, certain verbs have two separate, but similar-sounding forms, one of which is intransitive and one of which is transitive. An intransitive verb does not take a direct object. A transitive verb takes a direct object, which is always marked by the particle を.

a. Intransitive verb: (something) が or は　始まる (はじ) [begin] / 終わる (お) [finish, end]

試合が (しあい) or は　五時に　始まります。(はじ)　　The game will start at 5 o'clock.

b. Transitive verb: Subject は (something) を　始める (はじ) [begin] / 終わる (お) [finish]

私は　五時に　宿題を (しゅくだい)　始めました。(はじ)　　I started my homework at 5 o'clock.

▶))) MODELS

1. バスケットボールの 試合は 何時に 始まりますか。
   What time will the basketball game begin?

2. DVDを 始めて 下さい。
   Please start the video.

3. 映画は 何時ごろに 終わりますか。
   About what time will the movie end?

4. 先生は 授業を 早く 終わりました。
   The teacher finished class early.

READ/SPEAK Choose the correct word in the ( ) to complete the sentences.

1. 先生は 今日 授業を おそく (始めました / 始まりました)。

2. 授業は 今日 おそく (始めました / 始まりました)。

3. 明日 試合が ありますから、今日 練習を 早く (始まりました /
   終わりました)。

B Noun Modifiers

In Japanese, a noun follows the word that modifies it. Thus, verbs, い adjectives, な adjectives, nouns, and pre-nominatives (この, その, あの, どの, etc.) precede the nouns they modify. The plain form of a verb (dictionary, ない, た, or なかった) is used to modify a noun.

Verb (Plain Form)＋ Noun	始まる	時間	starting time
い Adjective＋ Noun	早い	時間	early time
な Adjective＋ な ＋ Noun	大事な	時間	important time
Noun＋ の ＋ Noun	朝の	時間	morning time
Pre-Nominative ＋ Noun	その	時間	that time

▶))) MODELS

1. 試合の/が 始まる 時間は 何時ですか。
   What time does the game start?

2. 今日の 試合は 大事な 試合です。
   Today's game is an important game.

3. その 試合は おもしろい 試合でした。
   That game was an interesting game.

READ/SPEAK Choose the correct particle in the ( ) to complete the sentences. X means no particle.

1. あの　足が　速い(の / な / X)　選手<ruby>選手<rt>せん</rt></ruby>は、だれですか。

2. あの　上手(の / な / X)　選手<ruby><rt>せん</rt></ruby>は、だれですか。

3. 十番の　ユニフォーム(の / な / X)　選手<ruby><rt>せん</rt></ruby>は、だれですか。

4. 十番の　ユニフォームを　着ている(の / な / X)　選手<ruby><rt>せん</rt></ruby>は、だれですか。

文化ノート　Culture Notes

Cheerleading

Outside of the U.S., Asia has become one of the world's most popular grounds for cheerleading. In particular, it has gained great popularity in Japan among girls in middle school, high school, and college. Since 1998, the International Federation of Cheerleading in Tokyo has organized a number of annual competitions. Many companies also sponsor cheerleading teams and competitions as well as utilize their talents for promotional work.

A women's cheerleading squad in Japan

Fans cheering at a soccer game

Traditional Japanese cheerleading, known as おうえんだん, has a long history in Japan, but recently is becoming less common. おうえんだん are mainly male cheer squads who shout cheers along with taiko drums, blaring horns, whistles, and megaphones. They also wave colorful flags and banners. Almost militaristic in tone, おうえんだん are highly competitive.

 Go online and view videos of Japanese cheerleading squads. Are they similar to American cheerleaders? View videos of おうえんだん. Write three differences between Western-style cheerleading and the traditional Japanese おうえんだん.

Language Note

The conjoining particle が combines two sentences. Although が is often translated as "but," it carries a far less contrastive meaning than the English "but." It may be used simply to connect two sentences together.

Ex. 今日　試合<ruby>試合<rt>しあい</rt></ruby>が　ありますが、行きませんか。

There is a game today. Wouldn't you like to go?

Can you create your own sentence using が?

アクティビティー Communicative Activities

ペアワーク

A. READ/SPEAK/LISTEN/WRITE Your friend is inviting you to a sports game. Ask him/her the following questions and create a schedule based on his/her answers on a separate sheet of paper.

1. 何の　試合が　ありますか。

2. どこの　チームと　どこの　チームが　試合を　しますか。

3. 試合は　どこで　ありますか。

4. 試合は　いつですか。

5. 試合の　始まる　時間は　何時ですか。

6. 試合は　何時ごろに　終わりますか。

7. 何時に　どこで　会いましょうか。

Authentic Reading

B. READ/WRITE Read this flyer about a sporting event in Japan and answer the following questions in Japanese on a separate sheet of paper.

UNDERSTAND

1. Is this a college soccer game or a professional soccer game?

2. Does it take place on a weekend?

IDENTIFY

3. What day and what time will the tickets be sold?

4. Are the ticket prices for the home team seats and the visitor seats the same?

5. What does 料金 mean?

APPLY

6. If you were in Osaka on this day, would you want to go see this game? Why or why not?

WORKBOOK page 99

J1リーグ　プロサッカー試合

東京レッズ　対　ガンバ大阪
5月2日(土曜日)
14:00開始 (12:00 開場)
会場:東京スタジアム2002

チケット発売
2月14日(土曜日)　10:00より

チケット料金
ホーム側応援エリア　S席　4300円
ホーム側指定席大人　3000円
ホーム側指定席小中高　1500円
ホーム側自由席大人　2100円
ホーム側自由席小中高　800円
（ビジター側料金は同じ）

会話 Dialogue

🔊 READ/LISTEN What time does Mari want to be picked up?

何時に　むかえに
行きましょうか。

六時ごろ　むかえに
来て　下さい。

文型 Sentence Patterns

READ Find one of these sentence patterns in the dialogue.

1. Person を むかえに 　　　　　　　go, come, return to pick up (someone)
2. Thing を 取りに 　　　　　　　　go, come, return to pick up (something)
3. Person を 連れて 　行く, 来る, 帰る　take, bring, take/bring home (someone)
4. Thing を 持って 　　　　　　　　take, bring, take/bring home (something)

単語 Vocabulary

1. (Person を) むかえに
行く

go to pick up (person)

2. (Person を) むかえに
来る

come to pick up (person)

3. (Person を) むかえに
帰る

return to pick up (person)

  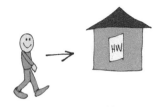

4. (Thing を) 取_とりに
行く

go to pick up (thing)

5. (Thing を) 取_とりに
来る

come to pick up (thing)

6. (Thing を) 取_とりに
帰る

return to pick up (thing)

7. (Place に) 寄_よる
[G1 よります／よって]

stop by, drop by (at a place)

8. (time) までに

by (a certain time)

七時までに　帰らなければ
なりません。
I have to go home by 7 o'clock.

9. そのころ

around that time

10. それは　いい　考_{かんが}えです。

That's a good idea.

11. どうぞ　よろしく
お願_{ねが}いします。

Thank you for doing a favor for me.

追加単語_{ついかたんご} Additional Vocabulary

1. 途中_{とちゅう}で　　　　on the way

2. 帰りに　　　　on the way home

🔊 **READ/LISTEN/SPEAK** Read these sentences in Japanese. Tell your partner who or what you will pick up or take home today.

クリーニング屋さんに
服を　取りに　行きました。

お母さんは　ジャックを
むかえに　行きました。

文法 Grammar

A Verbs of Bringing, Taking, and Picking Up

Personを　**Place** へ/に　むかえに　行く/来る/帰る

go, come, return to a place/ home to pick up (someone)

Thingを　**Place** へ/に　取りに　行く/来る/帰る

go, come, return to a place/home to pick up (something)

Personを　**Place** へ/に　連れて　行く/来る/帰る

take, bring to a place/home, take/bring (someone)

Thing を　**Place** へ/に　持って　行く/来る/帰る

take, bring to a place/home, take/bring (something)

This structure is used when the subject is going, coming, or returning to a place to pick up someone (or something animate) or something (inanimate). If the destination is away from the speaker, the verb should be 行く. If the direction of the movement is toward the speaker or subject, the verb should be 来る. If the destination is the speaker's or subject's home, the verb should be 帰る. If the direct object is animate, use むかえ (from the verb むかえます). If the direct object is inanimate, use 取り (from 取ります). Do not confuse this with the 連れて (つれて) and 持って forms, which are used to take or bring (not pick up) someone or something.

1. 試合の ユニフォームを 忘れて、うちへ 取りに 帰りました。
   I forgot my game uniform and returned home to pick it up.

2. 八時半ごろ 体育館へ むかえに 来て 下さい。
   Please come to pick me up at the gym around 8:30.

3. 友達を 映画に 連れて 行っても いいですか。
   May I take my friend to the movie?

4. パーティーに 何も 持って 来ないで 下さい。
   Please do not bring anything to the party.

READ/SPEAK Choose the correct verb in the ( ) to complete the sentences.

1. 忘れ物を （むかえ / 取り)に 来て 下さい。

2. 父は 車で 私を （むかえ / 取り)に 来て くれました。

3. フットボールの 試合に 友達を （連れて / 持って） 行きたいです。

文化ノート　Culture Notes

A. Baseball Player Etiquette
野球 選手の エチケット

The way baseball players interact with each other exemplifies the importance of respect in Japanese culture. Opposing teams bow to one another before and after games, balls are passed by hand to umpires, and players remove their caps and bow when approaching the home plate. Coaches are shown the utmost respect within the team, and younger players are expected to treat their older teammates with courtesy and respect.

Japanese fans at a soccer game

B. Spectator Etiquette at Sports Events スポーツ観戦者のエチケット

When you go to sports games in Japan, it is important to sit in your team's section with other fans. Japanese fans tend to remain quiet when the opponent is playing, but cheer enthusiastically when their team scores. Volunteers sit at the front of the cheering section and lead other fans in team cheers. There is no booing at games. At soccer games, losing teams and their fans stay after the games to help clean the stadiums.

How would you prepare a visitor from Japan to attend an athletic event at your school? Create a short video or a skit about what to do at a certain sporting event at your school and share it with your class.

Language Note

どうぞ　よろしく　おねがいします。

This versatile expression is handy to use whenever you request a favor. It is used when meeting a person for the first time, to request that the person treat you well in the future. It is also used in many other situations when a person thanks another ahead of time for doing him/her a favor. More casual versions of this expression are どうぞ　よろしく, or よろしく. Is there a similar phrase or expression you use when meeting someone for the first time in English?

> どうぞ
> よろしく
> おねがいします。

アクティビティー　Communicative Activities

ペアワーク

A. READ/SPEAK/LISTEN Interview your partner. Take turns.

1. たいてい　学校に　何時に　着きますか。
2. 朝（あさ）　学校へ　何で　来ますか。
3. 朝（あさ）　だれが　あなたを　学校へ　連れて　来ますか。
4. 学校へ　おべんとうを　持って　来ますか。
5. 毎日　学校へ　ケータイを　持って　来ますか。
6. たいてい　何時に　家へ　帰りますか。
7. だれが　学校へ　むかえに　来ますか。
8. 毎日　宿題（しゅくだい）を　全部（ぜんぶ）　家へ　持って　帰りますか。

B. READ/SPEAK/LISTEN/WRITE You call your friend and make plans to go out together on Saturday evening and offer to drive. Write out your plans on a separate sheet of paper.

質問	答え
1. 車で　むかえに　行きましょうか。	
2. どこで　会いましょうか。	
3. 私の　友達を　連れて（つ）　行っても　いいですか。	
4. 私の　車で　家へ　帰りましょうか。	
5. 家へ　何時に　帰りたいですか。	
6. 何時までに　家へ　帰らなければ　なりませんか。	

会話 Dialogue

🔊 READ/LISTEN Does Ken think his team will win the game?

今日の　試合は　かてますか。

さあ...　分かりません。

文型 Sentence Patterns

READ Find this sentence pattern in the dialogue.

Verb Potential Form

Group 1	飲みます	→	飲めます		can drink
Group 2	食べます	→	食べられます (or 食べれます)		can eat
Irregular Verb	来ます	→	来られます (or 来れます)		can come
	します	→	出来ます		can do

単語 Vocabulary

1. ゆうしょう(を)　する
   [IR します/して]

to win a championship

2. うそです(よ)。

That's not true.

Lit., It is a lie (you know).
うそでしょう? Are you kidding?

3. じょうだんです(よ)。

I'm just kidding.

Lit., It is a joke (you know).

追加単語 Additional Vocabulary
ついかたんご

1. けっしょうせん   a championship game
2. シュートする   to shoot [basketball]
3. ドリブルする   to dribble [basketball]
4. ファウルする   to foul
5. 点を　入れる   to score a point
6. まんてん   perfect score

読みましょう　Language in Context

 READ/LISTEN/SPEAK Read these sentences in Japanese. Say when a sports team you belonged to, a sports team at your school, or any other sports team you know, won an important game.

野球の　試合に優勝しました。

優勝出来て、本当にうれしいです。

文法　Grammar

A Verb Potential Form

 The potential verb form is used frequently in speaking, or in less formal writing situations, to express the capability or possibility of performing a certain action. When the potential form is used, the verb becomes intransitive. Therefore, when a transitive sentence is converted to the potential form, the noun which originally functioned as the direct object loses that function, and the particle を becomes が or は. More recent trends show a movement of retaining the を, though が is more widely accepted.

Example: おさしみを　食べます。→　おさしみが (or を)　食べられます。

All other particles are not affected. Example: 学校に　行けません。

* Verb Dictionary form＋ことが　出来ます is also used to express one's ability to do something.

Group 1 verbs

To obtain the potential form, change the final –i sound of the verb stem to the corresponding –e sound, then add ます or る. There is no potential form of the existence verbs います or あります or the verb わかります, which already means "can understand."

MODELS

[–i ます]	NAI FORM	MASU FORM	DIC. FORM	POTENTIAL	TA FORM
み verbs	のまない	のみます (drink)	のむ	のめる	のんだ
に verbs	しなない	しにます (die)	しぬ	しねる	しんだ
び verbs	あそばない	あそびます (play)	あそぶ	あそべる	あそんだ
い verbs	かわない	かいます (buy)	かう	かえる	かった
ち verbs	またない	まちます (wait)	まつ	まてる	まった
り verbs	つくらない	つくります (make)	つくる	つくれる	つくった
き verbs	かかない	かきます (write)	かく	かける	かいた
ぎ verbs	およがない	およぎます (swim)	およぐ	およげる	およいだ
し verbs	はなさない	はなします (speak)	はなす	はなせる	はなした

Group 2 [-IRU, -ERU] verbs

Group 2 verb potential forms are created simply by replacing ます by られます. Younger Japanese people tend to use –れます instead of the –られますending.

	NAI FORM	MASU FORM	DIC. FORM	POTENTIAL	TA FORM
[–e ます]	たべない	たべます (to eat)	たべる	たべられる	たべた
[One hiragana]	ねない	ねます (to sleep)	ねる	ねられる	ねた
[Special verbs]	おきない	おきます (to get up)	おきる	おきられる	おきた
	かりない	かります (to borrow)	かりる	かりられる	かりた
	おりない	おります (to get off)	おりる	おりられる	おりた

COMPARE: 見える "can be seen, visible" is not interchangeable with 見られる "can look at." 聞こえる "can be heard; audible" is not interchangeable with 聞ける "able to listen to."

Group 3 Irregular verbs

Only きます, します and noun + します verbs belong to this group. Young Japanese people tend to use これます instead of こられます.

	NAI FORM	MASU FORM	DIC. FORM	POTENTIAL	TA FORM
きます	こない	きます to come	くる	こられる	きた
します	しない	します to do	する	できる	した

◀))) MODELS

1. 「この　土曜日に　家へ　来られますか。」
   "Can you come to my house this Saturday?"

   「はい、もちろん　行けますよ。」
   "Yes, of course I can."

2. 父は　中国語が　話せますが、私は　話せません。
   My father can speak Chinese, but I cannot.

READ/WRITE Change the verb in the ( ) to the potential form. Write your answers on a separate sheet of paper.

1. 明日の　試合に　(かちます)か。
   しあい

2. おはしで　うどんが　(食べます)か。

3. 私は　(泳ぎます)。
   およ

4. 昨日　運転めんきょを　取りましたから、(運転します)よ。
   きのう　うんてん　　　　　　　　　　　　　　　　うんてん

5. 午後四時に　学校へ　むかえに　(来ます)か。

文化ノート　Culture Notes
ぶんか

Judo 柔道
じゅうどう

Judo literally means "the gentle way." It is one of the most popular martial arts in Japan and was developed in 1882 by Jigoro Kano, based on *jujitsu*. In the mid-1950's, judo became more widely recognized worldwide and the World Judo Championships were established. It became an official Olympic sport for men in 1964 at the Tokyo Olympics.

The object of judo is to throw your opponent to the ground, pin him/her down, or force a defeat with a joint lock or choke hold. Kano believed that judo was not simply a physical activity, but required the alignment of the martial artists' mind and spirit as well. A good *judoka* (judo practitioner) is able to overcome an opponent's attack, not through power but by skillfully adjusting to or evading the opponent.

 Search the Internet for a martial arts dojo in your city. Are there any? If so, what martial arts are practiced? Choose one and write a brief description. How does it differ from judo?

Language Note

The word うそ is translated as "lie," although it does not carry as serious or as negative a connotation as its English equivalent.「うそでしょう。」is used lightly among friends, much as English speakers would use, "Are you kidding?" or "Are you serious?" In casual conversation it may even be used to replace「そうですか。」. Both「うそです。」 and「じょうだんです。」(which literally means "It's a joke!") should only be used in informal situations, and never with people of higher status or a person you do not know well.

アクティビティー   Communicative Activities

ペアワーク

A. READ/SPEAK/LISTEN Take turns interviewing your partner. After your partner answers, respond with そうですか, 本当ですか, or うそでしょう.

1. サーフィンが　出来ますか。

2. スキーが　出来ますか。

3. スペイン語が　話せますか。

4. 十マイル　走れますか。

5. 日本料理が　作れますか。

6. ギターが　ひけますか。

クラスワーク

B. WRITE/SPEAK/LISTEN Write a list of five potential form questions on a separate sheet of paper. Circulate and ask your classmates if they are able to do these actions. Mark them off only if someone answers affirmatively. Share your findings with the class.

Ex. 質問：車の　運転が　出来ますか。

答え：はい、出来ます。 or いいえ、出来ません。

Aさん：「Bさんは　運転が　出来ます。」「Cさんは　出来ません。」

WORKBOOK　page 103

会話 Dialogue

🔊 **READ/LISTEN** What was the final score of the game? What does Mari think about it?

私は　チームに
かって　ほしいです。
スコアは　どうでしたか。

55対54で
かちましたよ。

それは
良かったですねえ。

文型 Sentence Patterns

READ Find this sentence pattern in the dialogue.

私は　チームに　かって　ほしいです。　　　I want (our) team to win.

単語 Vocabulary

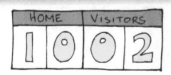

1. スコア

score

2. 55たい2

55 to 2

Aチームたい　Bチーム
A team vs. B team

3. あと〜

〜 more
あと　一点
one more point

4.

	Points
1	いってん
2	にてん
3	さんてん
4	よんてん
5	ごてん
6	ろくてん
7	ななてん
8	はってん
9	きゅうてん
10	じゅってん
？	なんてん

5. ドキドキします

is excited, is nervous

ドキドキ represents the sound of a heartbeat.

6. やったあ！

We did it!

[Used when a person accomplished a goal after hard work.]
やる is an informal equiv. of する.

ばんざい
7. 万歳！

Hurray!

Originally represented a cheer of "10,000 years" (まんざい) to the Emperor.

8. かった！かった！

(We) won! (We) won!

The plain form is used when talking to yourself.

9. ぜひ [Adverb]

by all means, definitely

読みましょう　Language in Context

🔊 **READ/LISTEN/SPEAK** Read these sentences in Japanese. Tell a partner which athletic team you would like to see win their next game.

チームに　かって　ほしいです。

やったあ！　かった！　ばんざい！

A Expressing Wanting Others to Do Something

Person 1 は + (Person 2 + に) + Verb [TE form] + ほしいです。

Person 1 wants Person 2 (not higher in status than Person 1) to do ~.

When the subject wants another person (Person 2) to do something, Person 2 is marked by に. The subject is usually the first person (I) in declarative sentences and the second person (you) in interrogative sentences. This construction is not used if Person 2 has a higher status.

Compare:

a. 私は　かちたいです。　　　　I want to win.

b. 私は　あなたに　かって　ほしいです。　　I want you to win.

◄)) MODELS

1. 私は　チームに　ぜひ　かって　ほしいです。
   I definitely want the team to win.

2. 私は　ぜひ　山中さんに　日本語を　教えて　ほしいです。
   I definitely want Ms. Yamanaka to teach me Japanese.

3. だれに　来て　ほしいですか。
   Who do you want to come (to something)?

READ/SPEAK Choose the correct particle in the ( ). Change the verb in the [ ] to the correct form.

1. 私達の　チーム( )　今日の　試合に　ぜひ　[かちます]　ほしいです。
   しあい

2. 私達は　ぜったい　今日の　試合( )　[かちます]　たいです。
   しあい

3. 私達は　ぜったい　ゆうしょうの　トロフィー( )　ほしいです。

ぶんか
文化ノート　Culture Notes

A. Japanese Proverb
「まけるが　かち」

This proverb means "Defeat is a win." A similar English expression might be, "Winning isn't everything." This proverb is used when despite a defeat or disappointment, you gain in some way from the experience.

B. Sports Anime and Manga
スポーツアニメとまんが

The popularity of anime and manga has skyrocketed in recent years, both in Japan and throughout the world. Among other genres, sports anime and manga featuring traditional martial arts, such as sumo, kendo, and judo as well as baseball, soccer, and tennis are immensely popular in Japan. These series often appeal to both men and women, sports fans and non-fans, and knowledge of the rules of the game is not required to enjoy the genre. A typical storyline features an underdog who overcomes his or her insecurities and flaws to emerge heroic.

Like most other manga, sports manga are usually first published in weekly or monthly anthology magazines, like the famous *Shonen Jump*「少年ジャンプ」. When a series becomes popular, these chapters are collected in larger volumes and may even be adapted into an anime series. Popular titles may continue for years, sometimes through sequels and side-stories. For example, the series *Prince of Tennis*「テニスのおうじさま」 has run for over 15 years and over 50 volumes since first appearing in *Shonen Jump*.

 Search for sports-related manga or anime online or at your local library or bookstore. Prepare a brief presentation about the series in Japanese to share with your class. Be sure to include information such as the author, year of publication, number of volumes in the series, main characters, and plot.

Language Note

Loan Words in Sports
Because many of the popular sports in Japan are of Western origin, the majority of the sports terminology used in Japan are borrowed words, especially sport names. Terms in baseball, a favorite sport of the Japanese, are frequently loan words. There are even some words that appear to be English, but were actually created in Japan, e.g., ナイター (nighter), which is a game played at night. Can you think of any Japanese loan words used in English?

Japanese	English
ベースボール	baseball
サッカー	soccer
テニス	tennis
ゴルフ	golf
フットボール	football
スキー	skiing
スケート	skating
バレーボール	volleyball
ストライク	strike
アウト	out
バッター	batter
ホームベース	home base
キャッチャー	catcher
ナイター	nighter

ペアワーク

A. READ/SPEAK/LISTEN You are going to a football game with your friend on Saturday night. Ask him/her the following questions. Take turns.

1. チケットを　買って　ほしいですか。

2. だれに　来て　ほしいですか。

3. 私の　友達を　連れて　行っても　いいですか。

4. むかえに　行きましょうか。

5. 何時に　むかえに　来て　ほしいですか。

6. どこで　会いましょうか。

7. ゲームは　何時に　始まりますか。

8. おうえんする　物を　持って来て　ほしいですか。

9. どちらの　チームの　方が　強いですか。

10. どちらの　チームに　かって　ほしいですか。

11. うちに　何時に　帰りたいですか。

12. 何時までに　家へ　帰らなければ　なりませんか。

クラスワーク

B. READ/WRITE/SPEAK/LISTEN Role play the following conversation using appropriate expressions and gestures. Add any additional lines that may be appropriate.

A: あっ、スコアは　５５対５４です。

B: あと　三分だけですよ。

A: 私達の　チームは　かてますか。

B: もちろん。ぜったい　かちますよ。

A: ドキドキしますね。

B: あと　一分！

A: あっ、シュートが　入った！

A & B: やったあ！かった！かった！ばんざい！

Review Questions

Ask your partner these questions in Japanese. Your partner should answer in Japanese. Check your answers using the audio.

Your Japanese class Review pages 273–274, 289

1. What time did Japanese class start today?

2. What time do you finish school today?

3. Did you begin tonight's Japanese homework already?

4. What does your Japanese teacher want you to do today?

Your day Review pages 279–280, 283–285, 289

5. Who brought you to school today?

6. Who will come to pick you up from school today?

7. Do you have to go to pick up your books from your locker after school?

8. Can you return home early today?

9. By what time do your parents want you to return home today?

Sporting events Review pages 273–274, 283–285

10. Where are the school's football games usually held?

11. What is the starting time for sports practice?

12. What kind of sports can you play?

13. Can you go to the next soccer game?

Text Chat

You will participate in a simulated exchange of text-chat messages. You should respond as fully and as appropriately as possible. You will have a conversation with Rin Okawa, a Japanese high school student, about a sporting event.

02月 20日　06:19 PM

私は　スポーツが　好きなんですが、
何も　出来ないんですよ。

Respond and ask for details.

02月 20日　06:23 PM

スポーツの　試合を　おうえんに
行きますか。

Respond and describe the details.

02月 20日　06:30 PM

次の　スポーツの　試合を
教えて　下さい。

Inform and provide details.

Can Do!
Now I can . . .

- ☐ discuss sporting events
- ☐ explain that I will pick up someone or something at a certain location
- ☐ relate what I can or cannot do
- ☐ express what I would like someone else to do

ラジオたいそう
Radio Exercises

Rajio taiso or "radio exercises" are calisthenics performed to music. They originated after World War II to encourage cooperation and unity. The custom of lining up together in neat rows for daily morning exercises continues today at schools and at certain companies.

Originally, people gathered around their radios or piped the radio music over public address systems into playgrounds or playing fields where the exercises took place. Today, you can still observe this morning ritual around schools, parks, and companies in Japan. However, you can also tune in to early morning television broadcasts and do the exercises in the privacy of your own home.

There are several versions of *rajio taiso*; most Japanese people are familiar with many of these versions. Often, instructions are called out as part of the lyrics to give cues as to which exercise to do and how. The exercises include familiar ones such as "jumping jacks," "windmill," and "touching toes."

There are 13 basic steps in the routine, beginning with extending and swinging the arms, leaning and twisting at the waist, and bending the knees and lifting the heels.

Senior citizens in Japan gather at a park for *rajio taiso* at 6:30 a.m.

For a visual guide on how to do some of the most common exercises in *rajio taiso*, visit the companion website at **cheng-tsui.com/adventuresinjapanese**. You can also search online for videos of *rajio taiso*.

日本昔話
Japanese Folktale

むかしばなし

9課

ねずみのよめいり Mouse Wedding

Can Do!
In this lesson you will learn to:

- read and perform a Japanese folktale
- quote others' statements
- express your opinions
- talk about elements of traditional Japanese folktales

Online Resources

cheng-tsui.com/adventuresinjapanese

- Audio
- Vocabulary Lists
- Vocabulary and *Kanji* Flashcards
- Study Guides
- Activity Worksheets

In this lesson you will learn how to perform a play of a traditional Japanese folktale. Review these words, phrases, and grammatical structures you already learned to help you talk about the aspects of storytelling.

めいし Nouns			
1. 日 （ひ）	day	4. 次 （つぎ）	next
2. 世界 （せかい）	world	5. (えらい)の	(great) one
3. 所 （ところ）	place	6. なぜ	why?

どうし Verbs	
7. 住んで いました [G1 すむ]	was living
8. 来て [IR くる / きて]	come
9. 言いました [G1 いう]	said
10. ～と 結婚したいんです [IR けっこんする]	want to marry~
11. ～を 下さい。	Please give me~.
12. 働きます [G1 はたらく]	work
13. 帰って 下さい [G1 かえる]	please return
14. 出かけました [G2 でかける]	left
15. もらって 下さい [G1 もらう]	please accept
16. いらっしゃいます [G1 いらっしゃる]	exist [polite]
17. ～に お願いしましょう [IR おねがいする]	let's ask ~ (a favor)
18. 開けて [G2 あける]	open
19. 結婚することが 出来ました [IR けっこんする]	could marry

-い けいようし I Adjectives	
20. 若くて [わかい]	young
21. 美しい （うつく）	beautiful

-な けいようし NA Adjectives	
22. だめ	no good

ふくし Adverbs			
23. 一番	the most (number one)	**24.** ずっと	always

Expressions	
25. Plain form + んです。	[offers an explanation to a listener]
26. おねがいします。	Please. I ask you a favor.
27. では、	And then, [Formal]
28. Sentence (reason) + から。	It is because (reason).

A. WRITE Write out what the mice are saying in each scene using the words, phrases, and grammatical structures you reviewed above.

1.

2.

3.

B. READ/WRITE Write the following English sentences in Japanese on a separate sheet of paper.

1. I was late this morning. (explanation)

2. Because I woke up late, I left my house at 9 o'clock.

3. And then, my train was late.

C. WRITE/SPEAK/LISTEN Imagine your life fifty years in the future. Write a short description of your life after graduating from high school in Japanese. Describe any higher education you obtained, where you lived, your job(s), and the kind of person you may have married, as well as information about your family. Keep your description to five sentences or less. Share it with your class.

In this lesson, you will learn some *kanji* related to nature.

	Kanji	Meaning	Readings	Examples	
123.	開	to open	あ (ける)	ドアを開けて下さい。	Please open the door. 門 + 开 → 开 = 開
124.	住	to live	す(む) ジュウ	日本に住んでいます。 住所	I'm living in Japan. address ヨ→イ + ◊ + 王→天 = 住
125.	美	beautiful	うつく(しい) ビ	美しい山 美術館 美人	a beautiful mountain art museum a beauty →羊 + →大 =美
126.	若	young	わか (い)	若い人	young people → ψψ + 右 = 若
127.	明	bright	あか (るい) あ (ける) *	明るい月 明けましておめでとう 明日	bright moon Happy New Year tomorrow ⊙ + ☽ =明
128.	力	power	ちから	力持ち	a strong person → → 力

Kanji	Meaning	Readings	Examples	
129. 風	wind	かぜ	つよ かぜ 強い風	strong wind → 風 →風
		フウ	たいふう 台風	typhoon
130. 世	world	セ	せ かい 世界	world → → 世
131. 界	boundary	カイ	せ かい 世界	world 田 + → ＝界
132. 次	next	つぎ	つぎ ひ 次の日	next day 二 + → ＝次
		ジ	じ ろう 次郎	Jiro [boy's name]

New Reading			
38. 生	ショウ	いっしょうけんめい 一生懸命	with utmost effort
	ジョウ	たんじょうび 誕生日	birthday
70. 話 story	はなし	はなし お話	story
	ばなし	むかしばなし 昔話	folk tale

Recognition Kanji
ひ さま お日様　sun

WORKBOOK page 199

Storytelling time with Mari

昔々 ある くらの中に、お金持ちの ねずみの お父さんと お母さんと 娘が 住んでいました。

チュウ子は 若くて 美しい 娘でした。

ある日、びんぼうな チュウ吉が チュウ子の 家に 来て、言いました。

お父さん、私は チュウ子さんと 結婚したいんです。チュウ子さんを 私に 下さい。

えっ、とんでもない。娘は 世界で 一番 えらい人と 結婚するんですよ。

お父さん、ぼく、一生懸命 働きます。だから、お願いします。

だめだめ。帰って 下さい。

次の日、お父さんは　お日様の
所へ　出かけました。

お日様、お日様、こんにちは。
私の　娘を　もらって　下さい。
お日様は　世界で　一番
えらい　方です。
お日様が　いらっしゃいますから、
この　世界は　明るいんです。

いや、世界で　一番
えらいのは、くもさんですよ。

えっ、なぜですか。

くもさんは　私を
かくして　しまいます。
だから、くもさんの方が
私より　ずっと
えらいんですよ。

なるほど。

では、くもさんに
お願いしましょう。

お父さんは　くもさんの
所へ　行きました。

くもさん、くもさん、こんにちは。
私の　娘を　もらって　下さい。
くもさんは　世界で　一番
えらい　方です。

いや、世界で
一番　えらいのは、
風さんですよ。

風さんは　私を
ふきとばして　しまいます。
だから、風さんの方が　私より
ずっと　えらいんですよ。

えっ、なぜですか。

なるほど。

では、風さんに
お願いしましょう。

 お父さんは
風さんの　所へ　行きました。

風さん、風さん、こんにちは。
私の　娘を　もらって　下さい。
風さんは　世界で　一番
えらい　方です。

いや、世界で
一番　えらいのは、
かべさんですよ。

えっ、なぜですか。

かべさんは　私の
力では　動きません。
だから、かべさんの方が
私より　ずっと
えらいんですよ。

なるほど。
では、かべさんに
お願いしましょう。

お父さんは　かべさんの
所へ　行きました。

かべさん、かべさん、
こんにちは。私の
娘（むすめ）を　もらって　下さい。
かべさんは　世界で　一番
えらい　方です。

いや、世界で
一番　えらいのは、
ねずみさんですよ。

えっ、
なぜですか。

ねずみさんは
ガリガリ　私に　穴（あな）を
開けて　しまいます。だから、
ねずみさんの方が　私より
ずっと　えらいんですよ。

なるほど。

　お父さんと
お母さんは　チュウ吉（きち）が
世界で　一番　えらいと
思（おも）いました。そして、
チュウ吉（きち）は　チュウ子と
とうとう　結婚（けっこん）することが
出来ました　とさ。

　　　おしまい。

304

会話 Dialogue

🔊 **READ/LISTEN** Would Ken rather be the Sun or the Cloud from the play?

文型 Sentence Patterns

READ Find one of these sentence patterns in the dialogue.

1. Noun に なります   become ~

2. Noun 1 の方が   Noun 2 より   〜です。   Noun 1 is more 〜 than Noun 2.

3. Noun 1 は   Noun 2 ほど   Negative predicate。   Noun 1 is not as 〜 as Noun 2.

単語 Vocabulary

1. 昔話
folktale

2. げき
(stage) play

3. ナレーター
narrator

4. お日様
_{ひさま}

sun [polite]

5. くも

cloud

6. かべ

wall

7. (お)金持ち
_{かね も}

rich person

8. びんぼう

poor [な Adj.]

9. 明るい
_{あか}

bright [い Adj.]

10. 暗い
_{くら}

dark [い Adj.]

11. えらい

great [い Adj.]

えらい is used to describe people.

12. ～に なります

[G1 なる]

become ～

追加単語 Additional Vocabulary
_{ついかたんご}

1. 嫁入り
_{よめ い}

wedding [A classical Japanese word. よめ is "bride," いり is derived from いります "to enter." Entering into a family as a bride was the equivalent of a marriage, or a wedding.]

2. 小道具
_{こどうぐ}

props

3. 紙芝居
_{かみしばい}

paper play [Japanese traditional storytelling using pictures]

🔊 **READ/LISTEN/SPEAK** Read these sentences in Japanese. What did you dress up as at Halloween, or when you were a child? (What did you "become?")

ハロウィンに　お姉_{ねえ}さんは
スノーホワイトに　妹_{いもうと}さんは
ウィッチに　なりました。

赤_{あか}ちゃんは　一歳に　なりました。
だから、よく　座_{すわ}れます。

文法_{ぶんほう}　Grammar

A Verb of Becoming に　なります

Noun に　なります　　　　to become ~

🔊 MODELS

1. 「何に　なりたいですか。」　　　"What do you want to be?"
   「医者_{いしゃ}に　なりたいです。」　　"I want to be a doctor."

2. 私は　十五才に　なりました。　I have turned 15 years old.

READ/SPEAK Choose the correct form of the verb in the ( ) based on the context of the sentences.

1. 弟_{おとうと}は　先週　げきで　お日様に　(なります / なりました / なりたいです)。
2. 弟_{おとうと}は　明日　十歳に　(なります / なりました / なりたいです)。
3. 弟_{おとうと}は　やきゅうのせん手に　(なります / なりました / なりたいです)。

文化ノート　Culture Notes

日本の 昔話: 桃太郎 Momotaro

Many Japanese folktales share storylines and themes similar to other tales throughout the world. Perhaps the most well-known Japanese folktale is the story of Momotaro, or Peach Boy.

Once there was an old woman who had no children. One day, while she was washing her clothes in the river, she saw a giant peach floating in the water toward her. She took it home, but when she and her husband opened the peach to eat it, out came a small boy whom they adopted as their son. They named him Momotaro, and he grew up to be a strong and courageous young man.

In those days, terrible ogres from far away Ogre Island terrorized villages. They came to Momotaro's village and stole treasures from the villagers. For the good of the village, Momotaro selflessly set out to fight them and bring the treasure back. Along the way, he befriended a dog, a monkey, and a pheasant, who united in order to help Momotaro fight the ogres. After a mighty struggle at the ogres' castle, Momotaro and his friends returned victorious with all the stolen treasures, and were hailed as heroes.

It is said that the story of Momotaro originated in Okayama Prefecture (located between Osaka and Hiroshima) where peaches are plentiful and millet dumplings are popular.

Be an anthropologist! Read the story of Momotaro and identify an important cultural value of Japan expressed in the story. Write a short essay explaining a value that the story presents, and how you think it is still important in contemporary Japan.

アクティビティー　Communicative Activities

ペアワーク

A. READ/SPEAK/LISTEN Ask your partner the following questions. Take turns.

1. 今年　何歳に　なりましたか。
2. 来年　何年生に　なりますか。
3. 日本語の　先生に　なりたいですか。
4. 医者に　なりたいですか。
5. 何に　なりたいですか。
6. ねずみのよめいりの　げきで　だれに　なりたいですか。

B. READ/SPEAK/LISTEN/WRITE Ask your partner comparison questions using the cues accompanying the pictures. Write the answers on a separate sheet of paper.

Ex. お父さん / チュウ吉, お金持ち

質問：お父さんと　チュウ吉と　どちらの　方が　お金持ちですか。

答え：お父さんの　方が　チュウ吉より　お金持ちです。

1. びんぼう

2. えらい

3. えらい

4. えらい

5. えらい

Authentic Reading

C. READ/WRITE Look at the book cover and answer the following questions.

UNDERSTAND

1. What type of book is this?

2. What do you think the story is about?

IDENTIFY

3. What is the title of the book?

4. Does it only include Japanese folktales?

APPLY

5. Create and illustrate a book cover of a folktale or fairytale from your own country and write the title in Japanese.

WORKBOOK　page 113

9課2
I finished all of my homework

<ruby>会話<rt>かいわ</rt></ruby> Dialogue

🔊 **READ/LISTEN** Did Ken finish all of his homework?

<ruby>文型<rt>ぶんけい</rt></ruby> Sentence Patterns

READ Find one of these sentence patterns in the dialogue.

1. Verb TE Form + しまいます   do ～ completely [regret, finality]

2. Sentence 1。だから or ですから、sentence 2。   Sentence 1. Therefore, sentence 2.

<ruby>単語<rt>たんご</rt></ruby> Vocabulary

1. (thing を) かくす
[G1 かくします]
to hide (thing)
[Transitive verb]

2. ふきとばす
[G1 ふきとばします]
to blow away
ふく to blow ＋とばす to fly

3. (thing が) <ruby>動<rt>うご</rt></ruby>く
[G1 うごきます]
(thing) moves
[Intransitive verb]

4. ガリガリ

chew away; gnaw

[Onomatopoetia]

5. あな(を) 開ける

[G2 あけます]

(to open up) a hole

<ruby>力<rt>ちから</rt></ruby>

6. 力

power, strength, ability
ちからが つよい
has strength; power

7. (Verb TE)＋しまいます

do ～ completely
食べて しまいました。 I ate (it) up.

8. だから、

Therefore,

[Informal]

9. ですから、

Therefore,

[Formal]

読ましょう Language in Context

🔊 **READ/LISTEN/SPEAK** Read these sentences in Japanese. Study the photo on the left.
In a complete sentence, say what you think the person drank (completely) with the meal.

日本<ruby>料理<rt>りょうり</rt></ruby>を <ruby>全部<rt>ぜんぶ</rt></ruby>
食べて しまいました。

クラスで サダコの げきを しました。

文法　Grammar

A Verb Extender しまいます

Verb TE form + しまいます

The verb TE plus extender しまいます has two interpretations, and some sentences may carry both nuances.

- It expresses the completion of an action. Sometimes the completion of the action may have been unexpected.

  Ex. 宿題を　して　しまいました。

  I completely finished my homework.

- It implies the speaker's regret about what has been done or a negative reaction to a completed action or event.

  Ex. 宿題を　車に　忘れて　しまいました。

  I forgot my homework in the car (by mistake).

MODELS

1. 弟は　私の　ケーキを　食べて　しまいました。
   My younger brother ate up all of my cake.

2. つかれて　いましたから、ゆうべは　早く　寝て　しまいました。
   I was tired, so I ended up going to bed early.

3. この　本を　全部　読んで　しまいました。
   I read this entire book.

READ/WRITE/SPEAK Change the word in the (　) to the correct form and choose the correct interpretation of しまいました in the [ ]. Write your answers on a separate sheet of paper.

1. 三時間の　DVDを　全部　(見ます)しまいました。

   [Completion, Regret]

2. よく　練習しましたが、　試合に　(まけます)しまいました。

   [Completion, Regret]

3. げきの　始まる　時間を　(忘れます)しまいました。

   [Completion, Regret]

B Providing Reasons with ですから / だから

Sentence 1 + から、sentence 2。 Sentence 1, so sentence 2.

Sentence 1。ですから、sentence 2。   Sentence 1. Therefore, sentence 2. [Formal]

Sentence 1。だから、sentence 2。   Sentence 1. Therefore, sentence 2. [Informal]

Note: In all cases, the reason must appear first.

MODELS

1. 昨日は　病気でした。ですから、宿題が　出来ませんでした。
   I was sick yesterday. Therefore, I could not do my homework. [Polite and formal]

2. 昨日は　病気でした。だから、宿題が　出来ませんでした。
   I was sick yesterday. Therefore, I could not do my homework. [Polite and informal]

3. 昨日は　病気でしたから、宿題が　出来ませんでした。
   Because I was sick yesterday, I could not do my homework. [Polite]

READ/SPEAK Choose the correct word in the ( ) to complete the sentences.

1. ケン：まりさん、明日　試験が　あります(ですから / だから / から)、
   今日　日本語の　勉強を　手伝って下さい。

2. ケン：先生、昨日　病気で　勉強出来ませんでした。(ですから /
   だから / から)、宿題を　明日　出しても　いいですか。

3. ケン：まりさん、今日　お金を　忘れて　しまいました。(ですから /
   だから / から)、5ドル　かして下さい。

文化ノート Culture Notes

日本の 昔話：花咲爺さん Hanasakajiisan

There once lived a kind old man and woman and their loyal dog Pochi.
One day, Pochi signaled to the old man that he should dig into a certain spot
in the ground. The old man dug, and gold coins burst out from the ground.
Seeing this, a greedy neighbor took Pochi and forced the dog to show him
where to find gold. However, the greedy neighbor only dug up worthless
trash. Angry at Pochi, the greedy neighbor killed him.

The kind old man and his wife were heartbroken and buried the dog, planting a sapling on his grave. The next day, they found a large tree towering over them. They cut down the tree and carved out a mortar to pound *mochi* rice cakes, since Pochi had loved *mochi*. As they pounded, the *mochi* turned into gold coins. The greedy neighbor came to borrow the mortar, but when he pounded *mochi*, the rice turned to trash.

Upset, the greedy neighbor burned the mortar as kindling. The kind old man was saddened and brought some of the ashes home in remembrance of Pochi. Just then, a gust of wind blew some of the ashes onto the shrubs and trees. To his delight, cherry blossoms burst into bloom.

A lord happened to be riding by and was so impressed that he rewarded the old man generously. Seeing this, the greedy neighbor ran home to gather some of the ashes. He climbed a tree and tossed the ashes onto the branches, but to his dismay, nothing happened, and the ashes blew into the eyes of the lord. The lord was very upset and punished the greedy neighbor.

 What lesson does the story of *Hanasakajiisan* teach? If this story were told in your country in contemporary times, how would the details change? Rewrite the story with the changed details and record it for others to listen to.

Language Note

Onomatopoeia

チューチュー

The Japanese language is filled with onomatopoetic expressions. Although many represent actual sounds, others are used as adverbs to describe actions, states, or feelings.

There are two categories of onomatopoetic expressions. The first describes actual sounds and is broken into two types, ぎせい語 (sounds made by living things), such as the cries of animals, and ぎおん語 (sounds made by inanimate things), such as the sound of a screeching car. For these types of words, *katakana* is generally used. The names チュー子 and チューきち are derived from the Japanese onomatopoetic cries of mice, which if you remember, is チューチュー.

The second category is ぎたい語, which express what one observes or feels through non-auditory means, or describe actions or emotions that do not necessarily involve sounds. An example would be にこにこ、which is used to describe a smile. For ぎたい語, *hiragana* is generally used. Look up some common English onomatopoeia and find the Japanese equivalents.

アクティビティー Communicative Activities

ペアワーク

A. READ/WRITE Match the pictures on the next page with the onomatopoetic words in the box. If you are unsure, make an educated guess. Write your answers on a separate sheet of paper.

ガリガリ,	フワフワ,	ギラギラ,	ザーザー,	ピューピュー,	ドキドキ

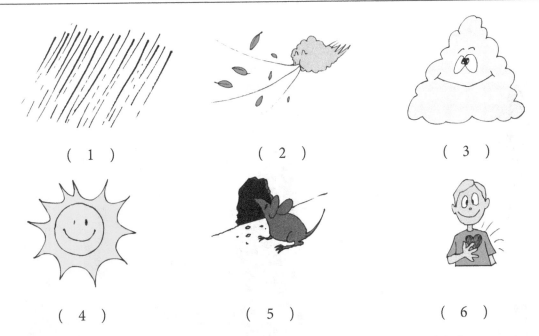

(1)   (2)   (3)

(4)   (5)   (6)

B. READ/SPEAK/LISTEN Convert the following sentences into the TE しまいました form. Your partner should comment using one of the expressions from the choices below. Take turns.

Ex. 宿題を　全部　しました。

Aさん: 宿題を　全部　して　しまいました。

Bさん: それは　良かったですねえ。

Choices: 「良かったですねえ。」「ざんねんでしたねえ。」「大変でしたね。」

1. 本を　全部　(読みました)。
2. 犬が　私の　宿題を　(食べました)。
3. 漢字も　単語も　全部　(おぼえました)。
4. 英語の　レポートを　(書きました)。
5. スマートフォンを　(なくしました)。
6. ポケットに　あなを　(開けました)。

WORKBOOK page 115

会話 <ruby>かいわ</ruby> Dialogue

🔊 **READ/LISTEN** What are Mari and Ken talking about? Who said what?

チュウ子の　お父さんは　何と　言いましたか。

お父さんは　「だめ　だめ」と　言いましたよ。

文型 <ruby>ぶんけい</ruby> Sentence Patterns

READ Find this sentence pattern in the dialogue.

マイクさんは　「おはよう」と　言いました。　　Mike said, "Good morning."

単語 Vocabulary

いっしょうけんめい
1. 一生懸命

with one's utmost effort

いっしょうけんめい　べんきょうして　います。

He is studying with his utmost effort.

2. とんでもない(です)。

That's impossible.

Don't mention it!

3. なるほど。

Indeed. I see.

4. 「〜」と　言いました。

(Someone) said, "〜."

と is a quotation particle.

5. えっ

Huh?

6. いや(っ)

No

Stronger negation than いいえ.
Used in speaking only.

---

7. 娘〔むすめ〕

(own) daughter, young lady

むすめさん (someone else's) daughter, young lady [polite]

8. 息子〔むすこ〕

(one's own) son

むすこさん (someone else's) son

追加単語 Additional Vocabulary

1. 主人　(own) husband; master [Lit., "main person"]

2. ご主人　(someone else's) husband

3. 家内　(own) wife [Lit., "inside the house"]

4. 奥さん　(someone else's) wife, a middle aged lady [Lit., "inner, far back"]

読みましょう　Language in Context

READ/LISTEN/SPEAK Read these sentences in Japanese. Using the same grammatical form as the caption, say how Yui, (the little girl in the picture on the left) would introduce her mother.

ゆう子さんは
「私の　娘です。」と　言いました。

桃太郎が　「こんにちは。」と
言っています。

文法 Grammar

A Quotation Marker と

「　　」と　言いました。

と is a particle used to mark a quotation. It follows the quotation. In Japanese, the marks 「　」 are the equivalent of English quotation marks " ".

(((MODELS

1. 父は　「今日は　遅く　帰るよ。」と　言いました。

   Dad said, "I will be home late today."

2. 友達は　「映画に　行かない。」と　言いました。

   My friend said, "I won't go to the movies."

READ/SPEAK Choose the character who would most likely say the following quotes.

1. (チュウ吉　/　お日様　/　風さん)は　「チュウ子さんと　結婚したいんです。」と　言いました。

2. (お日様　/　風さん　/　かべさん)は　「くもさんは　私を　かくしてしまいます。」と　言いました。

3. (お日様　/　くもさん　/　かべさん)は　「風さんは　私を　ふきとばして　しまいます。」と　言いました。

文化ノート Culture Notes

日本の　昔話：浦島太郎 Urashimataro

One day, Urashimataro, a young man from a fishing village in Japan, came upon a group of boys mistreating a young sea turtle on the beach. Urashimataro, a kind fellow, convinced the boys to stop torturing the sea turtle and gently sent it back into the sea.

The next day, as Urashimataro was out on his boat, he was greeted by a large sea turtle and the young sea turtle he had rescued. The larger sea turtle expressed her gratitude to Urashimataro and invited him to visit the undersea kingdom. They descended deep into the ocean and arrived at the Palace of the Dragon God. The young sea turtle, now a beautiful princess, greeted him. Urashimataro spent time enjoying the music, dance and wonderful food.

After a few days, Urashimataro thought of his mother and asked to be taken home. The sea turtle princess was sad to see Urashimataro go, and presented him with a gift, which he promised never to open. Urashimataro returned to his fishing village and noticed that everything had changed. The people did not recognize him. Indeed, those he spoke with recalled that a long time ago, there once lived a very kind fisherman by the name of Urashimataro. Devastated by the realization that he had been away for many years, Urashimataro decided to open the gift from the sea turtle princess. A puff of cloud emerged and Urashimataro felt his body grow wrinkled and bent, and his hair turned gray. From the sea, he heard, "Urashimataro! You broke your promise – you have now aged!"

 Aspects of the story Urashimataro may remind you of some Western folktales. Identify which stories they remind you of. Create a chart and identify the similarities and differences between the Western stories and Urashimataro. Share your observations with your class using your chart.

Language Note

とんでもない(です)。

This expression may be used in various contexts to mean, "That is impossible" or "That is crazy!" as well as "You're welcome!" or "Don't mention it." It can also be used to deny a compliment or words of praise. Why are Japanese people reluctant to accept praise?

アクティビティー Communicative Activities

ペアワーク

A. SPEAK/LISTEN Ask your partner what he/she wants to do over the weekend. Report to the class what he/she tells you.

質問：この　週末は　どんな　ことを　したいですか。

レポート：～さんは「　　　　　　　　」と　言いました。

B. READ/SPEAK/LISTEN You have a Japanese guest today. Interview him/her by asking the following questions. Your guest answers. Assume that your guest has at least two children.

1. お名前は？
2. お仕事は　何ですか。
3. お子さんが　いらっしゃいますか。
4. お子さんは　むす子さんですか。むすめさんですか。
5. (むす子さん)は　何歳ですか。何年生ですか。
6. (むすめさん)は　どんな　事が　上手ですか。
7. (むす子さん)は　一生けんめい　勉強して　いますか。

C. READ/SPEAK/LISTEN/WRITE Take turns asking your partner who in the story said the following quotes. Write the answers on a separate sheet of paper.

Ex. 質問：だれが「チュウ子さんを 下さい。」

　　　　　と 言いましたか。

　　答え：チュウ吉さんが 「チュウ子さんを

　　　　　下さい。」と 言いました。

質問	答え
1. 「ぼく、一生けんめい 働きます。」	
2. 「えっ、とんでもない。」	
3. 「世界で 一番 えらいのは くもさんですよ。」	
4. 「なるほど。では、くもさんに お願いしましょう。」	
5. 「風さんの 方が 私より もっと えらいです。」	
6. 「世界で 一番 えらいのは ねずみさんですよ。」	

Authentic Reading

D. READ/WRITE This is the first page of a Japanese folktale that you are familiar with. Read the story and answer the following questions in Japanese.

UNDERSTAND

1. What folktale is this?

2. Who are the two main characters?

IDENTIFY

3. What are they doing?

4. What do you think the onomatopoetic expression じゃぶじゃぶ means?

APPLY

5. If you were a character in the story, what would you do at this point and why?

WORKBOOK page 117

むかしむかし、ある所に
おじいさんとおばあさん
が住んでいました。
ある日、おじいさんは山へ
たきぎを取りに行きました。「それでは、
私はせんたくに。」とおばあさんはたらい
をかかえて、川へせんたくに行きました。
おばあさんが川ぎしで、じゃぶじゃぶ
せんたくをしていると、川上から大きい
ももがながれて来ました。

<ruby>会話<rt>かい わ</rt></ruby> Dialogue

🔊 **READ/LISTEN** What did Ken think about the story of the *Mouse Wedding*?

> この　お話を　どう　<ruby>思<rt>おも</rt></ruby>いますか。

> おもしろいと　<ruby>思<rt>おも</rt></ruby>います。

<ruby>文型<rt>ぶんけい</rt></ruby> Sentence Patterns

READ Find this sentence pattern in the dialogue.

Plain Form ＋と　<ruby>思<rt>おも</rt></ruby>います。　　　I think that ～.

<ruby>単語<rt>たん ご</rt></ruby> Vocabulary

1. <ruby>昔<rt>むかし</rt></ruby> <ruby>々<rt>むかし</rt></ruby>

long, long ago

2. ある（ところに）

(at) a certain (place)

ある　日 one day

3. とうとう

finally, at last [after much effort]

4. おしまい

the end

5. 思^{おも}います

[G1 おもう]
to think

6. (Noun/な Adj.)だ

[Plain form of copula
です]

好きだ。I like (you).

7. (Noun/な Adj.)だった

[Plain form of copula
でした]

好きだった。I liked (him/her).

追加単語^{ついかたんご} Additional Vocabulary

1. Sentence ＋ とさ。   and so it is [Used at the end of folktales.]

2. 年取^{としと}った人   an elderly person

読みましょう　Language in Context

🔊 **READ/LISTEN/SPEAK** Read these sentences in Japanese. Study both pictures and give your opinion of them using the と　思います pattern.

エイデン君^{くん}は　お茶^{ちゃ}が　おいしいと
思^{おも}いました。

竹内先生^{たけうち}は　柔道^{じゅうどう}が
とても　上手だと　思います。

A   Indicating Sentence Subjects

Indirect Quotation (Plain Form) ＋と 思います。　　think that 〜

言いました。　said that 〜

答えました。　answered that 〜

聞きました。　heard that 〜 ; asked that 〜

The subject of the sentence (the person who thinks, says, answers, etc.) is usually marked by は.
The subject of the quote, if different from the subject of the sentence, is followed by が.

	Formal form	Plain form	
Verb	行きます	行く	go, will go
	行きません	行かない	do not go, will not go
	行きました	行った	went
	行きませんでした	行かなかった	did not go
い **Adj.**	安いです	安い	is cheap
	安くないです	安くない	is not cheap
	安かったです	安かった	was cheap
	安くなかったです	安くなかった	was not cheap
な **Adj.**	好きです	好きだ	like
	好きじゃ (or では)ありません	好きじゃ (or では)ない	do not like
	好きでした	好きだった	liked
	好きじゃ (or では)ありませんでした	好きじゃ (or では)なかった	did not like
Noun	学生です	学生だ	is a student
	学生じゃ (or では)ありません	学生じゃ (or では)ない	is not a student
	学生でした	学生だった	was a student
	学生じゃ (or では)ありませんでした	学生じゃ (or では)なかった	was not a student

1. 明日　日本語の　試験が　あると　思います。
   I think there is a Japanese exam tomorrow.

2. 母は　今　四十五歳だと　思います。
   I think my mother is 45 years old now.

3. この　話は　おもしろいと　思います。
   I think this story is interesting.

4. 父は　前　ピアノが　上手だったと　聞きました。
   I heard that my father was good at the piano before.

5. 私は　パーティーへ　行かないと　言いました。
   I said that I will not go to the party.

READ/SPEAK Change the word in the (　) into the correct form.

1. 父は　今　(五十歳です)　と　思います。

2. 父は　大学に　(行きませんでした)　と　言いました。

3. 父の　家族は　むかし　(びんぼうでした)　と　聞きました。

4. 父の　お父さんは　あまり(えらくありませんでした)　と　聞きました。

5. 父は　明日　五十一歳に　(なります)　と　思います。

文化ノート　Culture Notes

A. 日本の昔話：かぐや姫 Princess Kaguya

There once was a poor old bamboo cutter and his wife who had always wished for a child. One day the old bamboo cutter came upon a bamboo stalk which seemed to be aglow. He cut into it and found a tiny baby girl inside. To his further surprise, golden coins gushed out from the bamboo stalk. The old man took the baby and the gold back to his home. He and his wife named the baby Princess Kaguya.

As the years passed, Princess Kaguya grew in beauty and grace. Many young suitors heard rumors of Princess Kaguya's beauty and came from far and wide to request her hand in marriage. The Princess agreed only to marry them if they could complete an impossible task; to bring her the bowl of the Buddha, and a jewel from a dragon's neck, among many more fabled items. The suitors, finding the tasks impossible, attempted to trick Princess Kaguya with fake items, but she was not fooled. Finally, the Emperor himself came to Princess Kaguya and begged her to marry him. She refused him also, saying, "I am not of this world. I cannot marry you, or anyone."

Every night thereafter Princess Kaguya would look up at the moon and cry. This went on for many months until finally she revealed to the old bamboo cutter and his wife that she was a princess of the moon, and that she would soon have to return to her birthplace and leave her life on Earth. She told them that the moon warriors would soon arrive to escort her. The old man and woman were deeply saddened by this news, which also reached the ears of the Emperor. He immediately called upon his soldiers to ward off the invaders.

When the moon warriors arrived with a carriage to carry the princess back home, the Emperor's soldiers attempted to attack them. However, they were blinded by the moon warriors' brilliance as they approached Earth. As the Emperor's soldiers lay defeated, Princess Kaguya, in her dazzling moon carriage, sadly departed from Earth.

B. Paper Storytelling かみしばい

Although rarely seen in Japan anymore, かみしばい, paper storytelling (large paper panel illustrations slid into a wooden frame) was a popular form of entertainment for children in the early 1900's. The かみしばい storytellers would call children to street corners with wooden clappers and those who purchased candies could sit in the best seats.

After the advent of television, かみしばい lost popularity. It is said, however, that modern まんが and アニメ originate from かみしばい.

 In a group, research another Japanese folktale and create your own かみしばい. Tell the story to your class in the traditional かみしばい storyteller fashion.

アクティビティー　Communicative Activities

ペアワーク

A. READ/SPEAK/LISTEN Each of the following is a scene from a popular Japanese folktale. Ask your partner which story each scene comes from. The folktale titles are listed below.

しつもん　　　　　　　　　むかし
質問：この　昔話は　何の　お話ですか。

Choices:

かぐやひめ	うらしまたろう	はなさかじいさん	ももたろう

（1）　　　　　　　　（2）　　　　　　　（3）　　　　　　　（4）

B. READ/SPEAK/LISTEN Read the information provided by まり and ケン. Then, take turns asking your partner the questions below. Use the と　言いました structure to answer his/her questions.

Ex.　まり：パーティーに　行きます。

　　　Aさん：まりさんは　パーティーに　行きますか。

　　　Bさん：はい、まりさんは　パーティーに　行くと　言いました。

昨日（きのう）の　宿題（しゅくだい）を　しました。

むかし、ピアノが　好きでした。

私は　今　十六歳です。

私は　いい　子どもでした。

パーティーに　行きました。

おもちが　好きじゃありません。

ぼくは　今　十五歳では　ありません。

ぼくは　いい　子どもでは　ありませんでした。

A.	答え
1. まりさんは　昨日（きのう）の　宿題（しゅくだい）を　しましたか。	
2. まりさんは　むかし　ピアノが　きらいでしたか。	
3. まりさんは　今　十六歳ですか。	
4. まりさんは　悪（わる）い　子どもでしたか。	

B.	答え
1. ケンさんは　パーティーに　行きましたか。	
2. ケンさんは　おもちが　好きですか。	
3. ケンさんは　十五歳ですか。	
4. ケンさんは　いい　子どもでしたか。	

C. READ/WRITE/SPEAK/LISTEN Based on the picture below, ask your partner what he/she thinks each person is about to do. Write the answers on a separate sheet of paper.

Ex. 質問：ゆきさんは　これから　何を　すると　思いますか。

答え：ゆきさんは　これから　泳ぐと　思います。

（魚を　つります to fish）

Now ask your partner what he/she thinks each person did.　Take turns.

Ex. 質問：ゆきさんは　何を　したと　思いますか。

答え：ゆきさんは　泳いだと　思います。

（ひやけを　します to get sunburned）

WORKBOOK　page 119

Lesson 9
Review

Review Questions

🔊 Ask your partner these questions in Japanese. Your partner should answer in Japanese. Check your answers using the audio.

About you   Review page 309

1. How old will you be next year?

2. What grade did you enter (become) this year?

3. In the future (しょうらい), what do you want to become (occupation)?

Folktales   Review pages 320, 325

4. Do you think Japanese folktales are interesting?

5. Among Japanese folktales, which do you like best?

6. Which do you like better, Japanese folktales or American folktales?

Mouse Wedding   Review pages 302–306, 309, 314–315, 320, 325

7. In ねずみのよめいり, who said that he wanted to marry チュウ子?

8. In ねずみのよめいり, what did Chuuko's father say to チュウ吉?

9. In ねずみのよめいり, who was the greatest?

10. Why was the Cloud stronger than the Sun?

11. Why was the Wind stronger than the Cloud?

12. Who (what character) do you want to be in the play? Why?

13. What do you think about the folktale ねずみのよめいり?

Text Chat

You will participate in a simulated exchange of text-chat messages. You should answer as fully and as appropriately as possible. You will have a conversation with Takuya Mori, a Japanese high school student, about Japanese folktales.

03月 07日　08:34 PM

何の　日本の　昔話を
知って　いますか。

Respond and give the details.

03月 07日　08:40 PM

ぼくは　桃太郎の　げきで
さるに　なりました。

Ask a question.

03月 07日　08:46 PM

日本の　昔話と　アメリカの　昔話とど
ちらの　方が　好きですか。

Respond and give a reason.

Can Do!
Now I can . . .

❏ read and perform a Japanese folktale

❏ quote others' statements

❏ express my opinions

❏ talk about elements of traditional Japanese folktales

Japanese Mythology

RESEARCH Use books, the Internet, or interview a Japanese member of your community to answer the following questions.

Determine

1. What is the oldest known literary source of Japanese myths and legends? How old is this source said to be?

2. What are the names of the two mythological deities who are said to be the creators of the islands of Japan?

3. Throughout much of Japan's history, the Imperial Family of Japan was believed to be the descendants of a Sun Goddess. What was her name?

4. What is a *kappa*?

5. What religions are entwined with many Japanese myths?

Compare

6. How is the creation story of your culture (or any other culture you are familiar with) different or similar to the creation story of Japan? Name at least two similarities and two differences.

7. What legends or myths about the sun are there in the Western culture (or any other culture you are familiar with)? Are there any universal themes about the role of the sun in different cultures?

Apply

8. Japan's relationship to its mythological past is still evident in much of the Japanese lifestyle today. Identify and explain at least two ways that Japan's mythological past is reflected in contemporary Japan. Can you think of any practice in your daily life that may be connected to ancient beliefs or myths from your culture or from your family's cultural heritage?

Extend Your Learning
CREATIVITY AND INNOVATION
In a small group, choose a folktale or fable from your own culture and rewrite it in Japanese. Adapt the story to include at least one element of Japanese culture that you have learned about in this lesson. Perform it as a skit for your class.

Giving Directions

✓ Can Do!
In this lesson you will learn to:

- give and follow street directions
- identify common places of interest
- ask for distances and lengths of travel time

Online Resources

cheng-tsui.com/
adventuresinjapanese

- Audio
- Vocabulary Lists
- Vocabulary and *Kanji* Flashcards
- Study Guides
- Activity Worksheets

Let's
Review

In this lesson you will learn how to ask for and give directions. Review these words, phrases, and grammatical structures you already learned to help you talk about getting around.

めいし Nouns

1. 道 (みち)	street, road		6. 次 (つぎ)	next	
2. 右	right (side)		7. 左	left (side)	
3. 建物 (たてもの)	building		8. 二十分くらい	about 20 minutes	
4. 所	place		9. 前 (まえ)	front	
5. かど	corner		10. 後ろ (うし)	behind	

どうし Verbs

11. まがって 下さい [G1 まがる]	please turn
12. 〜が 見えます [G2 見える]	〜 can be seen
13. 行きたいんです [G1 行く/行って]	want to go
14. 行くの [G1 行く]	going [Noun form]
15. 歩いて (ある) [G1 あるく]	walk
16. 歩いて (ある) 行くの [G1 あるいて 行きます]	go on foot [Noun form]

-い けいようし I Adjectives

17. 近い (ちか)	near		19. 高い	tall, high	
18. 白くて	is white [TE Form]		20. 速い (はや)	fast [speed]	

じょし Particles

21. (Place)に (thing)が あります	There is (thing) at (place).
22. 〜から	from 〜
23. (place)を	through, along (place)
24. (Place)で + Action verb	do 〜 at (place)
25. (Direction)に／へ + Direction verb	go 〜 to (direction)
26. (Mode of) transportation で + Direction verb	go by (mode of) transportation

ほかの Others			
27. それから、	And then,	**29.** たぶん	probably
28. 後で	later		

ぶんぽう Grammar	
30. Sentence (plain form) ＋ でしょう。	It is probably ～.
31. Noun 1 と　Noun 2 と(で)　どちらの　方が　～ですか。	Which is more ～, Noun 1 or Noun 2?
32. Noun 1 の方が　Noun 2 より　～です。	Noun 1 is more ～ than Noun 2.

ひょうげん Expressions	
33. ありがとう　ございました。	Thank you very much.
34. どう　いたしまして。	You are welcome.
35. そうですか。	Is that so?
36. そうですねえ ...	Let me see ... Well ...

A. READ/SPEAK Complete the following sentences with the correct particles in the ( ) based on the English sentences.

1. 図書館( )　勉強します。
   I study at the library.

2. 図書館( )　行きたいんですが、図書館( )　どこですか。
   I want to go to the library. Where is the library?

3. あそこ( )　図書館( )　あります。
   There is a library over there.

4. うち( )　近いです。
   It is near my house.

5. 図書館( )　バス( )　行きます。
   I will go to the library by bus.

B. READ/WRITE Write the following sentences in Japanese on a separate sheet of paper.

1. Which is faster, the bus or the train?

2. The train is faster than the bus.

3. The bus is probably slow.

Kanji
used in this lesson

In this lesson, you will learn the *kanji* related to getting around a city.

	Kanji	Meaning	Readings	Examples		
133.	多	many	おお (い) タ	ひと おお 人が多い た ぶん 多分	many people probably	
134.	少	few a little	すく (ない) すこ (し)	くるま 車が すく 少ない すこ 少し	few cars a little	
135.	止	to stop	と (まる)	と 止まって くだ 下さい。	Please stop.	
136.	歩	to walk	ある (く) ホ ポ	ある 歩きたい ほ どう 歩道 さん ぽ 散歩	want to walk sidewalk a walk	
137.	自	oneself	ジ	じ どう しゃ 自動車 じ てん しゃ 自転車 じ ゆう 自由	car bicycle free	
138.	道	road, way	みち ドウ	みち この道 じゅうどう 柔道 しょどう 書道	this road judo calligraphy	

	Kanji	Meaning	Readings	Examples	
139.	物	thing (tangible)	もの ブツ	食た べ物もの 着き 物もの 動どう 物ぶつ	food kimono (things to wear) animal
140.	公	public	コウ	公こう 園えん	park
141.	園	garden	エン	公こう 園えん 動どう 物ぶつ 園えん	park zoo
142.	近	near	ちか(い)	近ちか い所ところ	a near by place

Recognition Kanji

速はや い	fast	動どう 画が	online video
動うご かない	won't move	首くび	neck
動どう 物ぶつ 園えん	zoo		

WORKBOOK page 203

道に　まよいましたか

Are you lost?

あのう...
ちょっと、うかがいますが、
この　へんに　動物園が
ありますか。

ああ、動物園ですか。
ここから、近いですよ。

この　通り(とお)を
まっすぐ　行って、
二番目の　交差点(こうさ)で
右に　まがって
下さい。

あの 白くて 高い
建物(たて)の所ですか。

そうです、そうです。
あの　かどを　右に　まがって
下さい。それから、次の　交差点(こうさ)を
左に　まがると、　動物園の
入口が　見えます。

分かりました。
ありがとう　ございました。

どう
いたしまして。

それから、後で郵便局へ行きたいんですが、ここから歩いてどのぐらいかかりますか。

歩いて二十分ぐらいでしょう。

そうですか。バスで行くのと歩いて行くのとどちらの方が早いですか。

そうですねえ...今道がこんでいますから、多分歩く方が早いでしょうね。

どうもありがとうございました。

どういたしまして。

10課1
Excuse me, I have a question . . .

会話 Dialogue
かいわ

🔊 READ/LISTEN Where does the man want to go?

あのう… ちょっと うかがいますが、

この　へんに 動物園が ありますか。
どうぶつえん

ああ、 動物園ですか。 ここから、 近いですよ。
どうぶつえん

単語 Vocabulary

1. ちょっと うかがいますが . . .

[G1 うかがう]

Excuse me . . . I have a question . . .
うかがう is a humble equiv. of 聞きます

2. (この) へん

(this) area

3. 駐車場
ちゅう じょう
〔ちゅうしゃじょう〕

parking lot

IR ちゅうしゃする to park

4. 動物園
〔とうぶつえん〕
どうぶつえん

zoo

どうぶつ animals

5. 郵便局
〔ゆうびんきょく〕
ゆうびんきょく

post office

ゆうびん mail;
postal service
ゆうびんばこ mailbox

6. 美術館
〔びじゅつかん〕
びじゅつかん

art museum

びじゅつ fine arts

7. 駅
えき

(train/subway) station

8. 空港
くうこう

airport

9. ガソリンスタンド

gas station

ガソリン gas

10. コンビニ

convenience store

11. バス停
てい

bus stop

12. 地図
ちず

map

13. 町
まち

town

14. ああ

Oh!

ついかたんご
追加単語　Additional Vocabulary

むら
1. 村　　　village

2. ビル　　　building [tall, Western style]

の　ば
3. タクシー乗り場　　　taxi stand

こうばん
4. 交番　　　police box

🔊 **READ/LISTEN/SPEAK** Read these sentences in Japanese. Say whether there is a gas station near your school (or in the vicinity of where you are now).

ちょっと　うかがいますが、
このへんに　美術館が　ありますか。

あそこに　ガソリンスタンドが
あります。

文化ノート　Culture Notes

Post Offices

The postal system in Japan is very efficient. Post offices can be found in most cities and towns, and mailboxes are available in convenient areas. Public mailboxes are called ポスト, whereas ゆうびんばこ refers to home mailboxes. Public mailboxes are almost always red-orange in color and are identifiable with the symbol (〒) which resembles a katakana テ. In addition to postal services, such as the mailing of letters and parcels, and selling of stamps, postal services also include savings account services, electronic money transfers, and payments for utility and government bills. ATM machines are also available at post offices.

 Visit your local post office and ask about the services provided there. Do they offer the same services provided by Japanese post offices (money services, insurance, etc.)? Write a short essay comparing the services and functions of post offices in Japan and your own country.

アクティビティー　Communicative Activities

ペアワーク

A. READ/SPEAK/LISTEN Take turns asking your partner whether or not the following places are nearby.

質問：あのう... ちょっと　うかがいますが、この　へんに

　　　　〜が　ありますか。

答え：はい、あります。 or いいえ、ありません。

　　　 or さあ...　知りません。

Places Aさん wants to locate	Places Bさん wants to locate
1. えき	1. バスてい
2. 美じゅつかん	2. と書かん
3. 映画かん	3. くうこう
4. ちゅう車じょう	4. コンビニ
5. ガソリンスタンド	5. ゆうびんきょく

B. READ/SPEAK/LISTEN You want to do the following things.
Your partner suggests where to go.

Ex. I want to buy milk.

質問：牛乳を　買いたいんですが。
答え：じゃ、コンビニへ　行きましょう。

1. おいしい　コーヒーを　飲みたいです。	5. 電車に　のりたいです。
2. 日本に　この　手がみを　おくりたいです。	6. 安い　シャツを　買いたいです。
3. 美しい　えを　見たいです。	7. あたまが　いたくて、くすりが　ほしいです。
4. 車を　ちゅう車したいです。	8. おもしろい　映画を　見たいです。

<ruby>会話<rt>かいわ</rt></ruby> Dialogue

🔊 **READ/LISTEN** How many times must the man turn before he reaches his destination?

<ruby>文型<rt>ぶんけい</rt></ruby> Sentence Patterns

READ Find this sentence pattern in the dialogue.

Verb (Dictionary Form) ＋ と、〜   when, if

右に まがると、動物園が あります。   If you turn right, the zoo will be there.

<ruby>単語<rt>たんご</rt></ruby> Vocabulary

1. <ruby>通<rt>とお</rt></ruby>り
〔とおり〕

street, avenue

2. <ruby>交差点<rt>こうさ</rt></ruby>
〔こうさてん〕

intersection

3. 入口
〔いりぐち〕

entrance

4. 出口
〔でぐち〕

exit

5. <ruby>橋<rt>はし</rt></ruby>
〔はし〕

bridge

6. <ruby>向<rt>む</rt></ruby>こう
〔むこう〕

other side, beyond

7. まっすぐ

straight

8. 〜を　わたる
[G1 **わたります**]

to cross, go over 〜

9. 〜<ruby>側<rt>がわ</rt></ruby>
〔〜がわ〕

〜 side

<ruby>右<rt></rt></ruby>がわ right side, <ruby>左<rt></rt></ruby>がわ left side

10. <ruby>二番目<rt>ばん め</rt></ruby>

second (in order)

11. すると、

thereupon

<ruby>追加単語<rt>ついかたんご</rt></ruby>　Additional Vocabulary

1. <ruby>横断歩道<rt>おうだん</rt></ruby>〔おうだんほどう〕　　　　pedestrian crossing

🔊 **READ/LISTEN/SPEAK** Read these sentences in Japanese. Look at the photo on the right. Imagine what might be on the opposite side of the bridge and say it using the same grammatical form.

この　道を　まっすぐ　行くと、
ゆうびんきょくは　左に　あります。

橋<small>はし</small>を　わたると、右側<small>がわ</small>に
お寺が　あります。

文法<small>ぶんぽう</small>　Grammar

A Conditional "If" Conjunction と

Sentence 1 ＋ と、Sentence 2。　　**When/If/Whenever S1, S2.**

The conditional ("if") conjunction と follows a plain verb, noun, い adjective, or な adjective, either affirmative or negative. Affirmative nouns and な adjectives are followed by だ before と. It is often used to describe scientific principles or mathematical facts, static locations, or explainable natural occurrences. Sentence 2 is a logical or predictable follow-up of the preceding part of the sentence and does not usually express a command, request, suggestion, invitation, or volition. The final tense of Sentence 2 determines the tense of the sentence.

Verb	食べる		eat, will eat
	食べない		do not eat, will not eat
い Adjective	高い		is expensive
	高くない	＋ と	is not expensive
な Adjective	好きだ		like
	好きじゃない or 好きではない		do not like
Noun	学生だ		is a student
	学生じゃない or 学生ではない		is not a student

1. そのかどを 右に まがると、 レストランが ありますよ。
   If you turn right at that corner, there is a restaurant.

2. その橋を わたると、 映画館は すぐ そこですよ。
   If you cross that bridge, the movie theater is right there.

3. 日本語が 上手だと、 いろいろな 仕事が 出来ます。
   If you are good at Japanese, you can do various jobs.

4. 物は 高いと、 だれも 買いません。
   If things are expensive, nobody buys them.

READ/SPEAK Change the verb in the ( ) to the correct form.

1. その かどを 右に (まがります)と、コンビニが あります。

2. この 道を まっすぐ (行きます)と、左側に バス停があります。

3. あの 橋を (わたります)と、銀行は すぐ そこです。

4. 動画は (おもしろくありません)と、だれも 見ません。

5. 公園が (きれいです)と、歩く 人達が 多く なります。

文化ノート Culture Notes

A. Ueno Zoo 上野動物園

The most famous and popular zoo in Japan is undoubtedly Ueno Zoological Gardens, located in Tokyo. As the largest zoo in urban Tokyo, it boasts a wide variety of rare species from around the world. Its most popular attraction, however, is its pandas. The zoo is housed in Ueno Park, known for its picturesque Shinobazu Pond, which features a temple dedicated to the Goddess of Fortune. A five-storied pagoda and a tea ceremony house, as well as numerous museums and art galleries are also located in the park, making it a popular gathering place for cherry blossom-viewing parties in the spring.

B. Osaka Castle　大阪 城
<ruby>大阪<rt>さかじょう</rt></ruby>

Standing near the center of metropolitan Osaka is the grand and
historic Osaka Castle. The main structure is eight stories high, with
five stories visible from the outside, and three stories underground.
It is surrounded by a high, stone foundation which was used as
protection from invaders. Osaka Castle played a role throughout
much of Japan's military history until World War II. It was first constructed by the powerful shogun
Toyotomi Hideyoshi in 1597 and is most famous for its role in the unification of Japan during the
1600's. Today, Osaka Castle houses a museum that showcases the life of the castle, the story of
Toyotomi Hideyoshi, and the history of Osaka.

 Choose to research either Ueno Zoological Gardens or Osaka Castle. Select one aspect of
the site and describe it in Japanese along with a photo. In a small group, put together a
presentation and share it with your class. Be sure to include any new vocabulary words
you may have looked up to help with the presentation.

アクティビティー　Communicative Activities

ペアワーク

A. READ/WRITE Match the following sentences and connect them with と to form one logical and
meaningful sentence. Write your answers on a separate sheet of paper.

Ex:　　　日本へ　冬に　行きます。寒いです。

　　　　日本へ　冬に　行くと、寒いです。

1. 上野動物園に　行きます。	A. コンビニは　右に　あります。
2. 夜　八時です。	B. ドキドキします。
3. バスケットボールの　試合を　見ます。	C. たくさんの　人が　買いに　行きます。
4. 安いです。	D. くらいです。
5. 静かです。	E. 音楽が　よく　聞こえます。
6. 赤信号です。	F. パンダが　見えます。
7. 500メートルくらい　歩きます。	G. 交差点を　わたっては　いけません。

Authentic Reading

B. READ/WRITE Study the bus schedule below and answer the questions that follow in Japanese.

時	分（月曜日～金曜日）					時	分（土曜日・日祝日）			
7	11	21	34	44	55	7	12	26	50	
8	06	18	30	42	55	8	06	21	36	50
9	07	18	31	52		9	06	23	51	
10	13	34	57			10	19	34	49	
11	19	42				11	04	31	47	
12	05	28	49			12	05	17	47	
13	11	36				13	16	44		
14	01	26	52			14	02	23	46	
15	17	34	52			15	11	32	45	58
16	18	38	52			16	18	31	49	
17	09	26	41	54		17	17	45		
18	05	18	32	44	58	18	04	21	37	
19	22	45				19	06	23	36	52
20	06	29	51			20	18	47		
21	14	38				21	15	38		

31号【翠町】線　運行予定時刻表
比治山下・広島駅方面ゆき　※お忘れ物等のお問合わせ先
大州営業所 TEL(082)-281-9148
平成24年8月24日改正

広島バス㈱　　　　　上　段原中央

UNDERSTAND

1. Does the bus run every day?

2. On Wednesdays, what time does the first bus arrive?
   What time does the last bus arrive?

3. Does the bus run on the same schedule on weekends as weekdays?

IDENTIFY

4. What do you think 祝日 means?

APPLY

5. If you wanted to catch the bus by 1:30 pm on a weekday,
   how many buses would be available? How many buses would
   be available if it were a weekend or a holiday?

WORKBOOK page 129

10課3
Which is faster, to go by bus or to walk?

<ruby>会話<rt>かいわ</rt></ruby> Dialogue

🔊 READ/LISTEN What information does the Japanese tourist want to know?

<ruby>郵便局<rt>ゆうびんきょく</rt></ruby>は バスで 行くのと 歩いて 行くのと、どちらの 方が 早いですか。

バスで 行く 方が 早いでしょう。

<ruby>単語<rt>たんご</rt></ruby> Vocabulary

1. ～から ～まで
どのぐらい かかりますか。

How long does it take from ～ to ～? [Time]

2. ～から ～まで
どのぐらい ありますか。

How far is it from ～ to ～? [Distance]

<ruby>追加単語<rt>ついかたんご</rt></ruby> Additional Vocabulary

1. マイル　　　　mile(s)
2. キロ　　　　　kilometer(s)
3. メートル　　　meter(s)

4. センチ(メートル)　　centimeter(s)
5. ミリ(メートル)　　　millimeter(s)

🔊 **READ/LISTEN/SPEAK** Read these sentences in Japanese. Tell a partner how long it takes to get from your home to the nearest supermarket walking or by car.

うちから　駅(えき)まで　歩いて
15分ぐらい　かかります。

ここから　出口まで　あと
300メートルです。

文化ノート(ぶんか)　Culture Notes

A. Asking for Directions

The Japanese are usually very helpful when foreigners ask them for directions. Don't be surprised if they even accompany you to your destination! Police boxes (こうばん) are located conveniently throughout cities and villages and are good places to ask for directions. In certain cities such as Tokyo, knowing the address of a place is not necessarily helpful, as the numbering of addresses is not always systematic. In urban areas, there are also many people on the streets who may not necessarily know the area well. Therefore, it is best to stop at the police box and ask for assistance. Typically, the police box will have a very detailed map of the vicinity.

Information centers are also commonly found near stations and popular attractions. Maps and information about transportation systems in the area are available at these centers.

Recently, many phone apps (アプリ) are available to direct both natives and foreigners to their destinations. Map apps, train and subway system apps, hotel and restaurant guides, shopping apps, and travel guides can help anyone find their way around Japan!

 Find a map app (ちずのアプリ) in Japanese and look at a map of Tokyo. What similarities and differences do you notice between looking at a map app in Japanese and English? Share one difference and one similarity with your classmates.

B. Metric System

Japan uses the metric system, as does most of the world. Here is a conversion chart for distance:

U.S. measurements:	Metric system equivalent:
1 マイル (mile)	1.6 キロ (kilometers)
1 ヤード (yard)	.94 メートル (meters)
1 フィート (feet)	30.5 センチ (centimeters)
1 インチ (inch)	2.54 センチ (centimeters)

 Create a chart similar to the one above for weight, liquid or dry measurement. With the collective information gathered by your class, convert the following data into metric units:

1. Your height
2. The weight of your school bag
3. The amount of water you drink every day
4. Distance between your home and school
5. Amount of flour in two dozen chocolate chip cookies
6. The weight of an object of your choice

Language Note: 早い and 速い

The word はやい in Japanese has two separate usages, as reflected by the *kanji* used for each. 早い (はやい) is used when the time taken to complete a task was shorter than expected. For example, a bus is 早い when it arrives earlier than normal. 速い(はやい) is used to refer to the speed of an action. For example, if you win a race because you run fast, using 速い is appropriate. What are some examples of English words that sound the same but are spelled differently?

アクティビティー Communicative Activities

ペアワーク

A. READ/SPEAK/LISTEN/WRITE Ask your partner how far it is from his/her house to the following places. Record the answers on a separate sheet of paper in a chart like the one on the next page.

Ex. 家から　学校まで
しつもん
質問1：家から　学校まで　どのぐらい　ありますか。
こた
答え1：15マイルぐらいでしょう。
しつもん
質問2：家から　学校まで　どのぐらい　かかりますか。
こた
答え2：車で　30分ぐらい　かかります。

Places	Distance	Time and mode of transportation
Ex. 家から　学校まで	15マイル	車で　30分ぐらい
1. 家から　スーパーまで		
2. 家から　ガソリンスタンドまで		
3. 家から　映画かんまで		
4. 家から　ぎん行まで		
5. 家から　公園まで		

B. READ/SPEAK/LISTEN Take turns asking your partner for directions to the five places not given on your map below. Your partner's map is on the next page. He/she will give you directions. Check your answers to see if you communicated effectively.

Ex. 病院
いん

あのう...　ちょっと
うかがいますが、病院は
いん
どこですか。

病院ですね。寺町通りを　まっすぐ
いん　　　まちどお
行って、次の　交差点を
こう さ
右に　まがると、右側に　病院の
がわ　　　　いん
入口が　あります。

Ask for directions to:
1. 中学校
2. 花屋
   はな
3. レストラン
4. 本屋
5. ちゅう車じょう

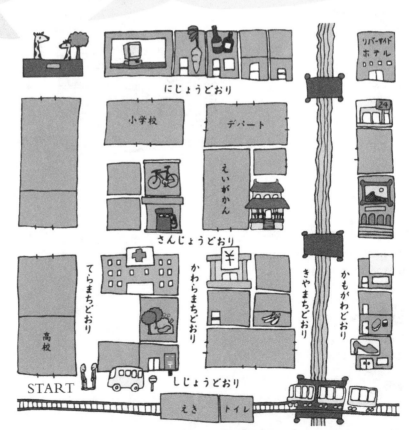

Ex. 病院
いん

あのう... ちょっと
うかがいますが、病院は
いん
どこですか。

病院ですね。寺町 通りを
いん   まちどお
まっすぐ 行って、次の 交差点を
こうさ
右に まがると、右側に 病院の
がわ   いん
入口が あります。

Ask for directions to:

1. 公園

2. カラオケ

3. 高校

4. 映画館
   かん

5. ホテル

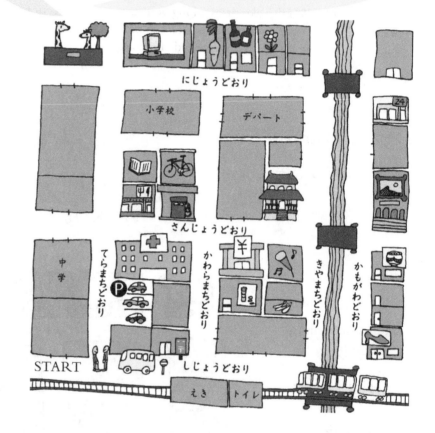

にじょうどおり

小学校   デパート

24

さんじょうどおり

中学   てらまちどおり   ¥   かわらまちどおり   きやまちどおり   かもがわどおり

START   しじょうどおり

えき   トイレ

クラスワーク

C. SPEAK/LISTEN Give directions in Japanese from the front gate of your school to
a nearby location (i.e., supermarket, convenience store, etc.). Have your classmates
guess your destination.

WORKBOOK page 131

 **READ/LISTEN** Where is the man going and what is the fastest way to get there?

<ruby>文型<rt>ぶんけい</rt></ruby> Sentence Patterns

READ Find one of these sentence patterns in the dialogue.

1. V1 (Dict. Form)＋のと　V2 (Dict.)＋のと　どちら／どっち(の方)が～ですか。

    Which is more ～, doing verb 1 or doing verb 2?

2. Verb 1 (Dict. Form)＋方が　Verb 2 (Dict. Form)＋(の)より　～です。

    Doing verb 1 is more ~ than doing verb 2.

3. Verb 1 (Dict. Form)＋のは　Verb 2 (Dict.Form)＋ほど　Negative predicate。

    Doing verb 1 is not as ~ doing verb 2.

1. こんで　います
[G1 こむ]
is crowded

2. すいて　います
[G1 すく]
is not crowded, is empty

ついかたんご
追加単語　Additional Vocabulary

1. ラッシュアワー　　　　　rush hour

こうそくどうろ
2. 高速道路　　　　　　　　freeway [Usually toll.]

読みましょう　Language in Context

🔊 READ/LISTEN/SPEAK　Read these sentences in Japanese. Tell a partner whether it is faster for you to go to school by bus or car.

ラッシュアワーに　道は
とても　こんでいます。

てん
自転車で　行く方が　歩くより
早いです。

文化ノート　Culture Notes

Rush Hour and Traffic

Morning and evening rush hours are challenging for Japanese commuters, particularly in the highly urban areas of Japan. ラッシュアワー on the trains, streets, and highways in Tokyo is perhaps the most extreme. Train and subway commuters are pushed into cars by station employees who work on the station platforms. Rush hour in the cities is generally from 7 to 9 a.m. and from 5 to 7 p.m. Heavy traffic on the streets and highways also commonly occurs on Saturdays, Sundays, and holidays. Large traffic signs are strategically placed on highways

A station attendant helps to push passengers onto a crowded train

leading to major cities to inform motorists where and how long the traffic is backed up. Commuters watch their televisions or check their smartphones for traffic updates on different routes before heading into the city.

Check the Internet for rush hour videos in urban centers in Japan. What advice would be useful for those unfamiliar with rush hour in Japan? Create a short informative video listing three pieces of advice for first time travelers to Japan about rush hour.

文法　Grammar

A Comparing Actions with のと

Verb (Dict. form) ＋のと　**Verb (Dict. form)** ＋のと　どちら／どっち(の方)が
〜ですか。

This pattern is used to compare two actions. The two actions expressed in their dictionary forms are both followed by the nominalizer の. The interrogative (question) word is どちら or どっち, which is always followed by the particle が.

MODELS

1. 外で　食べるのと　家で　食べるのと　どっちの方が　好きですか。
   Which is better, eating out or eating at home?

2. バスで　行くのと　タクシーで　行くのと　どちらの方が　早いですか。
   Which is faster, going by bus or going by taxi?

3. そうですねえ . . .　タクシーの方が　早いでしょう。
   Let's see . . . The taxi is probably faster.

READ/SPEAK Change the verb in the 〔 〕to the correct form, fill in the ( ) with the correct particle, and choose the correct word in the < >.

1. まり：ケン君、うちで　DVDを　〔見ます〕（ ）（ ）　映画館で
   映画を　〔見ます〕（ ）（ ）、<どちら　どっち>の　方が
   好きですか。

2. ケン：すみません。駅へ　行きたいんですが、ここから　バスで
   〔行きます〕（ ）（ ）〔歩きます〕（ ）（ ）、<どちら　どっち>の
   方が　早いですか。

B Subject Marker のは ─────

Verb (Dict. Form)＋のは　　**Verb (Dict. Form)**＋(の)より　〜です。

Verb (Dict. Form)＋(の)より　　**Verb (Dict. Form)**＋のは　〜です。

Verb (Dict. Form)＋方が　　**Verb (Dict. Form)**＋(の)より　〜です。

Verb (Dict. Form)＋(の)より　　**Verb (Dict. Form)**＋方が　〜です。

The two actions expressed in their dictionary forms. The greater action is marked by のは or 方が and the lesser alternative (い/な adjective) is followed by (の)より.

▶)) MODELS ▷

1. はしで　食べるのは　フォークで　食べるより　難しいです。
   It is more difficult to eat with chopsticks than to eat with a fork.

2. バスで　行く方が　歩くより　早いですよ。
   It is quicker to go by bus than to walk.

3. 買い物に　行くより　家に　いる方が　いいです。
   It is better to stay at home than to go shopping.

READ/SPEAK Change the verb in the 〔 〕into the correct form, and choose the correct particle in the ( ). X means no particle. There may be more than one correct answer.

1. 音楽を　〔聞きます〕(の / X)は、テレビを　〔見ます〕(の / X)
   より　好きです。

2. 自転車で　〔行きます〕(方が / より)、〔歩きます〕(方が / より)　早いです。

3. 〔歩きます〕(方が / より)、自転車で〔行きます〕(方が / より)　早いです。

C Negatively Comparing Actions

Verb (Dict. Form) ＋のは **Verb (Dict. Form)** ＋ほど **Negative predicate**。

Two actions may also be compared negatively. Verbs must be placed in their verb dictionary forms. The alternative followed by のは is the action which is not (い adjective / な adjective). The predicate must appear in its negative form. Often, this pattern is also used with the subject clause "as you think" or "as someone says." This clause precedes ほど in the dictionary form.

))) MODELS

1. 日本語を 話すのは 聞くほど 難しくありません。
   Speaking Japanese is not as difficult as hearing (understanding) it.

2. バスで 学校へ 行くのは 車で 行くほど 早くありません。
   Going to school by bus is not as fast as going by car.

3. 数学は あなたが 言うほど やさしくないです。
   Math is not as easy as you say.

READ/SPEAK Change the verb in the 〔 〕into the correct form, and choose the correct particle in the ( ). X means no particle. There may be more than one correct answer.

1. 漢字を 〔読みます〕(の / X)は、漢字を 〔書きます〕(の / X)
   (より / ほど) むずかしくないです。

2. 〔歩きます〕(の X)は、〔走ります〕(の / X) (より / ほど)
   速くないです。

3. 日本語を 〔話します〕(の / X)は スペイン語を
   〔話します〕(の / X) (より / ほど) 難しいです。

4. 高校の 後、大学へ 〔行きます〕(の / X)と 〔働きます〕(の / X)
   と、どっちの方が いいですか。

5. 大学へ 〔行きます〕(の / X)方が いいです。

6. 映画館で 映画を 〔見ます〕(の / X) 方が うちで DVDを
   〔見ます〕(の / X)より 好きですか

7. うちで DVDを〔見ます〕(の / X)は 映画館で 映画を 〔見ます〕
   (の / X)ほど 好きでは ありません。

アクティビティー　Communicative Activities

ペアワーク

A. READ/SPEAK/LISTEN Using the cues below, ask your partner which
means of transportation is faster. Assume that school is the starting
point. Answer based on fact. Take turns.

Ex. 映画館, 歩いて　行く, バスで　行く

質問：すみません、映画館へ　行きたいんですが、歩いて　行くのと

　　　　　バスで　行くのと　どちらの方が　早いですか。

答え：バスで　行く方が　歩いて　行くより　早いです。

1. 病院, 友達の　車で　行く, タクシーで　行く

2. ショッピングセンター, 車で　行く, バスで　行く

3. くうこう, バスで　行く, タクシーで　行く

4. 公園, 自てん車で　行く, 歩いて　行く

5. コンビニ, 歩いて　行く, バスで　行く

B. READ/SPEAK/LISTEN Ask your partner which he/she likes more using のと. He/she should
answer using 〜ほど. Take turns.

Ex. スポーツを　見る or スポーツを　する

質問：スポーツを　見るのと、　するのと　どちらの方が　好きですか。

答え：スポーツを　するのは　スポーツを　見るほど

　　　　　好きではありません。

1. 買物に　行く or 家で　テレビを　見る

2. 本を　読む or テレビゲームで　あそぶ

3. およぐ or バスケットボールを　する

4. 映画かんで　映画を　見る or 家で　DVDを　見る

5. 家で　食べる or レストランで　食べる

Authentic Reading

C. READ/WRITE/SPEAK/LISTEN Follow the Japanese GPS navigation route carefully and answer the questions below.

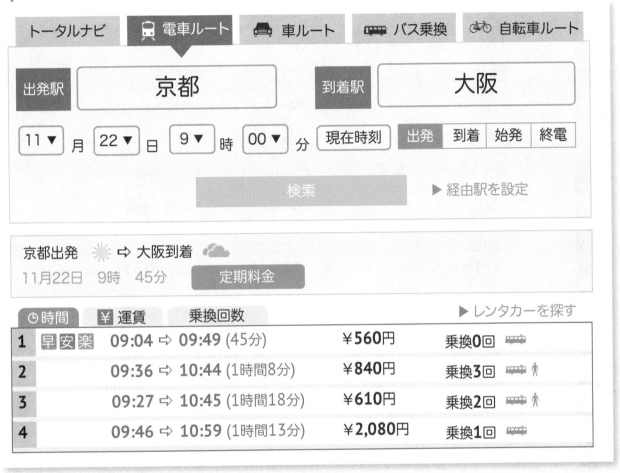

UNDERSTAND

1. What is the traveler's final destination?

2. When is he/she planning to leave?

3. Does he/she plan to go by bus, train, bicycle, or car?

IDENTIFY

4. What time should he/she leave to get there the fastest?

5. What is the cost of the most expensive ticket? The least expensive?

6. What do you think 乗換3回 means?

APPLY

7. If you were to choose one of these routes, which one would you choose and why?

WORKBOOK page 133

 Ask your partner these questions in Japanese. Your partner should answer in Japanese. Check your answers using the audio.

Directions   Review pages 338–339, 344

1. Excuse me, may I ask a question? Is there (an art museum) in this area?

2. I want to go to the university. Where is the bus stop?

3. Where is the hospital? Please show [use "teach"] it to me on this map.

4. When you go out (exit) from this building, what can you see?

Distances and Times   339, 344–345, 348, 355–357

5. I want to go to the convenience store. Which is faster, riding a bus or going on foot (by walking)?

6. How long does it take (to get) from (your) home to school?

7. About how far is it from (your) home to school?

8. Which is closer, going from here to the convenience store, or going from here to the post office?

9. If it is one mile, how many kilometers is it?

Your opinions   Review pages 344–345, 354–357

10. Which is better, writing with (your) right hand, or writing with (your) left hand?

11. When the traffic light is red, do you cross the street?

12. Is your classroom empty right now? Is it crowded?

Text Chat

You will participate in a simulated exchange of text-chat messages. You should respond as fully and as appropriately as possible. You will have a conversation with Takahiro Kojima, a visiting Japanese high school student, about your town.

03月 30日　10:12 PM

うちから　学校まで　どのぐらい
かかりますか。

Respond and give the details.

03月 30日　10:17 PM

うちから　学校まで　バスで
行くのと、自転車で　行くのと
どちらの　方が　早いですか。

Respond and give a reason.

03月 30日　10:24 PM

私は　週末に　なると、いつも
友達と　映画を　見に　行きます。

Comment and ask a question.

Can Do!
Now I can . . .

☐ give and follow street directions

☐ identify common places of interest

☐ ask for distances and lengths of travel time

Project Corner

うらない "Fortune-telling" Toy

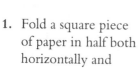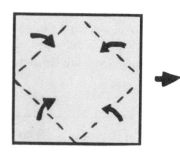

1. Fold a square piece of paper in half both horizontally and vertically.

2. Open up to the original square.

3. Fold each corner to the center along the creases.

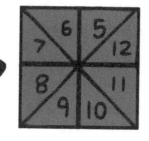

4. Turn the square over.

5. Fold each corner again toward the center so each corner meets at the center.

6. Number each triangle 5–12. Write a fortune on the reverse side of each triangle numbered 5–12.

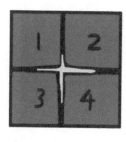

7. Turn over and write the numbers 1–4 on each square.

8. Open up the folded toy as shown. Place thumbs and forefingers under each pocket and open and close.

9. With a partner, take turns choosing numbers while the toy is being held in an open or closed position. Read each other's fortunes and enjoy!

日本料理
りょう り

Japanese Cooking

 Can Do!

In this lesson you will learn to:

- explain how to cook a simple dish
- communicate about things or actions done in excess
- describe a change of state

Online Resources

cheng-tsui.com/
adventuresinjapanese

- Audio
- Vocabulary Lists
- Vocabulary and *Kanji* Flashcards
- Study Guides
- Activity Worksheets

In this lesson you will learn how to cook a popular Japanese dish. Review these words, phrases, and grammatical structures you already learned to help you talk about the preparation of food.

めいし Nouns

1. 物〔もの〕	thing [tangible]	3. いっぱい	full
2. おなか	stomach	4. ぜんぶ	everything

どうし Verbs

5. 作り [G1 つくる]	make (stem form)
6. 教えて　下さい [G2 おしえる]	please teach me
7. 入れます [G2 いれる]	put in
8. 洗って [G1 あらう]	wash
9. なります [G1 なる]	become
10. 食べましょう [G2 たべる]	let's eat
11. 食べて　みましょう [G2 たべる]	let's try eating

-い けいようし I Adjectives

12. おいしそう〔おいしい〕	looks delicious

ふくし Adverbs

13. あつく〔あつい〕	hot	16. ちょっと	a little
14. よく	often, well	17. もう　少し	a little more
15. 小さく	small		

Others

18. どんな〜	what kind of 〜	**22.** このくらい？	This much?
19. そして、	And	**23.** どうですか。	How is it?
20. それから、	And then,	**24.** でも、	However,
21. どのくらい？	About how much?		

Expressions

25. そうですねえ . . .	Let me see . . .
26. じゃ、	Then, [Informal of では]
27. えっ、	What?
28. いただきます。	[Expression used before a meal]
29. はい、どうぞ。	Please go ahead (and eat).
30. ごちそうさま。	[Expression used after a meal]

ぶんぽう Grammar

31. 〜や〜や〜など	〜 and 〜 and 〜 etc.

WRITE Write out what Ken and Mari are saying in each scene using the words, phrases, and grammatical structures you reviewed above.

1.

2.

3.

Kanji
used in this lesson

In this lesson, you will learn the *kanji* used to describe cooking and cleaning.

	Kanji	Meaning	Readings	Examples	
143.	鳥	bird	とり	<ruby>小<rt>ちい</rt></ruby>さい<ruby>鳥<rt>とり</rt></ruby> — a small bird	
144.	台	counter counter for machine	タイ ダイ	<ruby>台<rt>たい</rt></ruby><ruby>風<rt>ふう</rt></ruby> — typhoon <ruby>台<rt>だい</rt></ruby><ruby>所<rt>どころ</rt></ruby> — kitchen <ruby>二<rt>に</rt></ruby><ruby>台<rt>だい</rt></ruby>の<ruby>車<rt>くるま</rt></ruby> — two cars	
145.	洗	to wash	あら(う) セン	<ruby>皿<rt>さら</rt></ruby>を<ruby>洗<rt>あら</rt></ruby>う — wash dishes <ruby>洗<rt>せん</rt></ruby><ruby>濯<rt>たく</rt></ruby>する — do laundry	
146.	作	to make	つく(る) サク	<ruby>作<rt>つく</rt></ruby>って<ruby>下<rt>くだ</rt></ruby>さい。 — Please make <ruby>作<rt>さく</rt></ruby><ruby>文<rt>ぶん</rt></ruby> — composition	
147.	使	to use	つか(う)	<ruby>辞<rt>じ</rt></ruby><ruby>書<rt>しょ</rt></ruby>の<ruby>使<rt>つか</rt></ruby>い<ruby>方<rt>かた</rt></ruby> — how to use a dictionary	
148.	知	to get to know	し(る)	<ruby>知<rt>し</rt></ruby>らない — I don't know	

	Kanji	Meaning	Readings		Examples	
149.	料	materials	リョウ	りょうり 料 理	cooking	米 + 🔑 → 斗 ＝料
150.	理	arrangement	リ	りょうり 料 理	cooking	王 + 田 + 土 ＝ 理
151.	長	long	なが(い)	なが みち 長い 道	a long road	🐚 → 長 → 長
152.	室	room	シツ	きょうしつ 教 室	classroom	⌂ → 宀 + 一 + レ + 土 ＝室

<table>
<tr><th colspan="3">New Reading</th><th colspan="2">Recognition Kanji</th></tr>
<tr><td>38.</td><td>生</td><td>raw　なま　<ruby>生卵<rt>なまたまご</rt></ruby>　a raw egg</td><td><ruby>本当<rt>ほん とう</rt></ruby></td><td>true</td></tr>
</table>

WORKBOOK page 207

まりさんと ケンさんの 料理　Cooking with Mari and Ken

すきやきの
作り方を　知って
いますか。

はい、
知って　いますよ。

じゃ、教えて　下さい。
始<small>はじ</small>めに　何を　しますか。

まず、
おなべを　熱<small>あつ</small>くして
あぶらを　入れて
下さい。

どんな　物を
入れますか。

そうですねえ…

牛肉や　糸こんにゃくや
野菜<small>やさい</small>などを　入れます。

ぼくが
切<small>き</small>りましょうか。

おねがいします。
牛肉は　うすく
切って、

そして、
野菜は　よく　洗って、
小さく　切って
下さいね。

糸こんにゃくは
半分に　切って
下さい。

それから、
牛肉を　入れて、
さとうと　しょうゆを
入れます。

どのくらい
入れますか。

このくらいですか。
味は　どうですか。

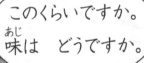

ちょっと　からすぎますね。
もう　少し　さとうを　入れて、
あまく　しましょう。
おいしく　なりますよ。

では、少し　入れます。

出来ましたよ。

To read an informal version of the conversation, go to cheng-tsui.com/adventuresinjapanese

会話　Dialogue
かいわ

🔊 **READ/LISTEN** Does Ken know how to make *sukiyaki*? Does Mari know how to make it?

すきやきの
作り方を　知って
いますか。

はい、知って
いますよ。

じゃ、教えて
下さい。

文型　Sentence Patterns
ぶんけい

READ Find this sentence pattern in the dialogue.

すきやきの　作り方　　　　　　　　　how to make *sukiyaki*

車の　運転の　し方　　　　　　　　how to drive a car
　　うんてん

単語　Vocabulary

1. 作り方
つく

how to make

2. すきやき

sukiyaki

3. 牛肉

beef

4. 豚肉
ぶた

pork

5. 鳥肉
とり
chicken (meat)

6. 卵
たまご
egg

7. 野菜
や さい
vegetable

8. 果物
く だ
fruit

9. 苺
いちご
strawberry

10. 糸こんにゃく
いと
shredded *konnyaku*

grey or transparent tuber root gelatin

11. 台 所
だいどころ
kitchen

追加単語　Additional Vocabulary
ついかたんご

1. 材 料　ingredients
ざいりょう

2. カップ　cup (measurement)

3. 大さじ　tablespoon
おお

4. 小さじ　teaspoon
こ

5. 二分の一　1/2
にぶん

6. まぜます [G2]　to mix [transitive]

7. トマト
tomato

8. じゃがいも
potato

9. にんじん
carrot

10. たまねぎ
round onion

11. きゅうり
cucumber

12. なす
eggplant

13. キャベツ
cabbage

14. レタス
lettuce

15. セロリ
celery

16. ピーマン
bell pepper

17. れんこん
lotus root

18. ねぎ   **19.** ほうれんそう   **20.** まめ   **21.** だいこん   **22.** ごぼう   **23.** りんご

green onion   spinach   peas; beans   radish   burdock   apple

24. オレンジ   **25.** グレープ   **26.** みかん   **27.** (よう)なし   **28.** さくらんぼ   **29.** すいか
                 フルーツ   or チェリー

orange   grapefruit   tangerine   (Western) pear   cherry   watermelon

30. バナナ   **31.** パイナップル   **32.** もも   **33.** ぶどう   **34.** メロン   **35.** かき

banana   pineapple   peach   grapes   melon   persimmon

読みましょう　Language in Context

🔊 **READ/LISTEN/SPEAK** Read these sentences in Japanese. Are you able to ride a motorcycle? Say whether you know or don't know how to ride one.

たまごやきの　作り方は
難（むずか）しいですね。

オートバイの　運転（うんてん）の　し方を
習（なら）っています。

A Verb Modifier 方〔かた〕

Something の **Verb [Stem form]** ＋ 方〔かた〕

When 〜方〔かた〕 is attached to a verb stem, it becomes a noun that is translated as "how to do (such and such)." Nouns preceding V-stem ＋ 方 must be followed by の.

 MODELS

1. すき焼きの　作り方を　教えて　下さい。
   Please teach me how to make *sukiyaki*.

2. 「この　漢字の　書き方を　知って　いますか。」
   "Do you know how to write this Chinese character?"

   「いいえ、知りません。」
   "No, I don't know (how)."

3. 漢字の　辞書の　使い方を　習いたいです。
   I want to learn how to use the *kanji* dictionary.

READ/SPEAK Fill in the ( ) with the correct particle and change the verb in [ ] to the correct form.

1. おはし(　)　[持ちます]方を　教えて下さい。

2. すきやき(　)　料理(　)　[します]方を　知っていますか。

3. 私は　ラーメン(　)　[作ります]方だけ　知っています。

4. 日本語(　)　勉強(　)　[します]方が　まだ　よく　分かりません。

文化ノート Culture Notes

すきやき Sukiyaki

Along with すし and てんぷら, すきやき is probably one of the most readily identifiable "Japanese" dishes. It is a relatively modern dish that has been in existence for only about a century, from around the time Japanese people began consuming beef.

すきやき is a type of なべもの or hot pot dish typically eaten during the colder months. The cooking of すきやき begins with preparing thin slices of beef, and a variety of ingredients, such as mushrooms, Chinese cabbage, tofu, leeks, and いとこんにゃく see pg. 372. The ingredients are boiled in a heavy pot called a なべ, which is heated on a small gas stove at the center of the table.

The かんさい (Western) and かんとう (Eastern) regions of Japan prepare すきやき differently. In かんさい, all of the ingredients are cooked together in a soup base called わりした that may be made of soy sauce, sugar, *mirin*, and sake. In かんとう, the beef is first grilled in the pot, and then seasoned with soy sauce and sugar. After the vegetables are cooked, a little sake and some water are added. After all of the food in the なべ is allowed to cook, those around the table enjoy the food in the pot. Dipping the hot foods from the pot in scrambled raw egg before consuming it is common.

 Search the Internet for other kinds of なべもの dishes. How are they different from すきやき? Find a photo of a different kind of なべもの, print it and write a short caption of the ingredients and how it is prepared in Japanese.

アクティビティー　Communicative Activities

クラスのみんなでビンゴゲーム

A. READ/WRITE/LISTEN Create a 5 x 5 Bingo style chart on a separate sheet of paper using the words below. Choose a classmate to call out the words in Japanese and play until someone wins with five consecutive words in a line (horizontal, vertical, or diagonal).

すきやき	牛肉	いちご	糸こんにゃく	台所
しゃぶしゃぶ	ぶた肉	りんご	にんじん	おさら
やき肉	鳥肉	みかん	いも	コップ
どんぶり	たまご	メロン	たまねぎ	ナイフ
うどん	かい (shellfish)	ようなし	レタス	フォーク
すし	やさい	バナナ	トマト	スプーン
ラーメン	くだ物	すいか	きゅうり	はし

ペアワーク

B. READ/SPEAK/LISTEN/WRITE Choose a dish below and ask your partner what you need to make each dish. He/she tells you the ingredients. Write them in Japanese on a separate sheet of paper.

Ex. ハムサンド

質問：ハムサンドを　作りたいんですが、何が　いりますか。

答え：ハムと　パンと　レタスが　いります。

Menu A	Menu B
1. たまごサンド	1. サラダ
2. フルーツサラダ	2. ハンバーガー
3. (Your choice)	3. (Your choice)

Authentic Reading

C. READ/WRITE Look at the prices of a melon at a Japanese supermarket and answer the following questions in Japanese on a separate sheet of paper.

UNDERSTAND

1. How much does this melon cost in yen?

2. How much does this melon cost in dollars? Check the conversion rate on the Internet.

3. Is this melon more expensive than a similar melon in your country?

IDENTIFY

4. The price in black is the price you pay at the register. How much is the tax on this melon?

APPLY

5. Would you buy this melon for yourself? Why or why not?

ペアワーク

D. READ/SPEAK/LISTEN/WRITE Create a chart like the one below on a separate sheet of paper. Ask your partner if he/she knows how to do the following things, then check the YES or NO column.

Ex. おすしの　作り方

質問：おすしの　作り方を　知って　いますか。

答え：はい、知って　います。or いいえ、知りません。

質問	はい	いいえ
1. ギターの　ひき方		
2. 車の　うんてんの　し方		
3. おはしの　使い方		
4. 料理の　し方		
5. すきやきの　作り方		
6. 日本の　着物の　着方		
7. サーフィンの　し方		
8. 漢字の　じ書の　使い方		
9. 洗たくの　し方		

WORKBOOK　page 141

会話 かいわ Dialogue

🔊 **READ/LISTEN** What is the first step in making *sukiyaki*?

始めに 何を しますか。

まず、おなべを 熱く して 下さい。

文型 ぶんけい Sentence Patterns

READ Find one of these sentence patterns in the dialogue.

1. 熱く ＋します。 (I) will make (it) hot. [I will heat it.]
2. きれい＋に＋します。 (I) will make (it) clean. [I will clean it.]
3. 小さく きって 下さい。 Please cut (them) small.
4. 半分に きって 下さい。 Please cut (them) in half.

単語 たんご Vocabulary

1. なべ

pot, pan

2. あぶら

oil

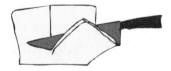

3. うすく

thin

Adverbial form of うすい

4. 厚く
（あつ）

thick

Adverbial form of あつい

5. 半分に
（はんぶん）

(in) half

半分 a half [noun]

6. 切る
（き）

[G1 きります]

to cut; slice

7. 熱く　します
（あつ）

to make hot; to heat

8. きれいに　します

to make clean; to clean

9. まず

First of all

10. 始めに
（はじ）

at the beginning

11. 次に
（つぎ）

next [Adverb]

12. 終わりに
（お）

at the end

追加単語　Additional Vocabulary
（ついかたんご）

1. フライパン　　　　　frying pan

2. ふっとうします [IR]　to boil

3. おきます [G1]　　　　to put; to place

4. おします [G1]　　　　to push; to press

5. その　後で　　　　　after that

6. その間　　　　　　　meanwhile
（あいだ）

READ/LISTEN/SPEAK Read these sentences in Japanese. Think of one of your favorite restaurants. Say what dish/food they are skilled at making.

すし屋さんは　すしを
上手に　作ります。

おなべを　熱^{あつ}く
して　います。

文法^{ぶんぽう}　Grammar

A Modifying Adjectives with する

い Adjective　（-く）　　　　　　する

な Adjective / Noun ＋に　　　　する

The verb "します" functions in this pattern as "to decide on a certain thing" or to make something (different from its present condition). The rules for this construction are exactly the same as those for the "なります" pattern. That is, い Adjectives take the -く form while な Adjectives are followed by に before the verb they modify. Often, this pattern includes or suggests a direct object.

◀》 MODELS

1. この　ピザを　少し　熱^{あつ}く　して　下さい。
   Please heat up this pizza.

2. 台所を　きれいに　しました。
   I cleaned up the kitchen.

3. 静^{しず}かに　して　下さい。
   Please be quiet.

4. すきやきに　しましょう。
   Let's have (decide on) *sukiyaki*.

READ/SPEAK Change the word in the ( ) into the correct form.

1. この　部屋は　暑いですねえ。少し　(すずしい)　しましょう。

2. 成績を　もっと　(いい)　しなければ　なりません。

3. この　食べ物は　私の　体を　(元気)　しました。

B Review of Adverbial Usage of Adjectives ——————

In Japanese, some adverbs are derived from adjectives.

Remember: Adverbs describe verbs, adjectives, and other adverbs. Adjectives describe nouns.

a. い Adjective (-い)　　　　　→　　い Adjective (-く)　Adverb

速い, 早い	is fast, is early	→	速く, 早く	fast, quickly, early
遅い	is slow, is late	→	遅く	slowly, late
うるさい	noisy	→	うるさく	noisily

b. な Adjective　　　　　　　→　　な Adjective ＋に　Adverb

静か	is quiet	→	静かに	quietly
きれい	is pretty, is clean	→	きれいに	neatly
急	is urgent, is sudden	→	急に	suddenly

MODELS ▷

1. 牛肉を　薄く　切って　下さい。
   Please cut the beef thinly.

2. 今日　早く　お昼を　食べたいです。
   I want to eat lunch early today.

3. もっと　静かに　食べて　下さい。
   Please eat more quietly.

READ/SPEAK Change the word in the ( ) into the correct adverbial form.

1. (早い)　料理を　始めましょう。

2. おはしを　(上手)　使えますよ。

3. シチューを　料理するのは、時間が　(長い)　かかります。

4. (自由)　好きな　物を　食べて　下さい。

文化ノート　Culture Notes

Dining Out in Japan

When dining out with others in Japan, seating arrangements are of particular importance. Certain positions at the table are considered seats of honor and are often given according to age or seniority. When in doubt, wait to be told where to sit by a member of your group.

The Japanese tend not to make special requests on how their food should be prepared. An exception is when ordering steak. Once it is time to eat, everyone waits until the most senior member of the group begins eating. It is also generally considered polite to pace your eating with the speed of others at your table.

Language Note

Cooking Terminology

Japanese verbs of cooking reflect a traditional diet, just as English reflects the Western traditions of food preparation. For example, in traditional Japanese cooking, roasting, baking and toasting were not common. Because there were no verbs to express these actions, the verb closest to this type of cooking, やきます (grilling, burning, or frying) was used. For example, ケーキを やきます (bake), パンをやきます (toast), 牛肉をやきます (sauté, grill, roast), たまごをやきます (fry).

Japanese vocabulary includes many different verbs which indicate boiling, depending on what is being boiled. For example, when boiling water, the verb わかす is used. For cooking (boiling) rice Japanese style, the verb たきます is used. The verb ゆでる is used to express boiling an egg. Other verbs that translate into "boil" are ゆがく and にる.

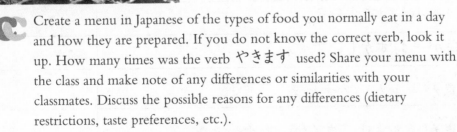

Create a menu in Japanese of the types of food you normally eat in a day and how they are prepared. If you do not know the correct verb, look it up. How many times was the verb やきます used? Share your menu with the class and make note of any differences or similarities with your classmates. Discuss the possible reasons for any differences (dietary restrictions, taste preferences, etc.).

アクティビティー　Communicative Activities

ペアワーク

A. READ/SPEAK/LISTEN You want to learn how to make *sukiyaki* and your partner knows how to prepare it. Give step-by-step cooking instructions using the –て下さい form. Switch roles.

Ex.　まず　野菜<small>やさい</small>を　小さく　切<small>き</small>ります。

　→まず　野菜<small>やさい</small>を　小さく　切<small>き</small>って　下さい。

1. まず、手を　洗います。

2. はじめに、やさいを　洗います。

3. 次に、やさいを　小さく　きります。

4. それから、牛肉を　うすく　きります。

5. それから、こんにゃくを　半分に　きります。

6. 次に、おなべを　あつく　します。

7. 次に、おなべに　あぶらを　入れます。

8. それから、牛肉を　おなべに　入れます。

B. READ/SPEAK/LISTEN You are on the newspaper staff at your school. Your teacher comments on the following things. Agree with your teacher and tell how you will improve next time.

Ex. 生徒：この　新聞<small>しん</small>は　みじかいですねえ。

　先生：そうですねえ。次は　新聞<small>しん</small>を　長く　します。

生徒	先生
1. スポーツインタビューは　長いですねえ。	
2. 英語の　まちがいが　多いですねえ。	
3. 字が　小さいですねえ。	
4. 英語が　むずかしいですねえ。	
5. 写真<small>しゃしん</small>が　少ないですねえ	
6. 写真<small>しゃしん</small>が　あまり　良くないですねえ	

Authentic Reading

READ/WRITE Read the recipe below for curry rice and answer the questions that follow.

カレーライスの作り方

材料：（12皿分）

カレー	1箱（250g）
肉（牛肉かぶた肉かチキン）	500g
玉ねぎ	中4個（800g）
じゃがいも	中4個（600g）
にんじん	中1本（200g）
サラダ油（またはバター）	大さじ3
水	1400ml（7カップ）

作り方：

1. あつ手のなべにサラダ油を入れ、熱くし、一口大に切った肉、野菜をよくいためます。

2. 水を入れ、ふっとうしたら、あくを取り、材料がやわらかくなるまで弱火～中火で　にこみます。

3. 火を止め、ルウをわって入れ、とかし、また弱(よわ)火でとろみがつくまでにこみます。

UNDERSTAND

1. What vegetables other than onions and potatoes do you need in order to prepare curry rice?

2. Should you add water after you cook the meat and vegetables, or should you boil the meat and vegetables in water from the beginning?

IDENTIFY

3. Does 12 皿分 mean that this recipe serves 12 people or that preparation time is 12 minutes?

4. What does 大さじ3 mean?

APPLY

5. You want to use this recipe to prepare a meal for your family of four people. How must you adjust this recipe in order to prepare the correct number of servings?

WORKBOOK page 143

会話 Dialogue
かいわ

🔊 **READ/LISTEN** What will Ken add to the dish? How will it taste?

もう 少し 砂糖を 入れて、あまく しましょう。おいしく なりますよ。

では、少し 入れましょう

文型 Sentence Patterns
ぶんけい

READ Find one of these sentence patterns in the dialogue.

1. おいしく なりました。   It has become delicious.
2. 静かに なりました。   It has become quiet.
しず
3. 医者に なりたいです。   I want to become a doctor.
いしゃ

1. さとう

sugar

2. しお

salt

3. こしょう

pepper

4. (お)す

vinegar

5. あまい

sweet

6. しおからい

salty

7. からい

spicy/hot

8. すっぱい

sour

9. (お)酒
〔おさけ〕

rice wine; liquor in general

10. 味
〔あじ〕

taste, flavor

11. 将来
〔しょうらい〕

future

12. 大人
〔おとな〕

adult

追加単語 Additional Vocabulary

1. にがい	bitter	5. マスタード	mustard
2. 調味料〔ちょうみりょう〕	seasonings	6. ドレッシング	dressing
3. マヨネーズ	mayonnaise	7. わさび	*wasabi*
4. ケチャップ	ketchup	8. ソース	sauce

🔊 **READ/LISTEN/SPEAK** Read these sentences in Japanese. Say what activity you want to become skilled at doing.

さとうを　入れると、あまく
なります。

バンドは　練習して、毎日
上手に　なっています。

文法 Grammar

A Verb of Becoming なる

い **Adjective (ー く)**　　　なる

な **Adjective/Noun +** に　なる

The verb "なります" may be modified by な adjectives, nouns or い adjectives. When modified by a な adjective or noun, the particle に follows the noun or な adjective. When modified by an い adjective, the adjective takes its adverbial form (- く form). Never use the - く form and に together.

🔊 MODELS

1. 背が　高く　なりましたねえ。
   You've grown tall, haven't you?

2. おそく　なって、すみません。
   I'm sorry to be late.

3. おすしが　好きに　なりました。
   I have come to like *sushi*.

4. 私は　将来　医者に　なりたいです。
   I want to become a doctor in the future.

READ/WRITE Change the word in the ( ) to the correct form. Write on a separate sheet of paper.

1. 私は　日本料理が　（好き）　なりました。

2. おすしを　作って　おいしかったから、（うれしい）　なりました。

3. そうじを　しましたから、台所が　とても　（きれい）　なりました。

4. よく　勉強^{べんきょう}しましたから、成績^{せいせき}が　（いい）　なりました。

5. 昨日^{きのう}、私は　（十六歳）　なりました。

文化^{ぶんか}ノート　Culture Notes

Seasonings　調味料^{ちょうみりょう}

The Japanese enjoy a host of diverse flavorings adopted through international cuisine. Traditional Japanese seasonings, however, are simple and limited. Almost all traditional Japanese dishes can be prepared using しょうゆ (soy sauce)、す (vinegar), cooking さけ、さとう (sugar)、みりん (heavily sweetened さけ)、しお (salt) and みそ (soy-bean paste).

だし, ねぎ, ごま, しょうゆ,
みりん, こんぶ
(dried seaweed)

Other seasonings that may be used for additional flavor are しちみとうがらし (a blend of seven spices including cayenne, pepper, and citrus)、わさび (Japanese horseradish), and からし (Japanese mustard). Also popular are さんしょ (Japanese pepper) and ゆずこしょう (a peppery spice with citron flavoring). ごま (sesame seeds) are also often used as garnish.

 Take a trip to your local supermarket and make a list of all the Japanese seasonings. Are there other varieties than those listed above? If so, do you think they are authentically Japanese or have they been adapted to suit the tastes of your country? Write a short observational essay on your findings and include the reasoning behind your thoughts.

Language Note

「すみません。おそくなりました。」Excuse me for being late.

In Japan, a lengthy explanation about the reason for lateness is not necessary unless requested. A simple apology, however, is expected. 「すみません。おそくなりました。」expressed sincerely with a bow, is used in this case. Students who are late to class may instead say, 「すみません、ちこくです。」

In an informal situation with friends, 「おそくなって、ごめん。」 is sufficient. On the opposite end of the spectrum, when one must show extreme apology to a person of very high status, 「おそくなって、もうしわけございません」 is used.

アクティビティー　Communicative Activities

ペアワーク

A. READ/SPEAK/LISTEN Tell your partner what seasoning to put in a certain dish and ask about the flavor. Your partner describes how the flavor has changed. Take turns.

Ex. わさび

Aさん：わさびを　入れて　下さい。味は　どうですか。

Bさん：からく　なりました。

1. しお	4. しょうゆ
2. こしょう	5. (お)さけ
3. (お)す	6. さとう

B. SPEAK/LISTEN Greet a Japanese person during the following seasons and comment on the weather. Take turns.

Ex. It has become warm (spring).

あなた：おはようございます。

日本人：おはようございます。

あなた：暖かく　なりましたねえ。

日本人：そうですねえ。春に　なりましたねえ。

1. It has become hot (summer).
2. It has become cool (fall).
3. It has become cold (winter).
4. It has become warm (spring).
5. It rains a lot during the rainy season (つゆ).

C. READ/SPEAK/LISTEN Tell your partner about something that has happened to you from the options below. He/she should respond appropriately with one of the comments listed below.

Ex. Aさん：成績が　良く　なりました。

せいせき

Bさん：それは　良かったですねえ。

それは　いいですねえ。

それは　良かったですねえ。

それは　ざんねんですねえ。

それは　ざんねんでしたねえ。

本当ですか。

大じょうぶですか。

1.	せいせきが　わるく　なりました。
2.	この　土曜日に　十六歳に　なります。
3.	私達の　チームは　つよく　なりました。
4.	おじいさんが　病気に　なりました。
5.	～が　上手に　なりました。
6.	私の　犬が　お母さんに　なりました。
7.	私は　トマトが　好きに　なりました。
8.	私達の　チームが　一番に　なりました。

D. READ/SPEAK/LISTEN/WRITE Recreate the chart below on a separate sheet of paper. Ask your partner whether he/she wants to become any of the following in the future. He/she should answer based on fact. Check はい or いいえ, and ask for the reason. Take turns.

Ex. 医者
質問1：将来　医者に　なりたいですか。
　答え1：はい、医者に　なりたいです。or
　　　　　いいえ、医者に　なりたくないです。
質問2：なぜですか。
　答え2：私は　血 (blood) が　こわいんです。

仕事	はい	いいえ	なぜ？
1. べんごし			
2. 先生			
3. しょうぼうし			
4. カウンセラー			
5. パイロット			
6. シェフ			
7. 大とうりょう (President of a country)			
8. ウェイター/ウェイトレス			

WORKBOOK　page 145

会話 Dialogue
かいわ

🔊 **READ/LISTEN** How does the *sukiyaki* taste?

文型 Sentence Patterns
ぶんけい

READ Find this sentence pattern in the dialogue.

食べ	＋すぎます。	(I) eat too much.
高	＋すぎます。	It's too expensive.
良	＋すぎます。	It's too good.
静か	＋すぎます。	It's too quiet.

しず

単語 Vocabulary

1. デザート

dessert

2. 生卵
なまたまご

raw egg

3. 気持ちが　悪い
わる

unpleasant; uncomfortable

4. 気持ちが　いい

pleasant, comfortable

5. 〜が　出来ました

6. (Object)を
(thing)に　つける
[G2 つけます]

かたづ
7. (Object)を　片付ける

[G2 かたづけます]

〜 is ready, 〜 is done

to dip (object) in (thing)

to clean up, put away

ついかたんご
追加単語　Additional Vocabulary

1. アイスクリーム　ice cream

3. クッキー　cookie

2. シャーベット　sherbet

まんじゅう
4. 饅頭　Japanese buns filled with
sweetened red beans

読みましょう　Language in Context

🔊 **READ/LISTEN/SPEAK** Read these sentences in Japanese. Say what food you last ate that you ate too much of.

くだ
日本の　果物は　高すぎます。　ケータイを　使いすぎます。

A Extender すぎます

Verb (Stem form) ／ い **Adjective (Stem form)** ／ な **Adjective** ＋すぎます

When the verb すぎます (to exceed) is attached to a verb stem, it is expressed in English as "to do (such and such) in excess." When attached to an adjective without its final –i or to a な Adjective, it is translated as "too . . . " The extender ～すぎます may be conjugated in any tense.

◀)) MODELS

1. アイスクリームを　食べすぎました。
   I ate too much ice cream.

2. あの　学生は　うるさすぎます。
   That student is too noisy.

3. この　犬は　頭（あたま）が　良すぎます。
   This dog is too smart.

4. あの　人は　テニスが　下手すぎます。
   That person is too unskillful at tennis.

5. ここは　静（しず）かすぎると　思います。
   I think this place is too quiet.

6. 勉強（べんきょう）しすぎないで　下さい。
   Please do not study too hard.

READ/SPEAK Change the word in the 〔 〕 to the correct form and choose the correct word in the (　).

1. すき焼（や）きは　〔おいしい〕すぎます。

2. 山本さんは　頭（あたま）が　〔いい〕すぎます。

3. 昨日（きのう）　パーティーの　料理を　〔作ります〕（すぎます / すぎました）。

4. 日本の　ケーキは　〔あまい〕（すぎます / すぎる）と　思（おも）います。

5. この　レストランは　〔有名（ゆうめい）〕（すぎて / すきで）、予約（よやく）出来ません。

6. あまい物を　〔食べます〕（すぎないで / すぎて）　下さい。

7. コンピューターを〔使います〕（すげる　すぎる）のは　良くないです。

文化ノート　Culture Notes

Desserts and Sweets

Although the Japanese diet is rice-based, the Japanese have come to enjoy ice cream, cakes, and pastries as much as Westerners do. Most sweets, however, are consumed as treats and not necessarily as desserts. Traditional sweets such as *manju*, *mochi*, or *senbei* were considered snacks, or sweets to accompany tea, and seasonal fruit was occasionally served at the end of a meal.

Western-style bakeries are quite popular in Japan. Many are small shops with open displays of a variety of freshly baked breads, cakes, and pastries. Customers typically choose their purchases by placing them on a tray. The tasty goods are then presented at the cashier's counter where they are packaged and paid for. Some bakeries also have a sit-down section where the food may be consumed, as at a café.

Be an entrepreneur! Search the Internet for a bakery in Japan and make a poster advertising the items sold there. Include the shop's name, a map of its location, and the pictures and names of the sweets sold there. Present it to your class as if it were the grand opening of the bakery and you are the shop owner.

アクティビティー Communicative Activities

ペアワーク

A. **READ/SPEAK/LISTEN** Your friend visits your room and complains about everything using the すぎます form.

Ex.　　この　部屋は　暑いです。

　→ この　部屋は　暑すぎます。

1. この　部屋は　くらいです。

2. この　部屋は　きたないです。

3. 音楽が　うるさいです。

4. この　動画は　長いです。

5. この　いすは　高いです。

B. READ/SPEAK/LISTEN Your friend loves to do the following things. You warn him/her not to do them in excess. Switch roles.

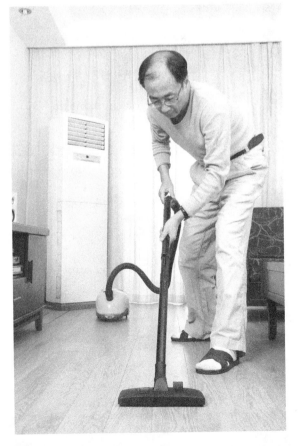

Ex. 友達　：私は　食べることが　大好きです。

あなた：でも、食べすぎないで　下さいよ。

友達	あなた
1. 私は　コーラを　飲むことが　大好きです。	
2. 私は　本を　読むことが　大好きです。	
3. 私は　動画を　見ることが　大好きです。	
4. 私は　テレビを　見ることが　大好きです。	
5. 私は　テレビゲームを　することが　大好きです。	

C. READ/SPEAK/LISTEN/WRITE Take turns interviewing your partner with the questions below. Write his/her answers on a separate sheet of paper.

1. 家で　たいてい　だれが　料理を　しますか。
2. 晩ご飯の　後で、だれが
   台所を　かたづけますか。
3. 時々　かたづけるのを
   手つだいますか。
4. 時々　おさらを　洗いますか。
5. 家ぞくに　晩ご飯を
   作ったことが　ありますか。
6. 今、すきやきの　作り方を
   知って　いますか。
7. すきやきを　生たまごに　つけて
   食べたことが　ありますか。
8. どんな　デザートが　好きですか。

Review Questions

Ask your partner these questions in Japanese. Your partner should answer in Japanese. Check your answers using the audio.

Making *Sukiyaki* Review pages 374, 379–380, 386–387

1. Do you know how to make *sukiyaki*?

2. Do you know how to eat *sukiyaki*?

3. Do (you) have to cut the vegetables small?

4. When (upon) heating the pot, what do (you) put in the pot?

5. What seasonings do (you) put in the *sukiyaki* that make it become delicious?

Your Food Preferences Review pages 372–373, 385, 393

6. Among fruits, what do you like best?

7. Which do you like better, eating vegetables or eating fruits?

8. Do you like eating sweet foods more than eating salty foods?

9. Do you like to eat spicy food?

10. Do you think making Japanese food is too difficult?

About You Review pages 374, 386, 393

11. Do you know how to drive a car?

12. Do you think you study too hard?

13. Has Japanese become difficult this year?

14. What do you want to become in the future?

Text Chat

You will participate in a simulated exchange of text-chat messages. You should answer as fully and as appropriately as possible. You will have a conversation with Nana Takahashi, a Japanese high school student, about cooking.

04月 19日　08:06 AM

私は　料理を　した　ことが
ありますが、とても　下手です。

Respond and ask a question.

04月 19日　08:11 AM

日本料理と　アメリカ料理と
どちらの　方が　おいしいと
思いますか。

Respond and give a reason.

04月 19日　08:22 AM

将来、シェフに　なりたいですか。

Respond and give a reason.

Can Do!
Now I can . . .

❑ explain how to cook a simple dish

❑ communicate about things or actions done in excess

❑ describe a change of state

Japanese Cuisine

RESEARCH Use books, the Internet, or interview a Japanese member of your community to answer the following questions.

Determine

1. What spices are used in traditional Japanese cooking?

2. What role do pickled vegetables play in the Japanese diet? What are some common kinds of pickled vegetables and when are they usually eaten?

3. What kinds of foods can be found in a traditional Japanese breakfast?

4. Name different types of main dishes available at a Japanese restaurant in your area.

Compare

5. Many traditional Japanese restaurants only serve specific dishes, like sushi or *yakitori*. For example at a すしや, you could not order udon or curry rice. Is there any equivalent in terms of American food?

6. What kind of meat and vegetables are most common in an American diet? What kind of meat and vegetables are most common in a Japanese diet?

7. Much like rice, soy food products, such as *miso*, *edamame*, and tofu, are a staple of the Japanese diet. What are some staple foods of your country's diet? Are soy food products common in your country?

Apply

8. Many Japanese restaurants display plastic models of their dishes in their windows. What do you think of this practice? Should U.S. restaurants adopt this practice?

Extend Your Learning
CREATIVITY AND TECHNOLOGY LITERACY
Choose a dish you are familiar with and translate the recipe into Japanese. Create an illustration or a short instructional video on how to cook the dish and give directions in Japanese.

母の日
Mother's Day

Can Do!
In this lesson you will learn to:

- list a sample of actions and descriptors
- use a conditional "if" statement
- communicate how you or another person does a favor for others
- express your gratitude and appreciation to others

Online Resources

cheng-tsui.com/
adventuresinjapanese

- Audio
- Vocabulary Lists
- Vocabulary and *Kanji* Flashcards
- Study Guides
- Activity Worksheets

In this lesson you will learn how to compose a letter that expresses appreciation. Review these words, phrases, and grammatical structures you already learned to help you talk about giving and receiving gifts or favors.

めいし Nouns

1. 母の日	Mother's Day	9. 先月	last month
2. 本屋	bookstore	10. 十四日	14th (of the month)
3. めがね	eyeglasses	11. ピアノ	piano
4. ネックレス	necklace	12. 部屋 (へや)	room
5. しゅみ	hobby	13. そば	nearby
6. 事	thing [intangible]	14. 何も + Neg.	(not) anything
7. 絵 (え)	painting, picture	15. 心 (こころ)	heart
8. 問題 (もんだい)	problem	16. 世界	world

どうし Verbs

17. ～に　つとめて　います [G2 つとめる]	is employed at ～
18. かけて　いて [G2 かける]	is wearing (glasses), (and)
19. Accessory ＋を　して　います [IR する]	is wearing (accessory)
20. りょ行をする [IR りょこうをします]	travel
21. およいだり [G1 およぐ]	swim [TARI form]
22. 手つだって [G1 てつだう]	help (and)
23. もらいます [G1 もらう]	receive
24. くれます [G2 くれる]	give (me)
25. あげません [G2 あげる]	do not give
26. そうじを　して [IR そうじを　する]	clean (and)
27. 洗たくを　して [IR せんたくを　する]	do laundry (and)

どうし Verbs		
28. あったら [G1 ある/あって]		if (I) have [TARA form]
29. れんしゅう(を)しました [IR れんしゅう(を)する]		practiced
30. 言ったことが ありません [G2 いう]		have never said

-い けいようし I Adjectives				
31. 背が 低くて	short [height]	34. かなしくて	sad
32. 明るい	bright	35. 暗い	dark
33. 悪い	bad	36. すばらしい	wonderful

-な けいようし NA Adjectives			
37. いろいろ	various	38. 大好き	like very much

ふくし Adverbs			
39. いつも	always	41. 一しょに	together
40. よく	often	42. 一生けんめい	with utmost effort

ぶんぽう Grammar	
43. Dictionary form＋こと	verb nominalization
44. 〜たことが ありません	have never done 〜

WRITE Write out what Ken is saying about his mother in each scene using the words, phrases, and grammatical structures you reviewed above.

In this lesson, you will learn the *kanji* used to describe thoughts and feelings.

	Kanji	Meaning	Readings	Examples		
153.	太	fat	ふと (る)	ふと 太って いる	is fat	大 ＋ ◊ ＝太
			タ	もも た ろう 桃太郎	Momotaro [name]	
154.	立	to stand	た (つ)	た 立って くだ 下さい。	Please stand.	
			リツ	きりつ 起立。	Stand.	
155.	泣	to cry	な (く)	な 泣いて いる	is crying	⫶⫶⫶ ＋ 立 ＝泣
156.	全	whole	ゼン	ぜんこく 全国	entire country	
157.	部	part	ブ	ぜんぶ 全部	everything	
			ヘ	へ や 部屋	room	

	Kanji	Meaning	Readings	Examples	
158.	仕	to serve	シ	しごと 仕事	job
				しかた 仕方が ない。	It cannot be helped.
159	心	heart	こころ	こころ いい心	a good heart 
			シン	しんぱい 心配する	worry
160	思	to think	おも (う)	いいと おも 思う	I think (it's) good
161.	悪	is bad	わる (い)	わる ひと 悪い人	a bad person
162.	絵	painting, picture	え	え か 絵を描く	to paint/ draw a picture 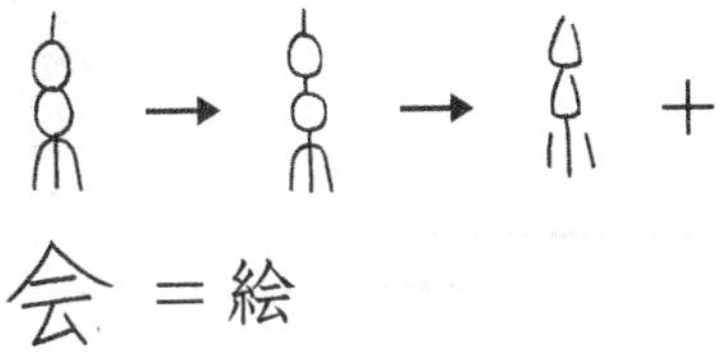

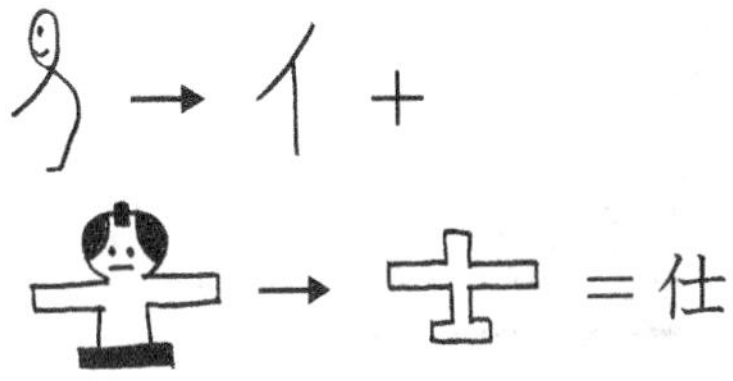

ヲ → イ +

→ 士 = 仕

→ 心 → 心

田 + 心 = 思

亜 + 心 = 悪

→ → +

会 = 絵

Recognition Kanji	
ぎんこう 銀行	bank

WORKBOOK page 211

お母さん、ありがとう

Happy Mother's Day, Mom!

ケン・ス

母は

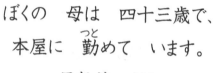

ぼくの 母は 四十三歳で、
本屋に 勤めて います。
　五年前 父と
離婚しました。
ぼくは 一人っ子です。

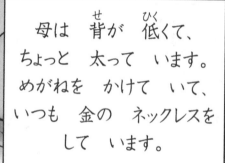

　母は 背が 低くて、
ちょっと 太って います。
めがねを かけて いて、
いつも 金の ネックレスを
して います。

　母の 趣味は
旅行を することです。
ひまな 時には 泳いだり、
犬と 散歩を したり、
　絵を かいたり
　　して います。

　いつも ニコニコ 笑って
いますから、家の 中が
明るいです。しかし、ぼくが
たまに 何か 悪い
ことを したら、おこります。

ぼくは　よく　母に
宿題を　手伝って
もらいます。母は
ぼくの　質問に　よく
答えて　くれます。

掃除も　洗濯も
して　くれます。問題が
あったら、いつも
助けて　くれます。

先月の　十四日に　ピアノの
コンクールが　あって、
ぼくは　一生懸命　練習
しましたが、三位でした。

悲しくて、自分の
部屋に　いました。

その　時、母が
あたたかい　飲み物を
持って　来て　くれました。

ぼくは　母に
何も　して　あげませんが、
母は　いつも　ぼくに
いろいろな　ことを
して　くれます。

ぼくは 心の 中で いつも
感謝していますが、母に 感謝の 言葉を
言ったことが ありません。
お母さん、ありがとう。ぼくは お母さんが
大好きです。

お母さん、ありがとう。
いつも ぼくに いろいろなことを
して くれて、かんしゃ して います。
お母さんは 世界で 一番 すばらしい
お母さんです。

ケン

会話 Dialogue
かいわ

🔊 **READ/LISTEN** What is Mari asking Ken?

文型 Sentence Patterns
ぶんけい

READ Find one of these sentence patterns in the dialogue.

1. Verb (Dictionary Form) ＋こと／の Verb nominalization

 2. Verbs "To Wear" (シャツを)　着ます　　　　(くつ, パンツを)　はきます
(めがねを)　かけます　　(ぼうしを)　かぶります
(ネックレスを)　します

単語 Vocabulary

1. 散歩(を)　する
さん
[IR さんぽ(を)　します]
to take a walk

2. 絵を　描く
か
[G1 かきます]
to draw, paint a picture

3. ニコニコ

smilingly

4. 笑う

[G1 わらいます]

to smile, laugh

5. 泣く

[G1 なきます]

to cry

6. おこる

[G1 おこります]

to become angry

おこっています is angry

7. しかる

[G1 しかります]

to scold

8. 離婚(を) する

[IR りこん(を) します]

to divorce

りこん(を)しています

is divorced

9. 金

gold

10. 銀

silver

11. ずっと

throughout, all the time

12. たまに

occasionally, once in a while

追加単語 Additional Vocabulary

1. 別居(を)します   to separate (from a partner); to live separately

READ/LISTEN/SPEAK Read these sentences in Japanese. Say what your hobby is using a verb.

母の　しゅみは　バーゲンで
安い　物を　買うことです。

森さんは　スーツを　着て、
ネクタイを　して、めがねを
かけて　います。

文法 Grammar

A Nominalizing Verbs

Verb (Dictionary Form)＋の／こと

By attaching の (matter) or こと to a verb in its dictionary form, one creates a nominal (noun) usage of a verb. At the end of a sentence, こと (not の) should be used.

MODELS

1. 私は　旅行するのが　好きです。
   I like traveling.

2. 日本語を　話すことは　難しいですが、楽しいです。
   Speaking Japanese is difficult, but it is fun.

3. 母の　趣味は　絵を　かくことです。
   My mother's hobby is drawing pictures.

READ/SPEAK Change the verb in the [   ] to the correct form and choose the correct word in the (   ).
In some cases, either response may be correct.

1. 母の　しゅみは、ピアノを [ひきます] (の / こと)です。

2. 毎日　[料理します] (の / こと)は、大変です。

3. 母と　[話します] (の / こと)が　好きです。

B Review of Japanese Verbs of Wearing

The Japanese verb for "to wear" varies according to where or how the clothing or accessory is worn. When wearing something above the waist or over the entire body, the verb きます is used. The verb はきます is used for things worn below the waist, します is used when wearing accessories. かぶります is used when things are worn on or draped over the head. The verb かけます is used for wearing glasses.

きます	will wear (above the waist, or on the entire body)
はきます	will wear (below the waist)
します	will wear (accessories)
かぶります	will wear (on or draped over the head)
かけます	will wear (glasses)

◀))) MODELS

1. 姉は　赤と　白の　ぼうしを　かぶって　います。
   My older sister is wearing a red and white hat.

2. 黒い　ドレスを　着て、むらさきの　くつを　はいて　います。
   She is wearing a black dress and purple shoes.

3. 母は　いつも　金の　ネックレスを　して　います。
   My mother always wears a gold necklace.

4. 私は　めがねを　かけて　います。
   I am wearing glasses. / I wear glasses.

READ/SPEAK Fill in the (   ) with the correct verb of wearing, using the correct verb form.

1. 母は　白い　シャツを　(　　)いて、青い　スカートを　(　　)います。

2. めがねを　(　　)いて、ネックレスを　(　　)います。

3. 時々　ぼうしを　(　　)います。

文化ノート　Culture Notes

The Japanese Family

Just as the American family has seen dramatic change over the past century, the structure and dynamics of the Japanese family have also changed. Traditionally, Japanese families included at least three generations living in one household. Families usually consisted of several children. Prior to World War II, the family was solidly patrilineal, with the eldest able-bodied male of the family serving as head of the household. He was the prime breadwinner, responsible for the welfare of all of the family members, and made most major decisions for those living under his roof. The role of the mother was to raise her children and tend to the daily needs of her family by doing housework, cooking, daily shopping, caring for in-laws, and managing the household budget.

After World War II, changes in the family structure occurred with the arrival of American influence. Such changes as equal rights for women, the decline of arranged marriages, and nuclear family households became prevalent. The father, still the primary wage earner, usually worked long hours and rarely spent time at home. The mother was still in charge of taking care of her family, though she now typically only tended to her husband's and children's needs and education.

Today there are even more changes, as younger fathers take more time to be with their families and shoulder more responsibilities in the home. More mothers work part-time outside of the home. The average number of children per family has dropped to between 1.2–1.4, a birthrate that has become a national concern. More young men and women choose not to get married and the divorce rate, which is still low by international standards, has grown in recent years.

 Research the evolution of family structure in your own culture within the last century. What changes have occurred in the most recent decades? Write a brief report comparing and contrasting traditional and modern families in Japan and in your own culture and share it with your class.

アクティビティー Communicative Activities

ペアワーク

A. READ/WRITE/SPEAK/LISTEN Recreate the drawing of the family tree below on a separate sheet of paper. Fill in the [ ] with the name of an imaginary friend and the ( ) with the hobbies of his/her family members chosen from the list in the box. Ask your partner what the hobbies of his/her friend's family members are and record the answers. Compare answers.
Ex.

質問1：友達の　名前は　何ですか。

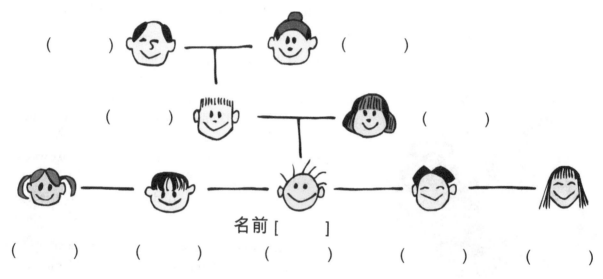

名前 [   ]

質問2：〜さんの　お母さんの　趣味は　何ですか。

Selection of hobbies:

1. 絵を　かく
2. しゃしんを　とる
3. さん歩を　する
4. およぐ
5. ねる
6. 食べる
7. バスケットボールを　する
8. ピアノを　ひく
9. (your choice)

B. SPEAK/LISTEN Share about your family with your partner. Include information such as your family members' relationship to you, their names, and each of their hobbies. Include yourself!

Ex. 「家族は　三人です。母の　名前は　メアリーです。」

「母の　趣味は　絵を　かく　ことです。」

「私は　本を　読むことが　好きです。」

C. READ/SPEAK/LISTEN Take turns interviewing your partner about a member of his/her family.

1. (family member) の	しゅみは　何ですか。	
2. (family member) は	せが　高いですか。ひくいですか。	
3. (family member) は	めがねを　かけて　いますか。	
4. (family member) は	いつも　ネックレスを　して　いますか。	
5. (family member) は	犬が　好きですか。	
6. (family member) は	よく　テレビを　見ますか。	
7. (family member) は	時々　おこりますか。	
8. (family member) は	時々　あなたを　しかりますか。	
9. (family member) は	いい　お母さんだと　思いますか。	

クラスワーク

D. WRITE/SPEAK/LISTEN What is everybody wearing today?

1. The teacher will distribute sheets of paper with a different number on each.

2. Write your name next to the number on the paper you receive and give it back to your teacher to be re-distributed.

3. Describe what the student whose name appears at the top of your paper is wearing from head to toe. Sign your name at the bottom of the paper.

4. The teacher will collect the papers and read only the numbers and descriptions to the class.

5. You and your classmates will guess which student is being described by writing one of your classmates' names beside the correct number on a chart.

6. After all the descriptions have been read, check your answers.

WORKBOOK　page 155

会話 Dialogue
<かいわ>

🔊 READ/LISTEN What does Ken's mother do in her free time?

お母さんは
ひまな　時に

何を　しますか。

泳いだり、
（およ）
犬と　散歩を　したり、
（さん）
絵を　かいたり
して　います。

文型 Sentence Patterns
<ぶんけい>

READ Find this sentence pattern in the dialogue.

　　〜たり　　　　〜たり　　します

およいだり　走ったり　します。　　　　We do such things as swimming and running.

あつかったり　さむかったり　します。　It is sometimes hot and sometimes cold.

はれだったり　くもりだったり　します。 It is sometimes sunny and sometimes cloudy.

単語 Vocabulary

1. 一人っ子
〔ひとりっこ〕

only child

2. 双子
（ふた）
〔ふたご〕

twin(s)

3. 五年前

five years ago

7.

Rank	

1	いちい
2	にい
3	さんい
4	よんい
5	ごい
6	ろくい
7	なない
8	はちい
9	きゅうい
10	じゅうい
?	なんい

4. ひ ま

[な Adj.]

free (time)

ひまな 時

when (someone) is free

5. その 時

[その とき]

at that time

6. コンクール

competition [music]

コンクールに 出ます

participate in a
competition

8. Sentence 1。 しかし、 Sentence 2。

Sentence 1. However, sentence 2.

[Formal expression of でも]

ついかたんご
追加単語 Additional Vocabulary

しょう
1. 賞   award; prize

せいかく
2. 性格   personality

読みましょう Language in Context

🔊 **READ/LISTEN/SPEAK** Read these sentences in Japanese. Say two things you do in your free time.

ひまな 時に、本屋で 本を
読みます。

けい子さんは 五年前に
とうきょう   けっこん
東京で 結婚しました。

A TARI Form (Listing Two or More Actions or States)

～たり　～たり　します/です

This sentence construction lists two or more verbs, い adjectives, な adjectives, or nouns in their –た forms, to which a り is attached. The two interpretations of this construction are "do such things as ～ and/or ～," or "sometimes ～ and sometimes ～." The たり forms are generally followed by forms of the verbs します, including the potential できます form, or forms of です. です endings are used more commonly used with い adjectives, な adjectives, and noun たり forms. The tense of the します or です ending determines the tense of the entire sentence. Although the listing of two actions or states is most common, more may be listed. Occasionally, only one たり form is used in a sentence. In such cases, the sentence can only be interpreted as "do such things as . . ."

 MODELS

1. 休みには　映画に　行ったり　コンサートに　行ったり　します。
   I go to movies and concerts on my days off.

2. 私の　成績は せいせき　良かったり　悪かったり　です。
   My grades are sometimes good and sometimes bad.

3. 生徒は　上手だったり　下手だったり　します。
   Some students are skillful and some students are unskillful.

4. 日本語の　先生は　日本人だったり　アメリカ人だったり　です。
   Teachers of Japanese are sometimes Japanese and sometimes American.

5. コーラを　飲んだり　しては　いけません。
   You should not do such things as drinking cola.

READ/SPEAK Change the words in the ( ) to their correct forms so the sentences mean "do such things as ～ and/or ～," or "sometimes ～ and sometimes ～."

1. ひまな　時に、公園を　(走ります)、テニスを　(します)　します。

2. 日本語の　宿題は しゅくだい　(多い)、(少ない)　です。

3. 食堂の どう　食事は　(好き)、(きらい)　します。

4. サッカーの　試合の しあい　場所は、 ば (学校)、(公園)　します。

5. 朝 あさ　私は　パンを　(食べます)、ジュースを　(飲みます)　します。

文化ノート　Culture Notes

A. Women in the Workforce

Although Japan ranks among the world's largest economies, it is also known to have one of the lowest percentages of women in the workforce. Traditional attitudes (such as the belief that women should remain in the home to raise children) have caused many women to leave the workforce after childbirth. Societal structures have also made it difficult for women to maintain full-time jobs, as work hours in Japan frequently run over 10 hours a day. The tax system also does not benefit families with two working adults.

One result of this reality is that families are choosing to have fewer or no children, which has contributed significantly to Japan's problematically low birthrate. At the current rate, Japan's population will drop by the millions in the next few decades.

The concern of the growing aging population with no younger people to support the economy has spurred the government to channel resources to support working mothers. Recent government initiatives have encouraged companies to cut their work hours and workweeks, and to provide daycare centers for children of company employees.

B. Japanese Television

Since its introduction in the 1950's, television has become an important part of the daily lives of the Japanese, with many Japanese companies, such as Sony, Panasonic, and Toshiba, producing some of the world's most popular television sets.

The most popular types of television shows in Japan are news programs, dramas, variety shows, sports programs, and trivia shows. Educational programs on history, nature and science as well as many bilingual, language education, and subtitled foreign programs also exist.

Morning television broadcasts are mainly news-oriented and geared toward working men. Many stay-at-home mothers tend to watch late morning through early afternoon programs, which feature human interest stories, followed by dramas and informational shows. From about 4:00 p.m., children-focused programs, such as cartoons and educational shows, run until the news begins again at about 6:00 p.m. Prime-time programs starring the most popular Japanese idols are shown from about 7:00 to 9:00 p.m., after which dramas that draw older audiences are broadcast. The late evening news begins at about 10:00 p.m., followed by shows for more mature audiences.

 Research a famous Japanese woman in the political, business, scientific, entertainment, historical, arts, or literary arena. Create a short slide show about the woman and any significant contributions she has made in her field and share it with your class.

Part 2 • What does your mother do in her free time?　417

アクティビティー　Communicative Activities

ペアワーク

A. SPEAK/LISTEN Take turns asking your partner what he/she does during the following times or at the following places. Name several activities.

Ex. 週末(まっ)

質問(しつもん)：週末(まっ)は　たいてい　どんな　ことを　しますか。

答え(こた)：週末(まっ)は　たいてい　映画を　見たり、友達と　会ったり　します。

1. 学校の　休み時間に
2. 学校の　後で
3. 晩(ばん)　家で
4. なつ休みに

B. SPEAK/LISTEN/WRITE Now ask your partner how his/her family members spend the weekend. He/she should name several activities. Write your partner's responses on a separate sheet of paper.

お父さん	お母さん
お兄(にい)さん	お姉(ねえ)さん
おとうとさん	いもうとさん

C. READ/SPEAK/LISTEN Interview your partner with the questions below.

1. 家族(ぞく)は　何人ですか。
2. 双子(ふたご)ですか。一人っ子ですか。
3. ひまな時に　どんなことを　して　いますか。
4. 五年前に　どんなことを　するのが　好きでしたか。
5. その時に　どんなことを　するのが　きらいでしたか。
6. 音楽(おんがく)の　コンクールに　出た　ことが　ありますか。
7. 学校の　やきゅうチームは、今　何位(い)ですか。
8. やきゅうの　チームを　おうえんしに　行きますか。

WORKBOOK page 157

<ruby>会話<rt>かいわ</rt></ruby>　Dialogue

🔊 **READ/LISTEN** When does Ken want to become a doctor?

大人に　なったら、
どんな　仕事を
したいですか。

そうですねえ...
<ruby>医者<rt>いしゃ</rt></ruby>に
なりたいです。

<ruby>文型<rt>ぶんけい</rt></ruby>　Sentence Patterns

READ Find this sentence pattern in the dialogue.

日本へ　行ったら、	If/When (I) go to Japan,
天気が　良かったら、	If/When the weather is good,
好きだったら、	If/When (you) like it,
明日だったら、	If/When (it) is tomorrow,

<ruby>単語<rt>たんご</rt></ruby>　Vocabulary

1. 自分
〔じぶん〕
oneself

2. 何か
〔なにか〕
something

3. <ruby>助<rt>たす</rt></ruby>ける
[G2 たすけます／たすけて]
to rescue, help

追加単語 *ついかたんご* Additional Vocabulary

1. 相談(を)します *そうだん* [IR]　　　　　　　　　　to consult

読みましょう　Language in Context

 READ/LISTEN/SPEAK Read these sentences in Japanese. Tell a partner what you can do if the weather is good in your city.

大人に　なったら、花屋さんに *はな*
なりたいです。

天気が　良かったら、新幹線の *かんせん*
窓から　富士山が　見えます。 *まど* *ふじ*

文法 *ぶんぽう*　Grammar

A Conditional Form -TARA

Verb (TA Form) ＋ら、

い **Adjective (ーかった)** ＋ら、

な **Adjective/Noun** ＋だった＋ら、

This conditional is formed by taking the plain past (TA forms) of verbs, い and な adjectives, and nouns, adding ら to the end of the first clause, then attaching a resulting clause to form one sentence. It is used to mean "if/when/after doing . . . , then . . ." The second clause generally expresses a wish, volition, suggestion, invitation, opinion, request, or emotion.

MODELS

1. 先生に　聞いたら、すぐ　分かりました。
   When (if) I asked my teacher, I understood it right away.

2. 天気が　良かったら、　ハイキングに　行きましょう。
   If the weather is good, let's go hiking.

3. はしを　使うのは　下手だったら、　使わなくても　いいです。

    If (you) are not skillful at using chopsticks, you do not have to use (them).

4. 四時だったら、　行けますよ。

    If it is at 4:00, I can go.

READ/SPEAK Change the words in the ( ) into the correct TARA form.

1. 日本へ　（行きます）、ぜひ　スカイツリ (Tokyo Skytree) を　見たいです。

2. 成績が　（悪いです）、かなしく　なります。
  せいせき

3. 本当に　（好きです）、がんばれます。

4. （病気です）、学校を　休んで　下さい。

文化ノート　Culture Notes
ぶんか

A. Japanese Proverb

「山より　高く、海より　深い　母の　愛」
   うみ　　ふか　　　あい

ふかい means "deep." This proverb means "A mother's love is higher than the mountains and deeper than the ocean."

B. Mother's Day and Father's Day in Japan

Although Mother's Day and Father's Day were not traditionally celebrated in Japan, through Western influence, both days are now observed by some families in Japan. Mother's Day, the more commonly celebrated of the two, is observed on the second Sunday of May and Father's Day on the third Sunday of June. Japanese children usually present their mothers with a bouquet of red carnations, handmade gifts, or cards on Mother's Day. Due to the popularity of red carnations, in recent years prices have skyrocketed and it is nearly impossible for young children to purchase them. On Father's Day, fathers may receive ties or other small gifts from their children. Families may also go out to eat at a restaurant to celebrate.

Research holidays in Japan on the Internet and choose one to report on. Share your report with your classmates. Include the origins of the holiday, who and/or what is celebrated, how the holiday is celebrated, and any other important information.

アクティビティー Communicative Activities

ペアワーク

A. READ/SPEAK/LISTEN Ask your partner what he/she would want to do in the following situations.

Ex. ひまな 時間が あったら、

しつもん
質問：今、ひまな 時間が あったら、何を したいですか。

1. 今 千ドル あったら、	4. 自分の 車が あったら、
2. 明日 学校が なかったら、	5. 大学生に なったら、
3. 日本へ 行けたら、	6. 大人に なったら、

Authentic Reading

B. READ/WRITE Look at the shopping Website and answer the following questions in Japanese on a separate sheet of paper.

UNDERSTAND

1. What kind of Website is this?

2. When would you purchase something from this Website?

IDENTIFY

3. If you bought both items with prices listed, what would the total cost be?

4. Who does this advertisement suggest you buy the more expensive chocolates for?

APPLY

5. If you were to order one of these items as a gift for your friend, which would you order?

WORKBOOK page 159

<ruby>会話<rt>かいわ</rt></ruby> Dialogue

🔊 READ/LISTEN What does Ken do for his mother? Does Ken's mother often do things for him?

<ruby>文型<rt>ぶんけい</rt></ruby> Sentence Patterns

READ Find one of these sentence patterns in the dialogue.

♻
1. Giver は　　Receiver (equal)　　　　に　　Something を　あげます。
2. Giver は　　Receiver (higher status)　に　　Something を　さしあげます。
3. Giver は　　Receiver (lower status)　に　　Something を　やります。
4. Giver は　　Receiver (me)　　　　　に　　Something を　くれます。
5. Receiver は　Giver　　　　　　　に／から Something を　もらいます。

1. Giver は　　Receiver (equal)　　　　に　　Verb (TE Form) あげます。
2. Giver は　　Receiver (lower status)　に　　Verb (TE Form) やります。
3. Giver は　　Receiver (me)　　　　　に　　Verb (TE Form) くれます。
4. Receiver は　Giver　　　　　　　に　　Verb(TE Form) もらいます。

1. 感謝(を)　する
かんしゃ
[IR かんしゃ(を)します]

to appreciate, thank
かんしゃ appreciation [noun]
Someone に　かんしゃを　して　います。
I am grateful to (someone).

2. 愛して　います
あい
[G1 あいします]

in love
あい love, affection [noun]

3. 言葉
ことば
〔ことば〕

words, language

追加単語　Additional Vocabulary
ついかたんご

1. 家事　　　chores, housework
か じ

2. 庭仕事　　yard work
にわしごと

読みましょう　Language in Context

🔊 READ/LISTEN/SPEAK Read these sentences in Japanese. Say what your father, or family member (other than your mother) does for you all the time.

母は　毎日　私に
お弁当を　作って　くれます。
べん

林 君は　女の子に　つるの
はやしくん
おり方を　教えて　あげて　います。
(つる crane, おります to fold)

文法 Grammar

 A Review of Verbs of Giving and Receiving

Giver は **Receiver (equal status)** に **Something** を あげます。

Giver は **Receiver (lower status)** に **Something** を やります。

Giver は **Receiver (me)** に **Something** を くれます。

Giver (outsider) は **Receiver (my family member)** に **Something** を くれます。

Receiver は **Giver** に／から **Something** を もらいます。

▶)) MODELS

1. 友達は 私に DVDを くれました。
   My friend gave me a DVD.

2. 私は 友達に (or から) お金を もらいました。
   I received some money from my friend.

3. これを あなたに あげます。
   I will give this to you.

4. 母は 毎日 犬に 食べ物を やります。
   My mother gives food to the dog every day.

◀)) READ/SPEAK Fill in the ( ) with the correct particle and the [ ] with the correct verb of giving and receiving from the list below.

Verbs of giving and receiving : 〔やります あげます くれます もらいます〕

1. 私は 毎日 犬( ) 食べ物( ) [   ]。

2. おばあさんは 時々 私( ) お金( ) [   ]。

3. 毎年 友達(or) 誕生日の プレゼント( ) [   ]。
   <small>たん</small>

4. 母の 日に 母( ) お花( ) [   ]。
   <small>はな</small>

5. 田中さんは 時々 妹 ( ) 本( ) [   ]。
   <small>いもうと</small>

B Giving and Receiving Favors

Giver	+は	Receiver (equal)	+に	Verb (TE Form) +あげます。
Giver	+は	Receiver (lower status)	+に	Verb (TE Form) +やります。
Giver	+は	Receiver (me)	+に/を	Verb (TE Form) +くれます。
Receiver +は		Giver	+に	Verb (TE Form) +もらいます。

The system of verbs of giving and receiving is very complex in Japanese. It is a reflection of Japanese society, which is structured hierarchically. Verbs differ depending on the relative status of the giver and receiver. あげます, やります, and くれます are all translated as "to give." However, あげます is used when the giver and receiver are of equal status. やります is used to express giving to someone or something lower in status. くれます is generally used when the receiver is the speaker. もらいます is used when the subject is the receiver.

When these verbs are attached to a verb in its TE form, the same general rules apply, except that one is now giving or receiving a favor instead of a gift. When the verbs of giving are used after a verb in its TE form, the favor is being done on the initiative of the giver. When もらいます is used in this construction, it is implied that the receiver of the favor initiated the favor (i.e., made a request), and as a result, receives the favor.

◄))) MODELS ▷

1. 私は 母に 晩ご飯を 作って あげました。
   I made dinner for my mother.

2. 妹 に 本を 読んで あげました。
   I read a book to my younger sister.

3. 父は 私を 学校に 連れて 行って くれます。
   My father takes me to school.

4. 友達は 私を 助けて くれました。
   My friend helped me (as a favor.)

5. 父は 私を 迎えに 来て くれました。
   My father came to pick me up (as a favor.)

6. 私は 友達に お金を 貸して もらいました。
   I had my friend lend me some money (as a favor.)

7. 私は 姉に 宿題を 手伝って もらいました。
   I asked my older sister to help me with my homework.

🔊 **READ/SPEAK** Choose the correct particle in the ( ), change the verb in the < > into the correct form and fill in the [ ] with the correct verb of giving and receiving from the list below.

Verbs of giving and receiving : やりました / あげました / くれました / もらいました

1. 友達は　私(を　に)　誕生日の　パーティーを　＜します＞

[　　　　　]。

2. 漢字の　読み方を　日本人の　友達(を　に)　＜教えます＞

[　　　　　　]。

3. 試験の　前に　私は　頭の　いい　友達(を　に)　＜手伝います＞

[　　　　　]。

4. 母は　昨日　私(を　に)　新しい　スマートフォンを　＜買います＞

[　　　　　]。

文化ノート　Culture Notes

Family Leisure Time

Until a few years ago, Japanese families rarely spent time together, as fathers worked late hours and children attended school six days a week. Recently however, most schools have moved to five-day weeks, and companies are starting to offer incentive programs for parental leave and extended vacation time. Other than on weekends, families enjoy time together during national holidays such as the first few days of the New Year, during Golden Week (the end of April to the beginning of May) and the *O-Bon* season (mid-August).

The most popular leisure activities for families include travel, dining out, and going for scenic drives. During the New Year and *O-Bon* seasons, many families return to their ancestral hometowns. Because so many people travel at these peak seasons, planes, trains, and highways are very crowded. Although most Japanese people choose to travel to domestic destinations, others enjoy traveling abroad. Within Japan, popular destinations are hot springs and mountain or ocean resorts. Families also frequent large theme parks near Tokyo and Osaka, or take part in outdoor activities such as hiking, camping, swimming, and skiing.

Write a short article similar to the one above about family leisure activities in your country and post it on a blog. Include your own photos and videos to augment the content of your article, or link to videos you find on the Internet.

アクティビティ Communicative Activities

ペアワーク

A. READ/SPEAK/LISTEN/WRITE Interview your partner and write his/her responses on a separate sheet of paper. If you do these things for your family, use 〜て あげます. If someone else does these things for you, use 〜て くれます. Compare your answers.

1. 家で だれが 料理を しますか。	
2. 家で だれが 家を そうじしますか。	
3. 家で だれが 洗たくを しますか。	
4. 家で だれが おさらを 洗いますか。	
5. 家で だれが 食物の 買物を しますか。	
6. 家で だれが にわ仕事を しますか。	
7. 家で だれが 車を 洗いますか。	

B. SPEAK/LISTEN Ask your partner what favors he/she asks of the following people.

Ex. お母さん

質問：〜さんは お母さんに 何を して もらいますか。

答え：私は 母に お昼ご飯を 作って もらいます。

1. お父さん	4. きょうだい
2. お母さん	5. 友達
3. おじいさんと おばあさん	6. 先生

C. SPEAK/LISTEN Now ask your partner what he/she does as a favor for the following people.

Ex. お母さん

質問：〜さんは お母さんに 何を して あげますか。

答え：私は 母に 時々 お皿を 洗って あげます。

1. お父さん	4. きょうだい
2. お母さん	5. 友達
3. おじいさんと おばあさん	6. ペット

D. READ/SPEAK/LISTEN/WRITE Take turns asking your partner if he/she is planning to do the following things on Mother's Day. Write his/her responses on a separate sheet of paper.

Ex. 花を　買う

質問：母の日に　お母さんに　花を　買って　あげるつもりですか。

答え：はい、花を　買って　あげるつもりです。or

　　　いいえ、花を　買って　あげないつもりです。

1. かんしゃの　カードを　書く	4. プレゼントを　買う
2. あさごはんを　作る	5. 家を　そうじ　する
3. レストランへ　つれて　行く	6. 何も　しない

Authentic Reading

E. READ/WRITE Read the card and answer the following questions.

UNDERSTAND

1. What did Erika give to her mother on Mother's Day?

2. What did Erika plan to do on Mother's Day?

3. For what reason does Erika appreciate her mother?

IDENTIFY

4. What does 花 mean?

APPLY

5. If you were to write a card to your mother or to another close family member, what would you tell that person that you appreciate most about him/her?

WORKBOOK page 161

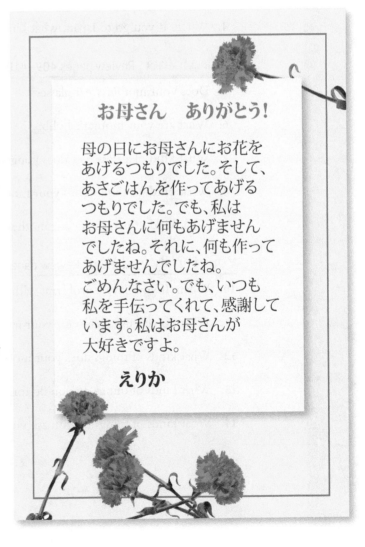

お母さん　ありがとう!

母の日にお母さんにお花を
あげるつもりでした。そして、
あさごはんを作ってあげる
つもりでした。でも、私は
お母さんに何もあげません
でしたね。それに、何も作って
あげませんでしたね。
ごめんなさい。でも、いつも
私を手伝ってくれて、感謝して
います。私はお母さんが
大好きですよ。

えりか

Review Questions

🔊 Ask your partner these questions in Japanese. Your partner should answer in Japanese. You may substitute "mother" with "father" or another family member. Check your answers using the audio.

About You   Review pages 409–410, 414, 416, 420

1. What kinds of things do you like to do on weekends?

2. What color do you like to wear?

3. Are you an only child?

4. When/If you go to Japan, what kinds of things do you want to do?

Your Mother   Review pages 409–410

5. Does your mother wear glasses?

6. What are your mother's hobbies?

7. What kind of accessories does your mother like to wear?

8. What kinds of things does your mother do on weekends?

9. What kind of person is your mother?

Your Family and You   Review pages 416, 420, 425–426

10. When/If you have a problem, with whom do you talk?

11. What do you usually do for your mother on Mother's Day?

12. What kinds of things does your mother/father do for you? [Favor]

13. What kinds of things do you do for your mother/father? [Favor]

14. What kinds of things do you ask your mother/father to do for you?

Text Chat

You will participate in a simulated exchange of text-chat messages. You should respond as fully and as appropriately as possible. You will have a conversation with Rina Fujiwara, a Japanese high school student, about her mother.

05月04日   08:32 AM

お母さんは　どんな人ですか。

Respond in detail.

05月04日   08:37 AM

お母さんの　趣味は　何ですか。

Name two and explain each.

05月04日   08:46 AM

お母さんは　あなたに　どんな
ことを　して　くれますか。

Respond and ask a question.

Can Do!
Now I can . . .

- ☐ list a sample of actions and descriptors
- ☐ use a conditional "if" statement
- ☐ communicate how I or another person does a favor for others
- ☐ express my gratitude and appreciation to others

母の日のカード
Mother's Day Card

母の日にお母さんに感謝(かんしゃ)のカードをおくりましょう。

おにんぎょうカード

Things you need:

はさみ	scissors
のり	glue stick
あかペン	red pen (for lips)
くろペン	black pen (for message)
あつがみ/マニラフォルダー	manila folder

ちよがみ	printed *origami* paper (for kimono)
くろのかみ	black paper (for hair and eyes)
いろがみ	colored paper (for ribbon and sash)
しろのあつがみ	small index card (for face)

リボン
hair ribbon

かお
face

かみ
hair

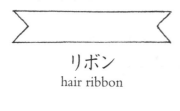

め

eyes
Use a hole puncher to cut
eyes or use a black pen.

きもの
kimono

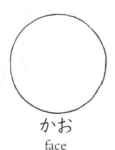

おび
sash

そで
sleeves

1. Trace and cut these patterns out on the appropriate type of paper.

2. Visit the companion website at **cheng-tsui.com/adventuresinjapanese** for a layout of the card frame. Assemble and glue pieces on paper that has been folded in half.

3. Write your Mother's Day message inside the card in Japanese.

Numbers and Counters

	Vol. 1. 1課5 1〜10, 100	4課2 percent パーセント	4課3 general counter 個	5課4 degrees 〜度	5課4 time(s) 〜回
一	いち	いっパーセント	いっこ	いちど	いっかい
二	に	にパーセント	にこ	にど	にかい
三	さん	さんパーセント	さんこ	さんど	さんかい
四	し, よん	よんパーセント	よんこ	よんど	よんかい
五	ご	ごパーセント	ごこ	ごど	ごかい
六	ろく	ろくパーセント	ろっこ	ろくど	ろっかい
七	しち, なな	ななパーセント	ななこ	ななど	ななかい
八	はち	はっパーセント	はっこ	はちど	はっかい
九	きゅう	きゅうパーセント	きゅうこ	きゅうど	きゅうかい
十	じゅう	じゅっパーセント	じゅっこ	じゅうど	じゅっかい
百	ひゃく	ひゃくパーセント	ひゃっこ	ひゃくど	ひゃっかい
?		なんパーセント	なんこ	なんど	なんかい

	6課4 bound objects 〜冊	7課4 floors 〜階	8課4 points 〜点	12課2 ranks 〜位
一	いっさつ	いっかい	いってん	いちい
二	にさつ	にかい	にてん	にい
三	さんさつ	さんかい	さんてん	さんい
四	よんさつ	よんかい	よんてん	よんい
五	ごさつ	ごかい	ごてん	ごい
六	ろくさつ	ろっかい	ろくてん	ろくい
七	ななさつ	ななかい	ななてん	なない
八	はっさつ	はっかい	はってん	はちい
九	きゅうさつ	きゅうかい	きゅうてん	きゅうい
十	じゅっさつ	じゅっかい	じゅってん	じゅうい
?	なんさつ	なんかい	なんてん	なんい

	Vol. 1. 7課2 Vol. 2. 5課4 minute(s) / (units of time) 〜分(間)	Vol. 1. 2課7 Vol. 2. 5課4 hour(s) 時	5課4 day(s) 〜日	5課4 week(s) 〜週間	Vol. 1. 2課6 Vol. 2. 5課4 month(s) 〜月	5課4 year(s) / (grade) 〜年(生)
一	いっぷん(かん)	いちじ*	いちにち	いっしゅうかん	いちがつ	いちねん* (生)
二	にふん(かん)	にじ*	ふつか*	にしゅうかん	にがつ	にねん* (生)
三	さんぷん(かん)	さんじ*	みっか*	さんしゅうかん	さんがつ	さんねん* (生)
四	よんぷん(かん)	よじ*	よっか*	よんしゅうかん	しがつ	よねん* (生)
五	ごふん(かん)	ごじ*	いつか*	ごしゅうかん	ごがつ	ごねん* (生)
六	ろっぷん(かん)	ろくじ*	むいか*	ろくしゅうかん	ろくがつ	ろくねん* (生)
七	ななふん(かん)	しちじ*	なのか*	ななしゅうかん	しちがつ	ななねん*
八	はっぷん(かん)	はちじ*	ようか*	はっしゅうかん	はちがつ	はちねん*
九	きゅうふん(かん)	くじ*	ここのか*	きゅうしゅうかん	くがつ	きゅうねん*
十	じゅっぷん(かん)	じゅうじ*	とおか*	じゅっしゅうかん	じゅうがつ	じゅうねん*
十一					じゅういちがつ	
十二					じゅうにがつ	
?	なんぷん(かん)	なんじ*	なんにち*	なんしゅうかん	なんがつ	なんねん* (生)

*Indicates that 間 may be added to express a unit of time

Vol. 1. 2課6 Days of the Month					
1	ついたち	11	じゅういちにち	21	にじゅういちにち
2	ふつか	12	じゅうににち	22	にじゅうににち
3	みっか	13	じゅうさんにち	23	にじゅうさんにち
4	よっか	14	じゅうよっか	24	にじゅうよっか
5	いつか	15	じゅうごにち	25	にじゅうごにち
6	むいか	16	じゅうろくにち	26	にじゅうろくにち
7	なのか	17	じゅうしちにち	27	にじゅうしちにち
8	ようか	18	じゅうはちにち	28	にじゅうはちにち
9	ここのか	19	じゅうくにち	29	にじゅうくにち
10	とおか	20	はつか	30	さんじゅうにち
?	なんにち			31	さんじゅういちにち

	2課 5 Flat Objects	2課 5 Round or Unclassified Objects	3課 1 People
一	いちまい	ひとつ	ひとり
二	にまい	ふたつ	ふたり
三	さんまい	みっつ	さんにん
四	よんまい	よっつ	よにん
五	ごまい	いつつ	ごにん
六	ろくまい	むっつ	ろくにん
七	ななまい	ななつ	ななにん
八	はちまい	やっつ	はちにん
九	きゅうまい	ここのつ	きゅうにん
十	じゅうまい	とお	じゅうにん
?	なんまい?	いくつ?	なんにん?

	Vol. 1. 8課3 Large, Mechanized Goods 〜台	Vol. 1. 8課3 Birds	Vol. 1. 8課3 Small Animals	Vol. 1. 8課3 Long, Cylindrical Objects 〜本	Vol. 1. 12課3 Cupfuls, Spoonfuls, Etc.
一	いちだい	いちわ	いっぴき	いっぽん	いっぱい
二	にだい	にわ	にひき	にほん	にはい
三	さんだい	さんわ	さんびき	さんぼん	さんばい
四	よんだい	よんわ	よんひき	よんほん	よんはい
五	ごだい	ごわ	ごひき	ごほん	ごはい
六	ろくだい	ろくわ	ろっぴき	ろっぽん	ろっぱい
七	ななだい	ななわ	ななひき	ななほん	ななはい
八	はちだい	はちわ	はっぴき	はっぽん	はっぱい
九	きゅうだい	きゅうわ	きゅうひき	きゅうほん	きゅうはい
十	じゅうだい	じゅうわ	じゅっぴき	じゅっぽん	じゅっぱい
?	なんだい?	なんわ?	なんびき?	なんぼん?	なんばい?

Verb Conjugations

	NAI form	MASU form	Dic. form	Potential	TE form	TA form	NAKATTA form
	informal, neg., nonpast	formal, nonpast	informal, nonpast	(Group 2 verb) L.8		informal, past	informal, neg., past

I. Group 1 Verbs

み	のまない	のみます	のむ	のめる	のんで	のんだ	のまなかった
に	しなない	しにます	しぬ	しねる	しんで	しんだ	しななかった
び	あそばない	あそびます	あそぶ	あそべる	あそんで	あそんだ	あそばなかった
い	かわない	かいます	かう	かえる	かって	かった	かわなかった
ち	またない	まちます	まつ	まてる	まって	まった	またなかった
り	かえらない	かえります	かえる	かえれる	かえって	かえった	かえらなかった
	*ない	あります	ある		あって	あった	*なかった
き	かかない	かきます	かく	かける	かいて	かいた	かかなかった
	いかない	いきます	いく	いける	*いって	*いった	いかなかった
ぎ	およがない	およぎます	およぐ	およげる	およいで	およいだ	およがなかった
し	はなさない	はなします	はなす	はなせる	はなして	はなした	はなさなかった

II. Group 2 Verbs

- e	たべない	たべます	たべる	たべられる	たべて	たべた	たべなかった
	みない	みます	みる	みられる	みて	みた	みなかった

Special verbs: おきます get up, かります borrow, おります get off, できます can do

III. Group 3 Irregular verbs

する	しない	します	する	できる	して	した	しなかった
くる	こない	きます	くる	こられる	きて	きた	こなかった

*Exceptional form

Abbreviations of Grammar Term References

A	い Adjective	atsui, takai, shiroi
Adv	Adverb	totemo, amari, sukoshi
C	Copula	desu, de, na
Da	Adjectival Derivative	-tai
Dv	Verbal Derivative	masu, mashoo, masen
Exp	Expression	chotto matte kudasai
N	Noun	hana, kuruma, enpitsu
Na	な Adjective	kirei, joozu, suki, yuumei
Nd	Dependent Noun	-doru, -han
Ni	Interrogative Noun	dare, doko, ikura
Num.	Number	ichi, juu, hyaku, sen
P	Particle	de, e, ni
Pc	Clause Particle	kara, ga
PN	Pre-Noun	donna, kono, ano
SI	Sentence Interjective	anoo, eeto
SP	Sentence Particle	ka, yo, ne, nee
V	Verb	
V1	Verb (group) 1	ikimasu, hanashimasu, nomimasu
V2	Verb (group) 2	tabemasu, nemasu, imasu
V3	Verb (group) 3 [irregular verb]	kimasu, shimasu

Appendix D

Japanese-English Glossary

Japanese (transliterated)	Japanese (かな)	Japanese (漢字)	Lesson	Type	English
A					
aa	ああ		II–10–1	SI	Oh!
abunai	あぶない	危ない	II–3–3	A	dangerous
abura	あぶら	油	II–11–2	N	oil
achira	あちら		II–4–4	N	over there, that one over there [polite equiv. of あそこ or あれ]
ageru	あげる		II–6–4	V2	(to) give (to an equal)
ai	あい	愛	II–12–4	N	love, affection
aida	あいだ	間	II–1–2	N	between
aishite iru	あいしている	愛している	II–12–4	V1	(to be in) love
aji	あじ	味	II–11–3	N	taste, flavor
aka	あか	赤	I–5–5	N	red
akachan	あかちゃん	赤ちゃん	II–1–3	N	baby
akai	あかい	赤い	I–6–3	A	red
akarui	あかるい	明るい	II–9–1	A	bright
akeru	あける	開ける	I–11–2	V2	to open
Akete kudasai.	あけてください。	開けて下さい。	I–2–2	Exp	Please open.
aki	あき	秋	I–10–4	N	autumn, fall
amai	あまい	甘い	II–11–3	A	sweet
amari	あまり	余り	I–5–4	Adv	(not) very
ame	あめ	飴	I–2–5	N	candy
ame	あめ	雨	I–1–6	N	rain
amerika	アメリカ		I–3–4	N	America
amerikajin	アメリカじん	アメリカ人	I–3–4	N	U.S. citizen
ana	あな	穴	II–9–2	N	hole
anata	あなた		I–2–4	N	you
anatano	あなたの		I–2–4	N	yours
ane	あね	姉	I–3–1	N	(my) older sister
ani	あに	兄	I–3–1	N	(my) older brother
ano	あの		I–2–4	PN	that ~ over there
anoo...	あのう...		I–2–1	SI	let me see . . . , well . . .
anzen	あんぜん	安全	II–3–3	Na	safe

Japanese (transliterated)	Japanese (かな)	Japanese (漢字)	Lesson	Type	English
ao	あお	青	I-5-5	N	blue, green
aoi	あおい	青い	I-6-3	A	blue
arabiago	アラビアご	アラビア語	I-4-1	N	Arabic language
arau	あらう	洗う	II-6-3	V1	(to) wash
are	あれ		I-1-5	N	that one over there
arigatoo	ありがとう		I-1-4	Exp	Thank you.
Arigatoo gozaimashita.	ありがとうございました。	有難うございました。	II-7-2	Exp	Thank you very much. [used after receiving something or after a completed action]
Arigatoo gozaimasu.	ありがとうございます。	有難うございます。	I-1-4	Exp	Thank you very much.
aru	ある		I-8-1	V1	(to) have, there is (inanimate obj.)
aru〜	ある 〜		II-9-4	PN	(a) certain 〜
(place de) arubaito(o) suru	(place で) アルバイト(を) する		II-1-1	V3	(to) work part-time (at 〜)
aruku	あるく	歩く	I-7-3	V1	(to) walk
asa	あさ	朝	I-4-3	N	morning
asagohan	あさごはん	朝ご飯	I-4-3	N	breakfast
asatte	あさって	明後日	I-9-3	N	day after tomorrow
ashi	あし	足	I-6-1	N	foot
ashi	あし	脚	I-6-1	N	leg
ashita	あした	明日	I-4-3	N	tomorrow
ashiyubi	あしゆび	足指	I-6-1	N	toe
asobu	あそぶ	遊ぶ	I-9-5	V1	(to) play, amuse (not for sports/music)
asoko	あそこ		I-2-5	N	over there
atama	あたま	頭	I-6-1	N	head
atarashii	あたらしい	新しい	I-8-4	A	new
atatakai	あたたかい	暖かい	I-12-4	A	warm
ato〜	あと〜	後〜	II-8-4	PN	〜 more
(〜no) ato de	(〜の) あとで	(〜の) 後で	I-10-5	Pp	after 〜
atsui	あつい	厚い	II-11-2	A	thick
atsui	あつい	暑い	I-1-6	IA	hot (temperature)
atsuku	あつく	厚く	II-11-2	Adv	thick
atsuku suru	あつくする	熱くする	II-11-2	V3	(to) heat, (to) make hot
au	あう	会う	I-10-5	V1	(to) meet

Japanese (transliterated)	Japanese (かな)	Japanese (漢字)	Lesson	Type	English
B					
baibai	バイバイ		I-12-5	Exp	bye bye
baiten	ばいてん	売店	I-4-4	N	snack bar; kiosk
〜ban	〜ばん	〜番	II-8-1	Nd	Number -
ban	ばん	晩	I-4-3	N	evening
bando	バンド		I-9-5	N	band
bangohan	ばんごはん	晩ご飯	I-4-3	N	dinner, supper
〜banme	〜ばんめ	〜番目	II-10-2	Nd	[in order]
Banzai!	ばんざい！	万歳！	II-8-4	Exp	Hurray!
baree(booru)	バレー(ボール)		I-5-3	N	volleyball
basho	ばしょ	場所	II-8-1	N	place, location
basu	バス		I-7-3	N	bus
basuketto(booru)	バスケット(ボール)		I-5-3	N	basketball
basutei	バスてい	バス停	II-10-1	N	bus stop
beddo	ベッド		I-8-5	N	bed
bengoshi	べんごし	弁護士	I-3-5	N	lawyer
benkyoo (o) suru	べんきょう(を) する	勉強(を) する	I-4-4	V3	(to) study
bentoo	べんとう	弁当	I-12-2	N	box lunch
bijutsu	びじゅつ	美術	I-9-1	N	art
bijutsukan	びじゅつかん	美術館	II-10-1	N	art museum
binboo	びんぼう	貧乏	II-9-1	Na	poor
boku	ぼく	僕	I-1-1	N	I (used by males)
bokutachi	ぼくたち	僕達	I-10-3	N	we [used by males.]
boorupen	ボールペン		I-2-3	N	ballpoint pen
booshi	ぼうし	帽子	I-2-3	N	cap, hat
bosuton	ボストン		I-7-5	N	Boston
burajiru	ブラジル		I-3-4	N	Brazil
buta	ぶた	豚	I-8-5	N	pig
butaniku	ぶたにく	豚肉	II-11-1	N	pork
byooin	びょういん	病院	I-3-5	N	hospital
byooki	びょうき	病気	I-10-1	N	illness, sickness
C					
chairo	ちゃいろ	茶色	I-5-5	N	brown color
chairoi	ちゃいろい	茶色い	I-6-3	A	brown
Chakuseki.	ちゃくせき。	着席。	I-1-3	Exp	Sit.
〜chan	〜ちゃん		II-1-3	Nd	[Suffix used with young animals or children instead of 〜さん.]

Japanese (transliterated)	Japanese (かな)	Japanese (漢字)	Lesson	Type	English
chichi	ちち	父	I-3-1	N	(my) father
chigau	ちがう	違う	II-1-4	V1	(to be) wrong, (to) differ
chiimu	チーム		I-10-3	N	team
chiisai	ちいさい	小さい	I-6-2	A	small
chika	ちか	地下	II-7-4	N	basement
chikai	ちかい	近い	I-8-5	A	near, close
chikaku	ちかく	近く	II-1-2	N	vicinity, nearby
chikara	ちから	力	II-9-2	N	power, strength, ability
chikatetsu	ちかてつ	地下鉄	I-7-3	N	subway
chikoku	ちこく	遅刻	I-1-3	Exp	tardy
chippu	チップ		II-4-2	N	tip
chizu	ちず	地図	II-10-1	N	map
chokoreeto	チョコレート		I-2-5	N	chocolate
chotto	ちょっと		I-4-1	Adv	a little [more colloquial than すこし]
Chotto matte kudasai.	ちょっとまってください。	ちょっと待って下さい。	I-1-4	Exp	Please wait a minute.
Chotto ukagaimasu ga . . .	ちょっとうかがいますが . . .		II-10-1	Exp	I have a question.
chuugaku	ちゅうがく	中学	I-3-3	N	intermediate school
chuugaku ichinensei	ちゅうがくいちねんせい	中学一年生	I-3-3	N	int. school 1st-year student
chuugaku ninensei	ちゅうがくにねんせい	中学二年生	I-3-3	N	int. school 2nd-year student
chuugaku sannensei	ちゅうがくさんねんせい	中学三年生	I-3-3	N	int. school 3rd-year student
chuugakusei	ちゅうがくせい	中学生	I-3-3	N	int. school student
chuugoku	ちゅうごく	中国	I-3-4	N	China
chuugokugo	ちゅうごくご	中国語	I-4-1	N	Chinese language
chuumon (o) suru	ちゅうもん(を) する	注文(を)する	II-4-2	V3	(to) order
Chuumon wa?	(ご)ちゅうもんは?	(御)注文は?	II-4-4	Exp	What is your order? May I take your order?
chuushajoo	ちゅうしゃじょう	駐車場	II-10-1	N	parking lot
D					
da	だ		II-9-4	C	[plain form of copula です]
~dai	~だい	~台	I-8-3	Nd	[counter for mechanized goods]
daidokoro	だいどころ	台所	II-11-1	N	kitchen
daigaku	だいがく	大学	I-10-5	N	college, university
daigakusei	だいがくせい	大学生	I-10-5	N	college student

Japanese (transliterated)	Japanese (かな)	Japanese (漢字)	Lesson	Type	English
daiji	だいじ	大事	I-10-4	Na	important
daijoobu	だいじょうぶ	大丈夫	I-10-1	Na	all right
daikirai	だいきらい	大嫌い	I-5-2	Na	dislike a lot, hate
daisuki	だいすき	大好き	I-5-2	Na	like very much, love
daitai	だいたい		II-4-2	Adv	generally
dakara	だから		II-9-2	SI	therefore [Informal]
〜dake	〜だけ		II-2-4	Nd	only 〜
dame	だめ	駄目	I-2-1	Na	no good
dansu	ダンス		I-5-1	N	dance, dancing
dare	だれ	誰	I-3-1	Ni	who?
〜dashite kudasai.	〜だしてください。	〜出して 下さい。	I-2-2	Exp	Please turn in 〜.
dasu	だす	出す	II-3-3	V1	(to) extend out, submit, take out
datta	だった		II-9-4	C	[plain form of copula でした]
[tool] de	[tool] で		I-4-5	P	[tool particle] by, with, on, in
[transportation] de	[transportation] で		I-7-3	P	by [transportation mode]
(〜no naka) de	(〜のなか) で	(〜の中) で	II-7-3	P	among 〜
[counter] de	[counter] で		I-12-2	P	[totalizing particle]
[place] de [action V]	[place] で [action V]		I-4-1	P	[doing something] at, in [a place]
deguchi	でぐち	出口	II-10-2	N	exit
dekakeru	(place を/から) でかける	出かける	II-3-4	V2	(to) leave, go out (from a place)
(〜ga) dekimashita	(〜が) できました	出来ました	II-11-4	V2	(〜 is) ready, (〜 is) done
(〜ga) dekiru	(〜 が) できる	出来る	II-5-1	V2	(to be) able to do 〜
demo	でも		I-4-1	SI	But [begins sentence]
densha	でんしゃ	電車	I-7-3	N	electric train
denwa	でんわ	電話	I-4-5	N	telephone
denwa bangoo	でんわばんごう	電話番号	II-1-1	N	telephone number
denwa o kakeru	でんわをかける	電話をかける	II-5-2	V2	(to) make a phone call
depaato	デパート		I-7-4	N	department store
(place o) deru	(place を) でる	(place を) 出る	II-3-2	V2	(to) leave (a place)
(shiai ni) deru	(しあいに)でる	(試合に)出る	II-8-1	V2	(to) participate in a (sports) game
〜deshoo	〜でしょう [falling intonation]		II-6-2	C	probably 〜

Japanese (transliterated)	Japanese (かな)	Japanese (漢字)	Lesson	Type	English
deshoo	〜でしょう [rising intonation]		II-6-2	C	Isn't it 〜?
desu	です		I-1-1	C	am, is, are
desukara	ですから		II-9-2	SI	therefore [formal]
dewa	では		I-12-1	Exp	well then [formal]
dezaato	デザート		II-11-4	N	dessert
dezain	デザイン		II-7-2	N	design
〜do	〜ど	〜度	II-5-4	Nd	[counter for degree(s), time(s)]
doa	ドア		I-2-2	N	door
dochira	どちら		II-4-4	Ni	where? [polite equiv. of どこ], which (one of two)?
dochiramo + neg.	どちらも + neg.		II-7-1	N	neither, not either
dokidoki suru	ドキドキする		II-8-4	V3	(to be) excited, (to be) nervous
doko	どこ		I-3-4	Ni	where?
doko emo	どこへも		I-7-4	Ni+P	(not to) anywhere
dokusho	どくしょ	読書	I-5-1	N	reading
donna〜?	どんな〜		I-5-2	PN	what kind of 〜?
dono〜?	どの〜		I-11-4	Nd	which 〜?
donogurai	どのぐらい		II-5-4	Ni	about how long/far/ often?
Donogurai arimasu ka.	どのぐらい ありますか。		II-10-3	Exp	How far is it? [distance]
Donogurai desu ka.	どのぐらいですか。		II-10-3	Exp	How long/far is it?
Donogurai kakarimasu ka.	どのぐらいかか りますか。		II-10-3	Exp	How long does it take? [time]
Doo desu ka .	どうですか。		I-7-5	Exp	How is it? [informal]
Doo itashimashite.	どういたしまして。		I-1-4	Exp	You are welcome.
Doo shimashita ka.	どうしましたか。		I-10-1	Exp	What happened?
doobutsuen	どうぶつえん	動物園	II-10-1	N	zoo
dooga	どうが	動画	II-5-2	N	online video
Doomo.	どうも。		I-1-4	Exp	Thank you.
dooshite?	どうして		I-9-3	Ni	why?
Doozo kochira e.	どうぞこちらへ。		II-4-4	Exp	This way, please.
Doozo yoroshiku.	どうぞよろしく。		I-1-1	N	Nice to meet you.

Japanese (transliterated)	Japanese (かな)	Japanese (漢字)	Lesson	Type	English
doraibaa	ドライバー		II-3-1	N	driver
dore	どれ		II-7-3	Ni	which one (of three or more)?
doru	ドル		I-11-4	Nd	dollar(s)
dotchi	どっち		II-7-1	Ni	which (one of two)? [informal]
doyoobi	どようび	土曜日	I-2-7	N	Saturday

E

Japanese (transliterated)	Japanese (かな)	Japanese (漢字)	Lesson	Type	English
e	えっ		II-9-3	SI	Huh?
[place] e	[place] へ		I-7-2	P	to [place]
e	え	絵	I-5-1	N	painting, drawing
ee	ええ		I-1-5	SI	yes [informal]
eeto...	ええと...		I-2-1	SI	let me see . . . , well . . .
eiga	えいが	映画	I-5-1	N	movie
eigakan	えいがかん	映画館	II-2-4	N	movie theater
eigo	えいご	英語	I-4-1	N	English
eki	えき	駅	II-10-1	N	train station
emu-saizu	エムサイズ		I-12-2	N	medium size
en	えん	円	I-11-4	Nd	yen
enjinia	エンジニア		I-3-5	N	engineer
enpitsu	えんぴつ	鉛筆	I-2-3	N	pencil
enpitsukezuri	えんぴつけずり	鉛筆削り	I-8-1	N	pencil sharpener
erai	えらい	偉い	II-9-1	A	great (person)
eru-saizu	エルサイズ		I-12-2	N	large size
esu-saizu	エスサイズ		I-12-2	N	small size

F

Japanese (transliterated)	Japanese (かな)	Japanese (漢字)	Lesson	Type	English
fooku	フォーク		I-12-3	N	fork
fukitobasu	ふきとばす	吹き飛ばす	II-9-2	V1	(to) blow away
fuku	ふく	服	II-2-1	N	clothing
fukuro	ふくろ	袋	II-7-4	N	(paper) bag
～fun	～ふん	～分	I-7-1	Nd	minute
fune	ふね	船	I-7-3	N	boat, ship
furaidopoteto	フライドポテト		I-12-2	N	french fries
furansu	フランス		I-3-4	N	France
furansugo	フランスご	フランス語	I-4-1	N	French language
furorida	フロリダ		I-7-5	N	Florida
furu	ふる	降る	II-6-2	V1	(rain, snow) fall
furui	ふるい	古い	I-8-4	A	old (not for person's age)

Japanese (transliterated)	Japanese (かな)	Japanese (漢字)	Lesson	Type	English
futago	ふたご	双子	II-12-2	N	twin
futari	ふたり	二人	I-3-1	N	two people
futatsu	ふたつ	二つ	I-2-5	N	two [general counter]
futoru	ふとる	太る	I-6-4	V1	(to become) fat
futsuka	ふつか	二日	I-2-6	N	2nd day of the month
futtobooru	フットボール		I-5-3	N	football
fuyu	ふゆ	冬	I-10-4	N	winter

G

Japanese (transliterated)	Japanese (かな)	Japanese (漢字)	Lesson	Type	English
[sentence] ga	[sentence] が		I-5-3	Pc	but
[subject] ga	[subject] が		I-7-3	P	[subject particle]
[sentence] ga. . .	[sentence] が. . .		II-5-2	Ps	[softens the statement.]
gaikokugo	がいこくご	外国語	I-9-1	N	foreign language
gakkoo	がっこう	学校	I-3-3	N	school
gakusei	がくせい	学生	I-3-3	N	student [college]
gamu	ガム		II-2-2	N	gum
ganbaru	がんばる	頑張る	I-10-4	V1	(to) do one's best
Ganbatte.	がんばって。	頑張って。	I-10-4	Exp	Good luck.
gareeji	ガレージ		I-8-5	N	garage
garigari	ガリガリ		II-9-2	Adv	chew away, gnaw [onomatopoetic]
～gatsu umare	～がつうまれ	～月生まれ	I-2-6	Nd	(month) born in
～gawa	～がわ	～側	II-10-2	Nd	(～) side
geemu	ゲーム		I-9-5	N	game
geemu(o) suru	ゲーム(を) する		I-9-5	V3	play a game
geki	げき	劇	II-9-1	N	(stage) play
genki	げんき	元気	I-1-6	Na	fine, healthy
(O)genki desu ka。	(お)げんきですか。	(お)元気ですか。	I-1-6	Exp	How are you?
getsuyoobi	げつようび	月曜日	I-2-7	N	Monday
gin	ぎん	銀	II-12-1	N	silver
giniro	ぎんいろ	銀色	I-5-5	N	silver color
ginkoo	ぎんこう	銀行	II-1-3	N	bank
gitaa	ギター		I-5-1	N	guitar
go	ご	五	I-1-4	Num.	five
gochisoo (o) suru	ごちそう(を)する		II-4-3	V3	(to) treat (SO)
gochisoosama	ごちそうさま		I-12-4	Exp	[expression after a meal]
gogatsu	ごがつ	五月	I-2-6	N	May
gogo	ごご	午後	I-7-1	N	p.m.
gohan	ごはん	ご飯	I-4-2	N	(cooked) rice

Japanese (transliterated)	Japanese (かな)	Japanese (漢字)	Lesson	Type	English
go-juu	ごじゅう	五十	I-1-5	Num.	fifty
gomi	ごみ		I-2-3	N	trash
gomibako	ごみばこ	ごみ箱	I-8-1	N	trash can
~goro	~ごろ		I-2-7	Nd	about (time)
gorufu	ゴルフ		I-5-3	N	golf
goryooshin	ごりょうしん	御両親	II-1-4	N	(SO else's) parents [polite]
gozen	ごぜん	午前	I-7-1	N	a.m.
guai ga warui	ぐあいがわるい	具合が悪い	II-5-1	A	condition is bad, feel sick
~gurai	~ぐらい		I-11-4	Nd	about ~ [Not used for time]
gurandokyanion	グランドキャニオン		I-7-5	N	Grand Canyon
guree	グレー		I-5-5	N	grey
gyuuniku	ぎゅうにく	牛肉	II-11-1	N	beef
gyuunyuu	ぎゅうにゅう	牛乳	I-4-2	N	(cow's) milk

H

Japanese (transliterated)	Japanese (かな)	Japanese (漢字)	Lesson	Type	English
ha	は	歯	I-6-1	N	tooth
hachi	はち	八	I-1-4	N	eight
hachigatsu	はちがつ	八月	I-2-6	N	August
hachi-juu	はちじゅう	八十	I-1-5	Num.	eighty
haha	はは	母	I-3-1	N	(my) mother
~hai	~はい	~杯	I-12-3	Nd	[counter for cupful, glassful, bowlful]
hai	はい		I-1-2	Exp	yes
Hai doozo.	はい、どうぞ。		I-2-5	Exp	Here, you are.
(place に) hairu	(place に) はいる	入る	II-3-2	V1	(to) enter (a place)
(~ga) hajimaru	(~が) はじまる	始まる	II-8-1	V1	(something will) begin, start
hajime ni	はじめに	始めに	II-11-2	Adv	(at the) beginning
Hajimemashite.	はじめまして。	初めまして。	I-1-1	Exp	How do you do? / Nice to meet you.
Hajimemashoo.	はじめましょう。	始めましょう。	I-1-3	Exp	Let's begin.
(~o) hajimeru	(~を) はじめる	始める	II-8-1	V2	(SO will) start, begin (something)
hajimete	はじめて	始めて	II-6-1	Adv.	(for the) first time
hako	はこ	箱	II-7-4	N	box
haku	はく	履く	II-2-1	V1	(to) wear [below the waist]
~han	~はん	~半	I-2-7	Nd	half
hana	はな	鼻	I-6-1	N	nose

Japanese (transliterated)	Japanese (かな)	Japanese (漢字)	Lesson	Type	English
hana	はな	花	I-8-3	N	flower
hanabi	はなび	花火	I-7-5	N	fireworks
hanasu	はなす	話す	I-4-1	V1	(to) speak, talk
hanaya	はなや	花屋	I-11-3	N	flower shop
hanbaagaa	ハンバーガー		I-12-2	N	hamburger
hanbun ni	はんぶんに	半分に	II-11-2	Adv	(in) half
harau	はらう	払う	II-4-2	V1	(to) pay
hare	はれ	晴れ	II-6-2	N	clear (weather)
haru	はる	春	I-10-4	N	spring
hashi	はし	橋	II-10-2	N	bridge
(o)hashi	(お)はし	(お)箸	I-12-3	N	chopsticks
hashiru	はしる	走る	I-10-5	V1	(to) run
hatachi	はたち	二十歳	I-3-1	N	twenty years old
(place de) hataraku	(place で) はたらく	働く	II-1-1	V1	(to) work (at 〜)
hatsuka	はつか	二十日	I-2-6	N	20th day of the month
hawai	ハワイ		I-7-5	N	Hawaii
hayai	はやい	早い	I-7-1	A	early
hayaku	はやく	速く	II-3-3	Adv	fast, quickly
hayaku	はやく	早く	I-10-2	Adv	early [used with a V]
(V Dic./NAI form) hazu desu	(V Dic./NAI form) はずです		II-5-3	Nd	I expect that he/she will do/will not do.
hen	へん	辺	II-10-1	N	area
hen	へん	変	II-5-1	Na	strange, weird, unusual
heta	へた	下手	I-5-3	Na	unskillful, poor at
heya	へや	部屋	I-8-5	N	room
hi	ひ	日	I-2-6	N	day
hidari	ひだり	左	II-1-2	N	left side
hidoi	ひどい	酷い	I-9-3	A	terrible
〜hiki	〜ひき	〜匹	I-8-3	Nd	[counter for small animals]
hikooki	ひこうき	飛行機	I-7-3	N	airplane
hiku	ひく	弾く	II-5-1	V1	(to) play (a string instrument)
hikui	ひくい	低い	I-6-1	A	short (height)
hima	ひま	暇	II-12-2	Na	(is) free (time)
hiroi	ひろい	広い	I-8-5	A	wide, spacious
(o)hiru	(お)ひる	(お)昼	I-4-3	N	daytime
hirugohan	ひるごはん	昼ご飯	I-4-3	N	lunch
hito	ひと	人	I-8-2	N	person

Japanese (transliterated)	Japanese (かな)	Japanese (漢字)	Lesson	Type	English
hitori	ひとり	一人	I-3-1	N	one person, alone
hitorikko	ひとりっこ	一人っ子	II-12-2	N	only child
hitotsu	ひとつ	一つ	I-2-5	N	one [general counter]
hodo + Neg.	ほど + neg.		II-7-2	P	not as ～ as
hoka	ほか		II-7-2	N	other
Hoka ni nani ka.	ほかになにか。	ほかに何か。	II-4-4	Exp	Anything else?
Hokkaidoo	ほっかいどう	北海道	II-1-1	N	Hokkaido
～hon	～ほん	～本	I-8-3	Nd	[counter for long cylindrical objects]
hon	ほん	本	I-2-3	N	book
Honshuu	ほんしゅう	本州	II-1-1	N	Honshu
hontoo	ほんとう	本当	I-3-1	N	true
Hontoo desu ka.	ほんとうですか。	本当ですか。	II-2-4	Exp	(Is it) true/real?
hontoo ni	ほんとうに	本当に	II-2-4	Adv	really, truly
honya	ほんや	本屋	I-11-3	N	bookstore
(～no) hoo	(～の) ほう	方	II-7-1	N	alternative
hoomuruumu	ホームルーム		I-9-1	N	homeroom
hoomusutei o suru	ホームステイをする		II-1-1	V3	do a homestaty
hoshii	ほしい	欲しい	I-9-4	A	want (something)
hottodoggu	ホットドッグ		I-12-2	N	hotdog
hyaku	ひゃく	百	I-1-5	Num.	hundred
hyaku-man	ひゃくまん	百万	I-11-4	N	one million

I

Japanese (transliterated)	Japanese (かな)	Japanese (漢字)	Lesson	Type	English
～i	～い	～位	II-12-2	Nd	[counter for rank]
ichi	いち	一	I-1-4	Num.	one
ichiban	いちばん	一番	II-7-3	Adv	the most
ichigatsu	いちがつ	一月	I-2-6	N	January
ichigo	いちご	苺	II-11-1	N	strawberry
ie	いえ	家	II-1-3	N	house
ii	いい		I-2-1	A	good
Ii desu nee.	いいですねえ。		I-9-3	Exp	How nice! [about a future event]
iie	いいえ		I-1-5	SI	no [formal]
Iie, kekkoo desu.	いいえ、けっこうです。	いいえ、結構です。	I-12-3	Exp	No, thank you.
Ikaga desu ka?	いかがですか。	如何ですか。	I-11-5	Ni	How about ~? [Polite exp. of どうですか]
ike	いけ	池	I-8-3	N	pond

Japanese (transliterated)	Japanese (かな)	Japanese (漢字)	Lesson	Type	English
ikemasen	いけません		II-2-2	V2	won't do, must not do
iku	いく	行く	I-7-2	V1	(to) go
(o)ikura?	(お)いくら?		I-11-4	Ni	How much? [cost]
ikutsu	いくつ		I-2-5	Ni	how many? [general counter]
(o)ikutsu?	(お)いくつ?		I-3-1	Ni	How old?
ima	いま	今	I-2-7	N	now
imooto	いもうと	妹	I-3-1	N	(my) younger sister
imootosan	いもうとさん	妹さん	I-3-2	N	(SO's) younger sister
indo	インド		I-3-4	N	India
inu	いぬ	犬	I-8-1	N	dog
Irasshaimase.	いらっしゃいませ。		II-4-4	Exp	Welcome.
(～ni) ireru	(～に) いれる	入れる	II-7-4	V2	(to) put in ～
iriguchi	いりぐち	入口	II-10-2	N	entrance
iro	いろ	色	I-5-5	N	color
iroiro	いろいろ		II-7-2	Na	various
iru	いる		I-8-1	V2	there is (animate obj.)
(～ga) iru	(～が) いる	要る	I-12-3	V1	(to) need ～
isha	いしゃ	医者	I-3-5	N	(medical) doctor
isogashii	いそがしい	忙しい	I-7-4	A	busy
issho ni	いっしょに	一緒に	I-4-4	Adv	together
isshookenmei	いっしょうけんめい	一生懸命	II-9-3	Adv	(with one's) utmost effort
isu	いす	椅子	I-8-1	N	chair
itadakimasu	いただきます		I-12-4	Exp	[expression before a meal]
itai	いたい	痛い	I-10-1	A	painful, sore
itoko	いとこ		II-6-4	N	cousin
itokonnyaku	いとこんにゃく	糸こんにゃく	II-11-1	N	shredded konnyaku
itsu	いつ		I-2-6	Ni	when?
itsuka	いつか	五日	I-2-6	N	5th day of the month
itsumo	いつも		I-4-2	Adv	always
itsutsu	いつつ	五つ	I-2-5	N	five [general counter]
iu	いう	言う	I-11-2	V1	(to) say
iya(tt)	いや(っ)		II-9-3	SI	No [stronger negation than いいえ]
iyaringu	イヤリング		II-2-1	N	earrings
J					
Ja	じゃ		I-12-1	Exp	Well then [informal]
jaketto	ジャケット		I-11-3	N	jacket

Japanese (transliterated)	Japanese (かな)	Japanese (漢字)	Lesson	Type	English
jama	じゃま	邪魔	I-6-5	Na	hindrance, nuisance
～ji	～じ	～時	I-2-7	Nd	[counter for hours (of day)]
jibun	じぶん	自分	II-12-3	N	oneself
jidoosha	じどうしゃ	自動車	I-7-3	N	car, vehicle
～jikan	～じかん	～時間	II-5-4	Nd	[counter for hours (unit of time)]
jikan	じかん	時間	II-8-1	N	time
jikoshookai(o) suru	じこしょうかい(を)する	自己紹介(を)する	II-1-3	V3	(to) do a self-introduction
jimusho	じむしょ	事務所	I-8-4	N	office
jinja	じんじゃ	神社	II-6-1	N	shrine (Shinto)
jisho	じしょ	辞書	I-2-3	N	dictionary
jitensha	じてんしゃ	自転車	I-7-3	N	bicycle
jiyuu	じゆう	自由	II-2-2	Na	free, liberal
jogingu	ジョギング		I-5-1	N	jogging
joodan	じょうだん	冗談	II-8-3	N	(a) joke
joozu	じょうず	上手	I-5-3	Na	skillful, (be) good at
jugyoo	じゅぎょう	授業	I-9-1	N	class, instruction
juu	じゅう	十	I-1-4	Num.	ten
juuden suru	じゅうでんする	充電する	II-5-2	V3	(to) charge (battery)
juugatsu	じゅうがつ	十月	I-2-6	N	October
juu-go	じゅうご	十五	I-1-5	Num.	fifteen
juu-hachi	じゅうはち	十八	I-1-5	Num.	eighteen
juu-ichi	じゅういち	十一	I-1-5	Num.	eleven
juuichigatsu	じゅういちがつ	十一月	I-2-6	N	November
juu-ku	じゅうく	十九	I-1-5	Num.	nineteen
juu-kyuu	じゅうきゅう	十九	I-1-5	Num.	nineteen
juu-man	じゅうまん	十万	I-11-4	Num.	hundred thousand
juu-nana	じゅうなな	十七	I-1-5	Num.	seventeen
juu-ni	じゅうに	十二	I-1-5	Num.	twelve
juunigatsu	じゅうにがつ	十二月	I-2-6	N	December
juu-roku	じゅうろく	十六	I-1-5	Num.	sixteen
juu-san	じゅうさん	十三	I-1-5	Num.	thirteen
juu-shi, juu-yon	じゅうし，じゅうよん	十四	I-1-5	Num.	fourteen
juu-shichi	じゅうしち	十七	I-1-5	Num.	seventeen
juusho	じゅうしょ	住所	II-1-1	N	address
juusu	ジュース		I-4-2	N	juice

Japanese (transliterated)	Japanese (かな)	Japanese (漢字)	Lesson	Type	English
K					
ka	か		I-1-3	SP	[question particle]
kabe	かべ	壁	II-9-1	N	wall
kaburu	かぶる		II-2-1	V1	(to) wear [on or draped over the head]
kado	かど	角	II-3-1	N	corner
kaeru	かえる	帰る	I-7-2	V1	(to) return (to a place)
kaesu	かえす	返す	II-4-3	V1	(to) return (something)
kafeteria	カフェテリア		I-4-4	N	cafeteria
kagaku	かがく	科学	I-9-1	N	science
～kagetsu	～かげつ	～か月	II-5-4	Nd	[counter for months]
kagi	かぎ	鍵	II-3-1	N	key
～kai	～かい	～階	II-7-4	Nd	[counter for floor]
kaimono	かいもの	買い物	I-7-4	N	shopping
kaimono(o)shi-masu	かいもの(を)します	買い物(を)します	I-7-4	V3	go shopping
kaisha	かいしゃ	会社	I-7-2	N	company
kaishain	かいしゃいん	会社員	I-3-5	N	company employee
Kaite kudasai.	かいてください。	書いて下さい。	I-2-2	Exp	Please write.
kakaru	かかる		II-7-4	V1	(to) require, to take (time)
kakeru	かける		II-2-1	V2	(to) wear [glasses]
kaku	かく	書く	I-4-5	V1	(to) write
(e o) kaku	(えを) かく	(絵を) 描く	II-12-1	V1	(to) draw, paint a picture
kakusu	かくす	隠す	II-9-2	V1	(to) hide (something)
kamaimasen	かまいません		II-2-2	V1	(I) do not mind if . . .
kami	かみ	紙	I-2-3	N	paper
kami (no ke)	かみ(のけ)	髪(の毛)	I-6-1	N	hair
kamoku	かもく	科目	I-9-1	N	subject
(gamu o) kamu	(ガムを)かむ		II-2-2	V1	(to) chew gum
kanashii	かなしい	悲しい	I-9-3	A	sad
(o)kane	(お)かね	(お)金	I-2-3	N	money
(o)kanemochi	(お)かねもち	(お)金持ち	II-9-1	N	rich person
(o)kanjoo	(お)かんじょう	(お)勘定	II-4-2	N	(a) check, bill
kankoku	かんこく	韓国	I-3-4	N	Korea
kankokugo	かんこくご	韓国語	I-4-1	N	Korean language
kansha (o) suru	かんしゃ(を) する	感謝(を)する	II-12-4	V3	(to) appreciate, thank
kao	かお	顔	I-6-1	N	face
[sentence] kara	[sentence] から		I-9-3	Pc	because～, since～, ～so

Japanese (transliterated)	Japanese (かな)	Japanese (漢字)	Lesson	Type	English
kara	～から		I-7-5	P	from～
karada	からだ	体	I-6-1	N	body
karai	からい	辛い	II-11-3	A	spicy, hot
kareeraisu	カレーライス		II-4-1	N	curry rice
kariru	かりる	借りる	II-2-3	V2	(to) borrow, (to) rent (from)
Kashite kudasai.	かしてください。	貸して下さい。	I-12-3	Exp	Please lend me ～.
(V stem +) kata	(V stem +)かた	方	II-11-1	N	how to do ～
kata	かた	方	I-8-2	Nd	person [polite form]
katazukeru	かたづける	片付ける	II-11-4	V2	(to) clean up, put away
katsu	かつ	勝つ	I-10-3	V1	(to) win
Katta! Katta!	かった！かった！	勝った！勝った！	II-8-4	Exp	(We) won! (We) won!
kau	かう	買う	I-11-3	V1	(to) buy
kawa	かわ	川	I-7-4	N	river
kawaii	かわいい	可愛い	I-6-5	A	cute
Kawaisoo ni.	かわいそうに。	可愛そうに。	I-10-1	Exp	How pitiful.
kayoobi	かようび	火曜日	I-2-7	N	Tuesday
kaze	かぜ	風	II-6-2	N	wind
kaze	かぜ	風邪	I-10-1	N	(a) cold
kaze o hiku	かぜをひく	風邪を引く	II-5-1	V1	(to) catch a cold
kazoku	かぞく	家族	I-3-1	N	(my) family
(go)kazoku	(ご)かぞく	(御)家族	I-3-2	N	(someone's) family
keetai	ケータイ/けいたい	携帯	I-4-5	N	cellular phone
keikan	けいかん	警官	I-3-5	N	police officer
(person to) kekkon (o) suru	(person と) けっこん(を) する	結婚(を)する	II-1-1	V3	(to be) married (to ～)
kenka (o) suru	けんか(を) する	喧嘩(を)する	II-3-2	V3	(to) have a fight
kesa	けさ	今朝	I-10-2	N	this morning
keshigomu	けしごム	消しゴム	I-2-3	N	eraser (rubber)
kesshite [+ Neg.]	けっして[+ Neg.]		II-3-2	Adv	never
ki	き	木	I-8-3	N	tree
ki o tsukeru	きをつける	気をつける	II-2-3	V2	(to be) careful
kibishii	きびしい	厳しい	I-6-4	A	strict
kiiro	きいろ	黄色	I-5-5	N	yellow color
kiiroi	きいろい	黄色い	I-6-3	A	yellow
Kiite kudasai.	きいてください。	聞いて下さい。	I-2-2	Exp	Please listen.
(～ ga) kikoeru	(～ が) きこえる	聞こえる	II-2-4	V2	～ can be heard
kiku	きく	聞く	I-4-4	V1	(to) listen, hear, (to) ask someone

Japanese (transliterated)	Japanese (かな)	Japanese (漢字)	Lesson	Type	English
kimasu	きます	来ます	I-7-2	V3	(to) come
kimochi ga ii	きもちがいい	気持ちがいい	II-11-4	A	pleasant, comfortable
kimochi ga warui	きもちがわるい	気持ちが悪い	II-11-4	A	unpleasant, uncomfortable
kin	きん	金	II-12-1	N	gold
kiniro	きんいろ	金色	I-5-5	N	gold color
kinoo	きのう	昨日	I-4-3	N	yesterday
kinyoobi	きんようび	金曜日	I-2-7	N	Friday
kirai	きらい	嫌い	I-5-2	Na	dislike
kirei	きれい		I-6-5	Na	pretty, clean, neat, nice
kirei ni suru	きれいにする		II-11-2	V3	(to) make clean, (to) clean
Kiritsu.	きりつ。	起立。	I-1-3	Exp	Stand.
kiru	きる	切る	II-11-2	V1	(to) cut, slice
kiru	きる	着る	II-2-1	V2	(to) wear [above the waist or on the entire body]
kisoku	きそく	規則	II-2-2	N	rule, regulation
kissaten	きっさてん	喫茶店	I-11-3	N	coffee shop
kitanai	きたない	汚い	I-6-5	A	dirty, messy
～ko	～こ	～個	II-4-3	Nd	[general counter]
kochira	こちら		II-4-4	N	here [polite equiv. of ここ]
kochira	こちら		II-7-1	N	this one [polite equiv. of これ]
kochira	こちら		I-3-4	N	this one [polite form]
kodomo	こども	子供	I-8-2	N	child
koe	こえ	声	I-6-1	N	voice
kokku	コック		I-3-5	N	cook
koko	ここ		I-2-5	N	here
kokonoka	ここのか	九日	I-2-6	N	9th day of the month
kokonotsu	ここのつ	九つ	I-2-5	N	nine [general counter]
kokoro	こころ	心	I-6-1	N	heart
komu	こむ	混む	II-10-3	V1	(to get) crowded
konban	こんばん	今晩	I-7-1	N	tonight
Konban wa.	こんばんは。	今晩は。	I-7-1	Exp	Good evening.
konbini	コンビニ		II-10-1	N	convenience store
kongetsu	こんげつ	今月	I-10-4	N	this month
konkuuru	コンクール		II-12-2	N	competition [music]
Konnichi wa.	こんにちは。	今日は。	I-1-2	Exp	Hello. Hi.
kono	この		I-2-4	PN	this
kono naka de	このなかで	この中で	II-7-3	PN+ N+P	among these

Japanese (transliterated)	Japanese (かな)	Japanese (漢字)	Lesson	Type	English
konpyuutaa	コンピューター		I-4-5	N	computer
konshuu	こんしゅう	今週	I-9-4	N	this week
kooen	こうえん	公園	II-1-3	N	park
koohii	コーヒー		I-4-2	N	coffee
kookoo	こうこう	高校	I-3-3	N	high school
kookoo ichinensei	こうこういちねんせい	高校一年生	I-3-3	N	H.S. 1st-year student
kookoo ninensei	こうこうにねんせい	高校二年生	I-3-3	N	H.S. 2nd-year student
kookoo sannensei	こうこうさんねんせい	高校三年生	I-3-3	N	H.S. 3rd-year student
kookoosei	こうこうせい	高校生	I-3-3	N	high school student
koora	コーラ		I-4-2	N	cola
koosaten	こうさてん	交差点	II-10-2	N	intersection
kootsuujiko	こうつうじこ	交通事故	II-3-1	N	traffic accident
koppu	コップ		I-12-3	N	cup
kore	これ		I-1-3	N	this one
korekara	これから		I-12-5	SI	from now on
koshoo	こしょう	胡椒	II-11-3	N	pepper (black)
kotae	こたえ	答え	II-1-4	N	answer
kotaeru	こたえる	答える	II-1-4	V2	(to) answer
koto	こと	事	I-5-3	N	thing [intangible]
kotoba	ことば	言葉	II-12-4	N	words, language
kotoshi	ことし	今年	I-9-5	N	this year
kowai	こわい	恐い	II-3-3	A	scary
ku	く	九	I-1-4	Num.	nine
kubi	くび	首	I-6-1	N	neck
kuchi	くち	口	I-6-1	N	mouth
kudamono	くだもの	果物	II-11-1	N	fruit
(〜o) kudasai.	(〜を)ください。	(〜を)下さい。	I-2-5	Exp	Please give me 〜.
kugatsu	くがつ	九月	I-2-6	N	September
kumo	くも	雲	II-9-1	N	cloud
kumori	くもり	曇り	II-6-2	N	cloudy (weather)
kuni	くに	国	II-7-3	N	country, nation
kuraberu	くらべる	比べる	II-7-2	V2	(to) compare
〜kurai	〜くらい		I-11-4	Nd	about 〜 [Not used for time]
kurai	くらい	暗い	II-9-1	A	dark
kurasu	クラス		I-9-1	N	class, instruction
kurejitto kaado	クレジットカード		II-7-4	N	credit card

Japanese (transliterated)	Japanese (かな)	Japanese (漢字)	Lesson	Type	English
kureru	くれる		II-6-4	V2	(to) give (to me or to my family)
kurisumasu	クリスマス		II-6-1	N	Christmas
kurisumasutsurii	クリスマスツリー		II-6-1	N	Christmas tree
kuro	くろ	黒	I-5-5	N	black
kuroi	くろい	黒い	I-6-3	A	black
kuruma	くるま	車	I-7-3	N	car, vehicle
kusuri	くすり	薬	I-10-2	N	medicine
kutsu	くつ	靴	I-11-3	N	shoes
kutsushita	くつした	靴下	II-2-1	N	socks
kuukoo	くうこう	空港	II-10-1	N	airport
kyandii	キャンディ		I-2-5	N	candy
kyanpu	キャンプ		I-7-4	N	camp
kyonen	きょねん	去年	I-9-5	N	last year
kyoo	きょう	今日	I-2-6	N	today
kyoodai	きょうだい	兄弟	I-3-1	N	(my) sibling(s)
kyookai	きょうかい	教会	II-6-1	N	church (Christian)
kyookasho	きょうかしょ	教科書	I-2-3	N	textbook
kyooshitsu	きょうしつ	教室	I-8-4	N	classroom
kyuu	きゅう	九	I-1-4	Num.	nine
kyuu ni	きゅうに	急に	II-3-3	Adv	suddenly
kyuu-juu	きゅうじゅう	九十	I-1-5	Num.	ninety
kyuukyuusha	きゅうきゅうしゃ	救急車	II-3-1	N	ambulance
Kyuushuu	きゅうしゅう	九州	II-1-1	N	Kyushu

M

Japanese (transliterated)	Japanese (かな)	Japanese (漢字)	Lesson	Type	English
maamaa	まあまあ		I-5-4	Adv	so-so
machi	まち	町	II-10-1	N	town
machigaeru	まちがえる	間違える	II-5-2	V2	(to) make a mistake
mada [+ Aff.]	まだ [+ Aff.]		II-1-3	Adv	still
mada desu [+Neg.]	まだです[+Neg.]		I-12-1	Exp	not yet
～made	～まで		I-7-5	P	to～; until ～
[time] made ni	[time] までに		II-8-2	P	by (a certain time)
mado	まど	窓	I-8-1	N	window
mae	まえ	前	I-3-5	N	front, before
(～no) mae ni	(～の)まえに	(～の)前に	I-10-5	Pp	before ～
(place de/o) magaru	(place で/を) まがる	曲がる	II-3-3	V1	(to) turn at/along (place)

Japanese (transliterated)	Japanese (かな)	Japanese (漢字)	Lesson	Type	English
～mai	～まい	～枚	I-2-5	Nd	[counter for flat objects]
mainen	まいねん	毎年	I-9-5	N	every year
mainichi	まいにち	毎日	I-4-2	N	every day
maishuu	まいしゅう	毎週	I-9-4	N	every week
maitoshi	まいとし	毎年	I-9-5	N	every year
maitsuki	まいつき	毎月	I-10-4	N	every month
makeru	まける	負ける	I-10-3	V2	(to) lose
(ichi)man	(いち)まん	(一)万	I-11-4	N	ten thousand
[V stem] masen ka.	[V stem] ませんか。		I-7-1	Dv	Won't you ～? [invitation]
[V stem] mashoo.	[V stem] ましょう。		I-7-1	Dv	Let's do ～. [suggestion]
massugu	まっすぐ		II-10-2	Adv	straight
mata	また	又	I-8-1	Adv	again
(Ja) mata ato de.	(じゃ)またあとで。	(じゃ)また後で。	I-12-5	Exp	(Well,) see you later.
Mata doozo.	またどうぞ。		II-7-4	Exp	Please come again.
matsu	まつ	待つ	I-11-2	V1	to wait
Mazu	まず		II-11-2	SI	First of all
mazui	まずい	不味い	I-11-5	A	unappetizing
me	め	目	I-6-1	N	eye
megane	めがね	眼鏡	II-2-1	N	eyeglasses
menyuu	メニュー		II-4-1	N	menu
michi	みち	道	II-3-1	N	street, road, way
midori	みどり	緑	I-5-5	N	green
～ga mieru	～が　みえる	～が　見える	I-2-1	V2	can seen; visible
migi	みぎ	右	II-1-2	N	right side
mijikai	みじかい	短い	I-6-2	A	short [not for height]
mikka	みっか	三日	I-2-6	N	3rd day of the month
mimi	みみ	耳	I-6-1	N	ear
miru	みる	見る	I-4-5	V2	(to) watch, look, see
(V TE form +) miru	(V TE form +) みる		II-4-3	Dv	try to (do)
miruku	ミルク		I-4-2	N	milk
(o)mise	(お)みせ	(お)店	I-11-2	N	store
miseru	みせる	見せる	I-11-2	V2	(to) show
Misete kudasai.	みせてください。	見せて下さい。	I-2-2	Exp	Please show me.
(o)misoshiru	(お)みそしる	(お)味噌汁	II-4-1	N	soup flavored with miso
Mite kudasai.	みてください。	見て下さい。	I-2-2	Exp	Please look.
mittsu	みっつ	三つ	I-2-5	N	three [general counter]
(o)miyage	(お)みやげ	(お)土産	II-7-4	N	souvenir gift

Japanese (transliterated)	Japanese (かな)	Japanese (漢字)	Lesson	Type	English
(o)mizu	(お)みず	(お)水	I-4-2	N	water
～mo	～も		I-3-3	P	also, too
mo [counter]	も		II-5-4	P	as many/long as ～
(o)mochi	(お)もち	(お)餅	II-6-1	N	pounded rice cake
mochiron	もちろん		II-5-3	SI	of course
mokuyoobi	もくようび	木曜日	I-2-7	N	Thursday
mon	もん	門	II-2-4	N	gate
mondai	もんだい	問題	II-5-1	N	problem
mono	もの	物	I-5-2	N	thing [tangible]
moo (ippai)	もう(いっぱい)	もう(一杯)	I-12-4	Adv	(one) more (cup)
moo [+Past Aff. V]	もう[+Past Aff. V]		I-12-1	Exp	already
moo [+ Neg.]	もう[+ Neg.]		II-1-3	Adv	(not) any more
moo sugu	もうすぐ		II-6-1	Adv	very soon
moo ichido	もういちど	もう一度	I-1-4	Adv	one more time
(person kara ～o) morau	(person から～を) もらう		II-5-2	V1	(to) receive ～ (from SO)
morau	もらう		II-6-4	V1	(to) receive
Moshi moshi.	もしもし。		II-5-2	Exp	Hello. (on the phone)
motsu	もつ	持つ	II-1-1	V1	(to) have, posess, carry
motte iku	もっていく	持って行く	II-6-3	V1	(to) take (thing)
motte kaeru	もってかえる	持って帰る	II-6-3	V1	(to) take/bring (thing) back home
motte kuru	もってくる	持って来る	II-6-3	V3	(to) bring (thing)
motto	もっと		II-7-1	Adv	more
muika	むいか	六日	I-2-6	N	6th day of the month
(person o) mukae ni iku	(person を) むかえ にいく	迎えに行く	II-8-2	V1	(to) go to pick up (person)
(person o) mukae ni kaeru	(person を) むかえ にかえる	迎えに帰る	II-8-2	V1	(to) return to pick up (person)
(person o) mukae ni kuru	(person を) むかえ にくる	迎えに来る	II-8-2	V3	(to) come to pick up (SO)
mukashibanashi	むかしばなし	昔話	II-9-1	N	folk tale
mukashimukashi	むかしむかし	昔々	II-9-4	N	long, long ago
mukoo	むこう	向こう	II-10-2	N	other side, beyond
murasaki	むらさき	紫	I-5-5	N	purple
mushiatsui	むしあつい	蒸し暑い	I-1-6	A	hot and humid
(o)musubi	(お)むすび	(お)結び	I-12-2	N	rice ball
musuko	むすこ	息子	II-9-3	N	(own) son
musukosan	むすこさん	息子さん	II-9-3	N	(SO else's) son

Japanese (transliterated)	Japanese (かな)	Japanese (漢字)	Lesson	Type	English
musume	むすめ	娘	II-9-3	N	(own) daughter, young lady
musumesan	むすめさん	娘さん	II-9-3	N	(SO else's) daughter, young lady [polite]
muttsu	むっつ	六つ	I-2-5	N	six [general counter]
muzukashii	むずかしい	難しい	I-9-2	A	difficult
N					
nabe	なべ	鍋	II-11-2	N	pot, pan
nado	など		I-9-5	Nd	etc.
nagai	ながい	長い	I-6-2	A	long
naifu	ナイフ		I-12-3	N	knife
naka	なか	中	II-1-2	N	inside
〜nakereba narimasen	〜なければ なりません		II-4-2	Dv	have to (do), should (do)
naku	なく	泣く	II-12-1	V1	(to) cry
〜nakutemo iidesu	〜なくてもいいです		II-4-2	Dv	do not have to (do), no need to (do)
nama tamago	なまたまご	生卵	II-11-4	N	raw egg
namae	なまえ	名前	I-3-1	N	name
(o)namae	(お)なまえ	(お)名前	I-3-2	N	(SO's) name
nan	なん	何	I-1-3	Ni	what?
nana	なな	七	I-1-4	Num.	seven
nana-juu	ななじゅう	七十	I-1-5	Num.	seventy
nanatsu	ななつ	七つ	I-2-5	N	seven [general counter]
nan-bai	なんばい	何杯	I-12-3	Ni	how many cups?
nanbiki	なんびき	何匹	I-8-3	Ni	how many [small animals]?
nanbon	なんぼん	何本	I-8-3	Ni	how many [long cylindrical objects]?
nandai	なんだい	何台	I-8-3	Ni	how many [mechanized goods]?
nandomo	なんども	何度も	II-5-4	Adv	many times
nan-gatsu	なんがつ	何月	I-2-6	Ni	what month?
nani	なに	何	I-1-3	Ni	what?
Nani o sashiagemashoo ka.	なにをさし あげましょうか。	何を差し 上げましょうか。	II-7-1	Exp	May I help you?
nanigo	なにご	何語	I-4-1	Ni	what language?
naniiro	なにいろ	何色	I-5-5	N	what color?
nani-jin	なにじん	何人	I-3-4	Ni	what nationality?

Japanese (transliterated)	Japanese (かな)	Japanese (漢字)	Lesson	Type	English
nanika	なにか	何か	II-12-3	N	something
nanimo [+ Neg. V]	なにも[+ Neg. V]	何も[+ Neg. V]	I-4-3	Ni+P	(not) anything
nanji	なんじ	何時	I-2-7	Ni	what time?
nan-nensei	なんねんせい	何年生	I-3-3	N	what grade?
nan-nichi	なんにち	何日	I-2-6	Ni	what day of the month?
nan-nin	なんにん	何人	I-3-1	Ni	how many people?
nanoka	なのか	七日	I-2-6	N	7th day of the month
nan-sai	なんさい	何歳/何才	I-3-1	Ni	How old?
nanwa	なんわ	何羽	I-8-3	Ni	how many [birds]?
nan-yoobi	なんようび	何曜日	I-2-7	Ni	what day of the week?
napukin	ナプキン		I-12-3	N	napkin
narau	ならう	習う	II-1-1	V1	(to) learn
nareetaa	ナレーター		II-9-1	N	narrator
narimasen	なりません		II-4-2	V1	(it) won't do
(〜ni) naru	(〜に) なる		II-9-1	V1	(to) become 〜
naruhodo	なるほど		II-9-3	Exp	Indeed! I see!
natsu	なつ	夏	I-10-4	N	summer
naze	なぜ		I-9-3	Ni	why?
ne	ね		I-6-5	SP	[sentence ending particle] isn't it?
(o)nedan	(お)ねだん	(お)値段	II-7-2	N	price
nekkuresu	ネックレス		II-2-1	N	necklace
neko	ねこ	猫	I-8-1	N	cat
nemui	ねむい	眠い	I-10-2	A	sleepy
〜nen	〜ねん	〜年	I-9-5	Nd	year
〜nen(kan)	〜ねんかん	〜年間	II-5-4	Nd	[counter for years]
nengajoo	ねんがじょう	年賀状	II-6-1	N	New Year's card
neru	ねる	寝る	I-7-2	V2	(to) sleep, go to bed
netsu	ねつ	熱	I-10-1	N	fever
nezumi	ねずみ	鼠	I-8-5	N	mouse
[activity] ni	[activity] に		I-7-2	P	to, for [activity]
[specific time] ni	[specific time] に		I-4-3	P	at [specific time]
〜ni	〜 に		II-5-4	P	per 〜
ni	に	二	I-1-4	Num.	two
〜ni 〜	〜 に 〜		II-4-1	P	〜 and 〜 (as a set)
[place] ni [+ direction V]	[place] に [+ direction V]		I-7-2	P	to [place]

Japanese (transliterated)	Japanese (かな)	Japanese (漢字)	Lesson	Type	English
[place] ni [+ existence V]	[place] に [+ existence V]		I-8-1	P	in, at [place]
~ni tsuite	~について		II-1-3	P+V	about (a topic)
~nichi	~にち	~日	I-2-6	Nd	day of the month
~nichi(kan)	~にち(かん)	~日(間)	II-5-4	Nd	[counter for days]
nichiyoobi	にちようび	日曜日	I-2-7	N	Sunday
nigate	にがて	苦手	I-5-3	Na	weak in
nigatsu	にがつ	二月	I-2-6	N	February
(o)nigiri	(お)にぎり	(お)握り	I-12-2	N	rice ball
nigirizushi	にぎりずし	握り鮨	II-4-1	N	bite-sized rectangles of sushi rice topped with fish, vegetables, or egg
nihon	にほん	日本	I-3-4	N	Japan
nihongo	にほんご	日本語	I-4-1	N	Japanese language
(~wa) nihongo de nan to iimasu ka.	(~は)にほんごで なんといいますか。	(~は)日本語で 何と言い ますか。	I-2-1	Exp	How do you say ~ in Japanese?
nihonjin	にほんじん	日本人	I-3-4	N	Japanese citizen
ni-juu	にじゅう	二十	I-1-5	Num.	twenty
nikoniko	ニコニコ		II-12-1	Adv	smilingly [onomatopoetic]
nikuudon	にくうどん	肉うどん	II-4-1	N	udon topped with beef
~nin	~にん	~人	I-3-1	Nd	[counter for people]
niwa	にわ	庭	I-8-5	N	garden, yard
no	の		I-3-1	P	[possessive and descriptive particle]
nodo	のど	喉	I-6-1	N	throat
Nodo ga karakara desu.	のどが カラカラです。	喉が カラカラです。	I-12-1	Exp	I am thirsty.
Nodo ga kawakimashita.	のどが かわきました。	喉が 渇きました。	I-12-1	Exp	I got thirsty.
nomimono	のみもの	飲み物	I-5-2	N	beverage
nomu	のむ	飲む	I-4-2	V1	(to) drink, (to) take (medicine)
nooto	ノート		I-2-3	N	notebook
(vehicle ni) noru	(vehicle に) のる	乗る	II-3-4	V1	(to) ride; (to) get on
nyuuyooku	ニューヨーク		I-7-5	N	New York

O

Japanese (transliterated)	Japanese (かな)	Japanese (漢字)	Lesson	Type	English
o	を		II-3-3	P	through, along
obaasan	おばあさん		I-3-2	N	grandmother, elderly woman

Japanese (transliterated)	Japanese (かな)	Japanese (漢字)	Lesson	Type	English
obasan	おばさん		II-6-4	N	aunt, middle-aged woman
oboeru	おぼえる	覚える	II-5-3	V2	(to) memorize
ocha	おちゃ	お茶	I-4-2	N	tea
Ohayoo.	おはよう。		I-1-2	Exp	Good morning. (informal)
Ohayoo gozaimasu.	おはようございます。		I-1-2	Exp	Good morning. (formal)
ohisama	おひさま	お日様	II-9-1	N	sun [polite]
oishasan	おいしゃさん	お医者さん	I-3-5	N	(medical) doctor (polite)
oishii	おいしい	美味しい	I-11-5	A	delicious
ojiisan	おじいさん		I-3-2	N	grandfather, elderly man
ojisan	おじさん		II-6-4	N	uncle, middle-aged man
okaasan	おかあさん	お母さん	I-3-2	N	(SO's) mother
Okinawa	おきなわ	沖縄	II-1-1	N	Okinawa
okiru	おきる	起きる	I-7-2	V2	(to) wake up, get up
okoru	おこる	怒る	II-12-1	V1	(to become) angry
oku	おく	置く	II-4-2	V1	(to) put, leave
okuru	おくる	送る	II-5-2	V1	(to) send
Omedetoo gozaimasu.	おめでとうございます。		I-2-6	Exp	Congratulations.
omoshiroi	おもしろい	面白い	I-9-2	A	interesting
omou	おもう	思う	II-9-4	V1	(to) think
onaji	おなじ	同じ	II-7-2	N	same
onaka	おなか	お腹	I-6-1	N	stomach
Onaka ga ippai desu.	おなかがいっぱいです。	お腹が一杯です。	I-12-4	Exp	I am full.
Onaka ga pekopeko desu.	おなかがペコペコです。	お腹がペコペコです。	I-12-1	Exp	I am hungry.
Onaka ga sukimashita.	おなかがすきました。	お腹が空きました。	I-12-1	Exp	I got hungry.
ondo	おんど	温度	II-6-2	N	temperature (general)
oneesan	おねえさん	お姉さん	I-3-2	N	(SO's) older sister
onegaishimasu	おねがいします	お願いします	I-1-4	Exp	please [request]
ongaku	おんがく	音楽	I-4-4	N	music
oniisan	おにいさん	お兄さん	I-3-2	N	(SO's) older brother
onna	おんな	女	I-8-2	N	female
onna no hito	おんなのひと	女の人	I-8-2	N	woman
onna no ko	おんなのこ	女の子	I-8-2	N	girl
ooen (o) suru	おうえん(を) する	応援(を)する	II-8-1	V3	(to) cheer
ooi	おおい	多い	I-9-4	A	many, much
ookii	おおきい	大きい	I-6-2	A	big

Japanese (transliterated)	Japanese (かな)	Japanese (漢字)	Lesson	Type	English
orenji(iro)	オレンジ(いろ)	オレンジ(色)	I-5-5	N	orange (color)
(vehicle kara/o) oriru	(vehicle から/を) おりる	降りる	II-3-4	V2	(to) get off, out of (vehicle)
oshieru	おしえる	教える	II-3-4	V2	(to) teach
oshimai	おしまい		II-9-4	N	(the) end
osoi	おそい	遅い	I-7-1	A	late
osoku	おそく	遅く	I-10-2	Adv	late [used with a V]
Osoku narimashita.	おそくなりました。	遅くなりました。	II-11-3	Exp	Sorry to be late.
Osuki desu ka.	おすきですか。	お好きですか。	II-7-1	Exp	Do you like it? [polite]
otoko	おとこ	男	I-8-2	N	male
otoko no hito	おとこのひと	男の人	I-8-2	N	man
otoko no ko	おとこのこ	男の子	I-8-2	N	boy
otona	おとな	大人	II-11-3	N	adult
otoosan	おとうさん	お父さん	I-3-2	N	(someone's) father
otooto	おとうと	弟	I-3-1	N	(my) younger brother
otootosan	おとうとさん	弟さん	I-3-2	N	(SO's) younger brother
otoshidama	おとしだま	お年玉	II-6-2	N	New Year's money (mainly given to children)
ototoi	おととい	一昨日	I-9-3	N	day before yesterday
otsuri	おつり	お釣	II-7-4	N	change (from a larger unit of money)
owari ni	おわりに	終わりに	II-11-2	Adv	(at the) end
Owarimashoo.	おわりましょう。	終わりましょう。	I-1-3	Exp	Let's finish.
(〜ga/o) owaru	(〜 が/を) おわる	終わる	II-8-1	V1	(something/SO) finish, end
oyakodonburi	おやこどんぶり	親子丼	II-4-1	N	chicken and egg over steamed rice
oyogu	およぐ	泳ぐ	I-9-5	V1	(to) swim

P

Japanese (transliterated)	Japanese (かな)	Japanese (漢字)	Lesson	Type	English
〜paasento	〜パーセント		II-4-2	Nd	percent
paatii	パーティー		I-7-4	N	party
pan	パン		I-4-2	N	bread
pantsu	パンツ		I-11-3	N	pants
pasokon	パソコン		I-4-5	N	personal computer
pasupooto	パスポート		II-2-3	N	passport
patokaa	パトカー		II-3-1	N	patrol car
piano	ピアノ		I-5-1	N	piano
piasu	ピアス		II-2-1	N	pierced earrings
pikunikku	ピクニック		I-7-4	N	picnic

Japanese (transliterated)	Japanese (かな)	Japanese (漢字)	Lesson	Type	English
pinku	ピンク		I-5-5	N	pink
piza	ピザ		I-12-2	N	pizza
〜pon	〜ぽん	〜本	I-8-3	Nd	[counter for long cylindrical objects]
puuru	プール		I-8-2	N	pool
R					
raamen	ラーメン		II-4-1	N	Chinese noodle soup
raigetsu	らいげつ	来月	I-10-4	N	next month
rainen	らいねん	来年	I-9-5	N	next year
raishuu	らいしゅう	来週	I-9-4	N	next week
raisukaree	ライスカレー		II-4-1	N	curry rice
rajio	ラジオ		I-4-5	N	radio
Rei.	れい。	礼。	I-1-3	Exp	Bow.
reji	レジ		II-4-2	N	cash register
renshuu	れんしゅう	練習	I-9-5	N	practice
renshuu(o) suru	れんしゅう(を) する	練習(を) する	I-10-5	V3	(to) practice
repooto	レポート		I-4-5	N	report, paper
resutoran	レストラン		I-7-4	N	restaurant
rikon (o) suru	りこん(を) する	離婚(を) する	II-12-1	V3	(to) divorce
rokkaa	ロッカー		I-8-4	N	locker
roku	ろく	六	I-1-4	Num.	six
rokugatsu	ろくがつ	六月	I-2-6	N	June
roku-juu	ろくじゅう	六十	I-1-5	Num.	sixty
rosanzerusu	ロサンゼルス		I-7-5	N	Los Angeles
ryokoo	りょこう	旅行	I-7-4	N	trip, traveling
ryokoo(o) suru	りょこう(を) する	旅行(を) する	I-7-4	V3	(to) travel
ryoo	りょう	寮	II-1-3	N	dormitory
ryoohoo	りょうほう	両方	II-7-1	N	both
ryoori (o) suru	りょうり(を) する	料理(を) する	II-6-3	V3	(to) cook
ryooshin	りょうしん	両親	II-1-4	N	(own) parents
ryukku	リュック		I-2-2	N	backpack
S					
saa . . .	さあ...		II-7-3	SI	Well . . . [Used when one is unsure of an answer.]
〜sai	〜さい	〜才/〜歳	I-3-1	Nd	[counter for age]
saifu	さいふ	財布	II-4-3	N	wallet
saizu	サイズ		I-12-2	N	size
sakana	さかな	魚	I-8-3	N	fish

Japanese (transliterated)	Japanese (かな)	Japanese (漢字)	Lesson	Type	English
(o)sake	(お)さけ	(お)酒	II-11-3	N	rice wine, liquor in general
sakkaa	サッカー		I-5-3	N	soccer
samui	さむい	寒い	I-1-6	A	cold
〜san	〜さん		I-1-2	Nd	Mr./Mrs./Ms.
san	さん	三	I-1-4	Num.	three
sandoitchi	サンドイッチ		I-12-2	N	sandwich
sanfuranshisuko	サンフランシスコ		I-7-5	N	San Francisco
sangatsu	さんがつ	三月	I-2-6	N	March
sangurasu	サングラス		II-2-1	N	sunglasses
san-juu	さんじゅう	三十	I-1-5	Num.	thirty
sanpo (o) suru	さんぽ(を) する	散歩(を) する	II-12-1	V3	(to) take a walk
(o)sara	(お)さら	(お)皿	I-12-3	N	plate, dish
sarada	サラダ		I-12-2	N	salad
(superior ni) sashiageru	(superior に) さしあげます	差し上げます	II-7-1	V2	(to) give (to a person of higher status)
satoo	さとう	砂糖	II-11-3	N	sugar
〜satsu	〜さつ	〜冊	II-6-4	Nd	[counter for bound objects]
sayoonara	さようなら		I-1-2	Exp	good-bye
se(i)	せ(い)	背	I-6-1	N	height
seeru(chuu)	セール(ちゅう)	セール(中)	II-7-2	N	(on) sale
seetaa	セーター		II-2-1	N	sweater
seifuku	せいふく	制服	II-2-1	N	(school) uniform
seiseki	せいせき	成績	I-9-3	N	grade(s)
seito	せいと	生徒	I-3-3	N	student [non-college]
sekai	せかい	世界	II-7-3	N	world
semai	せまい	狭い	I-8-5	A	narrow, small (area)
sen	せん	千	I-11-4	Num.	thousand
sengetsu	せんげつ	先月	I-10-4	N	last month
sensei	せんせい	先生	I-1-2	N	teacher, Mr./Mrs./Ms./Dr.
senshu	せんしゅ	選手	II-8-1	N	(sports) player
senshuu	せんしゅう	先週	I-9-4	N	last week
sentaku (o) suru	せんたく(を) する	洗濯(を)する	II-6-3	V3	(to do) laundry
〜sento	〜セント		I-11-4	Nd	〜cent(s)
shakai	しゃかい	社会	I-9-1	N	social studies
shashin	しゃしん	写真	I-2-3	N	photo
shashin o toru	しゃしんを　とる	写真を　撮る	II-6-1	V1	(to) take a photo
shatsu	シャツ		I-11-3	N	shirt
shi	し	市	II-7-3	N	city

Japanese (transliterated)	Japanese (かな)	Japanese (漢字)	Lesson	Type	English
shi, yon	し, よん	四	I-1-4	Num.	four
shiai	しあい	試合	I-10-3	N	(sports) game
shichi	しち	七	I-1-4	Num.	seven
shichigatsu	しちがつ	七月	I-2-6	N	July
shichi-juu	しちじゅう	七十	I-1-5	Num.	seventy
shigatsu	しがつ	四月	I-2-6	N	April
(o)shigoto	(お)しごと	(お)仕事	I-3-5	N	job
shiitoberuto o suru	シートベルトをする		II-3-4	V3	(to) wear a seat belt
shikaru	しかる	叱る	II-12-1	V1	(to) scold
Shikashi	しかし		II-2-2	SI	However [Formal equivalent of でも]
Shikata ga arimasen/nai.	しかたが ありません/ない。	仕方が ありません/ない。	II-5-3	Exp	(It) cannot be helped.
shiken	しけん	試験	I-2-5	N	exam
Shikoku	しこく	四国	II-1-1	N	Shikoku
shima	しま	島	II-7-3	N	island
(V TE form) shimau	(V TE form) しまう		II-9-2	V1	(to) do ～ completely [regret]
shimeru	しめる	閉める	I-11-2	V2	(to) close
Shimete kudasai.	しめてください。	閉めて下さい。	I-2-2	Exp	Please close.
shinbun	しんぶん	新聞	I-4-4	N	newspaper
shingoo	しんごう	信号	II-3-1	N	traffic lights
shinpai (o) suru	しんぱい(を) する	心配(を)する	II-3-2	V3	(to) worry
shinseki	しんせき	親戚	II-6-4	N	relatives
shinu	しぬ	死ぬ	I-10-1	V1	(to) die
shio	しお	塩	II-11-3	N	salt
shiokarai	しおからい	塩辛い	II-11-3	A	salty
shiro	しろ	白	I-5-5	N	white color
shiroi	しろい	白い	I-6-3	A	white
shita	した	下	II-1-2	N	under, below
shitsumon	しつもん	質問	II-1-4	N	question
shitsumon (o) suru	しつもん(を) する	質問(を)する	II-1-4	V3	(to) ask a question
shitte iru	しっている	知っている	II-1-1	V1	(to) know
shizuka	しずか	静か	I-6-5	Na	quiet
shizuka ni suru	しずかにする	静かにする	I-11-2	V3	to quiet down
Shizukani shite kudasai.	しずかにして ください。	静かにして 下さい。	I-2-2	Exp	Please be quiet.
shokudoo	しょくどう	食堂	I-4-4	N	cafeteria

Japanese (transliterated)	Japanese (かな)	Japanese (漢字)	Lesson	Type	English
shokuji	しょくじ	食事	I-7-4	N	meal, dining
shokuji(o) suru	しょくじ(を) する	食事(を) する	I-7-4	V3	(to) dine, have a meal
shoobooshi	しょうぼうし	消防士	I-3-5	N	firefighter
(o)shoogatsu	(お)しょうがつ	(お)正月	II-6-1	N	New Year
shookai(o) suru	しょうかい(を) する	紹介(を)する	II-1-3	V3	(to) introduce
shoomeisho	しょうめいしょ	証明書	II-2-3	N	I. D.
shoorai	しょうらい	将来	II-11-3	N	future
shootesuto	しょうテスト	小テスト	I-2-5	N	quiz
shootopantsu	ショートパンツ		II-2-1	N	shorts
shootsu	ショーツ		II-2-1	N	shorts
shufu	しゅふ	主婦	I-3-5	N	housewife
shukudai	しゅくだい	宿題	I-2-5	N	homework
shumi	しゅみ	趣味	I-5-1	N	hobby
shuu	しゅう	州	II-7-3	N	state
~shuukan	～しゅうかん	～週間	II-5-4	Nd	[counter for weeks]
shuumatsu	しゅうまつ	週末	I-9-4	N	weekend
soba	そば	傍	II-1-2	N	by, nearby
sochira	そちら		II-4-4	N	there, that one [polite equiv. of そこ or それ]
sokkusu	ソックス		II-2-1	N	socks
soko	そこ		I-2-5	N	there
sono	その		I-2-4	PN	that ～
sono koro	そのころ	その頃	II-8-2	PN+N	around that time
sono toki	そのとき	その時	II-12-2	PN+N	at that time
(V stem form +) soo desu	(V stem form +) そうです		II-4-1	SI	looks ～
soo desu	そうです		I-1-5	Exp	it is
Soo desu nee...	そうですねえ...		I-5-1	Exp	Let me see . . .
Soo desu nee.	そうですねえ。		I-1-6	Exp	Yes it is!
Soo desu ka.	そうですか。		I-3-1	Exp	Is that so? / I see.
Soo dewa/ ja arimasen.	そうでは/じゃありません。		I-1-5	Exp	It is not so.
sooji (o) suru	そうじ(を) する	掃除(を)する	II-6-3	V3	(to) clean up
sore	それ		I-1-5	N	that one
Sore wa ii kangae desu.	それはいいかんがえです。	それはいい考えです。	II-8-2	Exp	That is a good idea.
Soredake desu.	それだけです。		II-4-4	Exp	That's all.
sorekara	それから		I-7-2	SI	and then

Japanese (transliterated)	Japanese (かな)	Japanese (漢字)	Lesson	Type	English
Soreni	それに		I-9-4	SI	Moreover, besides
soretomo	それとも		I-6-4	SI	or
Soshite	そして		I-3-2	SI	And
soto	そと	外	I-8-1	N	outside
su	す	酢	II-11-3	N	vinegar
subarashii	すばらしい	素晴らしい	I-11-5	A	wonderful
～sugi	～すぎ	～過ぎ	I-7-1	Nd	after ～
(V stem form +) sugiru	(V stem form +) すぎる	過ぎる	II-11-4	V2	too ～
sugoi	すごい	凄い	I-11-5	A	terrible, terrific
suiei	すいえい	水泳	I-5-1	N	swimming
suiyoobi	すいようび	水曜日	I-2-7	N	Wednesday
sukaato	スカート		II-2-1	N	skirt
suki	すき	好き	I-5-2	Na	like
sukiyaki	すきやき	鋤焼き	II-11-1	N	*sukiyaki*
sukoa	スコア		II-8-4	N	score
sukoshi	すこし	少し	I-8-3	Adv	a few, a little
suku	すく		II-10-3	V1	(to become) empty
sukunai	すくない	少ない	I-9-4	A	few, little
sumaatofon	スマートフォン		I-4-5	N	smartphone
sumimasen	すみません		I-1-4	Exp	excuse me
(place ni) sumu	(place に) すむ	住む	II-1-1	V1	(to) live (in ～)
supein	スペイン		I-3-4	N	Spain
supeingo	スペインご	スペイン語	I-4-1	N	Spanish language
supiido o dasu	スピードをだす	出す	II-3-3	V1	(to) speed
supootsu	スポーツ		I-5-1	N	sports
suppai	すっぱい	酸っぱい	II-11-3	A	sour
supuun	スプーン		I-12-3	N	spoon
suru	する		I-4-4	V3	(to) do
suru	する		II-2-1	V3	(to) wear [accessories]
(～ni) suru	(～に) する		II-4-1	V3	(to) decide on ～
Suruto	すると		II-10-2	SI	Thereupon
sushiya	すしや	寿司屋	I-11-3	N	sushi shop/bar
(gomi o) suteru	(ごみを)すてる		II-2-2	V2	(to) litter, (to) throw away (garbage)
Sutoresu ga ippai desu.	ストレスが いっぱいです。		II-5-1	Exp	(Is) very stressed.
sutoroo	ストロー		I-12-3	N	straw
suugaku	すうがく	数学	I-9-1	N	math

Japanese (transliterated)	Japanese (かな)	Japanese (漢字)	Lesson	Type	English
suupaa	スーパー		I-11-3	N	supermarket
suwaru	すわる	座る	I-11-2	V1	(to) sit
Suwatte kudasai.	すわってください。	座って下さい。	I-2-2	Exp	Please sit.
suzushii	すずしい	涼しい	I-1-6	A	cool [temperature]
T					
tabemono	たべもの	食べ物	I-5-2	N	food
taberu	たべる	食べる	I-4-2	V2	(to) eat
tabun	たぶん	多分	II-6-2	Adv	probably
～tachi	～たち	～達	I-8-3	Nd	[suffix for animate plurals]
tadashii	ただしい	正しい	II-1-4	A	correct
～tai	～たい		I-10-2	Da	want (to do something)
～tai ～	～たい～	～対 ～	II-8-4	PN	～ to ～, ～ vs. ～
taigo	タイご	タイ語	I-4-1	N	Thai language
taihen	たいへん	大変	I-9-4	Na	hard, difficult
taiiku	たいいく	体育	I-9-1	N	P.E.
taiikukan	たいいくかん	体育館	II-8-1	N	gym
taipu(o) suru	タイプ(を) する		I-4-5	V3	(to) type
taitei	たいてい	大抵	I-4-2	Adv	usually
takai	たかい	高い	I-6-1	A	tall, expensive
takusan	たくさん	沢山	I-8-3	Adv	a lot, many
takushii	タクシー		I-7-3	N	taxi
tama ni	たまに		II-12-1	Adv	occasionally, once in a while
tamago	たまご	卵	II-11-1	N	egg
(o)tanjoobi	(お)たんじょうび	(お)誕生日	I-2-6	N	birthday
tanoshii	たのしい	楽しい	I-9-2	A	fun, enjoyable
(～o) tanoshimi ni shite imasu.	(～を)たのしみにしています。	(～を)楽しみにしています。	I-7-5	Exp	I am looking forward to (something)
tasukeru	たすける	助ける	II-12-3	V2	(to) rescue, (to) help
tatemono	たてもの	建物	I-8-4	N	building
tatsu	たつ	立つ	I-11-2	V1	(to) stand
Tatte kudasai.	たってください。	立って下さい。	I-2-2	Exp	Please stand.
te	て	手	I-6-1	N	hand
(o)tearai	(お)てあらい	(お)手洗い	I-8-2	N	bathroom, restroom
teeburu	テーブル		II-4-2	N	table
tegami	てがみ	手紙	I-4-5	N	letter
tekisuto	テキスト		I-2-3	N	textbook
～ten	～てん	～点	II-8-4	Nd	[counter for points]

Japanese (transliterated)	Japanese (かな)	Japanese (漢字)	Lesson	Type	English
tenisu	テニス		I-5-3	N	tennis
(o)tenki	(お)てんき	(お)天気	I-1-6	N	weather
(o)tera	(お)てら	(お)寺	II-6-1	N	temple (Buddhist)
terebi	テレビ		I-4-5	N	TV
terebigeemu	テレビゲーム		I-5-1	N	video game
tetsudau	てつだう	手伝う	II-6-3	V1	(to) help
tiishatsu	Tシャツ		II-2-1	N	T-shirt
tisshu	ティッシュ		I-2-5	N	tissue
[quotation] to	[quotation] と		II-9-3	P	[quotation particle]
to	と		I-3-2	P	and [between two nouns]
to	と	戸	I-8-1	N	door
toire	トイレ		I-8-2	N	bathroom, restroom
tokei	とけい	時計	I-11-3	N	watch, clock
～toki	～とき	～時	II-12-2	N	time, when ～
tokidoki	ときどき	時々	I-4-2	Adv	sometimes
tokoro	ところ	所	II-1-2	N	place
Tokorode	ところで		II-2-3	SI	By the way
toku ni	とくに	特に	II-1-4	Adv	especially
tokui	とくい	得意	I-5-3	Na	strong in, can do well
(place de/ni) tomaru	(place で/に) とまる	止まる	II-3-3	V1	(to) stop
tomodachi	ともだち	友達	I-4-1	N	friend
tonari	となり	隣	II-1-2	N	next to
Tondemonai.	とんでもない。		II-9-3	Exp	How ridiculous! That's impossible!
tonkatsu	とんかつ	豚カツ	II-4-1	N	pork cutlet
too	とお	十	I-2-5	N	ten [general counter]
tooi	とおい	遠い	I-8-5	A	far
tooka	とおか	十日	I-2-6	N	10th day of the month
tooku	とおく	遠く	II-1-2	N	far away
toori	とおり	通り	II-10-2	N	street, avenue
tootoo	とうとう		II-9-4	Adv	finally, at last [after much effort]
toranpu	トランプ		I-5-1	N	(playing) cards
tori	とり	鳥	I-8-3	N	bird
(thing o) tori ni iku	(thing を) とりにいく	取りに行く	II-8-2	V1	(to) go to pick up (thing)
(thing o) tori ni kaeru	(thing を) とりにかえる	取りに帰る	II-8-2	V1	(to) return to pick up (thing)

Japanese (transliterated)	Japanese (かな)	Japanese (漢字)	Lesson	Type	English
(thing o) tori ni kuru	(thing を) とりに くる	取りに来る	II-8-2	V3	(to) come to pick up (thing)
toriniku	とりにく	鳥肉	II-11-1	N	chicken (meat)
(kurasu o) toru	(クラスを) とる	(クラスを) 取る	II-5-3	V3	(to) take (a class)
(untenmenkyo o) toru	(うんてんめんきょを) とる	(運転免許を) 取る	II-5-3	V3	(to) get (a driver's license)
toshi o toru	としをとる	年を取る	I-6-4	V1	(to be) old (age)
toshokan	としょかん	図書館	I-4-4	N	library
totemo	とても		I-5-4	Adv	very
tsugi	つぎ	次	I-9-2	N	next
tsugi ni	つぎに	次に	II-11-2	Adv	next
tsuitachi	ついたち	一日	I-2-6	N	1st day of the month
tsukareru	つかれる	疲れる	I-10-2	V2	(to) tire
tsukau	つかう	使う	II-3-2	V1	(to) use
(obj. o thing ni) tsukeru	(obj. を thing に) つける		II-11-4	V2	(to) dip (object in thing)
(place ni) tsuku	(place に) つく	着く	II-3-4	V1	(to) arrive (at a place)
tsukue	つくえ	机	I-8-1	N	desk
tsukurikata	つくりかた	作り方	II-11-1	N	how to make
tsukuru	つくる	作る	II-6-1	V1	(to) make
tsumaranai	つまらない		I-9-2	A	boring, uninteresting
tsumetai	つめたい	冷たい	I-12-4	A	cold (to the touch)
(V Dic./NAI form) tsumori desu	(V Dic./NAI form) つもりです		II-5-3	Nd	plan/do not plan to do
tsurete iku	つれていく	連れて行く	II-6-3	V1	(to) take (animate)
tsurete kaeru	つれてかえる	連れて帰る	II-6-3	V1	(to) take/bring (animate) back home
tsurete kuru	つれてくる	連れて来る	II-6-3	V3	(to) bring (animate)
(place ni) tsutomeru	(place に) つとめる	勤める	II-1-1	V2	(to be) employed (at ～)
tsuyoi	つよい	強い	I-10-3	A	strong
U					
uchi	うち		I-4-1	N	house
ude	うで	腕	I-6-1	N	arm
udon	うどん		II-4-1	N	thick white noodles in broth
ue	うえ	上	II-1-2	N	on, top
(thing ga) ugoku	(thing が) うごく	動く	II-9-2	V1	(thing) (to) move
ukagau	うかがう	伺う	II-10-1	V1	(to) ask [polite equiv. of 聞く]

Japanese (transliterated)	Japanese (かな)	Japanese (漢字)	Lesson	Type	English
(place ni) umareru	(place に) うまれる	生まれる	II-1-1	V2	(to be) born (in 〜)
umi	うみ	海	I-7-4	N	beach, ocean, sea
un	うん		II-3-2	SI	yes [informal]
undoo	うんどう	運動	II-8-1	N	sports
undoo (o) suru	うんどう(を) する	運動(を)する	II-8-1	V3	(to) exercise
undoogutsu	うんどうぐつ	運動靴	II-8-1	N	sports shoes
undoojoo	うんどうじょう	運動場	II-8-1	N	athletic field
unten (o) suru	うんてん(を) する	運転(を)する	II-2-2	V3	(to) drive
untenmenkyo	うんてんめんきょ	運転免許	II-2-3	N	driver's license
untenshu	うんてんしゅ	運転手	II-3-1	N	driver
ureshii	うれしい	嬉しい	I-9-3	A	glad, happy
uru	うる	売る	II-7-4	V1	(to) sell
urusai	うるさい		I-6-5	A	noisy
ushiro	うしろ	後ろ	II-1-2	N	back, behind
uso	うそ	嘘	II-8-3	N	(a) lie
Uso deshoo.	うそでしょう。		II-8-3	Exp	Are you kidding? Are you serious?
usui	うすい	薄い	II-11-2	A	thin
usuku	うすく	薄く	II-11-2	Adv	thin
uta	うた	歌	I-5-1	N	song, singing
utau	うたう	歌う	I-9-5	V1	(to) sing
utsukushii	うつくしい	美しい	I-8-4	A	beautiful
uun	ううん		II-3-2	SI	no [informal]
uun	う〜ん		II-4-1	SI	Yummm . . .

W

Japanese (transliterated)	Japanese (かな)	Japanese (漢字)	Lesson	Type	English
〜wa	〜わ	〜羽	I-8-3	Nd	[counter for birds]
wa	は		I-1-1	P	[sentence topic-marking particle]
waa	わあ		I-11-5	SI	Wow!
waakushiito	ワークシート		I-2-5	N	worksheet
wakai	わかい	若い	I-6-4	A	young
wakaru	わかる	分かる	I-2-1	V1	(to) understand
wanpiisu	ワンピース		II-2-1	N	dress
warau	わらう	笑う	II-12-1	V1	(to) smile, laugh
warui	わるい	悪い	I-6-2	A	bad
wasureru	わすれる	忘れる	I-12-3	V2	(to) forget
(place o) wataru	(place を) わたる	渡る	II-10-2	V1	(to) cross, go over
watashi	わたし	私	I-1-1	N	I (used by anyone)
watashino	わたしの	私の	I-2-4	N	mine

Japanese (transliterated)	Japanese (かな)	Japanese (漢字)	Lesson	Type	English
watashitachi	わたしたち	私達	I-10-3	N	we
weitaa	ウェイター		I-3-5	N	waiter
weitoresu	ウェイトレス		I-3-5	N	waitress
Y					
[N1] ya [N2]	[N1] や [N2]		I-9-5	P	[Noun1] and [N2], etc.
yakiniku	やきにく	焼き肉	II-4-1	N	grilled meat
yakitori	やきとり	焼き鳥	II-4-1	N	grilled skewered chicken
yakyuu	やきゅう	野球	I-5-3	N	baseball
yama	やま	山	I-7-4	N	mountain
yaru	やる		II-6-4	V1	(to) give (to a person of lower status)
yasai	やさい	野菜	II-11-1	N	vegetable
yasashii	やさしい	易しい	I-9-2	A	easy
yasashii	やさしい	優しい	I-6-4	A	nice, kind
yasete imasu	やせています	痩せています	I-6-4	V2	thin
yasui	やすい	安い	I-11-5	A	cheap
(o)yasumi	(お)やすみ	(お)休み	I-7-5	N	day off, vacation
yasumijikan	やすみじかん	休み時間	I-9-1	N	(a) break
(～o) yasumimasu	(～を)やすみます	(～を)休みます	I-10-2	V1	(be) absent (from ～)
yasumu	やすむ	休む	I-10-2	V2	(to) rest
Yattaa.	やったあ。		II-8-4	Exp	We did it!
yattsu	やっつ	八つ	I-2-5	N	eight [general counter]
[sentence] yo	[sentence] よ		I-6-5	SP	[sentence ending particle] you know
yoi	よい	良い	I-6-2	A	good
Yokatta desu nee.	よかったですねえ。	良かった ですねえ。	I-9-3	Exp	How nice! [about a past event]
yokka	よっか	四日	I-2-6	N	4th day of the month
yoku	よく	良く	I-4-1	Adv	well, often
Yoku dekimashita.	よくできました。	良く出来ました。	I-2-2	Exp	Well done.
yomu	よむ	読む	I-4-4	V1	(to) read
Yonde kudasai.	よんでください。	読んで下さい。	I-2-2	Exp	Please read.
yon-juu	よんじゅう	四十	I-1-5	Num.	forty
yooka	ようか	八日	I-2-6	N	8th day of the month
～yori	～より		II-7-1	P	than ～
(place ni) yoru	(place に) よる	寄る	II-8-2	V1	(to) stop by, drop by (a place)
yoru	よる	夜	I-4-3	N	night
yottsu	よっつ	四つ	I-2-5	N	four [general counter]

Japanese (transliterated)	Japanese (かな)	Japanese (漢字)	Lesson	Type	English
yowai	よわい	弱い	I-10-3	A	weak
yoyaku (o) suru	よやく(を) する	予約(を) する	II-4-2	V3	(to) make reservations
yubi	ゆび	指	I-6-1	N	finger
yubiwa	ゆびわ	指輪	II-2-1	N	ring
yuki	ゆき	雪	II-6-2	N	snow
yukkuri	ゆっくり		I-1-4	Adv	slowly
yunifoomu	ユニフォーム		II-8-1	N	(sports) uniform
yuube	ゆうべ		I-10-2	N	last night
yuubinkyoku	ゆうびんきょく	郵便局	II-10-1	N	post office
yuugata	ゆうがた	夕方	I-4-3	N	late afternoon, early evening
yuumei	ゆうめい	有名	I-8-4	Na	famous
yuusho(o) suru	ゆうしょう(を) する	優勝(を) する	II-8-3	V3	(to) win a championship

Z

Japanese (transliterated)	Japanese (かな)	Japanese (漢字)	Lesson	Type	English
Zannen deshita.	ざんねんでした。	残念でした。	I-9-3	Exp	How disappointing! [about a past event]
Zannen desu ga . . .	ざんねんですが	残念ですが . . .	II-5-2	Exp	Sorry, but . . .
Zannen desu nee.	ざんねんですねえ。	残念ですねえ。	I-9-3	Exp	How disappointing! [about a future event]
zarusoba	ざるそば		II-4-1	N	buckwheat noodle dish
zasshi	ざっし	雑誌	I-4-4	N	magazine
zehi	ぜひ	是非	II-8-4	Adv	by all means, definitely
zeikin	ぜいきん	税金	II-7-4	N	tax
zenbu	ぜんぶ	全部	I-12-2	N	everything
zenzen [+ Neg. V]	ぜんぜん [+ Neg. V]	全然 [+ Neg. V]	I-5-4	Adv	(not) at all
zettai ni	ぜったいに	絶対に	II-2-2	Adv	absolutely
zubon	ズボン		II-2-1	N	pants
zutto	ずっと		II-12-1	Adv	throughout, all the time, by far

Appendix E

English-Japanese Glossary

English	Lesson	Type	Japanese (かな)	Japanese (漢字)
Particles				
[Noun1] and [N2], etc.	I-9-5	P	[N1] や [N2]	
[plain form of copula でした]	II-9-4	C	だった	
[plain form of copula です]	II-9-4	C	だ	
[possessive and descriptive particle]	I-3-1	P	の	
[question particle]	I-1-3	SP	か	
[quotation particle]	II-9-3	P	[quotation] と	
[sentence ending particle] isn't it?	I-6-5	SP	ね	
[sentence ending particle] you know	I-6-5	SP	[sentence] よ	
[sentence topic-marking particle]	I-1-1	P	は	
[softens the statement]	II-5-2	Ps	[sentence] が...	
[subject particle]	I-7-3	P	[subject] が	
[suffix for animate plurals]	I-8-3	Nd	～たち	～達
[Suffix used with young animals or children instead of - さん.]	II-1-3	Nd	～ちゃん	
[doing something] at, in [a place]	I-4-1	P	[place] で [action V]	
[tool particle] by, with, on, in	I-4-5	P	[tool] で	
[totalizing particle]	I-12-2	P	[counter] で	
A				
(a) few, a little	I-8-3	Adv	すこし	少し
(a) little [more colloquial than すこし]	I-4-1	Adv	ちょっと	
(a) lot, many	I-8-3	Adv	たくさん	沢山
a.m.	I-7-1	N	ごぜん	午前
(to be) able to do ～	II-5-1	V2	(～ が) できる	出来る
about (a topic)	II-1-3	P+V	～について	
about (time)	I-2-7	Nd	～ごろ	
about ～ [Not used for time]	I-11-4	Nd	～ぐらい，～くらい	
about how long/far/often?	II-5-4	Ni	どのぐらい	
(be) absent (from ～)	I-10-2	V1	(～を)やすみます	(～を)休みます
absolutely	II-2-2	Adv	ぜったいに	絶対に
address	II-1-1	N	じゅうしょ	住所
adult	II-11-3	N	おとな	大人
after ～	I-10-5	Pp	(～の) あとで	(～の) 後で
after ～	I-7-1	Nd	～すぎ	～過ぎ

English	Lesson	Type	Japanese (かな)	Japanese (漢字)
again	I-8-1	Adv	また	又
airplane	I-7-3	N	ひこうき	飛行機
airport	II-10-1	N	くうこう	空港
all right	I-10-1	Na	だいじょうぶ	大丈夫
already	I-12-1	Exp	もう[+Past Aff. V]	
also, too	I-3-3	P	〜も	
alternative	II-7-1	N	(〜 の) ほう	方
always	I-4-2	Adv	いつも	
am, is, are	I-1-1	C	です	
ambulance	II-3-1	N	きゅうきゅうしゃ	救急車
America	I-3-4	N	アメリカ	
among 〜	II-7-3	P	(〜のなか) で	(〜の中) で
among these	II-7-3	PN+ N+P	このなかで	この中で
And	I-3-2	SI	そして	
and [between two nouns]	I-3-2	P	と	
〜 and 〜 (as a set)	II-4-1	P	〜 に 〜	
and then	I-7-2	SI	それから	
(to become) angry	II-12-1	V1	おこる	怒る
(to) answer	II-1-4	V2	こたえる	答える
answer	II-1-4	N	こたえ	答え
(not) any more	II-1-3	Adv	もう+ [Neg. V]	
(not) anything	I-4-3	Ni+P	なにも[+ Neg. V]	何も[+ Neg. V]
Anything else?	II-4-4	Exp	ほかになにか。	ほかに何か。
(not to) anywhere	I-7-4	Ni+P	どこへも	
(to) appreciate, thank	II-12-4	V3	かんしゃ(を) する	感謝(を)する
April	I-2-6	N	しがつ	四月
Arabic language	I-4-1	N	アラビアご	アラビア語
Are you kidding? Are you serious?	II-8-3	Exp	うそでしょう。	
area	II-10-1	N	へん	辺
arm	I-6-1	N	うで	腕
around that time	II-8-2	PN+N	そのころ	その頃
(to) arrive (at a place)	II-3-4	V1	(place に) つく	着く
art	I-9-1	N	びじゅつ	美術
art museum	II-10-1	N	びじゅつかん	美術館
as many/long as 〜	II-5-4	P	も	
(to) ask [polite equiv. of 聞く]	II-10-1	V1	うかがう	伺う
(to) ask a question	II-1-4	V3	しつもん(を) する	質問(を)する
(to) ask someone	II-2-2	V1	(person に) きく	聞く

English	Lesson	Type	Japanese (かな)	Japanese (漢字)
at [specific time]	I-4-3	P	[specific time] に	
(not) at all	I-5-4	Adv	ぜんぜん [+ Neg. V]	全然 [+ Neg. V]
at that time	II-12-2	PN+N	そのとき	その時
athletic field	II-8-1	N	うんどうじょう	運動場
August	I-2-6	N	はちがつ	八月
aunt, middle-aged woman	II-6-4	N	おばさん	
autumn, fall	I-10-4	N	あき	秋

B

English	Lesson	Type	Japanese (かな)	Japanese (漢字)
baby	II-1-3	N	あかちゃん	赤ちゃん
back, behind	II-1-2	N	うしろ	後ろ
backpack	I-2-2	N	リュック	
bad	I-6-2	A	わるい	悪い
(paper) bag	II-7-4	N	ふくろ	袋
ballpoint pen	I-2-3	N	ボールペン	
band	I-9-5	N	バンド	
bank	II-1-3	N	ぎんこう	銀行
baseball	I-5-3	N	やきゅう	野球
basement	II-7-4	N	ちか	地下
basketball	I-5-3	N	バスケット(ボール)	
bathroom, restroom	I-8-2	N	(お)てあらい	(お)手洗い
bathroom, restroom	I-8-2	N	トイレ	
beach, ocean, sea	I-7-4	N	うみ	海
beautiful	I-8-4	A	うつくしい	美しい
because〜, since〜, 〜so	I-9-3	Pc	[sentence] から	
(to) become 〜	II-9-1	V1	(〜 に) なる	
bed	I-8-5	N	ベッド	
beef	II-11-1	N	ぎゅうにく	牛肉
before	I-3-5	N	まえ	前
before 〜	I-10-5	Pp	(〜の)まえに	(〜の)前に
(something will) begin, start	II-8-1	V1	(〜 が) はじまる	始まる
(at the) beginning	II-11-2	Adv	はじめに	始めに
between	II-1-2	N	あいだ	間
beverage	I-5-2	N	のみもの	飲み物
bicycle	I-7-3	N	じてんしゃ	自転車
big	I-6-2	A	おおきい	大きい
bird	I-8-3	N	とり	鳥
birthday	I-2-6	N	(お)たんじょうび	(お)誕生日
bite-sized rectangles of sushi rice topped with fish, vegetables, or egg	II-4-1	N	にぎりずし	握り鮨

English	Lesson	Type	Japanese (かな)	Japanese (漢字)
black	I-5-5	N	くろ	黒
black	I-6-3	A	くろい	黒い
(to) blow away	II-9-2	V1	ふきとばす	吹き飛ばす
blue	I-6-3	A	あおい	青い
blue, green	I-5-5	N	あお	青
boat, ship	I-7-3	N	ふね	船
body	I-6-1	N	からだ	体
book	I-2-3	N	ほん	本
bookstore	I-11-3	N	ほんや	本屋
boring, uninteresting	I-9-2	A	つまらない	
(to be) born (in ～)	II-1-1	V2	(place で) うまれる	生まれる
born in (month)	I-2-6	Nd	～がつうまれ	～月生まれ
(to) borrow, (to) rent (from)	II-2-3	V2	かりる	借りる
Boston	I-7-5	N	ボストン	
both	II-7-1	N	りょうほう	両方
Bow.	I-1-3	Exp	れい。	礼。
box	II-7-4	N	はこ	箱
box lunch	I-12-2	N	べんとう	弁当
boy	I-8-2	N	おとこのこ	男の子
Brazil	I-3-4	N	ブラジル	
bread	I-4-2	N	パン	
break	I-9-1	N	やすみじかん	休み時間
breakfast	I-4-3	N	あさごはん	朝ご飯
bridge	II-10-2	N	はし	橋
bright	II-9-1	A	あかるい	明るい
(to) bring (animate)	II-6-3	V3	つれてくる	連れて来る
(to) bring (thing)	II-6-3	V3	もってくる	持って来る
brown	I-6-3	A	ちゃいろい	茶色い
brown color	I-5-5	N	ちゃいろ	茶色
buckwheat noodle dish	II-4-1	N	ざるそば	
building	I-8-4	N	たてもの	建物
bus	I-7-3	N	バス	
bus stop	II-10-1	N	バスてい	バス停
busy	I-7-4	A	いそがしい	忙しい
But [begins sentence]	I-4-1	SI	でも	
but	I-5-3	Pc	[sentence]が	
(to) buy	I-11-3	V1	かう	買う
by (a certain time)	II-8-2	P	(time) までに	
by [transportation mode]	I-7-3	P	[transportation] で	

English	Lesson	Type	Japanese (かな)	Japanese (漢字)
by all means, definitely	II-8-4	Adv	ぜひ	是非
by far	II-7-1	Adv	ずっと	
By the way	II-2-3	SI	ところで	
by, nearby	II-1-2	N	そば	傍
bye bye	I-12-5	Exp	バイバイ	

C

English	Lesson	Type	Japanese (かな)	Japanese (漢字)
cafeteria	I-4-4	N	カフェテリア	
cafeteria	I-4-4	N	しょくどう	食堂
camp	I-7-4	N	キャンプ	
〜 can be heard	II-2-4	V2	(something が) きこえる	聞こえる
can be seen; visible	I-2-1	V2	〜が　みえる	〜が　見える
candy	I-2-5	N	あめ	飴
candy	I-2-5	N	キャンディ	
(It) cannot be helped.	II-5-3	Exp	しかたがありません/ない。	仕方がありません/ない。
cap, hat	I-2-3	N	ぼうし	帽子
car, vehicle	I-7-3	N	じどうしゃ	自動車
car, vehicle	I-7-3	N	くるま	車
(playing) cards	I-5-1	N	トランプ	
(to be) careful	II-2-3	V2	きをつける	気をつける
cash register	II-4-2	N	レジ	
cat	I-8-1	N	ねこ	猫
(to) catch a cold	II-5-1	V1	かぜをひく	風邪を引く
cellular phone	I-4-5	N	ケータイ/けいたい	携帯
c〜ent(s)	I-11-4	Nd	〜セント	
certain 〜	II-9-4	PN	ある 〜	
chair	I-8-1	N	いす	椅子
change (from a larger unit of money)	II-7-4	N	おつり	お釣
(to) charge (battery)	II-5-2	V3	じゅうでんする	充電する
cheap	I-11-5	A	やすい	安い
check, bill	II-4-2	N	(お)かんじょう	(お)勘定
(to) cheer	II-8-1	V3	おうえん(を) する	応援(を)する
chew away, gnaw [onomatopoetic]	II-9-2	Adv	ガリガリ	
(to) chew gum	II-2-2	V1	(ガムを)かむ	
chicken (meat)	II-11-1	N	とりにく	鳥肉
chicken and egg over steamed rice	II-4-1	N	おやこどんぶり	親子丼
child	I-8-2	N	こども	子供
China	I-3-4	N	ちゅうごく	中国

English	Lesson	Type	Japanese (かな)	Japanese (漢字)
Chinese language	I-4-1	N	ちゅうごくご	中国語
Chinese noodle soup	II-4-1	N	ラーメン	
chocolate	I-2-5	N	チョコレート	
chopsticks	I-12-3	N	(お)はし	(お)箸
Christmas	II-6-1	N	クリスマス	
Christmas tree	II-6-1	N	クリスマスツリー	
church (Christian)	II-6-1	N	きょうかい	教会
city	II-7-3	N	し	市
class, instruction	I-9-1	N	じゅぎょう	授業
class, instruction	I-9-1	N	クラス	
classroom	I-8-4	N	きょうしつ	教室
(to) clean up	II-6-3	V3	そうじ(を) する	掃除(を)する
(to) clean up, put away	II-11-4	V2	かたづける	片付ける
clear (weather)	II-6-2	N	はれ	晴れ
(to) close	I-11-2	V2	しめる	閉める
clothing	II-2-1	N	ふく	服
cloud	II-9-1	N	くも	雲
cloudy (weather)	II-6-2	N	くもり	曇り
coffee	I-4-2	N	コーヒー	
coffee shop	I-11-3	N	きっさてん	喫茶店
cola	I-4-2	N	コーラ	
(a) cold	I-10-1	N	かぜ	風邪
cold	I-1-6	A	さむい	寒い
cold (to the touch)	I-12-4	A	つめたい	冷たい
college student	I-10-5	N	だいがくせい	大学生
college, university	I-10-5	N	だいがく	大学
color	I-5-5	N	いろ	色
(to) come	I-7-2	V3	きます	来ます
(to) come to pick up (SO)	II-8-2	V3	(person を) むかえ にくる	迎えに来る
(to) come to pick up (thing)	II-8-2	V3	(thing を) とりにくる	取りに来る
company	I-7-2	N	かいしゃ	会社
company employee	I-3-5	N	かいしゃいん	会社員
(to) compare	II-7-2	V2	くらべる	比べる
competition [music]	II-12-2	N	コンクール	
computer	I-4-5	N	コンピューター	
Congratulations.	I-2-6	Exp	おめでとうございます	
convenience store	II-10-1	N	コンビニ	
(to) cook	II-6-3	V3	りょうり(を) する	料理(を)する

English	Lesson	Type	Japanese (かな)	Japanese (漢字)
cook	I-3-5	N	コック	
cool [temperature]	I-1-6	A	すずしい	涼しい
corner	II-3-1	N	かど	角
correct	II-1-4	A	ただしい	正しい
country, nation	II-7-3	N	くに	国
cousin	II-6-4	N	いとこ	
credit card	II-7-4	N	クレジットカード	
(to) cross, go over	II-10-2	V1	(place を) わたる	渡る
(to get) crowded	II-10-3	V1	こむ	混む
(to) cry	II-12-1	V1	なく	泣く
cup	I-12-3	N	コップ	
curry rice	II-4-1	N	カレーライス	
curry rice	II-4-1	N	ライスカレー	
(to) cut, slice	II-11-2	V1	きる	切る
cute	I-6-5	A	かわいい	可愛い

D

English	Lesson	Type	Japanese (かな)	Japanese (漢字)
dance, dancing	I-5-1	N	ダンス	
dangerous	II-3-3	A	あぶない	危ない
dark	II-9-1	A	くらい	暗い
(own) daughter, young lady	II-9-3	N	むすめ	娘
(SO else's) daughter, young lady [polite]	II-9-3	N	むすめさん	娘さん
day	I-2-6	N	ひ	日
day after tomorrow	I-9-3	N	あさって	明後日
day before yesterday	I-9-3	N	おととい	一昨日
day of the month	I-2-6	Nd	～にち	～日
day off, vacation	I-7-5	N	(お)やすみ	(お)休み
daytime	I-4-3	N	(お)ひる	(お)昼
December	I-2-6	N	じゅうにがつ	十二月
(to) decide on ～	II-4-1	V3	(～に) する	
delicious	I-11-5	A	おいしい	美味しい
department store	I-7-4	N	デパート	
design	II-7-2	N	デザイン	
desk	I-8-1	N	つくえ	机
dessert	II-11-4	N	デザート	
dictionary	I-2-3	N	じしょ	辞書
(to) die	I-10-1	V1	しぬ	死ぬ
difficult	I-9-2	A	むずかしい	難しい
(to) dine, have a meal	I-7-4	V3	しょくじ(を) する	食事(を) する
dinner, supper	I-4-3	N	ばんごはん	晩ご飯

English	Lesson	Type	Japanese (かな)	Japanese (漢字)
(to) dip (object in thing)	II-11-4	V2	(obj. を thing に) つける	
dirty, messy	I-6-5	A	きたない	汚い
dislike	I-5-2	Na	きらい	嫌い
dislike a lot, hate	I-5-2	Na	だいきらい	大嫌い
(to) divorce	II-12-1	V3	りこん(を) する	離婚(を) する
(to) do	I-4-4	V3	する	
(to) do 〜 completely [regret]	II-9-2	V1	(V TE form) しまう	
do a homestaty	II-1-1	V3	ホームステイをする	
(to) do a self-introduction	II-1-3	V3	じこしょうかい(を) する	自己紹介(を)する
do not have to (do), no need to (do)	II-4-2	Dv	〜なくてもいいです	
(I) do not mind if . . .	II-2-2	V1	かまいません	
(to) do one's best	I-10-4	V1	がんばる	頑張る
Do you like it? [polite]	II-7-1	Exp	おすきですか。	お好きですか。
(medical) doctor	I-3-5	N	いしゃ	医者
(medical) doctor (formal)	I-3-5	N	おいしゃさん	お医者さん
dog	I-8-1	N	いぬ	犬
dollar(s)	I-11-4	Nd	ドル	
door	I-2-2	N	ドア	
door	I-8-1	N	と	戸
dormitory	II-1-3	N	りょう	寮
(to) draw, paint a picture	II-12-1	V1	(えを) かく	(絵を) 描く
dress	II-2-1	N	ワンピース	
(to) drink	I-4-2	V1	のむ	飲む
(to) drive	II-2-2	V3	うんてん(を) する	運転(を)する
driver	II-3-1	N	ドライバー	
driver	II-3-1	N	うんてんしゅ	運転手
driver's license	II-2-3	N	うんてんめんきょ	運転免許

E

English	Lesson	Type	Japanese (かな)	Japanese (漢字)
ear	I-6-1	N	みみ	耳
early	I-7-1	A	はやい	早い
early [used with a V]	I-10-2	Adv	はやく	早く
earrings	II-2-1	N	イヤリング	
easy	I-9-2	A	やさしい	易しい
(to) eat	I-4-2	V2	たべる	食べる
egg	II-11-1	N	たまご	卵
eight	I-1-4	Num.	はち	八
eight [general counter]	I-2-5	N	やっつ	八つ

English	Lesson	Type	Japanese (かな)	Japanese (漢字)
eighteen	I-1-5	Num.	じゅうはち	十八
eighty	I-1-5	Num.	はちじゅう	八十
electric train	I-7-3	N	でんしゃ	電車
eleven	I-1-5	Num.	じゅういち	十一
(to be) employed (at 〜)	II-1-1	V2	(place に) つとめる	勤める
(to become) empty	II-10-3	V1	すく	
(at the) end	II-11-2	Adv	おわりに	終わりに
(the) end	II-9-4	N	おしまい	
engineer	I-3-5	N	エンジニア	
English	I-4-1	N	えいご	英語
(to) enter (a place)	II-3-2	V1	(place に) はいる	入る
entrance	II-10-2	N	いりぐち	入口
eraser (rubber)	I-2-3	N	けしごゴム	消しゴム
especially	II-1-4	Adv	とくに	特に
etc.	I-9-5	Nd	など	
evening	I-4-3	N	ばん	晩
every day	I-4-2	N	まいにち	毎日
every month	I-10-4	N	まいつき	毎月
every week	I-9-4	N	まいしゅう	毎週
every year	I-9-5	N	まいねん	毎年
every year	I-9-5	N	まいとし	毎年
everything	I-12-2	N	ぜんぶ	全部
exam	I-2-5	N	しけん	試験
(to be) excited, (to be) nervous	II-8-4	V3	ドキドキする	
Excuse me.	I-1-4	Exp	すみません。	
(to) exercise	II-8-1	V3	うんどう(を) する	運動(を)する
exit	II-10-2	N	でぐち	出口
expensive	I-11-5	A	たかい	高い
[expression after a meal]	I-12-4	Exp	ごちそうさま	
[expression before a meal]	I-12-4	Exp	いただきます	頂きます
(to) extend out, submit, take out	II-3-3	V1	だす	出す
eye	I-6-1	N	め	目
eyeglasses	II-2-1	N	めがね	眼鏡

F

English	Lesson	Type	Japanese (かな)	Japanese (漢字)
face	I-6-1	N	かお	顔
(rain, snow) fall	II-6-2	V1	ふる	降る
(my) family	I-3-1	N	かぞく	家族
(SO's) family	I-3-2	N	(ご)かぞく	(御)家族
famous	I-8-4	Na	ゆうめい	有名

English	Lesson	Type	Japanese (かな)	Japanese (漢字)
far	I-8-5	A	とおい	遠い
far away	II-1-2	N	とおく	遠く
fast, quickly	II-3-3	Adv	はやく	速く
(to become) fat	I-6-4	V1	ふとる	太る
(my) father	I-3-1	N	ちち	父
(SO's) father	I-3-2	N	おとうさん	お父さん
February	I-2-6	N	にがつ	二月
feel sick, condition is bad	II-5-1	A	ぐあいがわるい	具合が悪い
female	I-8-2	N	おんな	女
fever	I-10-1	N	ねつ	熱
few, little	I-9-4	A	すくない	少ない
fifteen	I-1-5	Num.	じゅうご	十五
fifty	I-1-5	Num.	ごじゅう	五十
finally, at last [after much effort]	II-9-4	Adv	とうとう	
fine, healthy	I-1-6	Na	げんき	元気
finger	I-6-1	N	ゆび	指
(something) finish, end	II-8-1	V1	(〜 が/を) おわる	終わる
firefighter	I-3-5	N	しょうぼうし	消防士
fireworks	I-7-5	N	はなび	花火
first of all	II-11-2	SI	まず	
(for the) first time	II-6-1	Adv	はじめて	始めて
fish	I-8-3	N	さかな	魚
five	I-1-4	Num.	ご	五
five [general counter]	I-2-5	N	いつつ	五つ
Florida	I-7-5	N	フロリダ	
flower	I-8-3	N	はな	花
flower shop	I-11-3	N	はなや	花屋
folk tale	II-9-1	N	むかしばなし	昔話
food	I-5-2	N	たべもの	食べ物
foot	I-6-1	N	あし	足
football	I-5-3	N	フットボール	
for everything / all	I-12-2	N	ぜんぶで	全部で
foreign language	I-9-1	N	がいこくご	外国語
(to) forget	I-12-3	V2	わすれる	忘れる
fork	I-12-3	N	フォーク	
forty	I-1-5	Num.	よんじゅう	四十
four	I-1-4	Num.	し, よん	四
four [general counter]	I-2-5	N	よっつ	四つ
fourteen	I-1-5	Num.	じゅうし, じゅうよん	十四

English	Lesson	Type	Japanese (かな)	Japanese (漢字)
France	I-3-4	N	フランス	
(is) free (time)	II-12-2	Na	ひま	暇
free, liberal	II-2-2	Na	じゆう	自由
french fries	I-12-2	N	フライドポテト	
French language	I-4-1	N	フランスご	フランス語
Friday	I-2-7	N	きんようび	金曜日
friend	I-4-1	N	ともだち	友達
from now on	I-12-5	SI	これから	
from〜	I-7-5	P	〜から	
front	II-1-2	N	まえ	前
fruit	II-11-1	N	くだもの	果物
(I am) full.	I-12-4	Exp	おなかが いっぱいです。	お腹が一杯です。
fun, enjoyable	I-9-2	A	たのしい	楽しい
future	II-11-3	N	しょうらい	将来

G

English	Lesson	Type	Japanese (かな)	Japanese (漢字)
game	I-9-5	N	ゲーム	
(sports) game	I-10-3	N	しあい	試合
garage	I-8-5	N	ガレージ	
garden, yard	I-8-5	N	にわ	庭
gate	II-2-4	N	もん	門
generally	II-4-2	Adv	だいたい	
(to) get (a driver's license)	II-5-3	V3	(うんてんめんきょを) とる	(運転免許を) 取る
(to) get off, out of (vehicle)	II-3-4	V2	(vehicle から/を) おりる	降りる
girl	I-8-2	N	おんなのこ	女の子
(to) give (to a person of higher status)	II-7-1	V2	(superior に) さし あげます	差し上げます
(to) give (to a person of lower status)	II-6-4	V1	やる	
(to) give (to an equal)	II-6-4	V2	あげる	
(to) give (to me or to my family)	II-6-4	V2	くれる	
glad, happy	I-9-3	A	うれしい	嬉しい
(to) go	I-7-2	V1	いく	行く
go shopping	I-7-4	V3	かいもの (を) します	買い物 (を) します
(to) go to pick up (person)	II-8-2	V1	(person を) むかえ にいく	迎えに行く
(to) go to pick up (thing)	II-8-2	V1	(thing を) とりにいく	取りに行く
gold	II-12-1	N	きん	金
gold color	I-5-5	N	きんいろ	金色
golf	I-5-3	N	ゴルフ	

English	Lesson	Type	Japanese (かな)	Japanese (漢字)
good	I-2-1	A	いい, よい	良い
Good evening.	I-7-1	Exp	こんばんは。	今晩は。
Good luck.	I-10-4	Exp	がんばって。	頑張って。
Good morning. (formal)	I-1-2	Exp	おはようございます。	
Good morning. (informal)	I-1-2	Exp	おはよう。	
Good-bye.	I-1-2	Exp	さようなら。	
grade	I-9-3	N	せいせき	成績
Grand Canyon	I-7-5	N	グランドキャニオン	
grandfather, elderly man	I-3-2	N	おじいさん	
grandmother, elderly woman	I-3-2	N	おばあさん	
great (person)	II-9-1	A	えらい	偉い
green	I-5-5	N	みどり	緑
grey	I-5-5	N	グレー	
grilled skewered chicken	II-4-1	N	やきとり	焼き鳥
guitar	I-5-1	N	ギター	
gum	II-2-2	N	ガム	
gym	II-8-1	N	たいいくかん	体育館

H

English	Lesson	Type	Japanese (かな)	Japanese (漢字)
H.S. 1st-year student	I-3-3	N	こうこういちねんせい	高校一年生
H.S. 2nd-year student	I-3-3	N	こうこうにねんせい	高校二年生
H.S. 3rd-year student	I-3-3	N	こうこうさんねんせい	高校三年生
hair	I-6-1	N	かみ(のけ)	髪(の毛)
(in) half	II-11-2	Adv	はんぶんに	半分に
half	I-2-7	Nd	〜はん	〜半
hamburger	I-12-2	N	ハンバーガー	
hand	I-6-1	N	て	手
hard, difficult	I-9-4	Na	たいへん	大変
(to) have	I-9-1	V1	ある	
(to) have a fight	II-3-2	V3	けんか(を) する	喧嘩(を)する
have to (do), should (do)	II-4-2	Dv	〜なければなりません	
(to) have, posess, carry	II-1-1	V1	もつ	持つ
Hawaii	I-7-5	N	ハワイ	
head	I-6-1	N	あたま	頭
heart	I-6-1	N	こころ	心
(to) heat, (to) make hot	II-11-2	V3	あつくする	熱くする
height	I-6-1	N	せ(い)	背
Hello. (on the phone)	II-5-2	Exp	もしもし。	
Hello. Hi.	I-1-2	Exp	こんにちは。	今日は。
(to) help	II-6-3	V1	てつだう	手伝う

English	Lesson	Type	Japanese (かな)	Japanese (漢字)
here	I-2-5	N	ここ	
here [polite equiv. of ここ]	II-4-4	N	こちら	
Here, you are.	I-2-5	Exp	はい、どうぞ。	
(to) hide (something)	II-9-2	V1	かくす	隠す
high school	I-3-3	N	こうこう	高校
high school student	I-3-3	N	こうこうせい	高校生
hindrance, nuisance	I-6-5	Na	じゃま	邪魔
hobby	I-5-1	N	しゅみ	趣味
Hokkaido	II-1-1	N	ほっかいどう	北海道
hole	II-9-2	N	あな	穴
homeroom	I-9-1	N	ホームルーム	
homework	I-2-5	N	しゅくだい	宿題
Honshu	II-1-1	N	ほんしゅう	本州
hospital	I-3-5	N	びょういん	病院
hot (temperature)	I-1-6	A	あつい	暑い
hot and humid	I-1-6	A	むしあつい	蒸し暑い
hotdog	I-12-2	N	ホットドッグ	
house	II-1-3	N	いえ	家
house	I-4-1	N	うち	
housewife	I-3-5	N	しゅふ	主婦
How about ~? [Polite exp. of どうですか]	I-11-5	Ni	いかがですか。	如何ですか。
How are you?	I-1-6	Exp	(お)げんきですか。	(お)元気ですか。
How disappointing! [about a future event]	I-9-3	Exp	ざんねんですねえ。	残念ですねえ。
How disappointing! [about a past event]	I-9-3	Exp	ざんねんでしたねえ。	残念でしたねえ。
How do you do? / Nice to meet you.	I-1-1	Exp	はじめまして。	初めまして。
How do you say ~ in Japanese?	I-2-1	Exp	(~は)にほんごでなんといいますか。	(~は)日本語で何と言いますか。
How far is it? [distance]	II-10-3	Exp	どのぐらいありますか。	
How is it? [informal]	I-7-5	Exp	どうですか。	
How long does it take? [time]	II-10-3	Exp	どのぐらいかかりますか。	
How long/far is it?	II-10-3	Exp	どのぐらいですか。	
how many [birds]?	I-8-3	Ni	なんわ	何羽
how many [long cylindrical objects]?	I-8-3	Ni	なんぼん	何本
how many [mechanized goods]?	I-8-3	Ni	なんだい	何台
how many [small animals]?	I-8-3	Ni	なんびき	何匹
how many cups?	I-12-3	Ni	なんばい	何杯
how many people?	I-3-1	Ni	なんにん	何人
how many? [general counter]	I-2-5	Ni	いくつ	
How much?	I-11-4	Ni	(お)いくら	

English	Lesson	Type	Japanese (かな)	Japanese (漢字)
How nice! [about a future event]	I-9-3	Exp	いいですねえ。	
How nice! [about a past event]	I-9-3	Exp	よかったですねえ。	良かったですねえ。
How old?	I-3-1	Ni	(お)いくつ	
How old?	I-3-1	Ni	なんさい	何歳／何才
How pitiful.	I-10-1	Exp	かわいそうに。	可愛そうに。
How ridiculous! That's impossible!	II-9-3	Exp	とんでもない。	
how to do ～	II-11-1	N	(Verb stem +)かた	方
how to make	II-11-1	N	つくりかた	作り方
However [Formal equivalent of でも]	II-2-2	SI	しかし	
Huh?	II-9-3	SI	えっ	
hundred	I-1-5	Num.	ひゃく	百
hundred thousand	I-11-4	Num.	じゅうまん	十万
(I am) hungry.	I-12-1	Exp	おなかがペコペコです。	お腹がペコペコです。
(I got) hungry.	I-12-1	Exp	おなかがすきました。	お腹が空きました。
Hurray!	II-8-4	Exp	ばんざい！	万歳!

I

English	Lesson	Type	Japanese (かな)	Japanese (漢字)
I (used by anyone)	I-1-1	N	わたし	私
I (used by males)	I-1-1	N	ぼく	僕
I am looking forward to (something)	I-7-5	Exp	(～を)たのしみにしています。	(～を)楽しみにしています。
I am thirsty.	I-12-1	Exp	のどがカラカラです。	喉がカラカラです。
I expect that he/she will do/will not do.	II-5-3	Nd	(V Dic./NAI form)はずです	
I got thirsty.	I-12-1	Exp	のどがかわきました。	喉が渇きました。
I have a question.	II-10-1	Exp	ちょっとうかがいますが...	
I. D.	II-2-3	N	しょうめいしょ	証明書
illness, sickness	I-10-1	N	びょうき	病気
important	I-10-4	Na	だいじ	大事
in, at [place]	I-8-1	P	[place] に[+ existence V]	
Indeed! I see!	II-9-3	Exp	なるほど	
India	I-3-4	N	インド	
inside	II-1-2	N	なか	中
int. school student	I-3-3	N	ちゅうがくせい	中学生
int. school 1st-year student	I-3-3	N	ちゅうがくいちねんせい	中学一年生
int. school 2nd-year student	I-3-3	N	ちゅうがくにねんせい	中学二年生

English	Lesson	Type	Japanese (かな)	Japanese (漢字)
int. school 3rd–year student	I-3-3	N	ちゅうがく さんねんせい	中学三年生
interesting	I-9-2	A	おもしろい	面白い
intermediate school	I-3-3	N	ちゅうがく	中学
intersection	II-10-2	N	こうさてん	交差点
(to) introduce	II-1-3	V3	しょうかい(を) する	紹介(を)する
Is that so? / I see.	I-3-1	Exp	そうですか。	
island	II-7-3	N	しま	島
Isn't it ～?	II-6-2	C	～でしょう [rising intonation]	
It is.	I-1-5	Exp	そうです。	
It is not so. [formal]	I-1-5	Exp	そうでは/ じゃありません。	

J

English	Lesson	Type	Japanese (かな)	Japanese (漢字)
jacket	I-11-3	N	ジャケット	
January	I-2-6	N	いちがつ	一月
Japan	I-3-4	N	にほん	日本
Japanese citizen	I-3-4	N	にほんじん	日本人
Japanese language	I-4-1	N	にほんご	日本語
job	I-3-5	N	(お)しごと	(お)仕事
jogging	I-5-1	N	ジョギング	
joke	II-8-3	N	じょうだん	冗談
juice	I-4-2	N	ジュース	
July	I-2-6	N	しちがつ	七月
June	I-2-6	N	ろくがつ	六月

K

English	Lesson	Type	Japanese (かな)	Japanese (漢字)
key	II-3-1	N	かぎ	鍵
kitchen	II-11-1	N	だいどころ	台所
knife	I-12-3	N	ナイフ	
(to) know	II-1-1	V1	しっている	知っている
Korea	I-3-4	N	かんこく	韓国
Korean language	I-4-1	N	かんこくご	韓国語
Kyushu	II-1-1	N	きゅうしゅう	九州

L

English	Lesson	Type	Japanese (かな)	Japanese (漢字)
large size	I-12-2	N	エルサイズ	
last month	I-10-4	N	せんげつ	先月
last night	I-10-2	N	ゆうべ	
last week	I-9-4	N	せんしゅう	先週
last year	I-9-5	N	きょねん	去年

English	Lesson	Type	Japanese (かな)	Japanese (漢字)
late	I-7-1	A	おそい	遅い
late [used with a V]	I-10-2	Adv	おそく	遅く
late afternoon, early evening	I-4-3	N	ゆうがた	夕方
(to do) laundry	II-6-3	V3	せんたく(を) する	洗濯(を)する
lawyer	I-3-5	N	べんごし	弁護士
(to) learn	II-1-1	V1	ならう	習う
(to) leave (a place)	II-3-2	V2	(place を) でる	出る
(to) leave, go out (from a place)	II-3-4	V2	(place を/から) でかける	出かける
left side	II-1-2	N	ひだり	左
leg	I-6-1	N	あし	脚
Let me see . . .	I-5-1	Exp	そうですねえ...	
let me see . . . , well . . .	I-2-1	SI	あのう...	
let me see . . . , well . . .	I-2-1	SI	ええと...	
Let's begin.	I-1-3	Exp	はじめましょう。	始めましょう。
Let's do 〜. [suggestion]	I-7-1	Dv	[V stem] ましょう。	
Let's finish.	I-1-3	Exp	おわりましょう。	終わりましょう。
letter	I-4-5	N	てがみ	手紙
library	I-4-4	N	としょかん	図書館
(a) lie	II-8-3	N	うそ	嘘
like	I-5-2	Na	すき	好き
like very much, love	I-5-2	Na	だいすき	大好き
(to) listen, hear, ask	I-4-4	V1	きく	聞く
(to) litter, (to) throw away (garbage)	II-2-2	V2	(ごみを)すてる	
(to) live (in 〜)	II-1-1	V1	(place に) すむ	住む
locker	I-8-4	N	ロッカー	
long	I-6-2	A	ながい	長い
long, long ago	II-9-4	N	むかしむかし	昔々
looks 〜	II-4-1	SI	(V stem form +) そうです	
Los Angeles	I-7-5	N	ロサンゼルス	
(to) lose	I-10-3	V2	まける	負ける
(to be in) love	II-12-4	V1	あいしている	愛している
love, affection	II-12-4	N	あい	愛
lunch	I-4-3	N	ひるごはん	昼ご飯

M

English	Lesson	Type	Japanese (かな)	Japanese (漢字)
magazine	I-4-4	N	ざっし	雑誌
(to) make	II-6-1	V1	つくる	作る
(to) make a mistake	II-5-2	V2	まちがえる	間違える

English	Lesson	Type	Japanese (かな)	Japanese (漢字)
(to) make a phone call	II-5-2	V2	でんわをかける	電話をかける
(to) make clean, (to) clean	II-11-2	V3	きれいにする	
(to) make reservations	II-4-2	V3	よやく(を) する	予約(を) する
male	I-8-2	N	おとこ	男
man	I-8-2	N	おとこのひと	男の人
many times	II-5-4	Adv	なんども	何度も
many, much	I-9-4	A	おおい	多い
map	II-10-1	N	ちず	地図
March	I-2-6	N	さんがつ	三月
(to be) married (to 〜)	II-1-1	V3	(person と) けっこん(を) する	結婚(を)する
math	I-9-1	N	すうがく	数学
May	I-2-6	N	ごがつ	五月
May I help you?	II-7-1	Exp	なにをさし あげましょうか。	何を差し 上げましょうか。
May I take your order? What is your order?	II-4-4	Exp	ごちゅうもんは。	御注文は。
meal, dining	I-7-4	N	しょくじ	食事
grilled meat	II-4-1	N	やきにく	焼き肉
medicine	I-10-2	N	くすり	薬
medium size	I-12-2	N	エムサイズ	
(to) meet	I-10-5	V1	あう	会う
(to) memorize	II-5-3	V2	おぼえる	覚える
menu	II-4-1	N	メニュー	
(cow's) milk	I-4-2	N	ぎゅうにゅう	牛乳
milk	I-4-2	N	ミルク	
(one) million	I-11-4	N	ひゃくまん	百万
mine	I-2-4	N	わたしの	私の
minute	I-7-1	Nd	〜ふん	〜分
Monday	I-2-7	N	げつようび	月曜日
money	I-2-3	N	(お)かね	(お)金
more	II-7-1	Adv	もっと	
〜 more	II-8-4	PN	あと〜	後〜
(one) more (cup)	I-12-4	Adv	もう(いっぱい)	もう(一杯)
moreover, besides	I-9-4	SI	それに	
morning	I-4-3	N	あさ	朝
(my) mother	I-3-1	N	はは	母
(SO's) mother	I-3-2	N	おかあさん	お母さん
mountain	I-7-4	N	やま	山
mouse	I-8-5	N	ねずみ	鼠

English	Lesson	Type	Japanese (かな)	Japanese (漢字)
mouth	I-6-1	N	くち	口
(thing) (to) move	II-9-2	V1	(thing が) うごく	動く
movie	I-5-1	N	えいが	映画
movie theater	II-2-4	N	えいがかん	映画館
Mr./Mrs./Ms.	I-1-2	Nd	〜さん	
music	I-4-4	N	おんがく	音楽
N				
name	I-3-1	N	なまえ	名前
(SO's) name	I-3-2	N	(お)なまえ	(お)名前
napkin	I-12-3	N	ナプキン	
narrator	II-9-1	N	ナレーター	
narrow, small (area)	I-8-5	A	せまい	狭い
near, close	I-8-5	A	ちかい	近い
neck	I-6-1	N	くび	首
necklace	II-2-1	N	ネックレス	
(to) need	I-12-3	V1	いる	要る
neither, not either	II-7-1	N	どちらも [+ Neg.]	
never	II-3-2	Adv	けっして [+ Neg.]	
new	I-8-4	A	あたらしい	新しい
New Year	II-6-1	N	(お)しょうがつ	(お)正月
New Year's card	II-6-1	N	ねんがじょう	年賀状
New Year's money (mainly given to children)	II-6-2	N	おとしだま	お年玉
New York	I-7-5	N	ニューヨーク	
newspaper	I-4-4	N	しんぶん	新聞
next	I-9-2	N	つぎ	次
next	II-11-2	Adv	つぎに	次に
next month	I-10-4	N	らいげつ	来月
next to	II-1-2	N	となり	隣
next week	I-9-4	N	らいしゅう	来週
next year	I-9-5	N	らいねん	来年
Nice to meet you.	I-1-1	N	どうぞよろしく。	
nice, kind	I-6-4	A	やさしい	優しい
night	I-4-3	N	よる	夜
nine	I-1-4	Num.	く	九
nine	I-1-4	Num.	きゅう	九
nine [general counter]	I-2-5	N	ここのつ	九つ
nineteen	I-1-5	Num.	じゅうく	十九
nineteen	I-1-5	Num.	じゅうきゅう	十九

English	Lesson	Type	Japanese (かな)	Japanese (漢字)
ninety	I-1-5	Num.	きゅうじゅう	九十
no [formal]	I-1-5	SI	いいえ	
no [informal]	II-3-2	SI	ううん	
No [stronger negation than いいえ]	II-9-3	SI	いや(っ)	
no good	I-2-1	Na	だめ	駄目
No, thank you.	I-12-3	Exp	いいえ、けっこうです。	いいえ、結構です。
noisy	I-6-5	A	うるさい	
nose	I-6-1	N	はな	鼻
not as ～ as	II-7-2	P	ほど [+ Neg.]	
not yet	I-12-1	Exp	まだ[+ Neg.]	
notebook	I-2-3	N	ノート	
November	I-2-6	N	じゅういちがつ	十一月
now	I-2-7	N	いま	今
number -	II-8-1	Nd	～ばん	～番

O

English	Lesson	Type	Japanese (かな)	Japanese (漢字)
occasionally, once in a while	II-12-1	Adv	たまに	
October	I-2-6	N	じゅうがつ	十月
of course	II-5-3	SI	もちろん	
office	I-8-4	N	じむしょ	事務所
Oh!	II-10-1	SI	ああ	
oil	II-11-2	N	あぶら	油
Okinawa	II-1-1	N	おきなわ	沖縄
(to be) old (age)	I-6-4	V1	としをとる	年を取る
old (not for person's age)	I-8-4	A	ふるい	古い
(my) older brother	I-3-1	N	あに	兄
(SO's) older brother	I-3-2	N	おにいさん	お兄さん
(my) older sister	I-3-1	N	あね	姉
(SO's) older sister	I-3-2	N	おねえさん	お姉さん
on, top	II-1-2	N	うえ	上
one	I-1-4	N	いち	一
one [general counter]	I-2-5	N	ひとつ	一つ
one more time	I-1-4	Adv	もういちど	もう一度
one person, alone	I-3-1	N	ひとり	一人
oneself	II-12-3	N	じぶん	自分
online video	II-5-2	N	どうが	動画
only ～	II-2-4	Nd	～だけ	
only child	II-12-2	N	ひとりっこ	一人っ子
Or	I-6-4	SI	それとも	
orange (color)	I-5-5	N	オレンジ(いろ)	オレンジ(色)

English	Lesson	Type	Japanese (かな)	Japanese (漢字)
(to) order	II-4-2	V3	ちゅうもん(を)する	注文(を)する
other	II-7-2	N	ほか	
other side, beyond	II-10-2	N	むこう	向こう
outside	I-8-1	N	そと	外
over there	I-2-5	N	あそこ	
over there, that one over there [polite equiv. of あそこ or あれ]	II-4-4	N	あちら	
P				
P.E.	I-9-1	N	たいいく	体育
p.m.	I-7-1	N	ごご	午後
painful, sore	I-10-1	A	いたい	痛い
painting, drawing	I-5-1	N	え	絵
pants	I-11-3	N	パンツ	
pants	II-2-1	N	ズボン	
paper	I-2-3	N	かみ	紙
(own) parents	II-1-4	N	りょうしん	両親
(SO else's) parents [polite]	II-1-4	N	ごりょうしん	御両親
park	II-1-3	N	こうえん	公園
parking lot	II-10-1	N	ちゅうしゃじょう	駐車場
(to) participate in a (sports) game	II-8-1	V2	(しあいに)でる	(試合に)出る
party	I-7-4	N	パーティー	
passport	II-2-3	N	パスポート	
patrol car	II-3-1	N	パトカー	
(to) pay	II-4-2	V1	はらう	払う
pencil	I-2-3	N	えんぴつ	鉛筆
pencil sharpener	I-8-1	N	えんぴつけずり	鉛筆削り
pepper (black)	II-11-3	N	こしょう	胡椒
per ～	II-5-4	P	～に	
percent	II-4-2	Nd	～パーセント	
person	I-8-2	N	ひと	人
person [polite form]	I-8-2	Nd	かた	方
personal computer	I-4-5	N	パソコン	
photo	I-2-3	N	しゃしん	写真
piano	I-5-1	N	ピアノ	
picnic	I-7-4	N	ピクニック	
pierced earrings	II-2-1	N	ピアス	
pig	I-8-5	N	ぶた	豚
pink	I-5-5	N	ピンク	
pizza	I-12-2	N	ピザ	

English	Lesson	Type	Japanese (かな)	Japanese (漢字)
place	II-1-2	N	ところ	所
place, location	II-8-1	N	ばしょ	場所
plan/do not plan to do	II-5-3	Nd	(V Dic./NAI form) つもりです	
plate, dish	I-12-3	N	(お)さら	(お)皿
(stage) play	II-9-1	N	げき	劇
(to) play (a string instrument)	II-5-1	V1	ひく	弾く
play a game	I-9-5	V3	ゲーム(を) する	
(to) play, amuse (not for sports/music)	I-9-5	V1	あそぶ	遊ぶ
(sports) player	II-8-1	N	せんしゅ	選手
pleasant, comfortable	II-11-4	A	きもちがいい	気持ちがいい
please [request]	I-1-4	Exp	おねがいします	お願いします
Please be quiet.	I-2-2	Exp	しずかにして ください。	静かにして 下さい。
Please close.	I-2-2	Exp	しめてください。	閉めて下さい。
Please come again.	II-7-4	Exp	またどうぞ。	
Please give me 〜.	I-2-5	Exp	(〜を)ください	(〜を)下さい
Please lend me 〜.	I-12-3	Exp	かしてください。	貸して下さい。
Please listen; ask.	I-2-2	Exp	きいてください。	聞いて下さい。
Please look.	I-2-2	Exp	みてください。	見て下さい。
Please open.	I-2-2	Exp	あけてください。	開けて下さい。
Please read.	I-2-2	Exp	よんでください。	読んで下さい。
Please show me.	I-2-2	Exp	みせてください。	見せて下さい。
Please sit.	I-2-2	Exp	すわってください。	座って下さい。
Please stand.	I-2-2	Exp	たってください。	立って下さい。
Please turn in 〜.	I-2-2	Exp	〜だしてください。	〜出して下さい。
Please wait a minute.	I-1-4	Exp	ちょっとまって ください。	ちょっと待って 下さい。
Please write.	I-2-2	Exp	かいてください。	書いて下さい。
police officer	I-3-5	N	けいかん	警官
pond	I-8-3	N	いけ	池
pool	I-8-2	N	プール	
poor	II-9-1	Na	びんぼう	貧乏
pork	II-11-1	N	ぶたにく	豚肉
pork cutlet	II-4-1	N	とんかつ	豚カツ
post office	II-10-1	N	ゆうびんきょく	郵便局
pot, pan	II-11-2	N	なべ	鍋
pounded rice cake	II-6-1	N	(お)もち	(お)餅
power, strength, ability	II-9-2	N	ちから	力
(to) practice	I-10-5	V3	れんしゅう(を) する	練習(を) する

English	Lesson	Type	Japanese (かな)	Japanese (漢字)
practice	I-9-5	N	れんしゅう	練習
pretty, clean, neat, nice	I-6-5	Na	きれい	
price	II-7-2	N	(お)ねだん	(お)値段
probably	II-6-2	Adv	たぶん	多分
probably 〜	II-6-2	C	〜でしょう [falling intonation]	
problem	II-5-1	N	もんだい	問題
purple	I-5-5	N	むらさき	紫
(to) put in 〜	II-7-4	V2	(〜 に) いれる	入れる
(to) put, leave	II-4-2	V1	おく	置く

Q

English	Lesson	Type	Japanese (かな)	Japanese (漢字)
question	II-1-4	N	しつもん	質問
quiet	I-6-5	Na	しずか	静か
(to) quiet down	I-11-2	V3	しずかにする	静かにする
quiz	I-2-5	N	しょうテスト	小テスト

R

English	Lesson	Type	Japanese (かな)	Japanese (漢字)
radio	I-4-5	N	ラジオ	
rain	I-1-6	N	あめ	雨
raw egg	II-11-4	N	なまたまご	生卵
(to) read	I-4-4	V1	よむ	読む
reading	I-5-1	N	どくしょ	読書
(〜 is) ready, (〜 is) done	II-11-4	V2	(〜が) できました	出来ました
really, truly	II-2-4	Adv	ほんとうに	本当に
(to) receive	II-6-4	V1	もらう	
(to) receive 〜 (from SO)	II-5-2	V1	(person から〜を) もらう	
red	I-5-5	N	あか	赤
red	I-6-3	A	あかい	赤い
relatives	II-6-4	N	しんせき	親戚
report, paper	I-4-5	N	レポート	
(to) require, to take (time)	II-7-4	V1	かかる	
(to) rescue, (to) help	II-12-3	V2	たすける	助ける
(to) rest	I-10-2	V1	やすむ	休む
restaurant	I-7-4	N	レストラン	
(to) return (something)	II-4-3	V1	かえす	返す
(to) return (to a place)	I-7-2	V1	かえる	帰る
(to) return to pick up (person)	II-8-2	V1	(person を) むかえに かえる	迎えに帰る
(to) return to pick up (thing)	II-8-2	V1	(thing を) とりに かえる	取りに帰る

English	Lesson	Type	Japanese (かな)	Japanese (漢字)
(cooked) rice	I-4-2	N	ごはん	ご飯
rice ball	I-12-2	N	(お)むすび	(お)結び
rice ball	I-12-2	N	おにぎり	お握り
rice wine, liquor in general	II-11-3	N	(お)さけ	(お)酒
rich person	II-9-1	N	(お)かねもち	(お)金持ち
(to) ride	II-3-4	V1	(vehicle に) のる	乗る
right (side)	II-1-2	N	みぎ	右
ring	II-2-1	N	ゆびわ	指輪
river	I-7-4	N	かわ	川
room	I-8-5	N	へや	部屋
rule, regulation	II-2-2	N	きそく	規則
(to) run	I-10-5	V1	はしる	走る

S

English	Lesson	Type	Japanese (かな)	Japanese (漢字)
sad	I-9-3	A	かなしい	悲しい
safe	II-3-3	Na	あんぜん	安全
salad	I-12-2	N	サラダ	
(on) sale	II-7-2	N	セール(ちゅう)	セール(中)
salt	II-11-3	N	しお	塩
salty	II-11-3	A	しおからい	塩辛い
same	II-7-2	N	おなじ	同じ
San Francisco	I-7-5	N	サンフランシスコ	
sandwich	I-12-2	N	サンドイッチ	
Saturday	I-2-7	N	どようび	土曜日
(to) say	I-11-2	V1	いう	言う
scary	II-3-3	A	こわい	恐い
school	I-3-3	N	がっこう	学校
science	I-9-1	N	かがく	科学
(to) scold	II-12-1	V1	しかる	叱る
score	II-8-4	N	スコア	
(Well,) see you later.	I-12-5	Exp	(じゃ)またあとで。	
(to) sell	II-7-4	V1	うる	売る
(to) send	II-5-2	V1	おくる	送る
September	I-2-6	N	くがつ	九月
seven	I-1-4	Num.	しち	七
seven	I-1-4	Num.	なな	七
seven [general counter]	I-2-5	N	ななつ	七つ
seventeen	I-1-5	Num.	じゅうなな	十七
seventeen	I-1-5	Num.	じゅうしち	十七
seventy	I-1-5	Num.	ななじゅう	七十

English	Lesson	Type	Japanese (かな)	Japanese (漢字)
seventy	I-1-5	Num.	しちじゅう	七十
Shikoku	II-1-1	N	しこく	四国
shirt	I-11-3	N	シャツ	
shoes	I-11-3	N	くつ	靴
shopping	I-7-4	N	かいもの	買い物
short (height)	I-6-1	A	ひくい	低い
short [not for height]	I-6-2	A	みじかい	短い
shorts	II-2-1	N	ショートパンツ	
shorts	II-2-1	N	ショーツ	
(to) show	I-11-2	V2	みせる	見せる
shredded konnyaku	II-11-1	N	いとこんにゃく	糸こんにゃく
shrine (Shinto)	II-6-1	N	じんじゃ	神社
(my) sibling(s)	I-3-1	N	きょうだい	兄弟
(〜) side	II-10-2	Nd	〜がわ	〜側
silver	II-12-1	N	ぎん	銀
silver color	I-5-5	N	ぎんいろ	銀色
(to) sing	I-9-5	V1	うたう	歌う
(to) sit	I-11-2	V1	すわる	座る
Sit.	I-1-3	Exp	ちゃくせき。	着席。
six	I-1-4	Num.	ろく	六
six [general counter]	I-2-5	N	むっつ	六つ
sixteen	I-1-5	Num.	じゅうろく	十六
sixty	I-1-5	Num.	ろくじゅう	六十
size	I-12-2	N	サイズ	
skillful, (be) good at	I-5-3	Na	じょうず	上手
skirt	II-2-1	N	スカート	
(to) sleep, go to bed	I-7-2	V2	ねる	寝る
sleepy	I-10-2	A	ねむい	眠い
slowly	I-1-4	Adv	ゆっくり	
small	I-6-2	A	ちいさい	小さい
small size	I-12-2	N	エスサイズ	
smartphone	I-4-5	N	スマートフォン	
(to) smile, laugh	II-12-1	V1	わらう	笑う
smilingly [onomatopoetic]	II-12-1	Adv	ニコニコ	
snack bar; kiosk	I-4-4	N	ばいてん	売店
snow	II-6-2	N	ゆき	雪
soccer	I-5-3	N	サッカー	
social studies	I-9-1	N	しゃかい	社会
socks	II-2-1	N	くつした	靴下

English	Lesson	Type	Japanese (かな)	Japanese (漢字)
socks	II-2-1	N	ソックス	
something	II-12-3	N	なにか	何か
sometimes	I-4-2	Adv	ときどき	時々
(own) son	II-9-3	N	むすこ	息子
(SO else's) son	II-9-3	N	むすこさん	息子さん
song, singing	I-5-1	N	うた	歌
Sorry to be late.	II-11-3	Exp	おそくなりました。	遅くなりました。
Sorry, but . . .	II-5-2	Exp	ざんねんですが	残念ですが . . .
so-so	I-5-4	Adv	まあまあ	
soup flavored with miso	II-4-1	N	(お)みそしる	(お)味噌汁
sour	II-11-3	A	すっぱい	酸っぱい
souvenir gift	II-7-4	N	(お)みやげ	(お)土産
Spain	I-3-4	N	スペイン	
Spanish language	I-4-1	N	スペインご	スペイン語
(to) speak, talk	I-4-1	V1	はなす	話す
(to) speed	II-3-3	V1	スピードをだす	出す
spicy, hot	II-11-3	A	からい	辛い
spoon	I-12-3	N	スプーン	
sports	I-5-1	N	スポーツ	
sports	II-8-1	N	うんどう	運動
sports shoes	II-8-1	N	うんどうぐつ	運動靴
spring	I-10-4	N	はる	春
(to) stand	I-11-2	V1	たつ	立つ
Stand.	I-1-3	Exp	きりつ。	起立。
(SO will) start, begin (something)	II-8-1	V2	(〜を) はじめる	始める
state	II-7-3	N	しゅう	州
still	II-1-3	Adv	まだ [+ Aff.]	
stomach	I-6-1	N	おなか	お腹
(to) stop	II-3-3	V1	(place で/に) とまる	止まる
(to) stop by, drop by (a place)	II-8-2	V1	(place に) よる	寄る
store	I-11-2	N	(お)みせ	(お)店
straight	II-10-2	Adv	まっすぐ	
strange, weird, unusual	II-5-1	Na	へん	変
straw	I-12-3	N	ストロー	
strawberry	II-11-1	N	いちご	苺
street, avenue	II-10-2	N	とおり	通り
street, road, way	II-3-1	N	みち	道
strict	I-6-4	A	きびしい	厳しい
strong	I-10-3	A	つよい	強い

English	Lesson	Type	Japanese (かな)	Japanese (漢字)
strong in, can do well	I-5-3	Na	とくい	得意
student [college]	I-3-3	N	がくせい	学生
student [non–college]	I-3-3	N	せいと	生徒
(to) study	I-4-4	V3	べんきょう(を) する	勉強(を) する
subject	I-9-1	N	かもく	科目
subway	I-7-3	N	ちかてつ	地下鉄
suddenly	II-3-3	Adv	きゅうに	急に
sugar	II-11-3	N	さとう	砂糖
sukiyaki	II-11-1	N	すきやき	鋤焼き
summer	I-10-4	N	なつ	夏
sun [polite]	II-9-1	N	おひさま	お日様
Sunday	I-2-7	N	にちようび	日曜日
sunglasses	II-2-1	N	サングラス	
supermarket	I-11-3	N	スーパー	
sushi shop/bar	I-11-3	N	すしや	寿司屋
sweater	II-2-1	N	セーター	
sweet	II-11-3	A	あまい	甘い
(to) swim	I-9-5	V1	およぐ	泳ぐ
swimming	I-5-1	N	すいえい	水泳

T

English	Lesson	Type	Japanese (かな)	Japanese (漢字)
table	II-4-2	N	テーブル	
(to) take (a class)	II-5-3	V3	(クラスを) とる	(クラスを) 取る
(to) take (animate)	II-6-3	V1	つれていく	連れて行く
(to) take (medicine)	I-10-2	V1	のむ	飲む
(to) take (thing)	II-6-3	V1	もっていく	持って行く
(to) take a photo	II-6-1	V1	しゃしんを　とる	写真を　撮る
(to) take a walk	II-12-1	V3	さんぽ(を) する	散歩(を) する
(to) take/bring (animate) back home	II-6-3	V1	つれてかえる	連れて帰る
(to) take/bring (thing) back home	II-6-3	V1	もってかえる	持って帰る
tall	I-6-1	A	たかい	高い
tardy	I-1-3	Exp	ちこくです。	遅刻です。
taste, flavor	II-11-3	N	あじ	味
tax	II-7-4	N	ぜいきん	税金
taxi	I-7-3	N	タクシー	
tea	I-4-2	N	おちゃ	お茶
(to) teach	II-3-4	V2	おしえる	教える
teacher, Mr./Mrs./Ms./Dr.	I-1-2	N	せんせい	先生
team	I-10-3	N	チーム	
telephone	I-4-5	N	でんわ	電話

English	Lesson	Type	Japanese (かな)	Japanese (漢字)
telephone number	II-1-1	N	でんわばんごう	電話番号
temperature (general)	II-6-2	N	おんど	温度
temple (Buddhist)	II-6-1	N	(お)てら	(お)寺
ten	I-1-4	N	じゅう	十
ten [general counter]	I-2-5	N	とお	十
ten thousand	I-11-4	N	(いち)まん	(一)万
tennis	I-5-3	N	テニス	
terrible	I-9-3	A	ひどい	酷い
terrible, terrific	I-11-5	A	すごい	凄い
textbook	I-2-3	N	きょうかしょ	教科書
textbook	I-2-3	N	テキスト	
Thai language	I-4-1	N	タイご	タイ語
than 〜	II-7-1	P	〜より	
Thank you very much.	I-1-4	Exp	ありがとう ございます。	
Thank you very much. [used after receiving something or after a completed action]	II-7-2	Exp	ありがとう。 ございました。	有難うござい ました。
Thank you.	I-1-4	Exp	ありがとう	
Thank you.	I-1-4	Exp	どうも。	
that 〜	I-2-4	PN	その	
that 〜 over there	I-2-4	PN	あの	
That is a good idea.	II-8-2	Exp	それはいい かんがえです。	それはいい 考えです。
that one	I-1-5	Num.	それ	
that one over there	I-1-5	Num.	あれ	
That's all.	II-4-4	Exp	それだけです。	
the most	II-7-3	Adv	いちばん	一番
there	I-2-5	N	そこ	
there is (animate obj.)	I-8-1	V2	います	
there is (inanimate obj.)	I-8-1	V1	ある	
there, that one [polite equiv. of そこ or それ]	II-4-4	N	そちら	
therefore [formal]	II-9-2	SI	ですから	
therefore [Informal]	II-9-2	SI	だから	
thereupon	II-10-2	SI	すると	
thick	II-11-2	A	あつい	厚い
thick	II-11-2	Adv	あつく	厚く
thick white noodles in broth	II-4-1	N	うどん	
thin	II-11-2	A	うすい	薄い

English	Lesson	Type	Japanese (かな)	Japanese (漢字)
thin	II–11–2	Adv	うすく	薄く
thin	I–6–4	V2	やせています	痩せています
thing [intangible]	I–5–3	N	こと	事
thing [tangible]	I–5–2	N	もの	物
(to) think	II–9–4	V1	おもう	思う
thirteen	I–1–5	Num.	じゅうさん	十三
thirty	I–1–5	Num.	さんじゅう	三十
this	I–2–4	PN	この	
this month	I–10–4	N	こんげつ	今月
this morning	I–10–2	N	けさ	今朝
this one	I–1–3	N	これ	
this one [polite equiv. of これ]	II–7–1	N	こちら	
this one [polite form]	I–3–4	N	こちら	
This way, please.	II–4–4	Exp	どうぞこちらへ。	
this week	I–9–4	N	こんしゅう	今週
this year	I–9–5	N	ことし	今年
thousand	I–11–4	Num.	せん	千
three	I–1–4	N	さん	三
three [general counter]	I–2–5	N	みっつ	三つ
throat	I–6–1	N	のど	喉
through, along	II–3–3	P	を	
throughout, all the time	II–12–1	Adv	ずっと	
Thursday	I–2–7	N	もくようび	木曜日
time	II–8–1	N	じかん	時間
time, when ～	II–12–2	N	～とき	～時
tip	II–4–2	N	チップ	
(to) tire	I–10–2	V2	つかれる	疲れる
tissue	I–2–5	N	ティッシュ	
to [place]	I–7–2	P	[place] へ	
to [place]	I–7–2	P	[place] に [+ direction V]	
to, for [activity]	I–7–2	P	[activity] に	
to～; until ～	I–7–5	P	～まで	
～ to ～, ～ vs. ～	II–8–4	PN	～たい～	～対 ～
today	I–2–6	N	きょう	今日
toe	I–6–1	N	あしゆび	足指
together	I–4–4	Adv	いっしょに	一緒に
tomorrow	I–4–3	N	あした	明日
tonight	I–7–1	N	こんばん	今晩

English	Lesson	Type	Japanese (かな)	Japanese (漢字)
too ~	II-11-4	V2	(V stem form +) すぎる	過ぎる
tooth	I-6-1	N	は	歯
town	II-10-1	N	まち	町
traffic accident	II-3-1	N	こうつうじこ	交通事故
traffic lights	II-3-1	N	しんごう	信号
train station	II-10-1	N	えき	駅
trash	I-2-3	N	ごみ	
trash can	I-8-1	N	ごみばこ	ごみ箱
(to) travel	I-7-4	V3	りょこう(を) する	旅行(を) する
(to) treat (SO)	II-4-3	V3	ごちそう(を)する	ご馳走(を)する
tree	I-8-3	N	き	木
trip, traveling	I-7-4	N	りょこう	旅行
true	I-3-1	N	ほんとう	本当
(Is it) true/real?	II-2-4	Exp	ほんとうですか。	本当ですか。
try to (do)	II-4-3	Dv	(Verb TE form +) みる	
T-shirt	II-2-1	N	Tシャツ	
Tuesday	I-2-7	N	かようび	火曜日
(to) turn at/along (place)	II-3-3	V1	(place で/を) まがる	曲がる
TV	I-4-5	N	テレビ	
twelve	I-1-5	Num.	じゅうに	十二
twenty	I-1-5	Num.	にじゅう	二十
twenty years old	I-3-1	N	はたち	二十歳
twin	II-12-2	N	ふたご	双子
two	I-1-4	Num.	に	二
two [general counter]	I-2-5	N	ふたつ	二つ
two people	I-3-1	N	ふたり	二人
(to) type	I-4-5	V3	タイプ(を) する	
U				
U.S. citizen	I-3-4	N	アメリカじん	アメリカ人
udon topped with beef	II-4-1	N	にくうどん	肉うどん
unappetizing	I-11-5	A	まずい	不味い
uncle, middle-aged man	II-6-4	N	おじさん	
under, below	II-1-2	N	した	下
(to) understand	I-2-1	V1	わかる	分かる
(school) uniform	II-2-1	N	せいふく	制服
(sports) uniform	II-8-1	N	ユニフォーム	
unpleasant, uncomfortable	II-11-4	A	きもちがわるい	気持ちが悪い
unskillful, poor at	I-5-3	Na	へた	下手

English	Lesson	Type	Japanese (かな)	Japanese (漢字)
(to) use	II-3-2	V1	つかう	使う
usually	I-4-2	Adv	たいてい	大抵
(with one's) utmost effort	II-9-3	Adv	いっしょうけんめい	一生懸命
V				
various	II-7-2	Na	いろいろ	
vegetable	II-11-1	N	やさい	野菜
(not) very	I-5-4	Adv	あまり	
very	I-5-4	Adv	とても	
very soon	II-6-1	Adv	もうすぐ	
(Is) very stressed.	II-5-1	Exp	ストレスが いっぱいです。	
vicinity, nearby	II-1-2	N	ちかく	近く
video game	I-5-1	N	テレビゲーム	
vinegar	II-11-3	N	す	酢
voice	I-6-1	N	こえ	声
volleyball	I-5-3	N	バレー(ボール)	
W				
(to) wait	I-11-2	V1	まつ	待つ
waiter	I-3-5	N	ウェイター	
waitress	I-3-5	N	ウェイトレス	
(to) wake up, get up	I-7-2	V2	おきる	起きる
(to) walk	I-7-3	V1	あるく	歩く
wall	II-9-1	N	かべ	壁
wallet	II-4-3	N	さいふ	財布
want (something)	I-9-4	A	ほしい	欲しい
want (to do something)	I-10-2	Da	～たい	
warm	I-12-4	A	あたたかい	暖かい
(to) wash	II-6-3	V1	あらう	洗う
watch, clock	I-11-3	N	とけい	時計
(to) watch, look, see	I-4-5	V2	みる	見る
water	I-4-2	N	(お)みず	(お)水
we	I-10-3	N	わたしたち	私達
we [used by males.]	I-10-3	N	ぼくたち	僕達
We did it!	II-8-4	Exp	やったあ。	
weak	I-10-3	A	よわい	弱い
weak in	I-5-3	Na	にがて	苦手
(to) wear [above the waist or on the entire body]	II-2-1	V2	きる	着る
(to) wear [accessories]	II-2-1	V3	する	
(to) wear [below the waist]	II-2-1	V1	はく	履く

English	Lesson	Type	Japanese (かな)	Japanese (漢字)
(to) wear [glasses]	II-2-1	V2	かける	
(to) wear [on or draped over the head]	II-2-1	V1	かぶる	
(to) wear a seat belt	II-3-4	V3	シートベルトをする	
weather	I-1-6	N	(お)てんき	(お)天気
Wednesday	I-2-7	N	すいようび	水曜日
weekend	I-9-4	N	しゅうまつ	週末
Welcome.	II-4-4	Exp	いらっしゃいませ。	
Well . . . [Used when one is unsure of an answer.]	II-7-3	SI	さあ. . .	
Well done.	I-2-2	Exp	よくできました。	良く出来ました。
Well then [formal]	I-12-1	Exp	では	
Well then [informal]	I-12-1	Exp	じゃ	
well, often	I-4-1	Adv	よく	良く
what color?	I-5-5	N	なにいろ	何色
what day of the month?	I-2-6	Ni	なんにち	何日
what day of the week?	I-2-7	Ni	なんようび	何曜日
what grade?	I-3-3	N	なんねんせい	何年生
What happened?	I-10-1	Exp	どうしましたか。	
what kind of ～?	I-5-2	PN	どんな～	
what language?	I-4-1	Ni	なにご	何語
what month?	I-2-6	Ni	なんがつ	何月
what nationality?	I-3-4	Ni	なにじん	何人
what time?	I-2-7	Ni	なんじ	何時
what?	I-1-3	Ni	なに	何
when?	I-2-6	Ni	いつ	
where?	I-3-4	Ni	どこ	
where? [polite equiv. of どこ]	II-4-4	Ni	どちら	
which (one of two)? [informal]	II-7-1	Ni	どっち	
which (one of two)? [polite]	II-7-1	Ni	どちら	
which ～?	I-11-4	Nd	どの～	
which one (of three or more)?	II-7-3	Ni	どれ	
white	I-6-3	A	しろい	白い
white color	I-5-5	N	しろ	白
who?	I-3-1	Ni	だれ	誰
why?	I-9-3	Ni	どうして	
why?	I-9-3	Ni	なぜ	
wide, spacious	I-8-5	A	ひろい	広い
(to) win	I-10-3	V1	かつ	勝つ
(to) win a championship	II-8-3	V3	ゆうしょう(を) する	優勝(を) する
wind	II-6-2	N	かぜ	風

English	Lesson	Type	Japanese (かな)	Japanese (漢字)
window	I-8-1	N	まど	窓
winter	I-10-4	N	ふゆ	冬
woman	I-8-2	N	おんなのひと	女の人
(We) won! (We) won!	II-8-4	Exp	かった!かった!	勝った!勝った!
wonderful	I-11-5	A	すばらしい	素晴らしい
(it) won't do	II-4-2	V1	なりません	
won't do, must not do	II-2-2	V2	いけません	
Won't you 〜? [invitation]	I-7-1	Dv	[V stem] ませんか	
words, language	II-12-4	N	ことば	言葉
(to) work (at 〜)	II-1-1	V1	(place で) はたらく	働く
(to) work part-time (at 〜)	II-1-1	V3	(place で) アルバイト (を) する	
worksheet	I-2-5	N	ワークシート	
world	II-7-3	N	せかい	世界
(to) worry	II-3-2	V3	しんぱい(を) する	心配(を)する
Wow!	I-11-5	SI	わあ	
(to) write	I-4-5	V1	かく	書く
(to be) wrong, (to) differ	II-1-4	V1	ちがう	違う

Y

English	Lesson	Type	Japanese (かな)	Japanese (漢字)
year	I-9-5	Nd	〜ねん	〜年
yellow	I-6-3	A	きいろい	黄色い
yellow color	I-5-5	N	きいろ	黄色
yen	I-11-4	Nd	えん	円
yes	I-1-2	Exp	はい	
yes [informal]	II-3-2	SI	うん	
yes [informal]	I-1-5	SI	ええ	
Yes it is!	I-1-6	Exp	そうですねえ。	
yesterday	I-4-3	N	きのう	昨日
you	I-2-4	N	あなた	
You are welcome.	I-1-4	Exp	どういたしまして。	
young	I-6-4	A	わかい	若い
(my) younger brother	I-3-1	N	おとうと	弟
(SO's) younger brother	I-3-2	N	おとうとさん	弟さん
(my) younger sister	I-3-1	N	いもうと	妹
(SO's) younger sister	I-3-2	N	いもうとさん	妹さん
yours	I-2-4	N	あなたの	
Yummm . . .	II-4-1	SI	う〜ん	

Z

English	Lesson	Type	Japanese (かな)	Japanese (漢字)
zoo	II-10-1	N	どうぶつえん	動物園

Appendix F

Kanji 漢字

Volume 1

Kanji with a + before them are new readings.

	1 一	2 二	3 三	4 四	5 五	6 日	名前	
3課	イチ, ひと (つ)	ニ, ふた (つ)	サン, みっ (つ)	シ, よ, よん, よっ (つ)	ゴ, いつ (つ)	ニチ, ひ, び, か	なまえ	
	7 六	8 七	9 八	10 九	11 十	12 月	明日	
4課	ロク, むっ (つ)	なな, シチ, なな (つ)	ハチ, やっ (つ)	キュウ, ク, ここの (つ)	ジュウ, とお	ガツ, ゲツ, つき	あした	
	13 火	14 水	15 木	16 金	17 土	18 本	曜	
5課	ひ, カ	みず, スイ	き, モク	かね, キン	つち, ド	もと, ホン, ポン, ボン	ヨウ	
	19 口	20 目	21 耳	22 手	23 父	24 母	上手	下手
6課	くち, ぐち, コウ	め, モク	みみ	て, シュ	ちち, とう	はは, かあ	じょうず	へた
	25 分	26 行	27 来	28 車	29 山	30 川	時	
7課	わ (かります), フン, プン, ブン	い (きます), コウ	き(ます)	くるま, シャ	やま, サン	かわ, がわ	ジ	

8課	[31] 人 ひと, ニン, ジン	[32] 子 こ	[33] 女 おんな	[34] 好 す(き)	[35] 田 た, だ	[36] 男 おとこ	私 わたし	
9課	[37] 先 セン	[38] 生 セイ	[39] 今 いま, コン	[40] 毎 マイ	[41] 年 とし, ネン	[42] 休 やす(み)	生徒 せいと	+来 ライ
10課	[43] 大 おお (きい), ダイ	[44] 小 ちい (さい), ショウ	[45] 中 チュウ, なか	[46] 早 はや (い)	[47] 学 ガク, がっ	[48] 校 コウ	高校 こうこう	
11課	[49] 白 しろ(い)	[50] 百 ヒャク, ピャク, ビャク	[51] 千 セン, ゼン	[52] 万 マン	[53] 円 エン	[54] 見 み (る)	犬 いぬ	太 ふと (る)
12課	[55] 天 テン	[56] 牛 ギュウ, うし	[57] 良 よ (い)	[58] 食 た(べる), ショク	[59] 言 い (う)	[60] 語 ゴ	何 なに, なん	+一 いっ

Volume 2

2課	⁶¹ 私 わたし, わたくし	⁶² 才 サイ	⁶³ 上 うえ, ジョウ	⁶⁴ 下 した, くだ(さい), カ	⁶⁵ 右 みぎ	歳 サイ	
	⁶⁶ 左 ひだり					+来 く(る), こ(ない)	+生 う(まれる)
3課	⁶⁷ 名 な, メイ	⁶⁸ 外 そと, ガイ	⁶⁹ 前 まえ, ゼン	⁷⁰ 話 はな(す), ワ	⁷¹ 書 か(く), ショ	夕 ゆう	漢字 かんじ
	⁷² 何 なに, なん					+手 シュ	
4課	⁷³ 門 モン	⁷⁴ 聞 き(く), ブン	⁷⁵ 雨 あめ	⁷⁶ 電 デン	⁷⁷ 魚 さかな	+牛 うし	
	⁷⁸ 肉 ニク	⁷⁹ 安 やす(い)	⁸⁰ 高 たか(い), コウ	⁸¹ 帰 かえ(る)	⁸² 買 か(う)		
5課	⁸³ 元 ゲン	⁸⁴ 気 キ	⁸⁵ 週 シュウ	⁸⁶ 間 あいだ, カン	⁸⁷ 出 で(る), だ(す)	病 ビョウ	度 ド
	⁸⁸ 午 ゴ	⁸⁹ 後 うし(ろ), あと(で), ゴ	⁹⁰ 飲 の(む)	⁹¹ 事 こと, ごと, ジ	⁹² 回 カイ		

6課	93 正	94 寺	95 時	96 待	97 持	明	玉
	ただ(しい), ショウ	てら, でら, ジ	とき, ジ	ま(つ)	も(つ)	あ(ける)	たま, だま
	98 教	99 会	100 着	101 雪	102 家	々	+火
	おし(える), キョウ	あ(う), カイ	き(る), つ(く)	ゆき	いえ, カ	*repeat	び
7課	103 英	104 国	105 犬	106 青	107 番	同	
	エイ	くに, ぐに, コク, ゴク	いぬ, ケン	あお	バン	おな(じ)	
	108 方	109 色	110 屋	111 売	112 読		
	かた, がた, ホウ	いろ	や	う(る)	よ(む), ドク		
8課	113 友	114 足	115 点	116 半	117 所	戸	達
	とも	あし	テン	ハン	ところ, ショ	と, ど	たち, だち
	118 映	119 画	120 取	121 入	122 走		
	エイ	ガ	と(る)	はい(る), い(れる), いり	はし(る)		
9課	123 開	124 住	125 美	126 若	127 明	様	
	あ(ける)	す(む), ジュウ	うつく (しい), ビ	わか(い)	あか (るい), あ(ける)	さま	
	128 力	129 風	130 世	131 界	132 次	+生	+話
	ちから	かぜ, フウ	セ	カイ	つぎ, ジ	ショウ, ジョウ	はなし, ばなし

10課	133 多 おお(い)，タ	134 少 すく(ない)， すこ(し)	135 止 と(まる)	136 歩 ある(く)， ホ， ポ	137 自 ジ	速 はや(い)	動 うご(く)， ドウ
	138 道 みち， ドウ	139 物 もの， ブツ	140 公 コウ	141 園 エン	142 近 ちか(い)	首 くび	
11課	143 鳥 とり	144 台 タイ， ダイ	145 洗 あら(う)， セン	146 作 つく(る)， サク	147 使 つか(う)	当 トウ	糸 いと
	148 知 し(る)	149 料 リョウ	150 理 リ	151 長 なが(い)	152 室 シツ	＋生 なま	
12課	153 太 ふと(る)， タ	154 立 た(つ)， リツ	155 泣 な(く)	156 全 ゼン	157 部 ブ， ヘ	銀 ギン	
	158 仕 シ	159 心 こころ， シン	160 思 おも(う)	161 悪 わる(い)	162 絵 エ		

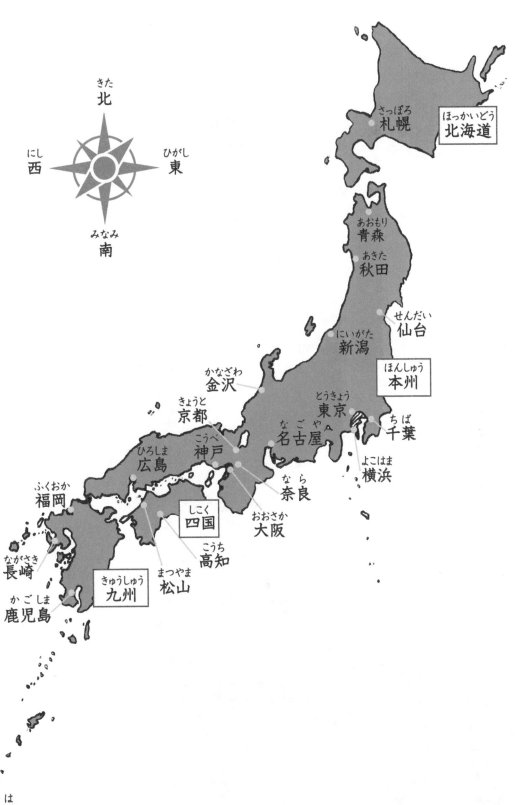

きた
北

にし　　　　　　　　　　　　ひがし
西　　　　　　　　　　　　東

みなみ
南

さっぽろ
札幌

ほっかいどう
北海道

あおもり
青森

あきた
秋田

せんだい
仙台

にいがた
新潟

ほんしゅう
本州

かなざわ
金沢

とうきょう
東京

ちば
千葉

きょうと
京都

な　ご　や
名古屋

こうべ
神戸

よこはま
横浜

ひろしま
広島

な　ら
奈良

ふくおか
福岡

しこく
四国

おおさか
大阪

ながさき
長崎

こうち
高知

まつやま
松山

きゅうしゅう
九州

か　ご　しま
鹿児島

おきなわ
沖縄

な　は
那覇